DIGITAL AND SOCIAL MEDIA MARKETING

DIGITAL AND SOCIAL MEDIA MARKETING

Carla Barbieri
Susan Slocum

Kruger Brentt
Publishers

2025

Kruger Brentt Publishers UK. LTD.
Company Number 9728962

Regd. Office: 68 St Margarets Road, Edgware, Middlesex HA8 9UU

ISBN: 978-1-78715-358-5

For information on all our publications visit our website at http://krugerbrentt.com/

PREFACE

In today's interconnected world, digital marketing and social media have become indispensable tools for businesses to reach and engage with their target audiences. From small startups to multinational corporations, organizations of all sizes are leveraging digital channels and social platforms to promote their products, build brand awareness, and drive customer engagement.

Digital marketing encompasses a wide range of online tactics and strategies aimed at promoting products or services through digital channels. Unlike traditional marketing methods, digital marketing leverages the power of the internet, mobile devices, and digital technologies to connect with consumers in real-time and on a global scale. From search engine optimization (SEO) and pay-per-click (PPC) advertising to email marketing and content marketing, digital marketing offers a diverse set of tools and techniques to attract, engage, and convert potential customers.

SEO involves optimizing a website's content and structure to improve its visibility and ranking in search engine results pages (SERPs). By targeting relevant keywords, optimizing meta tags, and building quality backlinks, businesses can increase organic traffic to their websites and enhance their online presence.

Content marketing focuses on creating valuable and relevant content to attract and engage target audiences. From blog posts and articles to videos and infographics, content marketing aims to provide valuable information, solve problems, and establish thought leadership, ultimately driving customer engagement and loyalty.

SMM involves using social media platforms such as Facebook, Instagram, Twitter, LinkedIn, and TikTok to connect with audiences, build relationships, and promote products or services. Through content sharing, community engagement, and targeted advertising, businesses can leverage social media to increase brand awareness, generate leads, and drive conversions.

Email marketing remains one of the most effective channels for reaching and nurturing leads. By sending targeted and personalized emails to subscribers, businesses can deliver relevant content, announce promotions, and build relationships with their audience, ultimately driving conversions and sales.

PPC advertising allows businesses to display ads on search engines and other online platforms and pay only when users click on their ads. By targeting specific keywords, demographics, and interests, businesses can reach highly relevant audiences and drive targeted traffic to their websites or landing pages.

Social media has revolutionized the way businesses interact with their customers and prospects. With billions of active users worldwide, social media platforms offer unparalleled opportunities for businesses to connect with their target audiences, build brand loyalty, and drive engagement. Through content sharing, community building, and influencer partnerships, businesses can leverage social media to humanize their brands, tell their stories, and foster meaningful connections with their audience.

Digital marketing and social media have transformed the way businesses connect with their audiences, enabling personalized interactions, targeted messaging, and measurable results. By leveraging the power of digital channels and social platforms, businesses can reach new heights of success in today's competitive marketplace, driving brand awareness, customer engagement, and business growth. As technology continues to evolve and consumer behaviors shift, businesses must stay agile, adapt their strategies, and embrace innovation to stay ahead of the curve in the ever-changing digital landscape.

This book explores the key concepts, strategies, and benefits of digital marketing and social media in the contemporary business landscape.

Carla Barbieri
Susan Slocum

CONTENTS

Preface v

1. Foundations of Digital Marketing 1

1.1 Introduction to Digital Marketing and Social Media 1

1.2 Evolution and Impact of Digital Channels in Marketing 33

1.3 Overview of Digital Marketing 37

1.4 Digital Marketing vs. Traditional Marketing 40

1.5 Key Components of Digital Marketing Strategy 44

1.6 Understanding the Digital Consumer Journey 49

2. Content Making 55

2.1 The Role of Content in Digital Marketing 55

2.2 Developing a Content Marketing Strategy 59

2.3 Content Types and Formats 62

2.4 Measuring Content Marketing Success 66

3. Social Media Marketing 71

3.1 Introduction to Social Media Platforms 71

3.2 Building a Social Media Strategy 143

3.3 Content Creation for Social Media 147

3.4 Community Management and Engagement 153

3.5 Social Media Analytics and Reporting 157

4. Search Engine Optimization (SEO) 161

4.1 Fundamentals of SEO 161

4.2 Keyword Research and Strategy 169

4.3 On-Page and Off-page SEO 173

4.4 Technical SEO and Website Optimization 177

4.5 Local SEO and Mobile Optimization 180

5. Pay-Per–Click (PPC) Advertising **183**

5.1 Introduction to PPC 183

5.2 Crafting Effective PPC Campaigns 188

5.3 Ad Platforms: Google Ads, Bing Ads, and Beyond 191

5.4 Conversions Rate Optimization for PPC 200

5.5 PPC Analytics and Optimization 204

6. Email Marketing **209**

6.1 The Power of Email in Digital Marketing 209

6.2 Developing an Email Marketing Strategy 212

6.3 Email Design and Content Best Practices 214

6.4 Segmentation, Personalization and Automation 219

6.5 Measuring Email Marketing Effectiveness 222

7. Mobile Marketing **227**

7.1 The Rise of Mobile Marketing 227

7.2 Mobile-Friendly Websites and SEO 230

7.3 SMS and Messaging Apps in Marketing 233

7.4 Mobile Apps and Location-Based Marketing 235

7.5 Mobile Analytics and Trends 238

8. Influencer Marketing **243**

8.1 Understanding in Influencer Marketing 243

8.2 Selection the Right Influencers 249

8.3 Crafting Collaborative Contents 252

8.4 Legal Considerations and Ethics 255

8.5 Measuring Influencer Campaign Success 258

9. Video Marketing **263**

9.1 The Impact of Video Content 263

9.2 Strategies for Video Marketing 266

9.3 Platforms for Video Marketing: youTube, Vimeo, Social Media 269

9.4 Live Streaming and Interactive Video Content 272

9.5 Video Analytics and Performance Measurement 274

10. Analytics and Data-Driven Marketing **277**

10.1 The Role of Data in Digital Marketing 277

10.2 Introduction to Digital Analytics Tools 280

10.3 Interpreting Data and KPIs 282

10.4 Applying Insights to Optimize Strategies 285
10.5 Privacy, Consent and Data Protection 288
11. Digital Marketing Tools and Technologies 293
11.1 Overview of Essential Digital Marketing Tools 293
11.2 Automation and Workflow Tools 296
11.3 AI and Machine Learning in Digital Marketing 298
11.4 Emerging Technologies and Their Applications 301
12. Creating an Integrated Digital Marketing Plan 307
12.1 Aligning Digital Channels and Tactics 307
12.2 Budgeting and Resource Allocation 310
12.3 Implementation and Project Management 313
12.4 Monitoring, Evaluation and Continuous Improvement 316
Conclusion 321
Recap of Key Learnings 321
Future Trends in Digital marketing and Social Media 323
Glossary 327
References 329
Index 333

CHAPTER 1

FOUNDATIONS OF DIGITAL MARKETING

1.1 INTRODUCTION TO DIGITAL MARKETING AND SOCIAL MEDIA

1.1.1 Digital Marketing

Digital marketing is the component of marketing that uses the Internet and online-based digital technologies such as desktop computers, mobile phones, and other digital media and platforms to promote products and services. Its development during the 1990s and 2000s changed the way brands and businesses use technology for marketing. As digital platforms became increasingly incorporated into marketing plans and everyday life, and as people increasingly used digital devices instead of visiting physical shops, digital marketing campaigns have become prevalent, employing combinations of search engine optimization (SEO), search engine marketing (SEM), content marketing, influencer marketing, content automation, campaign marketing, data-driven marketing, e-commerce marketing, social media marketing, social media optimization, e-mail direct marketing, display advertising, e-books, and optical disks and games have become commonplace. Digital marketing extends to non-Internet channels that provide digital media, such as television, mobile phones (SMS and MMS), callbacks, and on-hold mobile ringtones. The extension to non-Internet channels differentiates digital marketing from online marketing.

History

Digital marketing effectively began in 1990 when the Archie search engine was created as an index for FTP sites. In the 1980s, the storage capacity of computers was already large enough to store huge volumes of customer information. Companies started choosing online techniques, such as database marketing, rather than limited list brokers. Databases allowed companies to track customers' information more effectively, transforming the relationship between buyer and seller.

In the 1990s, the term *digital marketing* was coined. With the development of server/client architecture and the popularity of personal computers, Customer Relationship Management (CRM) applications became a significant factor in marketing technology. Fierce competition forced vendors to include more services in their software, such as marketing, sales, and service applications. Marketers were also able to own online customer data through eCRM software after the Internet was born. This led to the first clickable banner ad going live in 1994, which was the "You Will" campaign by AT&T, and over the first four months of it going live, 44% of all people who saw it clicked on the ad.

In the 2000s, with increasing numbers of Internet users and the birth of the iPhone, customers began searching for products and making decisions about their needs online first, instead of consulting a salesperson, which created a new problem for the marketing department of a company. In addition, a survey in 2000 in the United Kingdom found that most retailers still needed to register their own domain address. These problems encouraged marketers to find new ways to integrate digital technology into market development.

In 2007, marketing automation was developed as a response to the ever-evolving marketing climate. Marketing automation is the process by which software is used to automate conventional marketing processes. Marketing automation helped companies segment customers, launch multichannel marketing campaigns, and provide personalized information for customers., based on their specific activities. In this way, users' activity (or lack thereof) triggers a personal message that is customized to the user in their preferred platform. However, despite the benefits of marketing automation many companies are struggling to adapt it to their everyday uses correctly.

Digital marketing became more sophisticated in the 2000s and the 2010s, when the proliferation of devices capable of accessing digital media led to sudden growth. Statistics produced in 2012 and 2013 showed that digital marketing was still growing. With the development of social media in the 2000s, such as LinkedIn, Facebook, YouTube, and Twitter, consumers became highly dependent on digital electronics in their daily lives. Therefore, they expected a seamless user experience across different channels for searching product information. The change in customer behavior improved the diversification of marketing technology.

The term "Digital Marketing" was coined in the 1990s. Digital marketing was formally known as and referred to as 'online marketing', 'internet marketing', or 'web marketing'. Worldwide *digital marketing* has become the most commonly used term and has taken off in the business industry, especially after the year 2013. However in other countries like Italy, digital marketing is still known as *web marketing*. Digital media growth was estimated at 4.5 trillion online ads served annually with digital media spending at 48% growth in 2010. An increasing portion of advertising stems from businesses employing Online Behavioural Advertising (OBA) to tailor advertising for internet users, but OBA raises concerns about consumer privacy and data protection.

New Non-Linear Marketing Approach

Nonlinear marketing, a type of interactive marketing, is a long-term marketing approach that builds on businesses collecting information about an Internet user's online activities and trying to be visible in multiple areas.

Unlike traditional marketing techniques, which involve direct, one-way messaging to consumers (via print, television, and radio advertising), nonlinear digital marketing strategies are centered on reaching prospective customers across multiple online channels.

Combined with higher consumer knowledge and the demand for more sophisticated consumer offerings, this change has forced many businesses to rethink their outreach strategy and adopt or incorporate omnichannel, nonlinear marketing techniques to maintain sufficient brand exposure, engagement, and reach.

Nonlinear marketing strategies involve efforts to adapt the advertising to different platforms and to tailor the advertising to different individual buyers rather than a large coherent audience.

Tactics may include:

- Search engine optimization (SEO).
- Social media marketing.
- Video marketing.
- Email marketing.
- Blogging & affiliate marketing.
- Website marketing.
- Pay-per-click.
- Content marketing.
- Search engine marketing.

Some studies indicate that consumer responses to traditional marketing approaches are becoming less predictable for businesses. According to a 2018 study, nearly 90% of online consumers in the United States researched products and brands online before visiting the store or making a purchase.

The Global Web Index estimated that in 2018, a little more than 50% of consumers researched products on social media. Businesses often rely on individuals portraying their products in a positive light on social media, and may adapt their marketing strategy to target people with large social media followings in order to generate such comments. In this manner, businesses can use consumers to advertise their products or services, decreasing the cost for the company.

Brand Awareness

One of the key objectives of modern digital marketing is to raise brand awareness, the extent to which customers and the general public are familiar with and recognize a particular brand.

Enhancing brand awareness is important in digital marketing, and marketing in general, because of its impact on brand perception and consumer decision-making. According to the 2015 essay, "Impact of Brand on Consumer Behavior":

"Brand awareness, as one of the fundamental dimensions of brand equity, is often considered to be a prerequisite of consumers' buying decision, as it represents the main factor for including a brand in the consideration set. Brand awareness can also influence consumers' perceived risk assessment and their confidence in the purchase decision, due to familiarity with the brand and its characteristics."

Recent trends show that businesses and digital marketers are prioritizing brand awareness, focusing more on their digital marketing efforts on cultivating brand recognition and recall than in previous years. This is evidenced by a 2019 Content Marketing Institute study, which found that 81% of digital marketers have worked on enhancing brand recognition over the past year.

Another Content Marketing Institute survey revealed 89% of B2B marketers now believe improving brand awareness to be more important than efforts directed at increasing sales.

Increasing brand awareness is a focus of digital marketing strategy for a number of reasons:

- **The Growth of Online Shopping:** A survey by Statista projects 230.5 million people in the United States will use the internet to shop, compare, and buy products by 2021, up from 209.6 million in 2016. Research from business software firm Salesforce found 87% of people began searches for products and brands on digital channels in 2018.
- **The Role of Digital Interaction in Customer Behavior:** It's estimated that 70% of all retail purchases made in the U.S. are influenced to some degree by an interaction with a brand online.
- The Growing Influence and role of brand awareness in online consumer decision-making: 82% of online shoppers searching for services give preference to brands they know of.
- **The Use, Convenience, and Influence of Social Media:** A recent report by Hootsuite estimated there were more than 3.4 billion active users on social media platforms, a 9% increase from 2018. A 2019 survey by The Manifest states that 74% of social media users follow brands on

social sites, and 96% of people who follow businesses also engage with those brands on social platforms. According to Deloitte, one in three U.S. consumers are influenced by social media when buying a product, while 47% of millennials factor their interaction with a brand on social when making a purchase.

Online Methods Used to Build Brand Awareness

Digital marketing strategies may include the use of one or more online channels and techniques (omnichannel) to increase brand awareness among consumers.

Search Engine Optimization (SEO)

Search engine optimization techniques may be used to improve the visibility of business websites and brand-related content for common industry-related search queries. The importance of SEO to increase brand awareness is said to correlate with the growing influence of search results and search features like featured snippets, knowledge panels, and local SEO on customer behavior.

Search Engine Marketing (SEM)

SEM, also known as PPC advertising, involves the purchase of ad space in prominent, visible positions atop search results pages and websites. Search ads have been shown to have a positive impact on brand recognition, awareness and conversions. 33% of searchers who click on paid ads do so because they directly respond to their particular search query.

Social Media Marketing

Social media marketing has the characteristics of being in the marketing state and interacting with consumers all the time, emphasizing content and interaction skills. The marketing process needs to be monitored, analyzed, summarized and managed in real-time, and the marketing target needs to be adjusted according to the real-time feedback from the market and consumers. 70% of marketers list increasing brand awareness as their number one goal for marketing on social media platforms. Facebook, Instagram, Twitter, and YouTube are listed as the top platforms currently used by social media marketing teams. As of 2021, LinkedIn has been added as one of the most-used social media platforms by business leaders for its professional networking capabilities.

Content Marketing

56% of marketers believe personalization content – brand-centered blogs, articles, social updates, videos, landing pages – improves brand recall and engagement.

Developments and Strategies

One of the major changes that occurred in traditional marketing was the "emergence of digital marketing", this led to the reinvention of marketing strategies in order to adapt to this major change in traditional marketing.

As digital marketing is dependent on technology which is ever-evolving and fast-changing, the same features should be expected from digital marketing developments and strategies. This portion is an attempt to qualify or segregate the notable highlights existing and being used as of press time.

- **Segmentation:** More focus has been placed on segmentation within digital marketing, in order to target specific markets in both business-to-business and business-to-consumer sectors.
- **Influencer Marketing:** Important nodes are identified within related communities, known as influencers. This is becoming an important concept in digital targeting. Influencers allow brands to take advantage of social media and the large audiences available on many of these platforms. It is possible to reach influencers via paid advertising, such as Facebook Advertising or Google Ads campaigns, or through sophisticated sCRM (social customer relationship management) software, such as SAP C4C, Microsoft Dynamics, Sage CRM and Salesforce CRM. Many universities now focus, at Masters level, on engagement strategies for influencers.

To summarize, Pull digital marketing is characterized by consumers actively seeking marketing content while Push digital marketing occurs when marketers send messages without that content being actively sought by the recipients.

- **Online Behavioral Advertising:** Online behavioral advertising is the practice of collecting information about a user's online activity over time, "on a particular device and across different, unrelated websites, in order to deliver advertisements tailored to that user's interests and preferences." Such Advertisements are based on site retargeting are customized based on each user behavior and pattern.
- **Collaborative Environment:** A collaborative environment can be set up between the organization, the technology service provider, and the digital agencies to optimize effort, resource sharing, reusability and communications. Additionally, organizations are inviting their customers to help them better understand how to service them. This source of data is called user-generated content. Much of this is acquired via company websites where the organization invites people to share ideas that are then evaluated by other users of the site. The most popular ideas are evaluated and implemented in some form. Using this method of acquiring data and developing new products can foster the

organization's relationship with its customer as well as spawn ideas that would otherwise be overlooked. UGC is low-cost advertising as it is directly from the consumers and can save advertising costs for the organization.

- **Data-Driven Advertising:** Users generate a lot of data in every step they take on the path of customer journey and brands can now use that data to activate their known audience with data-driven programmatic media buying. Without exposing customers' privacy, users' data can be collected from digital channels (e.g.: when the customer visits a website, reads an e-mail, or launches and interact with a brand's mobile app), brands can also collect data from real-world customer interactions, such as brick and mortar stores visits and from CRM and sales engines datasets. Also known as people-based marketing or addressable media, data-driven advertising is empowering brands to find their loyal customers in their audience and deliver in real time a much more personal communication, highly relevant to each customers' moment and actions.

An important consideration today while deciding on a strategy is that the digital tools have democratized the promotional landscape.

- **Remarketing:** Remarketing plays a major role in digital marketing. This tactic allows marketers to publish targeted ads in front of an interest category or a defined audience, generally called searchers in web speak, they have either searched for particular products or services or visited a website for some purpose.
- **Game Advertising:** Game ads are advertisements that exist within computer or video games. One of the most common examples of in-game advertising is billboards appearing in sports games. In-game ads also might appear as brand-name products like guns, cars, or clothing that exist as gaming status symbols.

Six principles for building online brand content:

- Do not consider individuals as consumers;
- Have an editorial position;
- Define an identity for the brand;
- Maintain a continuity of contents;
- Ensure a regular interaction with audience; and
- Have a channel for events.

The new digital era has enabled brands to selectively target their customers that may potentially be interested in their brand or based on previous browsing interests. Businesses can now use social media to select the age range, location, gender, and interests of whom they would like their targeted post to be seen. Furthermore, based on a customer's recent search history they can be 'followed' on the internet so they see advertisements from similar brands, products, and services, This allows businesses to target the specific customers that they know and feel will most benefit from their product or service, something that had limited capabilities up until the digital era.

- **Tourism Marketing:** Advanced tourism, responsible and sustainable tourism, social media and online tourism marketing, and geographic information systems. As a broader research field matures and attracts more diverse and in-depth academic research

Ineffective Forms of Digital Marketing

Digital marketing activity is still growing across the world according to the headline global marketing index. A study published in September 2018, found that global outlays on digital marketing tactics are approaching $100 billion. Digital media continues to rapidly grow. While the marketing budgets are expanding, traditional media is declining. Digital media helps brands reach consumers to engage with their product or service in a personalized way. Five areas, which are outlined as current industry practices that are often ineffective are prioritizing clicks, balancing search and display, understanding mobiles, targeting, viewability, brand safety and invalid traffic, and cross-platform measurement. Why these practices are ineffective and some ways around making these aspects effective are discussed surrounding the following points.

Prioritizing Clicks

Prioritizing clicks refers to display click ads, although advantageous by being 'simple, fast and inexpensive' rates for display ads in 2016 is only 0.10 percent in the United States. This means one in a thousand click ads is relevant therefore having little effect. This displays that marketing companies should not just use click ads to evaluate the effectiveness of display advertisements.

Balancing Search and Display

Balancing search and display for digital display ads is important. marketers tend to look at the last search and attribute all of the effectiveness of this. This, in turn, disregards other marketing efforts, which establish brand value within the consumer's mind. ComScore determined through drawing on data online, produced by over one hundred multichannel retailers that digital display marketing poses strengths when compared with or positioned alongside, paid search. This is why it is advised that when someone clicks on a display ad the company opens a landing page, not its home page. A landing page typically has something to draw the customer in to search beyond this page. Commonly marketers see increased sales among people exposed to a search ad. But the fact of how many people you can reach with a display campaign compared to a search campaign should be considered. Multichannel retailers have an increased reach if the display is considered in synergy with search campaigns. Overall, both search and display aspects are valued as display campaigns build awareness for the brand so that more people are likely to click on these digital ads when running a search campaign.

Understanding Mobiles

Understanding mobile devices is a significant aspect of digital marketing because smartphones and tablets are now responsible for 64% of the time US consumers are online. Apps provide a big opportunity as well as challenge for the marketers because firstly the app needs to be downloaded and secondly the person needs to actually use it. This may be difficult as 'half the time spent on smartphone apps occurs on the individuals single most used app, and almost 85% of their time on the top four rated apps'. Mobile advertising can assist in achieving a variety of commercial objectives and it is effective due to taking over the entire screen, and voice or status is likely to be considered highly. However, the message must not be seen or thought of as intrusive. Disadvantages of digital media used on mobile devices also include limited creative capabilities, and reach. Although there are many positive aspects including the user's entitlement to select product information, digital media creating a flexible message platform and there is potential for direct selling.

Cross-Platform Measurement

The number of marketing channels continues to expand, as measurement practices are growing in complexity. A cross-platform view must be used to unify audience measurement and media planning. Market researchers need to understand how the Omni-channel affects consumer's behavior, although when advertisements are on a consumer's device this does not get measured. Significant aspects to cross-platform measurement involve deduplication and understanding that you have reached an incremental level with another platform, rather than delivering more impressions against people that have previously been reached. An example is 'ESPN and comScore partnered on Project Blueprint discovering the sports broadcaster achieved a 21% increase in unduplicated daily reach thanks to digital advertising'. Television and radio industries are the electronic media, which competes with digital and other technological advertising. Yet television advertising is not directly competing with online digital advertising due to being able to cross platform with digital technology. Radio also gains power through cross platforms, in online streaming content. Television and radio continue to persuade and affect the audience, across multiple platforms.

Targeting, Viewability, Brand Safety, and Invalid Traffic

Targeting, viewability, brand safety, and invalid traffic all are aspects used by marketers to help advocate digital advertising. Cookies are a form of digital advertising, which are tracking tools within desktop devices, causing difficulty, with shortcomings including deletion by web browsers, the inability to sort between multiple users of a device, inaccurate estimates for unique visitors, overstating reach, understanding frequency, problems with ad servers, which cannot distinguish between when cookies have been deleted and when consumers have not previously been exposed to an ad. Due to the inaccuracies influenced by cookies, demographics in the target market are low and vary. Another element, which is affected by digital marketing, is 'viewability' or whether the ad was actually seen by the consumer. Many ads are not seen by a consumer and may never reach the right demographic segment. Brand safety is another issue of whether or not the ad was produced in the context of being unethical or having offensive content. Recognizing fraud when an ad is exposed is another challenge marketers face. This relates to invalid traffic as premium sites are more effective at detecting fraudulent traffic, although non-premium sites are more so the problem.

Channels

Digital Marketing Channels are systems based on the Internet that can create, accelerate, and transmit product value from producer to a consumer terminal, through digital networks. Digital marketing is facilitated by multiple Digital Marketing channels, as an advertiser one's core objective is to find channels which result in maximum two-way communication and a better overall ROI for the brand. There are multiple digital marketing channels available namely:

- **Affiliate Marketing:** Affiliate marketing is perceived to not be considered a safe, reliable, and easy means of marketing through online platforms. This is due to a lack of reliability in terms of affiliates that can produce the demanded number of new customers. As a result of this risk and bad affiliates, it leaves the brand prone to exploitation in terms of claiming commission that isn't honestly acquired. Legal means may offer some protection against this, yet there are limitations in recovering any losses or investment. Despite this, affiliate marketing allows the brand to market towards smaller publishers and websites with smaller traffic. Brands that choose to use this marketing often should beware of such risks involved and look to associate with affiliates in which rules are laid down between the parties involved to assure and minimize the risk involved.
- **Display Advertising:** As the term implies, online display advertising deals with showcasing promotional messages or ideas to the consumer

on the internet. This includes a wide range of advertisements like advertising blogs, networks, interstitial ads, contextual data, ads on search engines, classified or dynamic advertisements, etc. The method can target specific audience tuning in from different types of locals to view a particular advertisement, the variations can be found as the most productive element of this method.

- **Email Marketing:** Email marketing in comparison to other forms of digital marketing is considered cheap. It is also a way to rapidly communicate a message such as their value proposition to existing or potential customers. Yet this channel of communication may be perceived by recipients to be bothersome and irritating especially to new or potential customers, therefore the success of email marketing is reliant on the language and visual appeal applied. In terms of visual appeal, there are indications that using graphics/visuals that are relevant to the message which is attempting to be sent, yet less visual graphics to be applied with initial emails are more effective in-turn creating a relatively personal feel to the email. In terms of language, the style is the main factor in determining how captivating the email is. Using a casual tone invokes a warmer, gentler and more inviting feel to the email, compared to a more formal tone.
- **Search Engine Marketing:** Search engine marketing (SEM) is a form of Internet marketing that involves the promotion of websites by increasing their visibility in search engine results pages (SERPs) primarily through paid advertising. SEM may incorporate Search engine optimization, which adjusts or rewrites website content and site architecture to achieve a higher ranking in search engine results pages to enhance pay per click (PPC) listings.
- **Social Media Marketing:** The term 'Digital Marketing' has a number of marketing facets as it supports different channels used in and among these, comes the Social Media. When we use social media channels (Facebook, Twitter, Pinterest, Instagram, Google+, etc.) to market a product or service, the strategy is called Social Media Marketing. It is a procedure wherein strategies are made and executed to draw in traffic for a website or to gain the attention of buyers over the web using different social media platforms.
- **Social Networking Service:** A social networking service is an online platform which people use to build social networks or social relations with other people who share similar personal or career interests, activities, backgrounds or real-life connections

- **In-Game Advertising:** In-Game advertising is defined as the "inclusion of products or brands within a digital game." The game allows brands or products to place ads within their game, either in a subtle manner or in the form of an advertisement banner. There are many factors that exist in whether brands are successful in the advertising of their brand/product, these being: Type of game, technical platform, 3-D and 4-D technology, game genre, congruity of brand and game, prominence of advertising within the game. Individual factors consist of attitudes towards placement advertisements, game involvement, product involvement, flow, or entertainment. The attitude towards the advertising also takes into account not only the message shown but also the attitude towards the game. Dependent on how enjoyable the game is will determine how the brand is perceived, meaning if the game isn't very enjoyable the consumer may subconsciously have a negative attitude towards the brand/product being advertised. In terms of Integrated Marketing Communication "integration of advertising in digital games into the general advertising, communication, and marketing strategy of the firm" is important as it results in a more clarity about the brand/ product and creates a larger overall effect.
- **Online Public Relations:** The use of the internet to communicate with both potential and current customers in the public realm.
- **Video Advertising:** This type of advertising in terms of digital/online means are advertisements that play on online videos e.g., YouTube videos. This type of marketing has seen an increase in popularity over time. Online Video Advertising usually consists of three types: Pre-Roll advertisements which play before the video is watched, Mid-Roll advertisements which play during the video, or Post-Roll advertisements which play after the video is watched. Post-roll advertisements were shown to have better brand recognition in relation to the other types, where-as "ad-context congruity/incongruity plays an important role in reinforcing ad memorability". Due to selective attention from viewers, there is the likelihood that the message may not be received. The main advantage of video advertising is that it disrupts the viewing experience of the video and therefore there is a difficulty in attempting to avoid them. How a consumer interacts with online video advertising can come down to three stages: Pre attention, attention, and behavioral decision. These online advertisements give the brand/business options and choices. These consist of length, position, adjacent video content which all directly affect the effectiveness of the produced advertisement time, therefore manipulating these variables will yield different results. The

length of the advertisement has shown to affect memorability where-as a longer duration resulted in increased brand recognition. This type of advertising, due to its nature of interruption of the viewer, it is likely that the consumer may feel as if their experience is being interrupted or invaded, creating negative perception of the brand. These advertisements are also available to be shared by the viewers, adding to the attractiveness of this platform. Sharing these videos can be equated to the online version of word by mouth marketing, extending number of people reached. Sharing videos creates six different outcomes: these being "pleasure, affection, inclusion, escape, relaxation, and control". As well, videos that have entertainment value are more likely to be shared, yet pleasure is the strongest motivator to pass videos on. Creating a 'viral' trend from a mass amount of a brand advertisement can maximize the outcome of an online video advert whether it be positive or a negative outcome.

- **Native Advertising:** This involves the placement of paid content that replicates the look, feel, and oftentimes, the voice of a platform's existing content. It is most effective when used on digital platforms like websites, newsletters, and social media. Can be somewhat controversial as some critics feel it intentionally deceives consumers.
- **Content Marketing:** This is an approach to marketing that focuses on gaining and retaining customers by offering helpful content to customers that improves the buying experience and creates brand awareness. A brand may use this approach to hold a customer's attention with the goal of influencing potential purchase decisions.
- **Sponsored Content:** This utilises content created and paid for by a brand to promote a specific product or service.
- **Inbound Marketing:** A market strategy that involves using content as a means to attract customers to a brand or product. Requires extensive research into the behaviors, interests, and habits of the brand's target market.
- **SMS Marketing:** Although the popularity is decreasing day by day, still SMS marketing plays huge role to bring new user, provide direct updates, provide new offers etc.
- **Push Notification:** In this digital era, Push Notification responsible for bringing new and abandoned customer through smart segmentation. Many online brands are using this to provide personalised appeals depending on the scenario of customer acquisition.

It is important for a firm to reach out to consumers and create a two-way communication model, as digital marketing allows consumers to give back feedback to the firm on a community-based site or straight directly to the firm via email. Firms should seek this long-term communication relationship by using multiple forms of channels and using promotional strategies related to their target consumer as well as word-of-mouth marketing.

Benefits of Digital Marketing

Possible benefits of digital marketing include:

- any information that is needed is accessible at any time and/or place;
- surpasses internet marketing and also possesses alternatives choices without the internet needed;
- top in presenting beneficial ways and features that reach, inform, engage, offer, and sell services and products to consumers;
- businesses can attain data that present target audiences based on their age, location, interests, and education;
- low investment, the cost per lead is 61% less expensive than traditional marketing; and
- able to reach every mobile user, there are over 14 billion worldwide mobile devices and with a projection to grow to almost 18 billion by the year 2024.

Self-Regulation

The ICC Code has integrated rules that apply to marketing communications using digital interactive media throughout the guidelines. Code self-regulation on the use of digital interactive media includes:

- Clear and transparent mechanisms to enable consumers to choose not to have their data collected for advertising or marketing purposes;
- Clear indication that a social network site is commercial and is under the control or influence of a marketer;
- Limits are set so that marketers communicate directly only when there are reasonable grounds to believe that the consumer has an interest in what is being offered;
- Respect for the rules and standards of acceptable commercial behavior in social networks and the posting of marketing messages only when the forum or site has clearly indicated its willingness to receive them;
- Special attention and protection for children.

Strategy

Planning

Digital marketing planning is a term used in marketing management. It describes the first stage of forming a digital marketing strategy for the wider digital marketing system. The difference between digital and traditional marketing planning is that it uses digitally based communication tools and technology such as Social, Web, Mobile, Scannable Surface. Nevertheless, both are aligned with the vision, the mission of the company and the overarching business strategy.

Stages of Planning

Using Dr. Dave Chaffey's approach, the digital marketing planning (DMP) has three main stages: Opportunity, Strategy, and Action. He suggests that any business looking to implement a successful digital marketing strategy must structure their plan by looking at opportunity, strategy and action. This generic strategic approach often has phases of situation review, goal setting, strategy formulation, resource allocation and monitoring.

Opportunity:

- To create an effective DMP, a business first needs to review the marketplace and set 'SMART' (Specific, Measurable, Actionable, Relevant, and Time-Bound) objectives. They can set SMART objectives by reviewing the current benchmarks and key performance indicators (KPIs) of the company and competitors. It is pertinent that the analytics used for the KPIs be customized to the type, objectives, mission, and vision of the company. Companies can scan for marketing and sales opportunities by reviewing their own outreach as well as influencer outreach. This means they have competitive advantage because they are able to analyse their co-marketers influence and brand associations.
- To seize the opportunity, the firm should summarize its current customers' personas and purchase journey from this they are able to deduce their digital marketing capability. This means they need to form a clear picture of where they are currently and how many resources, they can allocate for their digital marketing strategy i.e., labor, time, etc. By summarizing the purchase journey, they can also recognize gaps and growth for future marketing opportunities that will either meet objectives or propose new objectives and increase profit.

Strategy:

- To create a planned digital strategy, the company must review their digital proposition (what you are offering to consumers) and communicate it using digital customer targeting techniques. So, they must define online value proposition (OVP), this means the company must express clearly what they are offering customers online e.g., brand positioning.

- The company should also (re)select target market segments and personas and define digital targeting approaches.
- After doing this effectively, it is important to review the marketing mix for online options. The marketing mix comprises the 4Ps – Product, Price, Promotion, and Place. Some academics have added three additional elements to the traditional 4Ps of marketing Process, Place, and Physical appearance making it 7Ps of marketing.

Action:

- The third and final stage requires the firm to set a budget and management systems. These must be measurable touchpoints, such as the audience reached across all digital platforms. Furthermore, marketers must ensure the budget and management systems are integrating the paid, owned, and earned media of the company. The Action and final stage of planning also requires the company to set in place measurable content creation e.g. oral, visual or written online media.
- After confirming the digital marketing plan, a scheduled format of digital communications (e.g. Gantt Chart) should be encoded throughout the internal operations of the company. This ensures that all platforms used fall in line and complement each other for the succeeding stages of digital marketing strategy.

Understanding the Market

One way marketers can reach out to consumers and understand their thought process is through what is called an empathy map. An empathy map is a four-step process. The first step is through asking questions that the consumer would be thinking in their demographic. The second step is to describe the feelings that the consumer may be having. The third step is to think about what the consumer would say in their situation. The final step is to imagine what the consumer will try to do based on the other three steps. This map is so marketing teams can put themselves in their target demographics shoes. Web Analytics are also a very important way to understand consumers. They show the habits that people have online for each website. One particular form of these analytics is predictive analytics which helps marketers figure out what route consumers are on. This uses the information gathered from other analytics and then creates different predictions of what people will do so that companies can strategize on what to do next, according to the people's trends.

- **Consumer Behavior:** The habits or attitudes of a consumer that influences the buying process of a product or service. Consumer behavior impacts virtually every stage of the buying process specifically in relation to digital environments and devices.
- **Predictive Analytics:** A form of data mining that involves using existing data to predict potential future trends or behaviors. Can assist companies in predicting future behavior of customers.
- **Buyer Persona:** Employing research of consumer behavior regarding habits like brand awareness and buying behavior to profile prospective customers. Establishing a buyer persona helps a company better understand their audience and their specific wants/needs.
- **Marketing Strategy:** Strategic planning employed by a brand to determine potential positioning within a market as well as the prospective target audience. It involves two key elements: segmentation and positioning. By developing a marketing strategy, a company is able to better anticipate and plan for each step in the marketing and buying process.

Sharing Economy

The "sharing economy" refers to an economic pattern that aims to obtain a resource that is not fully used. Nowadays, the sharing economy has had an unimagined effect on many traditional elements including labor, industry, and distribution system. This effect is not negligible that some industries are obviously under threat. The sharing economy is influencing the traditional marketing channels by changing the nature of some specific concept including ownership, assets, and recruitment.

Digital marketing channels and traditional marketing channels are similar in function that the value of the product or service is passed from the original producer to the end user by a kind of supply chain. Digital Marketing channels, however, consist of internet systems that create, promote, and deliver products or services from producer to consumer through digital networks. Increasing changes to marketing channels has been a significant contributor to the expansion and growth of the sharing economy. Such changes to marketing channels has prompted unprecedented and historic growth. In addition to this typical approach, the built-in control, efficiency and low cost of digital marketing channels is an essential features in the application of sharing economy. Digital marketing channels within the sharing economy are typically divided into three domains including, e-mail, social media, and search engine marketing or SEM.

- **E-mail:** A form of direct marketing characterized as being informative, promotional, and often a means of customer relationship management. Organization can update the activity or promotion information to the user by subscribing the newsletter mail that happened in consuming. Success is reliant upon a company's ability to access contact information from its past, present, and future clientele.
- **Social Media:** Social media has the capability to reach a larger audience in a shorter time frame than traditional marketing channels. This makes social media a powerful tool for consumer engagement and the dissemination of information.
- **Search Engine Marketing or SEM:** Requires more specialized knowledge of the technology embedded in online platforms. This marketing strategy requires long-term commitment and dedication to the ongoing improvement of a company's digital presence.

Other emerging digital marketing channels, particularly branded mobile apps, have excelled in the sharing economy. Branded mobile apps are created specifically to initiate engagement between customers and the company. This engagement is typically facilitated through entertainment, information, or market transaction.

1.1.2 Social Media

Social media are interactive technologies that facilitate the creation, sharing and aggregation of content, ideas, interests, and other forms of expression through virtual communitie networks. Common features include:

- Online platforms that enable users to create and share content and participate in social networking.
- User-generated content—such as text posts or comments, digital photos or videos, and data generated through online interactions.
- Service-specific profiles that are designed and maintained by the social media organization.
- Social media helps the development of online social networks by connecting a user's profile with those of other individuals or groups.

The term *social* in regard to media suggests platforms enable communal activity. Social media can enhance and extend human networks. Users access social media through web-based apps or custom apps on mobile devices. These interactive platforms allow individuals, communities, and organizations to share, co-create, discuss, participate in, and modify user-generated or self-curated content. Social media are used to document memories, learn, and form friendships. They may be used to promote people, companies, products, and ideas. Social media can be used to consume, publish, or share news. Popular social media platforms with more than 100 million registered users include X, Facebook, WeChat, ShareChat, Instagram, Pinterest, QZone, Weibo, VK, Tumblr, Baidu Tieba, and LinkedIn. Depending on interpretation, other popular platforms that are sometimes referred to as social media services include YouTube, Letterboxd, QQ, Quora, Telegram, WhatsApp, Signal, LINE, Snapchat, Pinterest, Viber, Reddit, Discord, TikTok, Microsoft Teams.

Social media outlets differ from old media (e.g. newspapers, TV, and radio broadcasting) in many ways, including quality, reach, frequency, usability, relevancy, and permanence. Social media outlets operate in a *dialogic* transmission system (many sources to many receivers) while traditional media operate under a *monologic* transmission model (one source to many receivers). For instance, a newspaper is delivered to many subscribers, and a radio station broadcasts the same programs to a city.

Observers have noted a range of positive and negative impacts from social media. Social media can help to improve an individual's sense of connectedness with others and be an effective communication (or marketing) tool for corporations, entrepreneurs, non-profit organizations, advocacy groups, political parties, and governments. Social movements use social media for communicating and organizing. Social media has been criticized for a range of negative impacts on children and teenagers, including exposure to inappropriate content, exploitation by adults, sleep problems, attention problems, feelings of exclusion, and various mental health maladies.

History

The PLATO system was launched in 1960 at the University of Illinois and subsequently commercially marketed by Control Data Corporation. It offered early forms of social media features with innovations such as Notes, PLATO's message-forum application; TERM-talk, its instant-messaging feature; Talkomatic, perhaps the first online chat room; News Report, a crowdsourced online newspaper, and blog and Access Lists, enabling the owner of a note file or other application to limit access to a certain set of users, for example, only friends, classmates, or co-workers.

ARPANET, which came online in 1967, had by the late 1970s enabled exchange of non-government/business ideas and communication, as evidenced by the network etiquette (or "netiquette") described in a 1982 handbook on computing at MIT's Artificial Intelligence Laboratory. ARPANET evolved into the Internet in the 1990s. Usenet, conceived by Tom Truscott and Jim Ellis in 1979 at the University of North Carolina at Chapel Hill and Duke University, was the first open social media app, established in 1980. A precursor of the electronic bulletin board system (BBS), known as Community Memory, appeared by 1973. Mainstream BBSs arrived with the Computer Bulletin Board System in Chicago, which launched on February 16, 1978. Before long, most major US cities had more than one BBS, running on TRS-80, Apple II, Atari, IBM PC, Commodore 64, Sinclair, and similar personal computers. CompuServe, Prodigy, and AOL were three of the largest BBS companies and were the first to migrate to the Internet in the 1990s. Between the mid-1980s and the mid-1990s, BBSes numbered in the tens of thousands in North America alone. Message forums were the signature BBS phenomenon throughout the 1980s and early 1990s.

In 1991, Tim Berners-Lee integrated HTML hypertext software with the Internet, creating the World Wide Web. This breakthrough led to an explosion of blogs, list servers, and email services. Message forums migrated to the web, and evolved into Internet forums, supported by cheaper access as well as the ability to handle far more people simultaneously.

These early text-based systems expanded to include images and video in the 21st century, aided by digital cameras and camera phones.

The evolution of online services progressed from serving as channels for networked communication to becoming interactive platforms for networked social interaction with the advent of Web 2.0.

Social media started in the mid-1990s with the invention of platforms like GeoCities, Classmates.com, and SixDegrees.com. While instant messaging and chat clients existed at the time, SixDegrees was unique as it was the first online service designed for people to connect using their actual names instead of anonymously. It boasted features like profiles, friends lists, and school affiliations, making it "the very first social networking site".

The platform's name was inspired by the "six degrees of separation" concept, which suggests that every person on the planet is just six connections away from everyone else.

In the early 2000s, social media platforms gained widespread popularity with the likes of Friendster and Myspace, followed by Facebook, YouTube, and X.

Research from 2015 reported that globally, users spent 22% of their online time on social networks, likely fueled by the availability of smartphones. As of 2023 as many as 4.76 billion people used social media some 59% of the global population.

Definition

A 2015 review identified four features unique to social media services:

- Web 2.0 Internet-based applications.
- User-generated content
- User-created self profiles

- Social networks formed by connections between profiles, such as followers, groups, and lists.

In 2019, Merriam-Webster defined social media as “forms of electronic communication (such as websites for social networking and microblogging) through which users create online communities to share information, ideas, personal messages, and other content (such as videos).”

Services

Social media encompasses an expanding suite of services:

- Blogs (ex. HuffPost, Boing Boing).
- Business networks (ex. LinkedIn, XING).
- Collaborative projects (Mozilla, GitHub).
- Enterprise social networks (Yammer, Socialcast, Slack).
- Forums (Gaia Online, IGN).
- Microblogs (X, Tumblr, Weibo).
- Photo sharing (Pinterest, Flickr, Photobucket).
- Products/services review (Amazon, Upwork).
- Social bookmarking (Delicious, Pinterest).
- Social gaming (Fortnite, World of Warcraft).
- Social network (Facebook, Instagram, Baidu Tieba, VK, QZone, ShareChat, WeChat).
- Video sharing (YouTube, Vimeo).
- Virtual worlds (Second Life, Twinity).

Some services offer more than one type of service.

Mobile Social Media

Mobile social media refers to the use of social media on mobile devices such as phones and tablets. It is distinguished by its ubiquity, since users no longer have to be at desk in order to participate on a computer. Mobile services can further make use of the user’s immediate location to offer information, connections, or services relevant to that location.

According to Andreas Kaplan, mobile social media activities fall among four types:

- **Space-Timers (Location and Time-Sensitive):** Exchange of messages with relevance for a specific location at a specific point in time (posting about a traffic jam)

- **Space-Locators (Only Location Sensitive):** Posts/messages with relevance for a specific location, read later by others (e.g. a restaurant review)
- **Quick-Timers (only Time Sensitive):** Transfer of traditional social media mobile apps to increase immediacy (e.g. posting status updates)
- **Slow-Timers (Neither Location nor Time Sensitive):** Transfer of traditional social media applications to mobile devices (e.g., watching a video)

Elements and Function

Certain content has the potential to spread *virally*, an analogy for the way viral infections spread contagiously from individual to individual. One user spreads a post across their network, which leads those users to follow suit. A post from a relatively unknown user can reach vast numbers of people within hours. Virality is not guaranteed; few posts make the transition. Viral marketing campaigns are particularly attractive to businesses because they can achieve widespread advertising coverage at a fraction of the cost of traditional marketing campaigns. Nonprofit organizations and activists may also attempt to spread content virally. Social media sites provide specific functionality to help users re-share content, such as X's and Facebook's "like" option.

Bots are automated programs that operate on the internet. They automate many communication tasks. This has led to the creation of an industry of bot providers. Chatbots and social bots are programmed to mimic human interactions such as liking, commenting, and following. Bots have also been developed to facilitate social media marketing. Bots have led the marketing industry into an analytical crisis, as bots make it difficult to differentiate between human interactions and bot interactions. Some bots violate platforms' terms of use, which can result in bans and campaigns to eliminate bots categorically. Bots may even pose as real people to avoid prohibitions. 'Cyborgs'—either bot-assisted humans or human-assisted bots—are used for both legitimate and illegitimate purposes, from spreading fake news to creating marketing buzz. A common use claimed to be legitimate includes posting at a specific time. A human writes a post content and the bot posts it a specific time. In other cases, cyborgs spread fake news. Cyborgs may work as sock puppets, where one human pretends to be someone else, or operates multiple accounts, each pretending to be a person.

A multitude of United States patents are related to social media, growing rapidly. As of 2020, over 5000 social media patent applications had been published in the United States. Only slightly over 100 patents had been issued. As an instance of technological convergence, various social media platforms adapted functionality beyond their original scope, increasingly overlapping with each other. Examples are the social hub site Facebook launching an integrated video platform in May 2007, and Instagram, whose original scope was low-resolution photo sharing, introducing the ability to share quarter-minute 640×640 pixel videos (late extended to a minute with increased resolution). Instagram later implemented stories (short videos self-destructing after 24 hours), a concept popularized by Snapchat, as well as *IGTV*, for seekable videos. Stories were then adopted by YouTube. X, whose original scope was text-based microblogging, later adopted photo sharing, then video sharing, then a media studio for business users, after YouTube's Creator Studio.

The discussion platform Reddit added an integrated image hoster replacing the external image sharing platform Imgur, and then an internal video hosting service, followed by image galleries (multiple images in a single post), known from Imgur. Imgur implemented video sharing. YouTube rolled out a Community feature, for sharing text-only posts and polls.

Usage Statistics

A 2009 study suggested that individual differences may help explain who uses social media: extraversion and openness have a positive relationship with social media, while emotional stability has a negative sloping relationship with social media. A 2015 study reported that people with a higher social comparison orientation appear to use social media more heavily than people with low social comparison orientation.

Common Sense Media reported that children under age 13 in the United States use social networking services despite the fact that many social media sites require users to be 13 or older. In 2017, the firm conducted a survey of parents of children from birth to age 8 and reported that 4% of children at this age used social media sites such as Instagram, Snapchat, or (now-defunct) Musical.ly "often" or "sometimes". Their 2019 survey surveyed Americans ages 8–16 and reported that about 31% of children ages 8–12 use social media. In that survey, teens aged 16–18 were asked when they started using social media. the median age was 14, although 28% said they started to use it before reaching 13.

Social media played a role in communication during the COVID-19 pandemic. In June 2020, a survey by Cartoon Network and the Cyberbullying Research Center surveyed Americans tweens (ages 9–12) and reported that the most popular application was YouTube (67%). (as age increased, tweens were more likely to have used social media apps and games.) Similarly, Common Sense Media's 2020 survey of Americans ages 13–18 reported that YouTube was the most popular (used by 86% of 13- to 18-year-olds). As children aged, they increasingly utilized social media services and often used YouTube to consume content.

While adults were using social media before the COVID-19 pandemic, more started using it to stay socially connected and to get pandemic updates.

- "Social media have become popularly use to seek for medical information and have fascinated the general public to collect information regarding corona virus pandemics in various perspectives. During these days, people are forced to stay at home and the social media have connected and supported awareness and pandemic updates."

Healthcare workers and systems became more aware of social media as a place people were getting health information:

- "During the COVID-19 pandemic, social media use has accelerated to the point of becoming a ubiquitous part of modern healthcare systems."

This also led to the spread of disinformation. On December 11, 2020, the CDC put out a "Call to Action: Managing the Infodemic". Some healthcare organizations used hashtags as interventions and published articles on their X data:

- "Promotion of the joint usage of #PedsICU and #COVID19 throughout the international pediatric critical care community in tweets relevant to the coronavirus disease 2019 pandemic and pediatric critical care."

However others in the medical community were concerned about social media addiction, as it became an increasingly important context and therefore "source of social validation and reinforcement" and were unsure whether increased social media use was harmful.

Social Impacts and Regulation

The digital divide is the unequal access to digital technology, including smartphones, tablets, laptops, and the internet. The digital divide worsens inequality around access to information and resources. In the Information Age, people without access to the Internet and other technology are at a disadvantage, for they are unable or less able to connect with others, find and apply for jobs, shop, and learn.

People who are homeless, living in poverty, elderly people, and those living in rural communities may have limited access to the Internet; in contrast, urban middle class and upper-class people have easy access to the Internet. Another divide is between producers and consumers of Internet content, which could be a result of educational disparities. While social media use varies across age groups, a US 2010 study reported no racial divide.

According to the Pew Research Center and others, a majority of Americans at least occasionally receive news from social media. Because of recommendation algorithms that filter and display news content that matches users' political preferences, one potential impact is an increase in political polarization due to selective exposure. Political polarization is the divergence of political attitudes towards ideological extremes. Selective exposure occurs when an individual favors information that supports their beliefs and avoids information that conflicts with them. A 2016 study of U.S. elections revealed gender differences in the political use of X between candidates. On social media women discuss policy issues at a higher rate than males. The study concluded that an increase in female candidates correlated to an increase in the amount of attention paid to policy issues, potentially heightening polarization.

Efforts to combat selective exposure may increase political polarization. A study examining X activity paid Democrat and Republican participants to follow X users whose content was different from their political beliefs (Republicans received liberal content and Democrats received conservative content) over a six-week period. At the end of the study, both Democrat and Republican participants were reported to have increased political polarization in favor of their own parties, though only Republican participants had an increase that was statistically significant.

Though some research reported that social media increases political polarization, others reported that social media can persuade users to change their beliefs. A 2016 online survey of 1,024 U.S. users reported that individuals who use social media were more likely to have their political beliefs persuaded than those who did not. In particular, those using social media as a means to receive news were the most likely to change their beliefs. The persuasion reported by participants was influenced by their exposure to diverse viewpoints, in content they saw as well as political discussions they participated in. Another similar 2016 study conducted with 189 university students examined the persuasive effect of watching a political comedy video on Facebook, reporting that after watching comedian/political commentator John Oliver, participants were likely to be persuaded to change their viewpoint on the topic (either payday lending or the Ferguson protests) to one that was closer to Oliver. The persuasive effect was reported to be reduced if they viewed comments by Facebook users that contradicted Oliver.

Research has also reported that social media use may not affect polarization at all. A U.S. national survey of 1,032 participants reported that participants who used social media were more likely to be exposed to diverse people and opinions than others, although using social media was not correlated with a change in political polarization for these participants.

A 2017 study examining the potential polarizing effects of social media on the political views of its users suggested that a new way of engaging with social media must occur to avoid polarization. The authors stated that media literacy (described as methods that people can use to critique and create media) are valuable, and state that such skills must develop in order to be the most effective. In order to decrease polarization and encourage cooperation among social media users, Relevant skills included connecting with others in a caring way, embracing differences, and understanding the impact of social media on political, social, and cultural issues.

A 2018 study reported that social media increases the power of stereotypes. Stereotypes can have both negative and positive connotations. For example, during the COVID-19 pandemic, youth were accused of responsibility for spreading the disease. Elderly people get stereotyped as lacking knowledge of proper behavior on social media.

Social media allows for mass cultural exchange and intercultural communication, despite different ways of communicating in various cultures.

Social media has affected the way youth communicate, by introducing new forms of language. Novel acronyms save time, as illustrated by "LOL", which is the ubiquitous shortcut for "laugh out loud".

The hashtag was created to simplify searching for information and to allow users to highlight topics of interest in the hope of attracting the attention of others. Hashtags can be used to advocate for a movement, mark content for future use, and allow other users to contribute to a discussion.

For some young people, social media and texting have largely replaced in person communications, made worse by pandemic isolation, delaying the development of conversation and other social skills.

What is socially acceptable is now heavily based on social media. The American Academy of Pediatrics reported that bullying, the making of non-inclusive friend groups, and sexual experimentation have increased cyberbullying, privacy issues, and sending sexual images or messages. Sexting and revenge porn became rampant, particularly among minors, with legal implications and resulting trauma risk. However, adolescents can learn basic social and technical skills online. Social media, can strengthen relationships just by keeping in touch, making more friends, and engaging in community activities.

Content Moderation

Historically, platforms were responsible for moderating the content that they presented. They set rules for what was allowable, decided which content to promote and which to ignore. The US enacted the Communications Decency Act in 1996. Section 230 of that act exempted internet platforms from legal liability for content authored by third parties.

- No provider or user of an interactive computer service shall be treated as the publisher or speaker of any information provided by another information content provider." (47 U.S.C. § 230(c)(1)).—*US Congress, Communications Decency Act Section 230*

The European Union initially took a similar approach. However, in 2020, the European Commission presented two legislative proposals: The Digital Services Act (DSA) and the Digital Markets Act (DMA).

Both proposals were enacted in July 2022. The DSA entered into force on 17 February 2024, the DMA in March 2024. This legislation can be summarized in the following four objectives, articulated by MEPs:

- "What is illegal offline must also be illegal online".
- "Very large online platforms" must therefore, among other things:
  - delete illegal content (propaganda, election interference, hate crimes and online harms such as harassment and child abuse) and better protect fundamental rights,
  - redesign their systems to ensure a "high level of privacy, security and protection of minors", by prohibiting advertising based on personal data, designing recommender systems to minimize risks for children and demonstrating this to the European Commission via a risk assessment, and
  - not use sensitive personal data such as race, gender and religion to target advertising.

Violators could face a complete ban in Europe or fines of up to 6% of global sales. Such content moderation requires extensive investment by platform providers. Enforcement resources may not be sufficient to ensure compliance.

Tthe DSA allows a country to require information to be deleted that is illegal only in that jurisdiction. For example, Hungary could require a video to be deleted that is in part critical of its government, but the video would then be unavailable in other EU countries as well.

2018 Nobel Laureate Paul Romer advocated taxing negative externalities of social media platforms. Similar to a carbon tax – negative social effects could be compensated for by a financial levy on the platforms. Assuming that the tax did not deter the actions that produced the externalities, the revenue raised could be used to address them. However, consensus has yet to emerge on how to measure or mitigate the harms, nor to craft a tax,.

Another proposal is to invoke competition law. The idea is to restrict the platforms' market power by controlling mergers *ex ante* and tightening the law. This would be achieved through a supranational enforcement mechanism and the deterrent effect of high fines.

Business Models

The business model of most social media platforms is based on selling slots to advertisers. Platforms provide access to data about each user, which allows them to deliver adds that are individually relevant to them. This strongly incents platforms to arrange their content so that users view as much content as possible, increasing the number of ads that they see. Platforms such as X add paid user subscriptions in part to reduce their dependence on advertising revenues.

Criticism, Debate and Controversy

The enormous reach and impact of social media has naturally led to a stream of criticism, debate, and controversy. Criticisms include platform capabilities, content moderation and reliability, impact on concentration, mental health, content ownership, and the meaning of interactions, and poor cross-platform interoperability, decrease in face-to-face interactions, cyberbullying, sexual predation, particularly of children, and child pornography.

In 2007 Andrew Keen wrote, "Out of this anarchy, it suddenly became clear that what was governing the infinite monkeys now inputting away on the Internet was the law of digital Darwinism, the survival of the loudest and most opinionated. Under these rules, the only way to intellectually prevail is by infinite filibustering."

Social media has become a regular source of news and information. A 2021 Pew Research Center poll reported roughly 70% of users regularly get news from social media, despite the presence of fake news and misinformation. Platforms typically do not take responsibility for content accuracy, and many do not vet content at all, although in some cases, content the platform finds problematic is deleted or access to it is reduced. Content distribution algorithms otherwise typically ignore substance, responding instead to the contents' virality.

In 2018, researchers reported that fake news spread almost 70% faster than truthful news on X. Social media bots on social media increase the reach of both true and false content and if wielded by bad actors misinformation can reach many more users. Some platforms attempt to discover and block bots, with limited success. Fake news seems to receive more user engagement, possibly because it is relatively novel, engaging users' curiosity and increasing spread. Fake news often propagates in the immediate aftermath of an event, before conventional media are prepared to publish.

Social media mining is the process of obtaining data from user-generated content on social media in order to extract actionable patterns, form conclusions about users, and act upon the information. Mining supports targeting advertising to users or academic research. The term is an analogy to the process of mining for minerals. Mining companies sift through raw ore to find the valuable minerals; likewise, social media mining sifts through social media data in order to discern patterns and trends about matters such as social media usage, online behaviour, content sharing, connections between individuals, buying behaviour. These patterns and trends are of interest to companies, governments and not-for-profit organizations, as such organizations can use the analyses for tasks such as design strategies, introduce programs, products, processes or services.

Social media mining uses concepts from computer science, data mining, machine learning, and statistics. Mining is based on social network analysis, network science, sociology, ethnography, optimization and mathematics. It attempts to formally represent, measure and model patterns from social media data. In the 2010s, major corporations, governments and not-for-profit organizations began mining to learn about customers, clients and others.

Platforms such as Google, Facebook (partnered with Datalogix and BlueKai) conduct mining to targe users with advertising. Scientists and machine learning researchers extract insights and design product features.

Users may not understand how platforms use their data. Users tend to click through Terms of Use agreements without reading them, leading to ethical questions about whether platforms adequately protect users' privacy.

During the 2016 United States presidential election, Facebook allowed Cambridge Analytica, a political consulting firm linked to the Trump campaign, to analyze the data of an estimated 87 million Facebook users to profile voters, creating controversy when this was revealed.

Malcolm Gladwell considers the role of social media in revolutions and protests to be overstated. He concluded that while social media makes it easier for activists to express themselves, that expression likely has no impact beyond social media. What he called "high-risk activism" involves strong relationships, coordination, commitment, high risks, and sacrifice. Gladwell claimed that social media are built around weak ties and argues that "social networks are effective at increasing participation—by lessening the level of motivation that participation requires." According to him, "Facebook activism succeeds not by motivating people to make a real sacrifice, but by motivating them to do the things that people do when they are not motivated enough to make a real sacrifice."

Disputing Gladwell's theory, a 2018 survey reported that people who are politically expressive on social media are more likely to participate in offline political activity.

Social media content is generated by users. However, content ownership is defined by the Terms of Service to which users agree. Platforms control access to the content, and may make it available to third parties.

Although platform's terms differ, generally they all give permission to utilize users' copyrighted works at the platform's discretion.

After its acquisition by Facebook in 2012, Instagram revealed it intended to use content in ads without seeking permission from or paying its users. It then reversed these changes, with then-CEO Kevin Systrom promising to update the terms of service. Privacy rights advocates warn users about the collection of their personal data. Information is captured without the user's knowing consent. Data may be applied to law enforcement or other governmental purposes. Information may be offered for third party use.

Young people are prone to sharing personal information that can attract predators.

While social media users claim to want to keep their data private, their behavior does not reflect that concern, as many users expose significant personal data on their profiles.

In addition, platforms collect data on user behaviors that are not part of their personal profiles. This data is made available to third parties for purposes that include targeted advertising.

A 2014 Pew Research Center survey reported that 91% of Americans "agree" or "strongly agree" that people have lost control over how personal information is collected and used. Some 80% of social media users said they were concerned about advertisers and businesses accessing the data they share on social media platforms, and 64% said the government should do more to regulate advertisers. In 2019, UK legislators criticized Facebook for not protecting certain aspects of user data.

In 2019 the Pentagon issued guidance to the military, Coast Guard and other government agencies that identified "the potential risk associated with using the TikTok app and directs appropriate action for employees to take in order to safeguard their personal information." As a result, the military, Coast Guard, Transportation Security Administration, and Department of Homeland Security banned the installation and use of TikTok on government devices.

In 2020 The US government attempted to ban TikTok and WeChat from the States over national security concerns. However, a federal court blocked the move. In 2024, the US Congress passed a low directing TikTok's parent company ByteDance to divest the service or see the service banned from operating in the US. The company sued, challenging the constitutionality of the ban.

Internet addiction disorder (IAD), also known as problematic internet use or pathological internet use, is problematic, compulsive use of the internet, particularly social media, that impairs individual function over a prolonged period of time. Young people are at particular risk of developing internet addiction disorder, with case studies highlighting students whose academic performance declines as they spend more time online. Some experience health consequences from loss of sleep as they stay up to continue scrolling, chatting, and gaming.

Excessive Internet use is not recognized as a disorder by the World Health Organization, the *Diagnostic and Statistical Manual of Mental Disorders (DSM-5)* or the *International Classification of Diseases (ICD-11)*. However, gaming disorder appears in the *ICD-11*. Controversy around the diagnosis includes whether the disorder is a separate clinical entity, or a manifestation of underlying psychiatric disorders. Definitions are not standardized or agreed upon, complicating the development of evidence-based recommendations.

Users under 30 access the Internet more than other age groups and experience a higher risk of overuse.

In 2011 the term "Facebook addiction disorder" (FAD) emerged. FAD is characterized by compulsive use of Facebook. A 2017 study investigated a correlation between excessive use and narcissism, reporting "FAD was significantly positively related to the personality trait narcissism and to negative mental health variables (depression, anxiety, and stress symptoms)".

In 2020, the documentary *The Social Dilemma* reported the concerns of mental health experts and former employees of social media companies over social media's pursuit of addictive use. For example, when a user has not visited Facebook for some time, the platform varies its notifications, attempting to lure them back. It also raises concerns about the correlation between social media use and child and teen suicidality.

Turning off social media notifications may help reduce social media use. For some users, changes in web browsing can be helpful in compensating for self-regulatory problems. For instance, a study involving 157 online learners on massive open online courses examined the impact of such an intervention. The study reported that providing support in self-regulation was associated with a reduction in time spent online, particularly on entertainment.

Whether to restrict the use of phones and social media among young people has been debated since smartphones became ubiquitous. A study of Americans aged 12-15, reported that teenagers who used social media over three hours/day doubled their risk of negative mental health outcomes, including depression and anxiety. Platforms have not tuned their algorithms to prevent young people from viewing inappropriate content. A 2023 study of Australian youth reported that 57% had seen disturbingly violent content, while nearly half had regular exposure to sexual images. Further, youth are prone to misuse social media for cyberbullying.

As result, phones have been banned from some schools, and some schools have blocked social media websites. In 2024, Florida banned the use of social media by minors.

Social media often features in political struggles. In some countries, Internet police or secret police monitor or control citizens' use of social media. For example, in 2013 some social media was banned in Turkey after the Taksim Gezi Park protests. Both X and YouTube were temporarily suspended in the country by a court's decision.

A law granted immunity to Telecommunications Directorate (TİB) personnel. The TİB was also given the authority to block access to specific websites without a court order. Yet TİB's 2014 blocking of X was ruled by the constitutional court to violate free speech.

In the 2014 Thai coup d'état, the public was explicitly instructed not to 'share' or 'like' dissenting views on social media or face prison. In July of that year, in response to WikiLeaks' release of a secret suppression order made by the Victorian Supreme Court, media lawyers were quoted in the Australian media to the effect that "anyone who tweets a link to the WikiLeaks report, posts it on Facebook, or shares it in any way online could also face charges". On 27 July 2020, in Egypt, two women were sentenced to two years of imprisonment for posting TikTok videos, which the government claims are "violating family values".

Internet censorship in the United States is the suppression of information published or viewed on the Internet in the United States. The First Amendment of the United States Constitution protects freedom of speech and expression against federal, state, and local government censorship.

Free speech protections allow little government-mandated Internet content restrictions. However, the Internet is highly regulated, supported by a complex set of legally binding and privately mediated mechanisms.

Gambling, cyber security, and the dangers to children who frequent social media are important ongoing debates. Significant public resistance to proposed content restriction policies has prevented measures used in some other countries from taking hold in the US

Many government-mandated attempts to regulate content have been barred, often after lengthy legal battles. However, the government has exerted pressure indirectly. With the exception of child pornography, content restrictions tend to rely on platforms to remove/suppress content, following state encouragement or the threat of legal action.

Intellectual property protections yielded a system that predictably removes infringing materials. The US also seizes domains and computers, at times without notification.

While the dominant social media platforms are not interoperable, open source protocols such as ActivityPub have been adopted by platforms such as Mastodon, GNU social, Diaspora, and Friendica. They operate as a loose federation of mostly volunteer-operated servers, called the Fediverse. However, in 2019, Mastodon blocked Gab from connecting to it, claiming that it spread violent, right-wing extremism. In December 2019, X CEO Jack Dorsey advocated an "open and decentralized standard for social media". He joined Bluesky to bring it to reality.

Deplatforming, (no-platforming), a form of Internet censorship of an individual or group by preventing them from posting on the platforms they use to share their information/ideas. This typically involves suspension, outright bans, or reducing spread (shadow banning).

As early as 2015, platforms such as Reddit began to enforce selective bans based, for example, on terms of service that prohibit "hate speech". The most notorious examples of deplatforming were Twitter's ban of then-US President Donald Trump shortly after and the *New York Post* during the 2020 presidential election.

According to *LikeWar: The Weaponization of Social Media*, the use of effective social media marketing techniques includes not only celebrities, corporations, and governments, but also extremist groups. The use of social media by ISIS and Al-Qaeda has been used to influence public opinion where it operates and gain the attention of sympathizers. Social media platforms and encrypted-messaging applications have been used to recruit members, both locally and internationally. Platforms have endured backlash for allowing this content. Extreme nationalist groups, and more prominently, US right-wing extremists have used similar online tactics. As many traditional social media platforms banned hate speech, several platforms became popular among right-wing extremists to carry out planning and communication including of events; these application became known as "Alt-tech". Platforms such as Telegram, Parler, and Gab were used during the January 6 United States Capitol attack, to coordinate attacks. Members shared tips on how to avoid law enforcement and their plans on carrying out their objectives; some users called for killing law enforcement officers and politicians.

1.2 EVOLUTION AND IMPACT OF DIGITAL CHANNELS IN MARKETING

The landscape of marketing has undergone a significant transformation with the advent and evolution of digital channels. From the early days of the internet to the contemporary era dominated by social media, mobile applications, and sophisticated data analytics, digital channels have revolutionized how businesses engage with consumers. This shift has not only enhanced the reach and effectiveness of marketing campaigns but also altered the fundamental principles of marketing strategies.

The evolution of digital channels has fundamentally reshaped the marketing landscape. From the early days of email marketing and simple websites to the sophisticated, data-driven, and highly interactive strategies of today, digital channels have enabled businesses to connect with consumers in more meaningful and impactful ways. As technology continues to advance, the future of digital marketing promises even greater innovation, offering endless possibilities for businesses to reach and engage their audiences. The key to success in this dynamic environment lies in staying adaptable, leveraging data and technology, and consistently delivering value to consumers through personalized and relevant experiences.

1.2.1 The Early Stages of Digital Marketing

The inception of digital marketing can be traced back to the 1990s with the commercialization of the internet. The introduction of the World Wide Web brought about a new dimension for businesses to connect with their audience. Early digital marketing efforts were primarily focused on email marketing and simple websites. Email marketing, with its ability to reach consumers directly, quickly became a popular tool. However, these initial forays were often marked by a lack of personalization and high levels of spam. Websites in the early days served as digital brochures, providing information about products and services without much interactivity. Banner ads were among the first forms of online advertising, appearing on websites in a static and often intrusive manner. Despite their rudimentary nature, these early digital marketing efforts laid the groundwork for more sophisticated and interactive methods that would follow.

1.2.2 The Rise of Search Engines and SEO

The late 1990s and early 2000s saw the emergence of search engines, most notably Google. The development of search engine algorithms transformed how information was accessed on the internet, giving rise to Search Engine Optimization (SEO). SEO became a crucial aspect of digital marketing, as businesses strived to appear at the top of search engine results pages (SERPs). This shift marked the beginning of content-driven marketing, where creating valuable and relevant content became essential for improving search rankings and attracting organic traffic. Pay-per-click (PPC) advertising also emerged during this period, with Google AdWords (now Google Ads) launching in 2000. PPC allowed businesses to bid on keywords and display ads in search results, providing a more targeted and measurable approach to online advertising compared to traditional banner ads.

1.2.3 The Social Media Revolution

The mid-2000s heralded the social media revolution with the launch of platforms such as Facebook, Twitter, and LinkedIn. Social media fundamentally changed how businesses interacted with consumers. These platforms enabled two-way communication, allowing brands to engage with their audience in real-time. Social media marketing became a powerful tool for building brand awareness, fostering customer loyalty, and driving engagement. The rise of social media influencers also added a new dimension to digital marketing. Influencers, with their large and engaged followings, became valuable partners for brands looking to reach niche audiences authentically. This shift emphasized the importance of trust and credibility in marketing, as consumers increasingly relied on recommendations from influencers over traditional advertising.

1.2.4 The Mobile Era

The proliferation of smartphones in the late 2000s and early 2010s ushered in the mobile era. Mobile devices became the primary means of accessing the internet, leading to the development of mobile-friendly websites and applications. Mobile marketing strategies, including SMS marketing, in-app advertising, and location-based marketing, emerged to cater to the on-the-go consumer. The integration of mobile technology with digital marketing allowed for more personalized and contextual advertising. For instance, geo-targeting enabled businesses to deliver location-specific offers and promotions, enhancing the relevance and effectiveness of marketing campaigns.

1.2.5 Data-Driven Marketing and Analytics

The digital age brought an unprecedented amount of data, enabling businesses to gain deeper insights into consumer behavior and preferences. The use of data analytics became a cornerstone of digital marketing, allowing for more informed decision-making and targeted strategies. Tools like Google Analytics and various customer relationship management (CRM) systems provided valuable metrics and analytics, helping marketers track the performance of campaigns and optimize them in real-time. The ability to segment audiences based on demographics, behavior, and interests allowed for highly personalized marketing efforts. Personalized email campaigns, targeted ads, and customized content became standard practices, significantly improving engagement and conversion rates.

1.2.6 The Emergence of Content Marketing

Content marketing emerged as a dominant strategy in the 2010s, emphasizing the creation and distribution of valuable, relevant, and consistent content to attract and retain a clearly defined audience. Blogs, videos, podcasts, and infographics became essential tools for storytelling and brand building. Content marketing not only helped improve SEO but also established brands as thought leaders and trusted sources of information. The rise of video content, in particular, transformed digital marketing. Platforms like YouTube and later TikTok created opportunities for brands to reach vast audiences through engaging and shareable video content. Live streaming also gained popularity, allowing for real-time interaction and engagement with consumers.

1.2.7 The Role of Artificial Intelligence and Automation

In recent years, artificial intelligence (AI) and automation have further revolutionized digital marketing. AI-powered tools and algorithms have enhanced various aspects of marketing, from chatbots providing instant customer support to predictive analytics forecasting consumer behavior. Machine learning has enabled more sophisticated targeting and personalization, ensuring that marketing messages are delivered to the right audience at the right time. Automation has streamlined many marketing processes, such as email marketing, social media posting, and ad campaigns. Marketing automation platforms like HubSpot and Marketo allow businesses to automate repetitive tasks, nurture leads, and measure the effectiveness of campaigns more efficiently.

1.2.8 The Impact of Digital Channels on Marketing

The evolution of digital channels has had a profound impact on marketing, transforming it in several key ways:

- **Enhanced Reach and Accessibility**: Digital channels have enabled businesses to reach a global audience. The internet's accessibility means that even small businesses can compete with larger corporations on a more level playing field.
- **Improved Targeting and Personalization**: The ability to collect and analyze data has allowed for highly targeted and personalized marketing efforts. Businesses can segment their audience and deliver tailored messages, improving engagement and conversion rates.
- **Real-Time Interaction and Engagement**: Social media and mobile technology have facilitated real-time interaction between brands and consumers. This immediacy has enhanced customer service, fostered brand loyalty, and enabled quicker responses to market trends and consumer feedback.
- **Cost-Effectiveness:** Digital marketing often proves to be more cost-effective than traditional marketing methods. Pay-per-click advertising, social media marketing, and content marketing typically offer higher returns on investment, especially for small and medium-sized enterprises.
- **Measurability and Analytics**: The digital landscape provides extensive metrics and analytics, allowing marketers to measure the effectiveness of their campaigns accurately. This data-driven approach enables continuous optimization and better allocation of marketing budgets.
- **Innovative Formats and Channels**: The evolution of digital channels has introduced innovative formats and platforms, from immersive video content to interactive social media features. These innovations have opened new avenues for creativity and engagement in marketing.

1.3 OVERVIEW OF DIGITAL MARKETING

Digital marketing refers to the use of digital channels and technologies to promote products, services, or brands to a target audience. This broad field encompasses a wide range of strategies and techniques aimed at engaging consumers, driving sales, and building brand awareness in the online world. With the rapid advancement of technology and the increasing reliance on the internet, digital marketing has become an essential component of modern business strategies.Digital marketing has transformed the way businesses connect with consumers, offering unprecedented opportunities for reach, engagement, and growth. By leveraging various digital channels and strategies, businesses can create targeted, personalized, and cost-effective marketing campaigns that drive results. However, navigating the dynamic digital landscape requires continuous learning, adaptation, and a data-driven approach. As technology continues to evolve, staying ahead of trends and embracing innovation will be key to thriving in the digital marketing realm.

1.3.1 The Core Components of Digital Marketing

Digital marketing comprises various components, each with its unique functions and benefits. Understanding these core elements is crucial for crafting effective marketing strategies.

- **Search Engine Optimization (SEO):** SEO involves optimizing a website to rank higher in search engine results pages (SERPs) organically. It focuses on improving site structure, content quality, and user experience to increase visibility for relevant search queries. Key SEO techniques include keyword research, on-page optimization (meta tags, headers, content), off-page optimization (backlinks), and technical SEO (site speed, mobile-friendliness).
- **Content Marketing:** Content marketing centers on creating and distributing valuable, relevant, and consistent content to attract and engage a target audience. It includes blogs, articles, videos, infographics, podcasts, and social media posts. The goal is to provide useful information that addresses the audience's needs, thereby building trust and credibility with potential customers.
- **Social Media Marketing:** Social media marketing involves using social media platforms like Facebook, Twitter, Instagram, LinkedIn, and TikTok to promote products or services. It encompasses both organic activities (posting, engaging with followers) and paid advertising (sponsored posts, ads). Social media marketing helps increase brand awareness, drive website traffic, and foster customer loyalty through direct interaction.

- **Pay-Per-Click (PPC) Advertising:** PPC is a model of internet marketing where advertisers pay a fee each time their ad is clicked. Google Ads is the most popular PPC platform, but social media platforms like Facebook and LinkedIn also offer PPC advertising. PPC allows for precise targeting based on keywords, demographics, interests, and behavior, making it an effective tool for driving immediate traffic and conversions.
- **Email Marketing:** Email marketing involves sending targeted messages to a group of subscribers via email. It is a powerful tool for nurturing leads, building relationships, and encouraging repeat business. Effective email marketing campaigns often include personalized content, segmented lists, automated workflows, and performance tracking to ensure relevancy and engagement.
- **Affiliate Marketing:** Affiliate marketing is a performance-based strategy where businesses reward affiliates for driving traffic or sales through their marketing efforts. Affiliates, often bloggers or influencers, promote the business's products or services on their platforms and earn a commission for every sale or lead generated. This approach leverages the reach and credibility of affiliates to expand the business's market presence.
- **Influencer Marketing:** Influencer marketing involves collaborating with influencers—individuals with a large and engaged following in a specific niche—to promote a product or service. Influencers create content that showcases the brand to their audience, leveraging their credibility and relationship with followers to drive engagement and conversions. This strategy is particularly effective in reaching younger demographics and niche markets.
- **Online Public Relations (PR):** Online PR involves managing and influencing an organization's reputation and presence across digital platforms. This includes engaging with online publications, bloggers, and social media influencers to generate positive coverage, handling online reviews, and managing crisis communications. Effective online PR strategies help build a positive brand image and enhance visibility in the digital space.
- **Mobile Marketing:** Mobile marketing focuses on reaching audiences on their mobile devices through SMS, mobile apps, push notifications, and mobile-optimized websites. With the increasing use of smartphones, mobile marketing has become a critical aspect of digital strategies, enabling businesses to engage with consumers wherever they are.

1.3.2 The Benefits of Digital Marketing

Digital marketing offers numerous advantages over traditional marketing methods. These benefits highlight why businesses, both large and small, are investing heavily in digital strategies.

- **Global Reach:** Digital marketing enables businesses to reach a global audience. Unlike traditional marketing, which is often limited by geography, digital channels allow for worldwide exposure, making it easier to expand into new markets.
- **Cost-Effectiveness:** Compared to traditional marketing methods such as TV or print advertising, digital marketing is generally more cost-effective. Platforms like social media and email marketing offer affordable options for businesses with limited budgets, while PPC allows for precise budget control and spending based on performance.
- **Measurability and Analytics:** Digital marketing provides access to extensive metrics and analytics, enabling businesses to track the performance of their campaigns in real-time. Tools like Google Analytics, social media insights, and email marketing software offer valuable data on user behavior, engagement, and conversion rates. This data-driven approach allows for continuous optimization and better decision-making.
- **Targeted Advertising:** Digital marketing enables precise targeting based on demographics, interests, behavior, and location. This ensures that marketing messages are delivered to the most relevant audience, increasing the likelihood of engagement and conversions. Personalized marketing efforts, driven by data analytics, further enhance the effectiveness of campaigns.
- **Enhanced Engagement:** Digital channels facilitate direct interaction with consumers, fostering greater engagement and building stronger relationships. Social media platforms, in particular, allow for real-time communication, enabling businesses to respond to queries, address concerns, and engage in conversations with their audience.
- **Flexibility and Adaptability:** Digital marketing campaigns can be easily adjusted and optimized based on performance data. This flexibility allows businesses to respond quickly to market trends, consumer feedback, and competitive pressures. Unlike traditional marketing, where changes can be costly and time-consuming, digital marketing offers agility and responsiveness.

- **Higher Conversion Rates:** Digital marketing strategies, particularly those that leverage targeted and personalized content, often result in higher conversion rates. Techniques like retargeting—showing ads to users who have previously visited a website—help keep the brand top-of-mind and encourage users to complete desired actions, such as making a purchase.

1.3.3 Challenges in Digital Marketing

Despite its numerous benefits, digital marketing also presents several challenges that businesses must navigate.

- **Increasing Competition:** As more businesses recognize the value of digital marketing, the competition for online visibility and consumer attention has intensified. Standing out in a crowded digital landscape requires innovative strategies, high-quality content, and consistent engagement.
- **Rapid Technological Changes:** The digital marketing landscape is constantly evolving with new technologies, platforms, and tools emerging regularly. Keeping up with these changes and adapting strategies accordingly can be challenging for businesses, especially those with limited resources.
- **Data Privacy Concerns:** With the increasing collection and use of consumer data, privacy concerns have become a significant issue. Regulations such as the General Data Protection Regulation (GDPR) in Europe and the California Consumer Privacy Act (CCPA) in the US impose strict requirements on how businesses collect, store, and use data. Compliance with these regulations is essential to avoid legal repercussions and maintain consumer trust.
- **Managing Multi-Channel Campaigns:** Effectively managing and integrating campaigns across multiple digital channels can be complex. Each platform has its unique features, audience, and best practices, requiring tailored approaches to maximize effectiveness. Coordinating these efforts to ensure a cohesive and consistent brand message is crucial for success.

1.4 DIGITAL MARKETING VS. TRADITIONAL MARKETING

Marketing is a fundamental aspect of any business strategy, designed to promote products, services, or brands to attract and retain customers. The advent of digital technology has brought about a significant shift in marketing practices, leading to the development of digital marketing. Traditional marketing, which encompasses conventional advertising methods such as print, television, radio, and outdoor advertising, has been the cornerstone of marketing for decades. In contrast, digital marketing leverages the internet and electronic devices to reach and engage consumers.

Digital marketing and traditional marketing each have their unique strengths and challenges. Digital marketing offers precise targeting, cost-effectiveness, flexibility, and robust analytics, making it a powerful tool for modern businesses. Traditional marketing, on the other hand, excels in broad reach and credibility, especially through established media channels. By understanding the differences and potential synergies between these two approaches, businesses can craft comprehensive marketing strategies that maximize their reach, engagement, and impact. As the marketing landscape continues to evolve, an integrated approach that leverages the strengths of both traditional and digital methods will be key to achieving sustainable growth and success.

1.4.1 Definitions

Traditional Marketing

Traditional marketing refers to conventional forms of advertising and promotion, including print ads (newspapers, magazines), broadcast ads (television, radio), direct mail (catalogs, brochures), outdoor ads (billboards, posters), and face-to-face marketing (events, trade shows). These methods rely on physical media and direct interactions to reach consumers.

Digital Marketing

Digital marketing involves the use of digital channels and technologies to promote products or services. This includes search engine optimization (SEO), content marketing, social media marketing, pay-per-click (PPC) advertising, email marketing, affiliate marketing, influencer marketing, and online public relations. Digital marketing relies on the internet and electronic devices to engage consumers.

1.4.2 Reach and Targeting

Traditional Marketing

Traditional marketing has a broad reach, especially through mediums like television, radio, and print. It is effective for mass marketing campaigns aimed at a wide audience. However, its targeting capabilities are limited. While demographic targeting is possible to some extent (e.g., choosing specific magazines or TV channels), traditional marketing generally lacks the precision of digital marketing in reaching specific consumer segments.

Digital Marketing

Digital marketing excels in precise targeting. It allows businesses to target specific demographics, interests, behaviors, and geographic locations. Tools like Google Ads and Facebook Ads provide advanced targeting options, enabling marketers to reach the right audience with tailored messages. This level of precision increases the likelihood of engagement and conversion, making digital marketing highly efficient.

1.4.3 Cost and Budgeting

Traditional Marketing

Traditional marketing can be expensive, particularly for television and radio ads, which require significant investment in production and airtime. Print ads, billboards, and direct mail campaigns also entail substantial costs. Additionally, measuring the return on investment (ROI) for traditional marketing campaigns can be challenging, as tracking and analytics are limited.

Digital Marketing

Digital marketing is generally more cost-effective than traditional marketing. Online advertising platforms offer flexible budgeting options, allowing businesses to set daily or campaign-specific budgets. Digital marketing campaigns can be scaled up or down based on performance and budget availability. Furthermore, digital marketing provides comprehensive analytics and tracking tools, enabling businesses to measure ROI accurately and optimize their spending.

1.4.4 Engagement and Interaction

Traditional Marketing

Traditional marketing is often one-way communication, with limited opportunities for interaction between the brand and the consumer. While some traditional methods, like events and trade shows, offer face-to-face interaction, most traditional ads (TV, radio, print) do not facilitate direct engagement.

Digital Marketing

Digital marketing fosters two-way communication and interaction. Social media platforms, in particular, enable real-time engagement, allowing brands to interact with consumers through comments, messages, and posts. Email marketing and live chat support further enhance customer engagement by providing personalized responses and immediate assistance. This interactive nature of digital marketing helps build stronger relationships and trust with consumers.

1.4.5 Flexibility and Adaptability

Traditional Marketing

Traditional marketing campaigns require significant planning and lead time. Once an ad is placed in a magazine or aired on TV, making changes or adjustments is difficult and costly. This lack of flexibility can be a disadvantage in responding to market changes or consumer feedback promptly.

Digital Marketing

Digital marketing offers unparalleled flexibility and adaptability. Campaigns can be quickly modified based on performance data and feedback. For example, PPC ads can be adjusted in real-time, social media posts can be updated instantly, and email campaigns can be segmented and tailored with ease. This agility allows businesses to stay responsive to market trends and consumer needs, ensuring more effective marketing strategies.

1.4.6 Measurement and Analytics

Traditional Marketing

Measuring the effectiveness of traditional marketing campaigns can be challenging. While methods like coupon codes or customer surveys provide some insights, tracking overall campaign performance and ROI is often imprecise. This lack of detailed analytics makes it difficult to assess which aspects of a campaign are successful and which need improvement.

Digital Marketing

Digital marketing provides robust analytics and measurement tools. Platforms like Google Analytics, social media insights, and email marketing software offer detailed data on user behavior, engagement, and conversion rates. Marketers can track key performance indicators (KPIs) such as click-through rates, bounce rates, and customer acquisition costs. This data-driven approach enables continuous optimization and more informed decision-making.

1.4.7 Longevity and Sustainability

Traditional Marketing

Traditional marketing methods like print ads, billboards, and TV commercials have a finite lifespan. Once the ad run is over, its impact diminishes. While some campaigns may leave a lasting impression, the overall longevity is limited, and maintaining visibility requires continuous investment.

Digital Marketing

Digital marketing content, such as blogs, videos, and social media posts, can have a longer lifespan. High-quality content can continue to attract and engage audiences long after it is published, providing ongoing value. SEO-optimized content, in particular, can drive organic traffic over time, enhancing sustainability and long-term impact without continuous expenditure.

1.4.8 Examples and Case Studies

Traditional Marketing Example

Coca-Cola's "Share a Coke" campaign utilized traditional marketing channels like television commercials, billboards, and in-store displays to great effect. The campaign personalized Coke bottles with popular names, encouraging consumers to purchase and share them. While it successfully generated buzz and sales, it required significant investment in traditional advertising methods.

Digital Marketing Example

Dollar Shave Club's launch video is a prime example of successful digital marketing. The video, shared on YouTube and social media, went viral due to its humorous and relatable content. It garnered millions of views, drove massive traffic to the website, and significantly boosted subscriptions. The campaign's success was driven by its digital strategy, leveraging the viral nature of social media to achieve widespread reach and engagement at a relatively low cost.

1.4.9 Integrating Traditional and Digital Marketing

While digital marketing offers many advantages, traditional marketing still holds value, particularly for reaching specific demographics and enhancing brand credibility. An integrated approach that combines both traditional and digital methods can yield the best results.

Synergy Example

A retail brand might use traditional marketing to build broad brand awareness through TV commercials and print ads while simultaneously running digital campaigns on social media and search engines to engage younger, tech-savvy consumers. Events and trade shows can be promoted through both channels, leveraging traditional media for local reach and digital media for broader visibility and interaction.

1.5 KEY COMPONENTS OF DIGITAL MARKETING STRATEGY

A well-crafted digital marketing strategy is essential for businesses aiming to succeed in the competitive online landscape. A comprehensive strategy involves multiple components, each playing a crucial role in reaching, engaging, and converting the target audience.

A successful digital marketing strategy encompasses a variety of components, each contributing to a comprehensive and cohesive plan. From audience research and SEO to social media marketing and data analysis, these elements work together to reach, engage, and convert the target audience. By understanding and integrating these key components, businesses can create effective digital marketing strategies that drive growth and achieve their objectives in the ever-evolving online landscape.

1.5.1 Audience Research and Segmentation

Understanding the target audience is the foundation of any digital marketing strategy. Audience research involves gathering data on potential customers, including demographics, interests, behavior, and preferences. This information helps businesses create detailed buyer personas, which are semi-fictional representations of their ideal customers. Segmentation further divides the audience into distinct groups based on specific criteria such as age, location, purchasing behavior, or interests. By segmenting the audience, businesses can tailor their marketing messages and campaigns to resonate with each group, increasing the relevance and effectiveness of their efforts.

1.5.2 Search Engine Optimization (SEO)

SEO is the process of optimizing a website to rank higher in search engine results pages (SERPs) for relevant keywords. Effective SEO strategies drive organic traffic to the website, enhancing visibility and credibility.

Key Aspects of SEO Include:

- **Keyword Research:** Identifying the search terms that potential customers use to find products or services similar to those offered by the business.
- **On-Page Optimization:** Ensuring that the website's content, meta tags, headers, and images are optimized for target keywords.
- **Off-Page Optimization:** Building high-quality backlinks from reputable websites to improve the website's authority and ranking.
- **Technical SEO:** Enhancing the website's technical aspects, such as site speed, mobile-friendliness, and secure connections (HTTPS).

1.5.3 Content Marketing

Content marketing focuses on creating and distributing valuable, relevant, and consistent content to attract and engage a target audience. High-quality content builds trust, establishes authority, and drives organic traffic to the website.

Forms of Content Include:

- **Blog Posts:** Informative articles that address common questions or provide solutions to problems faced by the target audience.
- **Videos:** Engaging visual content that can explain complex topics, showcase products, or tell the brand's story.
- **Infographics:** Visual representations of data or information that are easy to understand and share.
- **E-books and Whitepapers:** In-depth guides or reports that offer valuable insights on industry-specific topics.
- **Podcasts:** Audio content that can reach audiences who prefer listening over reading or watching.

1.5.4 Social Media Marketing

Social media marketing involves using platforms like Facebook, Twitter, Instagram, LinkedIn, and TikTok to promote products or services, engage with customers, and build brand awareness. Each platform has its unique features and audience, requiring tailored strategies to maximize impact.

Key elements of social media marketing include:

- **Content Creation:** Developing engaging and shareable content, such as posts, stories, and videos.
- **Community Management:** Interacting with followers, responding to comments, and managing the brand's online reputation.
- **Social Media Advertising:** Running paid campaigns to target specific demographics and achieve marketing objectives like increased website traffic or sales.

1.5.5 Pay-Per-Click (PPC) Advertising

PPC advertising is a model where businesses pay a fee each time their ad is clicked. This method provides immediate visibility and drives targeted traffic to the website.

Popular PPC platforms include:

- **Google Ads:** Allows businesses to display ads on Google's search results and across its vast network of partner websites.
- **Social Media Ads:** Platforms like Facebook, Instagram, and LinkedIn offer advanced targeting options based on user demographics, interests, and behavior.

1.5.6 Email Marketing

Email marketing is a powerful tool for nurturing leads, building relationships, and encouraging repeat business. It involves sending targeted messages to a list of subscribers who have opted in to receive communications from the brand.

Effective email marketing strategies include:

- **Segmentation:** Dividing the email list into segments based on criteria such as purchase history, engagement level, or demographics to send more personalized messages.
- **Automation:** Using email marketing software to automate sending welcome emails, follow-ups, and promotional campaigns.
- **Personalization:** Tailoring email content to the recipient's preferences and behavior to increase engagement and conversion rates.

1.5.7 Affiliate Marketing

Affiliate marketing is a performance-based strategy where businesses reward affiliates (partners) for driving traffic or sales through their marketing efforts. Affiliates, often bloggers or influencers, promote the business's products or services on their platforms and earn a commission for every sale or lead generated.

Key components of affiliate marketing include:

- **Affiliate Recruitment:** Identifying and partnering with affiliates who have a relevant and engaged audience.
- **Commission Structure:** Establishing a clear and attractive commission structure to incentivize affiliates.
- **Tracking and Reporting:** Using affiliate tracking software to monitor performance and ensure accurate commission payments.

1.5.8 Influencer Marketing

Influencer marketing involves collaborating with influencers—individuals with a large and engaged following in a specific niche—to promote a product or service.

Influencers create content that showcases the brand to their audience, leveraging their credibility and relationship with followers to drive engagement and conversions.

Steps in influencer marketing include:

- **Identifying Influencers:** Finding influencers whose audience aligns with the target market.
- **Building Relationships:** Engaging with influencers to establish trust and mutually beneficial partnerships.

- **Measuring Impact:** Tracking the performance of influencer campaigns using metrics such as reach, engagement, and conversions.

1.5.9 Online Public Relations (PR)

Online PR involves managing and influencing an organization's reputation and presence across digital platforms. This includes engaging with online publications, bloggers, and social media influencers to generate positive coverage, handling online reviews, and managing crisis communications.

Key activities in online PR include:

- **Press Releases:** Distributing newsworthy information about the business to online media outlets.
- **Media Outreach:** Building relationships with journalists and bloggers to secure coverage.
- **Reputation Management:** Monitoring and responding to online reviews and feedback to maintain a positive brand image.

1.5.10 Analytics and Data Analysis

Analytics and data analysis are critical components of a digital marketing strategy. They involve tracking, measuring, and analyzing the performance of marketing campaigns to gain insights and make data-driven decisions.

Essential analytics tools include:

- **Google Analytics:** Provides detailed data on website traffic, user behavior, and conversion rates.
- **Social Media Analytics:** Offers insights into the performance of social media campaigns, including engagement rates and audience demographics.
- **Email Marketing Analytics:** Tracks metrics such as open rates, click-through rates, and conversions to assess the effectiveness of email campaigns.

1.5.11 Conversion Rate Optimization (CRO)

CRO involves optimizing the website and marketing campaigns to increase the percentage of visitors who complete desired actions, such as making a purchase or filling out a form.

This process involves analyzing user behavior, conducting A/B tests, and implementing changes to improve the user experience.

Key CRO techniques include:

- **Landing Page Optimization**: Creating and refining landing pages to improve relevance and clarity.
- **A/B Testing**: Comparing different versions of a webpage or ad to determine which performs better.
- **User Feedback:** Collecting and analyzing feedback from users to identify pain points and areas for improvement.

1.5.12 Mobile Marketing

Mobile marketing focuses on reaching audiences on their mobile devices through SMS, mobile apps, push notifications, and mobile-optimized websites. With the increasing use of smartphones, mobile marketing has become a critical aspect of digital strategies.

Key mobile marketing tactics include:

- **Responsive Design**: Ensuring that websites and emails are optimized for mobile devices.
- **App Marketing**: Promoting mobile apps through app stores, social media, and other channels.
- **SMS Marketing**: Sending targeted text messages with offers, updates, or reminders to engage customers.

1.6 UNDERSTANDING THE DIGITAL CONSUMER JOURNEY

The digital consumer journey refers to the process consumers go through when interacting with brands online, from initial awareness to final purchase and beyond. Understanding this journey is crucial for businesses aiming to optimize their digital marketing strategies and enhance customer satisfaction.

Understanding the digital consumer journey is essential for businesses aiming to optimize their digital marketing strategies and enhance customer satisfaction. By recognizing the stages of the journey, identifying key touchpoints, and providing a seamless, personalized experience, brands can effectively engage and convert consumers, fostering loyalty and advocacy. As the digital landscape continues to evolve, staying attuned to consumer needs and preferences will remain crucial for achieving long-term success in digital marketing.

1.6.1 Stages of the Digital Consumer Journey

The digital consumer journey can be broadly divided into five stages: Awareness, Consideration, Decision, Retention, and Advocacy. Each stage represents a different phase in the consumer's interaction with the brand, and understanding these stages helps businesses tailor their marketing efforts effectively.

Awareness

In the awareness stage, consumers become aware of a brand, product, or service. This stage is crucial as it marks the first point of contact between the consumer and the brand. Digital channels play a significant role in creating awareness, with methods such as social media marketing, content marketing, search engine optimization (SEO), and online advertisements.

- **Social Media Marketing:** Platforms like Facebook, Instagram, Twitter, and LinkedIn are powerful tools for reaching potential customers. Brands can create engaging content, run targeted ad campaigns, and participate in trending conversations to increase visibility.
- **Content Marketing:** Blogs, videos, infographics, and other content forms help attract and inform potential customers. High-quality, relevant content that addresses consumer pain points can drive organic traffic and build brand awareness.
- **SEO:** Optimizing website content for search engines helps brands appear in relevant search queries, increasing the likelihood of being discovered by potential customers.
- **Online Advertisements:** Pay-per-click (PPC) ads, display ads, and social media ads can target specific demographics and interests, ensuring that the brand message reaches the right audience.

Consideration

During the consideration stage, consumers evaluate different options and conduct research to find the best solution to their needs. They compare products, read reviews, seek recommendations, and engage with brand content to make informed decisions.

- **Website and Landing Pages:** Well-designed, informative websites and landing pages that clearly convey product benefits and features help consumers in their research process.
- **Email Marketing:** Sending personalized emails with relevant content, product information, and offers can keep potential customers engaged and guide them through the decision-making process.
- **Social Proof:** Reviews, testimonials, and user-generated content on social media and review sites build trust and credibility, influencing consumer choices.
- **Webinars and Demos:** Offering free webinars, product demos, or consultations can provide in-depth information and address specific consumer queries, helping them make informed decisions.

Decision

In the decision stage, consumers are ready to make a purchase. At this point, businesses need to remove any remaining barriers and make the purchasing process as smooth as possible.

- **Clear Calls to Action (CTAs):** Prominent and persuasive CTAs on product pages, emails, and ads guide consumers towards making a purchase.
- **User Experience (UX):** A seamless, intuitive website design with easy navigation, fast loading times, and a straightforward checkout process enhances the user experience and reduces cart abandonment.
- **Payment Options:** Offering multiple payment options, including credit cards, digital wallets, and buy-now-pay-later services, caters to diverse consumer preferences.
- **Retargeting Ads:** Retargeting campaigns can remind consumers of products they viewed or added to their cart but did not purchase, encouraging them to complete the transaction.

Retention

The retention stage focuses on maintaining a relationship with the customer after the initial purchase. Retaining customers is more cost-effective than acquiring new ones, and loyal customers are likely to make repeat purchases and refer others.

- **Customer Support:** Providing excellent customer service through live chat, email, phone, and social media ensures that customers feel valued and supported.
- **Loyalty Programs:** Rewarding repeat customers with points, discounts, or exclusive offers incentivizes them to continue purchasing from the brand.
- **Personalized Communications:** Sending personalized emails, product recommendations, and special offers based on past purchases keeps customers engaged and fosters loyalty.
- **Follow-Up Surveys:** Collecting feedback through post-purchase surveys helps identify areas for improvement and shows customers that their opinions are valued.

Advocacy

In the advocacy stage, satisfied customers become brand advocates, sharing their positive experiences with others and influencing potential customers. Advocacy is a powerful form of marketing, as people trust recommendations from friends and family more than traditional advertisements.

- **Referral Programs:** Encouraging customers to refer friends and family by offering incentives such as discounts or rewards can drive new customer acquisition.
- **User-Generated Content:** Encouraging customers to share their experiences, reviews, and photos on social media and the brand's website can amplify positive word-of-mouth marketing.
- **Engaging with Advocates:** Recognizing and engaging with brand advocates through social media shoutouts, special offers, or exclusive access to new products helps strengthen their loyalty and advocacy efforts.

1.6.2 Key Touchpoints in the Digital Consumer Journey

Throughout the digital consumer journey, consumers interact with various touchpoints that influence their perceptions and decisions. Identifying and optimizing these touchpoints is crucial for providing a seamless, positive experience.

- **Website:** The website is often the primary touchpoint where consumers learn about the brand, research products, and make purchases. Ensuring a user-friendly design, informative content, and smooth navigation is essential.
- **Social Media:** Social media platforms are key touchpoints for engagement, customer service, and brand awareness. Active, responsive, and strategic use of social media can significantly impact consumer perceptions and loyalty.
- **Email:** Email remains a powerful touchpoint for personalized communication, nurturing leads, and driving repeat purchases. Regular, relevant, and engaging email campaigns can keep the brand top-of-mind for consumers.
- **Search Engines:** Search engines are critical touchpoints for discovery and research. Optimizing for SEO ensures that the brand appears in relevant search results, driving organic traffic and visibility.
- **Online Reviews and Forums:** Consumers often turn to online reviews and forums to gather information and opinions about products and services. Encouraging satisfied customers to leave positive reviews and addressing any negative feedback promptly can influence potential buyers.

1.6.3 Importance of a Seamless and Personalized Experience

In today's competitive digital landscape, providing a seamless and personalized experience is key to standing out and retaining customers. Consumers expect brands to understand their needs and preferences, offering relevant content, recommendations, and services.

Seamlessness

Ensuring that the transition between different stages and touchpoints is smooth enhances the overall experience. For example, a consumer should be able to move from a social media ad to a product page and complete a purchase without friction. Consistent branding, intuitive design, and fast load times across all digital channels contribute to a seamless experience.

Personalization

Tailoring content and interactions to individual consumer preferences can significantly enhance engagement and loyalty. Personalization can be achieved through:

- **Data Analytics:** Leveraging data analytics to understand consumer behavior, preferences, and purchase history enables personalized marketing efforts.
- **AI and Machine Learning:** Using AI and machine learning algorithms to deliver personalized product recommendations, content, and offers based on consumer behavior.
- **Segmentation:** Segmenting the audience and tailoring messages to different segments ensures relevance and resonance.

CHAPTER 2
CONTENT MAKING

2.1 THE ROLE OF CONTENT IN DIGITAL MARKETING

In the rapidly evolving digital landscape, content has emerged as the cornerstone of successful marketing strategies. Content marketing involves creating and distributing valuable, relevant, and consistent content to attract and engage a target audience. This approach not only helps in building brand awareness but also fosters customer loyalty and drives conversions.

Content is the backbone of digital marketing, playing a crucial role in attracting, engaging, and converting audiences. By understanding the various forms of content, the benefits it offers, and best practices for creating and distributing it, businesses can develop effective content marketing strategies. In the competitive digital landscape, high-quality, relevant content not only drives traffic and conversions but also builds brand authority and fosters long-term customer loyalty. As consumer preferences and technologies continue to evolve, staying agile and continuously optimizing content strategies will be key to sustained success in digital marketing.

2.1.1 Understanding Content in Digital Marketing

Content in digital marketing refers to any information that is created and shared with the aim of engaging and influencing an audience. This includes blog posts, videos, social media updates, infographics, podcasts, webinars, e-books, and more. The primary goal of content is to provide value to the audience, addressing their needs, interests, and pain points.

2.1.2 Forms of Content in Digital Marketing

Content can take various forms, each serving different purposes and engaging audiences in unique ways. Here are some of the most popular types of content used in digital marketing:

- **Blog Posts:** Blog posts are a foundational element of content marketing. They allow brands to share in-depth information, insights, and updates on topics relevant to their industry. Regularly updated blogs help improve search engine rankings, drive organic traffic, and establish authority.

- **Videos:** Video content is highly engaging and can effectively convey complex information in an easily digestible format. Videos can be used for product demonstrations, tutorials, customer testimonials, brand stories, and more. Platforms like YouTube, Instagram, and TikTok have made video a crucial component of digital marketing strategies.
- **Social Media Content:** Social media platforms are essential for content distribution and audience engagement. Posts, stories, reels, and live videos on platforms like Facebook, Instagram, Twitter, and LinkedIn allow brands to connect with their audience in real time. Social media content should be visually appealing, shareable, and tailored to the platform's audience.
- **Infographics:** Infographics are visual representations of information or data. They are an effective way to simplify complex topics and make them easily understandable. Infographics are highly shareable and can help increase brand visibility and engagement.
- **Podcasts:** Podcasts have gained popularity as a medium for sharing information and insights in an audio format. They allow brands to reach audiences who prefer listening over reading or watching. Podcasts can cover a wide range of topics, including industry news, interviews, and educational content.
- **E-books and Whitepapers:** E-books and whitepapers are long-form content pieces that provide in-depth information on specific topics. They are often used to generate leads by offering valuable content in exchange for contact information. These resources help establish authority and trust in the industry.
- **Webinars:** Webinars are live or recorded online seminars that allow brands to engage with their audience in real-time. They are an effective way to provide educational content, demonstrate products, and interact with potential customers. Webinars can also be repurposed into other content formats, such as blog posts and videos.

2.1.3 Benefits of Content in Digital Marketing

Content marketing offers numerous benefits that contribute to the overall success of digital marketing strategies. Here are some of the key advantages:

- **Increased Brand Awareness:** High-quality, valuable content helps increase brand visibility and awareness. By consistently producing and sharing content that resonates with the target audience, brands can establish a strong online presence and attract new customers.

- **Improved Search Engine Rankings:** Search engine optimization (SEO) is closely tied to content marketing. Creating relevant, keyword-rich content helps improve search engine rankings, driving organic traffic to the website. Regularly updated content signals to search engines that the website is active and relevant.
- **Audience Engagement and Loyalty:** Content that addresses the needs and interests of the audience fosters engagement and builds trust. Engaged audiences are more likely to become loyal customers, returning to the brand for information, products, and services.
- **Lead Generation and Conversion:** Content marketing is an effective tool for lead generation. By offering valuable content, such as e-books or webinars, in exchange for contact information, brands can build a list of potential customers. Nurturing these leads with targeted content can guide them through the sales funnel, ultimately driving conversions.
- **Thought Leadership and Authority:** Consistently producing high-quality content positions brands as thought leaders in their industry. Sharing insights, research, and expertise helps establish authority and credibility, making the brand a trusted source of information.
- **Cost-Effective Marketing:** Compared to traditional advertising methods, content marketing is cost-effective. While it requires an investment of time and resources, the long-term benefits and return on investment (ROI) are substantial. Content can continue to drive traffic and engagement long after it is published.

2.1.4 Best Practices for Content Marketing

To maximize the impact of content in digital marketing, it is essential to follow best practices. Here are some key strategies for creating and distributing effective content:

- **Understand Your Audience:** Knowing the target audience is crucial for creating relevant content. Conduct audience research to understand their needs, preferences, and pain points. Develop detailed buyer personas to guide content creation and ensure that it resonates with the intended audience.
- **Create Valuable and Relevant Content:** Content should provide value to the audience. Focus on addressing their questions, solving their problems, and offering insights that are relevant to their interests. High-quality content that is informative, entertaining, or educational will attract and engage the audience.

- **Consistency is Key:** Consistency is vital for building and maintaining an audience. Develop a content calendar to plan and schedule content production and distribution. Regularly updated content keeps the audience engaged and signals to search engines that the website is active.
- **Optimize for Search Engines:** Incorporate SEO best practices into content creation. Conduct keyword research to identify relevant search terms and integrate them naturally into the content. Use meta tags, headers, and alt text for images to enhance search engine visibility.
- **Leverage Multiple Formats and Channels:** Diversify content formats to reach a broader audience. Use a mix of blog posts, videos, infographics, podcasts, and social media content to cater to different preferences. Distribute content across multiple channels to maximize reach and engagement.
- **Engage with Your Audience:** Content marketing is not just about creating content but also about engaging with the audience. Respond to comments, answer questions, and participate in discussions on social media and other platforms. Building a community around the brand fosters loyalty and trust.
- **Analyze and Optimize:** Regularly analyze content performance using analytics tools. Track metrics such as traffic, engagement, conversion rates, and social shares to measure the effectiveness of content. Use these insights to optimize future content strategies and improve ROI.

2.1.5 Case Studies of Successful Content Marketing

Examining successful content marketing campaigns provides valuable insights into best practices and strategies. Here are two notable examples:

- **Red Bull:** Red Bull's content marketing strategy revolves around extreme sports, adventure, and lifestyle. The brand creates high-quality videos, blog posts, and social media content that resonate with its target audience. Red Bull's content not only promotes its products but also aligns with the interests and passions of its consumers, fostering a strong brand community.
- **HubSpot:** HubSpot, a leader in inbound marketing, offers a wealth of valuable content, including blog posts, e-books, webinars, and tutorials. By providing comprehensive resources and tools for marketers, HubSpot positions itself as a thought leader in the industry. The brand's content-driven approach has helped it attract and nurture a loyal customer base.

2.2 DEVELOPING A CONTENT MARKETING STRATEGY

A well-developed content marketing strategy is essential for any business looking to attract, engage, and convert its target audience. It involves a comprehensive plan that guides the creation, distribution, and management of content to achieve specific marketing objectives.

Developing a content marketing strategy involves a series of thoughtful and strategic steps, from defining objectives and understanding the audience to creating high-quality content and measuring performance. By following these steps and continuously refining your approach, you can create a content marketing strategy that effectively engages your audience, drives business goals, and establishes your brand as a trusted authority in your industry. Content marketing is a dynamic and evolving field, and staying adaptable and innovative is key to long-term success.

2.2.1 Step 1: Define Your Objectives

The first step in developing a content marketing strategy is to define clear and measurable objectives. These objectives should align with the broader marketing and business goals of the organization. Common objectives for content marketing include:

- **Increasing Brand Awareness:** Making more people aware of your brand and its offerings.
- **Driving Website Traffic:** Attracting visitors to your website through engaging content.
- **Generating Leads:** Capturing contact information from potential customers.
- **Building Customer Loyalty:** Enhancing relationships with existing customers.

Clearly defined objectives provide a focus for your content marketing efforts and a basis for measuring success.

2.2.2 Step 2: Understand Your Audience

Understanding your audience is crucial for creating content that resonates and engages. Start by conducting thorough audience research to gather insights into their demographics, interests, behaviors, and pain points. This can be achieved through various methods, including:

- **Surveys and Questionnaires:** Directly asking your audience about their preferences and needs.
- **Social Media Insights:** Analyzing data from social media platforms to understand audience engagement and behavior.

- **Website Analytics:** Using tools like Google Analytics to track visitor behavior and identify popular content.
- **Customer Feedback:** Gathering feedback from current customers to understand their experiences and expectations.

Based on this research, create detailed buyer personas that represent your ideal customers. These personas will guide your content creation, ensuring it is relevant and valuable to your target audience.

2.2.3 Step 3: Conduct a Content Audit

A content audit involves evaluating your existing content to identify what is performing well, what needs improvement, and where there are gaps. This process helps you make informed decisions about future content creation and ensures that your strategy builds on past successes.

To conduct a content audit:

- **Inventory Your Content:** List all existing content assets, including blog posts, videos, infographics, e-books, and social media posts.
- **Analyze Performance:** Use analytics tools to assess the performance of each content piece based on metrics such as traffic, engagement, conversions, and shares.
- **Identify Gaps:** Determine if there are any topics or formats that are missing or underrepresented in your content library.
- **Evaluate Quality:** Assess the quality of your content in terms of accuracy, relevance, and engagement.

Based on the audit results, decide which content to keep, update, repurpose, or retire.

2.2.4 Step 4: Develop a Content Plan

A content plan outlines what content will be created, when, and how it will be distributed. This plan ensures that your content marketing efforts are organized and aligned with your objectives.

Key elements of a content plan include:

- **Content Topics:** Identify the key topics that will resonate with your audience and support your objectives. These topics should address the needs and interests of your buyer personas.
- **Content Calendar:** Create a calendar that schedules content production and publication. This calendar helps maintain consistency and ensures that content is published at optimal times.

- **Content Formats**: Decide on the types of content you will create, such as blog posts, videos, infographics, podcasts, or e-books. Diversifying content formats can help reach a broader audience.
- **Content Creation Process**: Outline the steps involved in creating content, from ideation to publication. Assign responsibilities to team members and set deadlines to ensure timely delivery.

2.2.5 Step 5: Create High-Quality Content

The success of your content marketing strategy hinges on the quality of the content you produce. High-quality content is engaging, informative, and valuable to your audience. Here are some best practices for creating effective content:

- **Focus on Value**: Ensure that your content addresses the needs and interests of your audience. Provide solutions to their problems, answer their questions, and offer valuable insights.
- **Tell a Story**: Use storytelling techniques to make your content more relatable and engaging. Stories can evoke emotions and create a stronger connection with your audience.
- **Use Visuals**: Incorporate visuals such as images, infographics, and videos to enhance the appeal of your content. Visual content is more likely to be shared and remembered.
- **Maintain Consistency**: Consistent branding, tone, and style across all content pieces help reinforce your brand identity and build trust with your audience.
- **Optimize for SEO**: Implement SEO best practices to improve the visibility of your content in search engine results. This includes using relevant keywords, creating compelling meta descriptions, and optimizing headings and images.

2.2.6 Step 6: Distribute Your Content

Creating great content is only half the battle; you also need to ensure it reaches your target audience. Content distribution involves sharing your content across various channels to maximize its reach and impact. Common distribution channels include:

- **Owned Media**: Channels you control, such as your website, blog, and email newsletters. Regularly update your website and blog with fresh content and promote it through your email list.
- **Social Media**: Share your content on social media platforms like Facebook, Twitter, LinkedIn, Instagram, and Pinterest. Tailor your

content to fit the platform and engage with your audience through comments and shares.

- **Earned Media:** Third-party channels, such as guest blogs, influencer partnerships, and press coverage. Collaborate with industry influencers and publications to expand your reach.
- **Paid Media:** Paid advertising channels, such as Google Ads, social media ads, and sponsored content. Use targeted advertising to reach specific segments of your audience.

2.2.7 Step 7: Measure and Analyze Performance

Measuring the performance of your content marketing efforts is crucial for understanding what works and what doesn't. Use analytics tools to track key performance indicators (KPIs) that align with your objectives. Common KPIs include:

- **Traffic:** The number of visitors to your website or content pages.
- **Engagement:** Metrics such as likes, shares, comments, and time spent on content.
- **Lead Generation:** The number of leads captured through content offers, such as e-book downloads or webinar registrations.
- **Conversions:** The number of conversions or sales resulting from content interactions.
- **SEO Performance:** Rankings, organic traffic, and backlinks generated by your content.

Regularly review these metrics to identify trends, strengths, and areas for improvement. Use the insights gained to refine your content strategy and optimize future content.

2.2.8 Step 8: Continuously Improve

Content marketing is an ongoing process that requires continuous improvement. Stay updated with industry trends, audience preferences, and new technologies to keep your content strategy relevant and effective. Encourage feedback from your audience and team members to identify areas for enhancement. Experiment with new content formats, topics, and distribution channels to discover what resonates best with your audience.

2.3 CONTENT TYPES AND FORMATS

In the digital marketing landscape, the types and formats of content used can significantly influence the success of a campaign. Different content types serve various purposes and engage audiences in unique ways. Understanding the diverse array of content types and formats available is crucial for crafting an effective content marketing strategy.

The diverse array of content types and formats available in digital marketing allows brands to engage with their audience in multiple ways. Each type serves different purposes and can be used strategically to achieve specific marketing objectives. By understanding the benefits and best practices for each content type, businesses can create a comprehensive content marketing strategy that effectively attracts, engages, and converts their target audience. The key to success lies in delivering high-quality, relevant content that resonates with the audience and aligns with the overall marketing goals. As the digital landscape continues to evolve, staying adaptable and continuously experimenting with new content types and formats will be crucial for sustained success in digital marketing.

2.3.1 Blog Posts

Blog posts are one of the most common and versatile forms of content in digital marketing. They allow businesses to share in-depth information on a variety of topics relevant to their industry and audience.

- **Benefits:** Blog posts help improve search engine rankings through SEO, establish authority, and drive organic traffic to the website. They also provide valuable content that can be shared on social media and used to nurture leads.
- **Utilization:** Blog posts should be informative, well-researched, and engaging. They can cover how-to guides, industry news, opinion pieces, case studies, and more. Regularly updating the blog with fresh content helps maintain audience interest and improve SEO performance.

2.3.2 Videos

Videos are highly engaging and can effectively convey complex information in an easily digestible format. They cater to the growing preference for visual content among consumers.

- **Benefits:** Videos can significantly boost engagement, increase time spent on a website, and improve conversion rates. They are also highly shareable on social media, increasing brand visibility.
- **Utilization:** Videos can be used for product demonstrations, tutorials, customer testimonials, brand stories, and behind-the-scenes looks. Platforms like YouTube, Instagram, TikTok, and Facebook are ideal for video distribution. Ensuring high production quality and concise messaging is key to effective video content.

2.3.3 Infographics

Infographics are visual representations of information or data designed to make complex information more understandable and engaging.

- **Benefits:** Infographics are highly shareable and can drive significant traffic to a website. They simplify complex data, making it easier for audiences to grasp key points quickly.
- **Utilization:** Infographics should be visually appealing, well-organized, and informative. They are ideal for presenting statistics, timelines, processes, and comparisons. Sharing infographics on social media and including them in blog posts can enhance their reach and impact.

2.3.4 Social Media Posts

Social media posts are essential for engaging with audiences on platforms like Facebook, Twitter, Instagram, LinkedIn, and Pinterest.

- **Benefits:** Social media posts facilitate direct interaction with audiences, increasing brand visibility and engagement. They can drive traffic to other content types, such as blog posts and videos.
- **Utilization:** Effective social media content includes images, short videos, polls, stories, and updates. Posts should be tailored to the platform's audience and optimized for engagement. Consistency, responsiveness, and leveraging trending topics can enhance social media performance.

2.3.5 E-books and Whitepapers

E-books and whitepapers are long-form content pieces that provide in-depth information on specific topics. They are often used as lead magnets to capture contact information from potential customers.

- **Benefits:** E-books and whitepapers help establish authority and credibility. They provide valuable, detailed content that can nurture leads and guide them through the sales funnel.
- **Utilization:** These content types should be well-researched, professionally designed, and offer actionable insights. Promoting them through website landing pages, email marketing, and social media can help generate leads and build an audience.

2.3.6 Webinars and Online Courses

Webinars and online courses are interactive forms of content that provide valuable educational opportunities to audiences.

- **Benefits:** Webinars and online courses foster direct interaction with the audience, offering real-time engagement and feedback. They can build trust and authority while generating leads and driving conversions.

- **Utilization:** Topics should be relevant and offer significant value to the audience. Promoting webinars and courses through email marketing, social media, and partnerships can increase attendance. Recording and repurposing the content for future use can extend its lifespan.

2.3.7 Podcasts

Podcasts are audio content that allows brands to share information, stories, and insights in a format that audiences can consume on the go.

- **Benefits:** Podcasts reach audiences who prefer listening over reading or watching. They can build a loyal audience and establish the brand as an industry thought leader.
- **Utilization:** Podcasts should be engaging, well-produced, and cover topics of interest to the target audience. Regular episodes, guest interviews, and cross-promotion with other content types can enhance their impact.

2.3.8 Case Studies

Case studies provide detailed examples of how a product or service has successfully solved a problem for a customer.

- **Benefits:** Case studies build credibility and trust by showcasing real-world success stories. They provide social proof and can influence purchasing decisions.
- **Utilization:** Effective case studies should include a clear problem statement, solution description, and measurable results. Including quotes from satisfied customers and data-backed outcomes can enhance their persuasive power.

2.3.9 User-Generated Content

User-generated content (UGC) includes reviews, testimonials, social media posts, and other content created by customers.

- **Benefits:** UGC builds trust and authenticity, as it comes directly from customers. It can increase engagement and provide valuable social proof.
- **Utilization:** Encouraging customers to share their experiences and leveraging UGC in marketing campaigns can boost brand credibility. Featuring UGC on social media, websites, and other marketing channels can enhance its impact.

2.3.10 Emails and Newsletters

Emails and newsletters are direct communication channels that allow brands to share updates, offers, and valuable content with their audience.

- **Benefits:** Email marketing is highly effective for nurturing leads, driving conversions, and maintaining customer relationships. It provides a direct line of communication with the audience.
- **Utilization:** Emails should be personalized, relevant, and offer clear value to the recipient. Segmentation and automation can enhance the effectiveness of email campaigns. Regular newsletters keep the audience informed and engaged.

2.3.11 Interactive Content

Interactive content includes quizzes, polls, surveys, and interactive infographics that engage the audience through active participation.

- **Benefits:** Interactive content increases engagement and time spent on the website. It provides valuable insights into audience preferences and behaviors.
- **Utilization:** Creating interactive content that is fun, relevant, and easy to use can capture the audience's attention. Promoting it through social media and email marketing can extend its reach.

2.3.12 Guides and Tutorials

Guides and tutorials provide step-by-step instructions on how to accomplish specific tasks or solve problems.

- **Benefits:** Guides and tutorials establish authority and provide immediate value to the audience. They can drive organic traffic through SEO and increase engagement.
- **Utilization:** These content types should be detailed, easy to follow, and visually supported with images or videos. Promoting them through blogs, social media, and email can enhance their visibility.

2.4 MEASURING CONTENT MARKETING SUCCESS

Content marketing is an essential strategy for engaging audiences, building brand awareness, and driving conversions. However, to ensure its effectiveness and make data-driven decisions, it is crucial to measure the success of your content marketing efforts. This involves tracking key performance indicators (KPIs), analyzing data, and continuously optimizing strategies based on insights.

Measuring content marketing success is crucial for understanding the effectiveness of your efforts and making data-driven decisions. By setting clear objectives, selecting relevant KPIs, and using the right tools, you can gain valuable insights into your content's performance. Regularly monitoring and analyzing data, conducting A/B tests, and gathering qualitative feedback are essential practices for optimizing your content strategy.

Successful brands like HubSpot and Buffer demonstrate the importance of a comprehensive approach to measurement, combining both quantitative and qualitative insights.

By following these best practices, you can ensure your content marketing efforts drive meaningful results and contribute to your overall business goals.

2.4.1 Setting Clear Objectives

Before diving into the metrics and methods for measuring success, it is important to establish clear, measurable objectives for your content marketing strategy. These objectives should align with your broader business goals and provide a roadmap for your content efforts. Common objectives include:

- **Increasing Brand Awareness:** Reaching a larger audience and making more people aware of your brand.
- **Driving Website Traffic:** Attracting more visitors to your website through engaging content.
- **Boosting Sales:** Encouraging conversions and purchases.
- **Enhancing Customer Loyalty:** Building stronger relationships with existing customers.
- **Establishing Thought Leadership:** Positioning your brand as an authority in your industry.

Having clear objectives allows you to select the appropriate KPIs and metrics to measure your success.

2.4.2 Key Performance Indicators (KPIs)

KPIs are specific metrics used to track the performance of your content marketing efforts. They provide insights into how well your content is achieving its objectives. Here are some essential KPIs for measuring content marketing success:

Traffic Metrics

Traffic metrics help you understand how many people are visiting your content and where they are coming from. Key traffic metrics include:

- **Page Views:** The total number of times a page has been viewed.
- **Unique Visitors:** The number of distinct individuals visiting your content.

- **Traffic Sources:** The origins of your traffic, such as organic search, social media, direct visits, or referral links.

These metrics help gauge the reach of your content and identify the most effective channels for driving traffic.

Engagement Metrics

Engagement metrics indicate how your audience is interacting with your content. They help assess the quality and relevance of your content. Key engagement metrics include:

- **Time on Page:** The average amount of time visitors spend on a page.
- **Bounce Rate:** The percentage of visitors who leave your site after viewing only one page.
- **Pages per Session:** The average number of pages a visitor views in a single session.
- **Social Shares:** The number of times your content is shared on social media platforms.
- **Comments and Interactions:** The number and quality of comments, likes, and other interactions on your content.

High engagement indicates that your content resonates with your audience and keeps them interested.

Conversion Metrics

Conversion metrics measure the effectiveness of your content in driving desired actions, such as lead generation or sales. Key conversion metrics include:

- **Conversion Rate:** The percentage of visitors who take a desired action, such as filling out a form or making a purchase.
- **Lead Generation:** The number of leads captured through content offers, such as e-books, webinars, or newsletter sign-ups.
- **Sales:** The number of sales or revenue generated from content marketing efforts.

These metrics directly tie your content to business outcomes, providing a clear picture of its impact on your bottom line.

SEO Metrics

Search engine optimization (SEO) metrics help evaluate how well your content is performing in search engine results and driving organic traffic. Key SEO metrics include:

- **Keyword Rankings:** The positions of your target keywords in search engine results pages (SERPs).

- **Organic Traffic**: The number of visitors coming to your site from search engines.
- **Backlinks**: The number and quality of external links pointing to your content.

Improving these metrics enhances your content's visibility and reach in search engines.

2.4.3 Tools for Measuring Content Marketing Success

Several tools can help you track and analyze your content marketing performance. Here are some popular ones:

- **Google Analytics**: A powerful tool for tracking website traffic, user behavior, and conversion metrics. It provides detailed insights into how visitors interact with your content.
- **Google Search Console**: Useful for monitoring your site's presence in Google search results. It helps track keyword rankings, organic traffic, and indexing issues.
- **Social Media Analytics**: Platforms like Facebook Insights, Twitter Analytics, and LinkedIn Analytics provide data on engagement, reach, and audience demographics for your social media content.
- **Email Marketing Tools**: Tools like Mailchimp, HubSpot, and Constant Contact offer analytics on email open rates, click-through rates, and conversions.
- **Content Management Systems (CMS)**: CMS platforms like WordPress and HubSpot offer built-in analytics and integrations with other tools to track content performance.

2.4.4 Best Practices for Measuring Content Marketing Success

To effectively measure content marketing success, follow these best practices:

- **Set SMART Goals:** Ensure your objectives are Specific, Measurable, Achievable, Relevant, and Time-bound (SMART). This clarity helps you track progress and make informed decisions.
- **Select Relevant KPIs:** Choose KPIs that align with your objectives. For example, if your goal is lead generation, focus on metrics like conversion rates and leads captured.
- **Regularly Monitor and Analyze Data:** Regularly review your metrics to identify trends, strengths, and areas for improvement. Use tools like dashboards and reports to visualize data and track performance over time.

- **A/B Testing:** Conduct A/B tests to compare different versions of your content and determine what works best. This helps optimize your content for better performance.
- **Audience Segmentation:** Segment your audience based on demographics, behavior, or other criteria to gain deeper insights. Tailoring content to specific segments can improve engagement and conversions.
- **Benchmarking:** Compare your performance against industry benchmarks or competitors to gauge your success. This helps set realistic goals and identify areas where you can improve.
- **Qualitative Feedback:** In addition to quantitative metrics, gather qualitative feedback through surveys, interviews, and social media interactions. This provides valuable insights into audience preferences and perceptions.

2.4.5 Case Studies of Successful Measurement

Examining successful case studies can provide practical insights into measuring content marketing success. Here are two examples:

HubSpot

HubSpot, a leading inbound marketing and sales platform, uses a comprehensive approach to measure content marketing success. They track various KPIs, including organic traffic, leads generated, and conversion rates. By regularly analyzing data and conducting A/B tests, HubSpot continuously optimizes its content strategy. This data-driven approach has helped them significantly increase their website traffic and lead generation.

Buffer

Buffer, a social media management tool, focuses on engagement metrics to measure the success of their content marketing efforts. They use tools like Google Analytics and social media analytics to track traffic, social shares, and user interactions. Buffer also collects qualitative feedback through surveys and social media interactions. By combining quantitative data with qualitative insights, Buffer effectively tailors its content to meet audience needs, resulting in high engagement and customer satisfaction.

CHAPTER 3
SOCIAL MEDIA MARKETING

3.1 INTRODUCTION TO SOCIAL MEDIA PLATFORMS

Social media platforms have revolutionized the way individuals and businesses communicate, interact, and share information. They serve as powerful tools for marketing, customer engagement, and brand building. Social media platforms offer diverse opportunities for businesses to connect with their audiences, build brand awareness, and drive engagement. By understanding the unique features and best practices for each platform, businesses can tailor their strategies to maximize impact. Choosing the right platforms, creating high-quality content, and continuously measuring performance are key to achieving success in the dynamic world of social media marketing.

3.1.1 Facebook

Facebook is a social media and social networking service owned by the American technology conglomerate Meta. Created in 2004 by Mark Zuckerberg with four other Harvard College students and roommates Eduardo Saverin, Andrew McCollum, Dustin Moskovitz, and Chris Hughes, its name derives from the face book directories often given to American university students. Membership was initially limited to Harvard students, gradually expanding to other North American universities. Since 2006, Facebook allows everyone to register from 13 years old, except in the case of a handful of nations, where the age limit is 14 years. As of December 2022, Facebook claimed almost 3 billion monthly active users. As of October 2023, Facebook ranked as the 3rd most visited website in the world, with 22.56% of its traffic coming from the United States. It was the most downloaded mobile app of the 2010s.

Facebook can be accessed from devices with Internet connectivity, such as personal computers, tablets and smartphones. After registering, users can create a profile revealing information about themselves.

They can post text, photos and multimedia which are shared with any other users who have agreed to be their friend or, with different privacy settings, publicly. Users can also communicate directly with each other with Messenger, join common-interest groups, and receive notifications on the activities of their Facebook friends and the pages they follow.

The subject of numerous controversies, Facebook has often been criticized over issues such as user privacy (as with the Cambridge Analytica data scandal), political manipulation (as with the 2016 U.S. elections) and mass surveillance. Facebook has also been subject to criticism over psychological effects such as addiction and low self-esteem, and various controversies over content such as fake news, conspiracy theories, copyright infringement, and hate speech. Commentators have accused Facebook of willingly facilitating the spread of such content, as well as exaggerating its number of users to appeal to advertisers.

History

Zuckerberg built a website called "Facemash" in 2003 while attending Harvard University. The site was comparable to Hot or Not and used "photos compiled from the online face books of nine Houses, placing two next to each other at a time and asking users to choose the 'hotter' person". Facemash attracted 450 visitors and 22,000 photo-views in its first four hours.

The site was sent to several campus group listservs, but was shut down a few days later by Harvard administration. Zuckerberg faced expulsion and was charged with breaching security, violating copyrights and violating individual privacy. Ultimately, the charges were dropped. Zuckerberg expanded on this project that semester by creating a social study tool.

A "face book" is a student directory featuring photos and personal information. In 2003, Harvard had only a paper version along with private online directories. Zuckerberg told *The Harvard Crimson*, "Everyone's been talking a lot about a universal face book within Harvard.... I think it's kind of silly that it would take the University a couple of years to get around to it. I can do it better than they can, and I can do it in a week." In January 2004, Zuckerberg coded a new website, known as "TheFacebook", inspired by a *Crimson* editorial about Facemash, stating, "It is clear that the technology needed to create a centralized Website is readily available... the benefits are many." Zuckerberg met with Harvard student Eduardo Saverin, and each of them agreed to invest $1,000 ($1,613 in 2023 dollars) in the site. On February 4, 2004, Zuckerberg launched "TheFacebook", originally located at thefacebook.com.

Six days after the site launched, Harvard seniors Cameron Winklevoss, Tyler Winklevoss, and Divya Narendra accused Zuckerberg of intentionally misleading them into believing that he would help them build a social network called HarvardConnection.com. They claimed that he was instead using their ideas to build a competing product. The three complained to the *Crimson* and the newspaper began an investigation. They later sued Zuckerberg, settling in 2008 for 1.2 million shares (worth $300 million at Facebook's IPO, or $398 million in 2023 dollars).

Membership was initially restricted to students of Harvard College. Within a month, more than half the undergraduates had registered. Dustin Moskovitz, Andrew McCollum, and Chris Hughes joined Zuckerberg to help manage the growth of the website. In March 2004, Facebook expanded to Columbia, Stanford and Yale. It then became available to all Ivy League colleges, Boston University, NYU, MIT, and successively most universities in the United States and Canada.

In mid-2004, Napster co-founder and entrepreneur Sean Parker—an informal advisor to Zuckerberg—became company president. In June 2004, the company moved to Palo Alto, California. Sean Parker called Reid Hoffman to fund Facebook. However, Reid Hoffman was too busy launching LinkedIn so he set Facebook up with PayPal co-founder Peter Thiel, who gave Facebook its first investment later that month. In 2005, the company dropped "the" from its name after purchasing the domain name Facebook.com for US$200,000 ($312,012 in 2023 dollars). The domain had belonged to AboutFace Corporation.

In May 2005, Accel Partners invested $12.7 million ($19.8 million in 2023 dollars) in Facebook, and Jim Breyer added $1 million ($1.56 million in 2023 dollars) of his own money. A high-school version of the site launched in September 2005. Eligibility expanded to include employees of several companies, including Apple Inc. and Microsoft.

In May 2006, Facebook hired its first intern, Julie Zhuo. After a month, Zhuo was hired as a full-time engineer. On September 26, 2006, Facebook opened to everyone at least 13 years old with a valid email address.

By late 2007, Facebook had 100,000 pages on which companies promoted themselves. Organization pages began rolling out in May 2009. On October 24, 2007, Microsoft announced that it had purchased a 1.6% share of Facebook for $240 million ($353 million in 2023 dollars), giving Facebook a total implied value of around $15 billion ($22 billion in 2023 dollars). Microsoft's purchase included rights to place international advertisements.

In May 2007, at the first f8 developers conference, Facebook announced the launch of the Facebook Developer Platform, providing a framework for software developers to create applications that interact with core Facebook features. By the second annual f8 developers conference on July 23, 2008, the number of applications on the platform had grown to 33,000, and the number of registered developers had exceeded 400,000.

The website won awards such as placement into the "Top 100 Classic Websites" by *PC Magazine* in 2007, and winning the "People's Voice Award" from the Webby Awards in 2008. In early 2008, Facebook became EBITDA profitable, but was not cash flow positive yet.

On July 20, 2008, Facebook introduced "Facebook Beta", a significant redesign of its user interface on selected networks. The Mini-Feed and Wall were consolidated, profiles were separated into tabbed sections, and an effort was made to create a cleaner look. Facebook began migrating users to the new version in September 2008. In July 2008, Facebook sued StudiVZ, a German social network that was alleged to be visually and functionally similar to Facebook.

In October 2008, Facebook announced that its international headquarters would locate in Dublin, Ireland. A January 2009 Compete.com study ranked Facebook the most used social networking service by worldwide monthly active users. China blocked Facebook in 2009 following the Ürümqi riots.

In 2009, Yuri Milner's DST (which later split into DST Global and Mail.ru Group), alongside Uzbek Russian metals magnate Alisher Usmanov, invested $200 million in Facebook when it was valued at $10 billion. A separate stake was also acquired by Usmanov's USM Holdings on another occasion. According to the New York Times in 2013, "Mr. Usmanov and other Russian investors at one point owned nearly 10 percent of Facebook, though precise details of their ownership stakes are difficult to assess." It was later revealed in 2017 by the Paradise Papers that lending by Russian state-backed VTB Bank and Gazprom's investment vehicle partially financed these 2009 investments, although Milner was reportedly unaware at the time.

In May 2009, Zuckerberg said of the $200 million Russian investment, "This investment is purely buffer for us. It is not something we needed to get to cash flow positive." In September 2009, Facebook became cash flow positive ahead of schedule after closing a roughly $200 million gap in operating profitability.

In 2010, Facebook won the Crunchie "Best Overall Startup Or Product" award for the third year in a row.

The company announced 500 million users in July 2010. Half of the site's membership used Facebook daily, for an average of 34 minutes, while 150 million users accessed the site from mobile devices. A company representative called the milestone a "quiet revolution". In October 2010 groups were introduced. In November 2010, based on SecondMarket Inc. (an exchange for privately held companies' shares), Facebook's value was $41 billion ($57.3 billion in 2023 dollars). The company had slightly surpassed eBay to become the third largest American web company after Google and Amazon.com.

On November 15, 2010, Facebook announced it had acquired the domain name fb.com from the American Farm Bureau Federation for an undisclosed amount. On January 11, 2011, the Farm Bureau disclosed $8.5 million ($11.5 million in 2023 dollars) in "domain sales income", making the acquisition of FB.com one of the ten highest domain sales in history.

In February 2011, Facebook announced plans to move its headquarters to the former Sun Microsystems campus in Menlo Park, California. In March 2011, it was reported that Facebook was removing about 20,000 profiles daily for violations such as spam, graphic content and underage use, as part of its efforts to boost cyber security. Statistics showed that Facebook reached one trillion page views in the month of June 2011, making it the most visited website tracked by DoubleClick. According to a Nielsen study, Facebook had in 2011 become the second-most accessed website in the U.S. behind Google.

In March 2012, Facebook announced App Center, a store selling applications that operate via the website. The store was to be available on iPhones, Android devices, and for mobile web users.

Facebook's initial public offering came on May 17, 2012, at a share price of US$38 ($50.00 in 2023 dollars). The company was valued at $104 billion ($138 billion in 2023 dollars), the largest valuation to that date. The IPO raised $16 billion ($21.2 billion in 2023 dollars), the third-largest in U.S. history, after Visa Inc. in 2008 and AT&T Wireless in 2000. Based on its 2012 income of $5 billion ($6.64 billion in 2023 dollars), Facebook joined the Fortune 500 list for the first time in May 2013, ranked 462. The shares set a first-day record for trading volume of an IPO (460 million shares). The IPO was controversial given the immediate price declines that followed, and was the subject of lawsuits, while SEC and FINRA both launched investigations.

Zuckerberg announced at the start of October 2012 that Facebook had one billion monthly active users, including 600 million mobile users, 219 billion photo uploads and 140 billion friend connections.

On October 1, 2012, Zuckerberg visited Russian Prime Minister Dmitry Medvedev in Moscow to stimulate social media innovation in Russia and to boost Facebook's position in the Russian market.

On January 15, 2013, Facebook announced Facebook Graph Search, which provides users with a "precise answer", rather than a link to an answer by leveraging data present on its site. Facebook emphasized that the feature would be "privacy-aware", returning results only from content already shared with the user. On April 3, 2013, Facebook unveiled Facebook Home, a user-interface layer for Android devices offering greater integration with the site. HTC announced HTC First, a phone with Home pre-loaded.

On April 15, 2013, Facebook announced an alliance across 19 states with the National Association of Attorneys General, to provide teenagers and parents with information on tools to manage social networking profiles. On April 19 Facebook modified its logo to remove the faint blue line at the bottom of the "F" icon. The letter F moved closer to the edge of the box.

Following a campaign by 100 advocacy groups, Facebook agreed to update its policy on hate speech. The campaign highlighted content promoting domestic violence and sexual violence against women and led 15 advertisers to withdraw, including Nissan UK, House of Burlesque, and Nationwide UK. The company initially stated, "while it may be vulgar and offensive, distasteful content on its own does not violate our policies". It took action on May 29.

On June 12, Facebook announced that it was introducing clickable hashtags to help users follow trending discussions, or search what others are talking about on a topic. San Mateo County, California, became the top wage-earning county in the country after the fourth quarter of 2012 because of Facebook. The Bureau of Labor Statistics reported that the average salary was 107% higher than the previous year, at $168,000 a year ($222,961 in 2023 dollars), more than 50% higher than the next-highest county, New York County (better known as Manhattan), at roughly $110,000 a year ($145,986 in 2023 dollars).

Facebook joined Alliance for Affordable Internet (A4AI) in October, as it launched. The A4AI is a coalition of public and private organizations that includes Google, Intel and Microsoft. Led by Sir Tim Berners-Lee, the A4AI seeks to make Internet access more affordable to ease access in the developing world.

The company celebrated its 10th anniversary during the week of February 3, 2014. In January 2014, over one billion users connected via a mobile device. As of June, mobile accounted for 62% of advertising revenue, an increase of 21% from the previous year. By September Facebook's market capitalization had exceeded $200 billion ($257 billion in 2023 dollars).

Zuckerberg participated in a Q&A session at Tsinghua University in Beijing, China, on October 23, where he attempted to converse in Mandarin. Zuckerberg hosted visiting Chinese politician Lu Wei, known as the "Internet czar" for his influence in China's online policy, on December 8.

As of 2015, Facebook's algorithm was revised in an attempt to filter out false or misleading content, such as fake news stories and hoaxes. It relied on users who flag a story accordingly. Facebook maintained that satirical content should not be intercepted. The algorithm was accused of maintaining a "filter bubble", where material the user disagrees with and posts with few likes would be deprioritized. In November, Facebook extended paternity leave from 4 weeks to 4 months.

On April 12, 2016, Zuckerberg outlined his 10-year vision, which rested on three main pillars: artificial intelligence, increased global connectivity, and virtual and augmented reality. In July, a US$1 billion suit was filed against the company alleging that it permitted Hamas to use it to perform assaults that cost the lives of four people. Facebook released its blueprints of Surround 360 camera on GitHub under an open-source license. In September, it won an Emmy for its animated short "Henry". In October, Facebook announced a fee-based communications tool called Workplace that aims to "connect everyone" at work. Users can create profiles, see updates from co-workers on their news feed, stream live videos and participate in secure group chats.

Following the 2016 U.S. presidential election, Facebook announced that it would combat fake news by using fact checkers from sites like FactCheck.org and Associated Press (AP), making reporting hoaxes easier through crowdsourcing, and disrupting financial incentives for abusers.

On January 17, 2017, Facebook COO Sheryl Sandberg planned to open Station F, a startup incubator campus in Paris, France. On a six-month cycle, Facebook committed to work with ten to 15 data-driven startups there. On April 18, Facebook announced the beta launch of Facebook Spaces at its annual F8 developer conference. Facebook Spaces is a virtual reality version of Facebook for Oculus VR goggles. In a virtual and shared space, users can access a curated selection of 360-degree photos and videos using their avatar, with the support of the controller. Users can access their own photos and videos, along with media shared on their newsfeed. In September, Facebook announced it would spend up to US$1 billion on original shows for its Facebook Watch platform. On October 16, it acquired the anonymous compliment app tbh, announcing its intention to leave the app independent.

In October 2017, Facebook expanded its work with Definers Public Affairs, a PR firm that had originally been hired to monitor press coverage of the company to address concerns primarily regarding Russian meddling, then mishandling of user data by Cambridge Analytica, hate speech on Facebook, and calls for regulation. Company spokesman Tim Miller stated that a goal for tech firms should be to "have positive content pushed out about your company and negative content that's being pushed out about your competitor". Definers claimed that George Soros was the force behind what appeared to be a broad anti-Facebook movement, and created other negative media, along with America Rising, that was picked up by larger media organisations like *Breitbart News*. Facebook cut ties with the agency in late 2018, following public outcry over their association. Posts originating from the Facebook page of *Breitbart News*, a media organization previously affiliated with Cambridge Analytica, were among the most widely shared political content on Facebook.

In May 2018 at F8, the company announced it would offer its own dating service. Shares in competitor Match Group fell by 22%. Facebook Dating includes privacy features and friends are unable to view their friends' dating profile. In July, Facebook was charged £500,000 by UK watchdogs for failing to respond to data erasure requests. On July 18, Facebook established a subsidiary named Lianshu Science & Technology in Hangzhou City, China, with $30 million ($36.4 million in

2023 dollars) of capital. All its shares are held by Facebook Hong. Approval of the registration of the subsidiary was then withdrawn, due to a disagreement between officials in Zhejiang province and the Cyberspace Administration of China. On July 26, Facebook became the first company to lose over $100 billion ($121 billion in 2023 dollars) worth of market capitalization in one day, dropping from nearly $630 billion to $510 billion after disappointing sales reports. On July 31, Facebook said that the company had deleted 17 accounts related to the 2018 U.S. midterm elections. On September 19, Facebook announced that, for news distribution outside the United States, it would work with U.S. funded democracy promotion organizations, International Republican Institute and the National Democratic Institute, which are loosely affiliated with the Republican and Democratic parties. Through the Digital Forensic Research Lab Facebook partners with the Atlantic Council, a NATO-affiliated think tank. In November, Facebook launched smart displays branded Portal and Portal Plus (Portal+). They support Amazon's Alexa (intelligent personal assistant service). The devices include video chat function with Facebook Messenger.

In August 2018, a lawsuit was filed in Oakland, California claiming that Facebook created fake accounts in order to inflate its user data and appeal to advertisers in the process.

In January 2019, the 10-year challenge was started asking users to post a photograph of themselves from 10 years ago (2009) and a more recent photo.

Criticized for its role in vaccine hesitancy, Facebook announced in March 2019 that it would provide users with "authoritative information" on the topic of vaccines. A study published in the journal *Vaccine* of advertisements posted in the three months prior to that found that 54% of the anti-vaccine advertisements on Facebook were placed by just two organisations funded by well-known anti-vaccination activists. The Children's Health Defense/World Mercury Project chaired by Robert F. Kennedy Jr. and Stop Mandatory Vaccination, run by campaigner Larry Cook, posted 54% of the advertisements. The ads often linked to commercial products, such as natural remedies and books.

In March 2019, the perpetrator of the Christchurch mosque shootings in New Zealand used Facebook to stream live footage of the attack as it unfolded. Facebook took 29 minutes to detect the livestreamed video, which was eight minutes longer than it took police to arrest the gunman. About 1.3m copies of the video were blocked from Facebook but 300,000 copies were published and shared. Facebook has promised changes to its platform; spokesman Simon Dilner told Radio New Zealand that it could have done a better job. Several companies, including the ANZ and ASB banks, have stopped advertising on Facebook after the company was widely condemned by the public. Following the attack, Facebook began blocking white nationalist, white supremacist, and white separatist content, saying that they could not be meaningfully separated. Previously, Facebook had only blocked overtly supremacist content. The older policy had been condemned by civil rights groups, who described these movements as functionally indistinct. Further bans were made in mid-April 2019, banning several British far-right organizations and associated individuals from Facebook, and also banning praise or support for them.

NTJ's member Moulavi Zahran Hashim, a radical Islamist imam believed to be the mastermind behind the 2019 Sri Lanka Easter bombings, preached on a pro-ISIL Facebook account, known as "Al-Ghuraba" media.

On May 2, 2019, at F8, the company announced its new vision with the tagline "the future is private". A redesign of the website and mobile app was introduced, dubbed as "FB5". The event also featured plans for improving groups, a dating platform, end-to-end encryption on its platforms, and allowing users on Messenger to communicate directly with WhatsApp and Instagram users.

On July 31, 2019, Facebook announced a partnership with University of California, San Francisco to build a non-invasive, wearable device that lets people type by simply imagining themselves talking.

On August 13, 2019, it was revealed that Facebook had enlisted hundreds of contractors to create and obtain transcripts of the audio messages of users. This was especially common of Facebook Messenger, where the contractors frequently listened to and transcribed voice messages of users. After this was first reported on by Bloomberg News, Facebook released a statement confirming the report to be true, but also stated that the monitoring program was now suspended.

On September 5, 2019, Facebook launched Facebook Dating in the United States. This new application allows users to integrate their Instagram posts in their dating profile.

Facebook News, which features selected stories from news organizations, was launched on October 25. Facebook's decision to include far-right website *Breitbart News* as a "trusted source" was negatively received.

On November 17, 2019, the banking data for 29,000 Facebook employees was stolen from a payroll worker's car. The data was stored on unencrypted hard drives and included bank account numbers, employee names, the last four digits of their social security numbers, salaries, bonuses, and equity details. The company did not realize the hard drives were missing until November 20. Facebook confirmed that the drives contained employee information on November 29. Employees were not notified of the break-in until December 13, 2019.

On March 10, 2020, Facebook appointed two new directors Tracey Travis and Nancy Killefer to their board of members.

In June 2020, several major companies including Adidas, Aviva, Coca-Cola, Ford, HP, InterContinental Hotels Group, Mars, Starbucks, Target, and Unilever, announced they would pause adverts on Facebook for July in support of the Stop Hate For Profit campaign which claimed the company was not doing enough to remove hateful content. The BBC noted that this was unlikely to affect the company as most of Facebook's advertising revenue comes from small- to medium-sized businesses.

On August 14, 2020, Facebook started integrating the direct messaging service of Instagram with its own Messenger for both iOS and Android devices. After the update, an update screen is said to pop up on Instagram's mobile app with the following message, "There's a New Way to Message on Instagram" with a list of additional features.

As part of the update, the regular DM icon on the top right corner of Instagram will be replaced by the Facebook Messenger logo.

On September 15, 2020, Facebook launched a climate science information centre to promote authoritative voices on climate change and provide access of "factual and up-to-date" information on climate science. It featured facts, figures and data from organizations, including the Intergovernmental Panel on Climate Change (IPCC), Met Office, UN Environment Programme (UNEP), National Oceanic and Atmospheric Administration (NOAA) and World Meteorological Organization (WMO), with relevant news posts.

After the 2020 U.S. presidential election, Facebook temporarily increased the weight of ecosystem quality in its news feed algorithm.

Facebook was sued by the Federal Trade Commission as well as a coalition of several states for illegal monopolization and antitrust. The FTC and states sought the courts to force Facebook to sell its subsidiaries WhatsApp and Instagram. The suits were dismissed by a federal judge on June 28, 2021, who stated that there was not enough evidence brought in the suit to determine Facebook to be a monopoly at this point, though allowed the FTC to amend its case to include additional evidence. In its amended filings in August 2021, the FTC asserted that Facebook had been a monopoly in the area of personal social networks since 2011, distinguishing Facebook's activities from social media services like TikTok that broadcast content without necessarily limiting that message to intended recipients.

In response to the proposed bill in the Australian Parliament for a News Media Bargaining Code, on February 17, 2021, Facebook blocked Australian users from sharing or viewing news content on its platform, as well as pages of some government, community, union, charity, political, and emergency services. The Australian government strongly criticised the move, saying it demonstrated the "immense market power of these digital social giants".

On February 22, Facebook said it reached an agreement with the Australian government that would see news returning to Australian users in the coming days. As part of this agreement, Facebook and Google can avoid the News Media Bargaining Code adopted on February 25 if they "reach a commercial bargain with a news business outside the Code".

Facebook has been accused of removing and shadow banning content that spoke either in favor of protesting Indian farmers or against Narendra Modi's government. India-based employees of Facebook are at risk of arrest.

On February 27, 2021, Facebook announced Facebook BARS app for rappers.

On June 29, 2021, Facebook announced Bulletin, a platform for independent writers. Unlike competitors such as Substack, Facebook would not take a cut of subscription fees of writers using that platform upon its launch, like Malcolm Gladwell and Mitch Albom. According to *The Washington Post* technology writer Will Oremus, the move was criticized by those who viewed it as an tactic intended by Facebook to force those competitors out of business.

In October 2021, owner Facebook, Inc. changed its company name to Meta Platforms, Inc., or simply "Meta", as it shifts its focus to building the "metaverse". This change does not affect the name of the Facebook social networking service itself, instead being similar to the creation of Alphabet as Google's parent company in 2015.

In November 2021, Facebook stated it would stop targeting ads based on data related to health, race, ethnicity, political beliefs, religion and sexual orientation. The change will occur in January and will affect all apps owned by Meta Platforms.

In February 2022, Facebook's daily active users dropped for the first time in its 18-year history. According to Facebook's parent Meta, DAUs dropped to 1.929 billion in the three months ending in December, down from 1.930 billion the previous quarter. Furthermore, the company warned that revenue growth would slow due to competition from TikTok and YouTube, as well as advertisers cutting back on spending.

On March 10, 2022, Facebook announced that it will temporarily ease rules to allow violent speech against 'Russian invaders'. Russia then banned all Meta services, including Instagram.

In September 2022, Jonathan Vanian, a Technology Reporter for CNBC, wrote a piece on CNBC.com about the recent struggles Facebook was experiencing, writing "Users are jumping ship and advertisers are reducing their spending, leaving Meta poised to report its second straight drop in quarterly revenue." He also cited poor leadership decisions devoting resources to the metaverse, writing "CEO Mark Zuckerberg spends much of his time proselytizing the metaverse, which may be the company's future but accounts for virtually none of its near-term revenue and is costing billions of dollars a year to build." He also detailed accounts from analysts predicting a "death spiral" for Facebook stock as users leave, ad impressions increase, and the company chases revenue.

On October 4, 2021, Facebook had its worst outage since 2008. The outage was global in scope, and took down all Facebook properties, including Instagram and WhatsApp, from approximately 15:39 UTC to 22:05 UTC, and affected roughly three billion users. Security experts identified the problem as a BGP withdrawal of all of the IP routes to their Domain Name (DNS) servers which were all self-hosted at the time. The outage also affected all internal communications systems used by Facebook employees, which disrupted restoration efforts.

The outage cut off Facebook's internal communications, preventing employees from sending or receiving external emails, accessing the corporate directory, and authenticating to some Google Docs and Zoom services. The outage had a major impact on people in the developing world, who depend on Facebook's "Free Basics" program, affecting communication, business and humanitarian work.

Facebook's chief technology officer, Mike Schroepfer, wrote an apology after the downtime had extended to several hours, saying, "Teams are working as fast as possible to debug and restore as fast as possible."

On November 2, 2021, Facebook announced it would shut down its facial recognition technology and delete the data on over a billion users. Meta later announced plans to implement the technology as well as other biometric systems in its future products, such as the metaverse.

The shutdown of the technology will reportedly also stop Facebook's automated alt text system, used to transcribe media on the platform for visually impaired users.

In February 2023, Meta CEO Mark Zuckerberg announced that Meta would start selling blue "verified" badges on Instagram and Facebook.

Features

Facebook posts can have an unlimited number of characters. They can also have images and videos. Users can "friend" users, both sides must agree to being friends. Post can be changed to be seen by everyone (public), friends, people in a certain group (group) or by selected friends (private).

Users can also join groups. Groups are composed of persons with shared interests. For example, they might go to the same sporting club, live in the same suburb, have the same breed of pet or share a hobby. Posts posted in a group can be seen only by those in a group, unless set to public. Users can also buy, sell or swap things on Facebook Marketplace or in a Buy, Swap and Sell group. Facebook users can also advertise events on Facebook. Events advertised can be offline, on a website other than Facebook or on Facebook.

Website

The site's primary color is blue as Zuckerberg is red–green colorblind, a realization that occurred after a test taken around 2007. Facebook was initially built using PHP, a popular scripting language designed for web development. PHP was used to create dynamic content and manage data on the server side of the Facebook application. Zuckerberg and co-founders chose PHP for its simplicity and ease of use, which allowed them to quickly develop and deploy the initial version of Facebook. As Facebook grew in user base and functionality, the company encountered scalability and performance challenges with PHP. In response, Facebook engineers developed tools and technologies to optimize PHP performance. One of the most significant was the creation of the HipHop Virtual Machine (HHVM). This significantly improved the performance and efficiency of PHP code execution on Facebook's servers.

Facebook is developed as one monolithic application. According to an interview in 2012 with Facebook build engineer Chuck Rossi, Facebook compiles into a 1.5 GB binary blob which is then distributed to the servers using a custom BitTorrent-based release system. Rossi stated that it takes about 15 minutes to build and 15 minutes to release to the servers. The build and release process has zero downtime. Changes to Facebook are rolled out daily.

Facebook used a combination platform based on HBase to store data across distributed machines. Using a tailing architecture, events are stored in log files, and the logs are tailed. The system rolls these events up and writes them to storage. The user interface then pulls the data out and displays it to users. Facebook handles requests as AJAX behavior. These requests are written to a log file using Scribe (developed by Facebook).

Data is read from these log files using Ptail, an internally built tool to aggregate data from multiple Scribe stores. It tails the log files and pulls data out. Ptail data are separated into three streams and sent to clusters in different data centers (Plugin impression, News feed impressions, Actions (plugin + news feed)). Puma is used to manage periods of high data flow (Input/Output or IO). Data is processed in batches to lessen the number of times needed to read and write under high demand periods. (A hot article generates many impressions and news feed impressions that cause huge data skews.) Batches are taken every 1.5 seconds, limited by memory used when creating a hash table.

Data is then output in PHP format. The backend is written in Java. Thrift is used as the messaging format so PHP programs can query Java services. Caching solutions display pages more quickly. The data is then sent to MapReduce servers where it is queried via Hive. This serves as a backup as the data can be recovered from Hive. Facebook uses its own content delivery network or "edge network" under the domain fbcdn.net for serving static data. Until the mid-2010s, Facebook also relied on Akamai for CDN services.

On March 20, 2014, Facebook announced a new open-source programming language called Hack. Before public release, a large portion of Facebook was already running and "battle tested" using the new language.

Each registered user on Facebook has a personal profile that shows their posts and content. The format of individual user pages was revamped in September 2011 and became known as "Timeline", a chronological feed of a user's stories, including status updates, photos, interactions with apps and events. The layout let users add a "cover photo". Users were given more privacy settings. In 2007, Facebook launched Facebook Pages for brands and celebrities to interact with their fanbases. 100,000 Pages launched in November. In June 2009, Facebook introduced a "Usernames" feature, allowing users to choose a unique nickname used in the URL for their personal profile, for easier sharing.

In February 2014, Facebook expanded the gender setting, adding a custom input field that allows users to choose from a wide range of gender identities. Users can also set which set of gender-specific pronoun should be used in reference to them throughout the site. In May 2014, Facebook introduced a feature to allow users to ask for information not disclosed by other users on their profiles. If a user does not provide key information, such as location, hometown, or relationship status, other users can use a new "ask" button to send a message asking about that item to the user in a single click.

News Feed appears on every user's homepage and highlights information including profile changes, upcoming events and friends' birthdays. This enabled spammers and other users to manipulate these features by creating illegitimate events or posting fake birthdays to attract attention to their profile or cause. Initially, the News Feed caused dissatisfaction among Facebook users; some complained it was too cluttered and full of undesired information, others were concerned that it made it too easy for others to track individual activities (such as relationship status changes, events, and conversations with other users). Zuckerberg apologized for the site's failure to include appropriate privacy features. Users then gained control over what types of information are shared automatically with friends. Users are now able to prevent user-set categories of friends from seeing updates about certain types of activities, including profile changes, Wall posts and newly added friends.

On February 23, 2010, Facebook was granted a patent on certain aspects of its News Feed. The patent covers News Feeds in which links are provided so that one user can participate in the activity of another user. The sorting and display of stories in a user's News Feed is governed by the EdgeRank algorithm.

The Photos application allows users to upload albums and photos. Each album can contain 200 photos. Privacy settings apply to individual albums. Users can "tag", or label, friends in a photo. The friend receives a notification about the tag with a link to the photo. This photo tagging feature was developed by Aaron Sittig, now a Design Strategy Lead at Facebook, and former Facebook engineer Scott Marlette back in 2006 and was only granted a patent in 2011.

On June 7, 2012, Facebook launched its App Center to help users find games and other applications.

On May 13, 2015, Facebook in association with major news portals launched "Instant Articles" to provide news on the Facebook news feed without leaving the site.

In January 2017, Facebook launched Facebook Stories for iOS and Android in Ireland. The feature, following the format of Snapchat and Instagram stories, allows users to upload photos and videos that appear above friends' and followers' News Feeds and disappear after 24 hours.

On October 11, 2017, Facebook introduced the 3D Posts feature to allow for uploading interactive 3D assets. On January 11, 2018, Facebook announced that it would change News Feed to prioritize friends/family content and de-emphasize content from media companies.

In February 2020, Facebook announced it would spend $1 billion ($1.18 billion in 2023 dollars) to license news material from publishers for the next three years; a pledge coming as the company falls under scrutiny from governments across the globe over not paying for news content appearing on the platform. The pledge would be in addition to the $600 million ($706 million in 2023 dollars) paid since 2018 through deals with news companies such as *The Guardian* and *Financial Times*.

In March and April 2021, in response to Apple announcing changes to its iOS device's Identifier for Advertisers policy, which included requiring app developers to directly request to users the ability to track on an opt-in basis, Facebook purchased full-page newspaper advertisements attempting to convince users to allow tracking, highlighting the effects targeted ads have on small businesses. Facebook's efforts were ultimately unsuccessful, as Apple released iOS 14.5 in late April 2021, containing the feature for users in what has been deemed "App Tracking Transparency".

Moreover, statistics from Verizon Communications subsidiary Flurry Analytics show 96% of all iOS users in the United States are not permitting tracking at all, and only 12% of worldwide iOS users are allowing tracking, which some news outlets deem "Facebook's nightmare", among similar terms.

Despite the news, Facebook has stated that the new policy and software update would be "manageable".

The "like" button, stylized as a "thumbs up" icon, was first enabled on February 9, 2009, and enables users to easily interact with status updates, comments, photos and videos, links shared by friends, and advertisements. Once clicked by a user, the designated content is more likely to appear in friends' News Feeds. The button displays the number of other users who have liked the content. The like button was extended to comments in June 2010. In February 2016, Facebook expanded Like into "Reactions", choosing among five pre-defined emotions, including "Love", "Haha", "Wow", "Sad", or "Angry". In late April 2020, during the COVID-19 pandemic, a new "Care" reaction was added.

Facebook Messenger is an instant messaging service and software application. It began as Facebook Chat in 2008, was revamped in 2010 and eventually became a standalone mobile app in August 2011, while remaining part of the user page on browsers.

Complementing regular conversations, Messenger lets users make one-to-one and group voice and video calls. Its Android app has integrated support for SMS and "Chat Heads", which are round profile photo icons appearing on-screen regardless of what app is open, while both apps support multiple accounts, conversations with optional end-to-end encryption and "Instant Games". Some features, including sending money and requesting transportation, are limited to the United States. In 2017, Facebook added "Messenger Day", a feature that lets users share photos and videos in a story-format with all their friends with the content disappearing after 24 hours; Reactions, which lets users tap and hold a message to add a reaction through an emoji; and Mentions, which lets users in group conversations type @ to give a particular user a notification.

In April 2020, Facebook began rolling out a new feature called Messenger Rooms, a video chat feature that allows users to chat with up to 50 people at a time. In July 2020, Facebook added a new feature in Messenger that lets iOS users to use Face ID or Touch ID to lock their chats. The feature is called App Lock and is a part of several changes in Messenger regarding privacy and security. On October 13, 2020, the Messenger application introduced cross-app messaging with Instagram, which was launched in September 2021. In addition to the integrated messaging, the application announced the introduction of a new logo, which will be an amalgamation of the Messenger and Instagram logo.

Businesses and users can interact through Messenger with features such as tracking purchases and receiving notifications, and interacting with customer service representatives. Third-party developers can integrate apps into Messenger, letting users enter an app while inside Messenger and optionally share details from the app into a chat. Developers can build chatbots into Messenger, for uses such as news publishers building bots to distribute news. The M virtual assistant (U.S.)

scans chats for keywords and suggests relevant actions, such as its payments system for users mentioning money. Group chatbots appear in Messenger as "Chat Extensions". A "Discovery" tab allows finding bots, and enabling special, branded QR codes that, when scanned, take the user to a specific bot.

Facebook's data policy outlines its policies for collecting, storing, and sharing user's data. Facebook enables users to control access to individual posts and their profile through privacy settings. The user's name and profile picture (if applicable) are public.

Facebook's revenue depends on targeted advertising, which involves analyzing user data to decide which ads to show each user. Facebook buys data from third parties, gathered from both online and offline sources, to supplement its own data on users. Facebook maintains that it does not share data used for targeted advertising with the advertisers themselves. The company states:

- "We provide advertisers with reports about the kinds of people seeing their ads and how their ads are performing, but we don't share information that personally identifies you (information such as your name or email address that by itself can be used to contact you or identifies who you are) unless you give us permission. For example, we provide general demographic and interest information to advertisers (for example, that an ad was seen by a woman between the ages of 25 and 34 who lives in Madrid and likes software engineering) to help them better understand their audience. We also confirm which Facebook ads led you to make a purchase or take an action with an advertiser."

As of October 2021, Facebook claims it uses the following policy for sharing user data with third parties:

- Apps, websites, and third-party integrations on or using our Products.
- When you choose to use third-party apps, websites, or other services that use, or are integrated with, our Products, they can receive information about what you post or share. For example, when you play a game with your Facebook friends or use a Facebook Comment or Share button on a website, the game developer or website can receive information about your activities in the game or receive a comment or link that you share from the website on Facebook. Also, when you download or use such third-party services, they can access your public profile on Facebook, and any information that you share with them. Apps and websites you use may receive your list of Facebook friends if you choose to share it with them. But apps and websites you use will not be able to receive any other information about your Facebook friends from you,

or information about any of your Instagram followers (although your friends and followers may, of course, choose to share this information themselves). Information collected by these third-party services is subject to their own terms and policies, not this one.

- Devices and operating systems providing native versions of Facebook and Instagram (i.e. where we have not developed our own first-party apps) will have access to all information you choose to share with them, including information your friends share with you, so they can provide our core functionality to you.
- **Note:** We are in the process of restricting developers' data access even further to help prevent abuse. For example, we will remove developers' access to your Facebook and Instagram data if you haven't used their app in 3 months, and we are changing Login, so that in the next version, we will reduce the data that an app can request without app review to include only name, Instagram username and bio, profile photo and email address. Requesting any other data will require our approval.

Facebook will also share data with law enforcement if needed to. Facebook's policies have changed repeatedly since the service's debut, amid a series of controversies covering everything from how well it secures user data, to what extent it allows users to control access, to the kinds of access given to third parties, including businesses, political campaigns and governments. These facilities vary according to country, as some nations require the company to make data available (and limit access to services), while the European Union's GDPR regulation mandates additional privacy protections.

On July 29, 2011, Facebook announced its Bug Bounty Program that paid security researchers a minimum of $500 ($677.00 in 2023 dollars) for reporting security holes. The company promised not to pursue "white hat" hackers who identified such problems. This led researchers in many countries to participate, particularly in India and Russia.

Reception

Facebook's rapid growth began as soon as it became available and continued through 2018, before beginning to decline.

Facebook passed 100 million registered users in 2008, and 500 million in July 2010. According to the company's data at the July 2010 announcement, half of the site's membership used Facebook daily, for an average of 34 minutes, while 150 million users accessed the site by mobile.

In October 2012, Facebook's monthly active users passed one billion, with 600 million mobile users, 219 billion photo uploads, and 140 billion friend connections. The

2 billion user mark was crossed in June 2017. In November 2015, after skepticism about the accuracy of its "monthly active users" measurement, Facebook changed its definition to a logged-in member who visits the Facebook site through the web browser or mobile app, or uses the Facebook Messenger app, in the 30-day period prior to the measurement. This excluded the use of third-party services with Facebook integration, which was previously counted.

From 2017 to 2019, the percentage of the U.S. population over the age of 12 who use Facebook has declined, from 67% to 61% (a decline of some 15 million U.S. users), with a higher drop-off among younger Americans (a decrease in the percentage of U.S. 12- to 34-year-olds who are users from 58% in 2015 to 29% in 2019). The decline coincided with an increase in the popularity of Instagram, which is also owned by Meta.

The number of daily active users experienced a quarterly decline for the first time in the last quarter of 2021, down to 1.929 billion from 1.930 billion, but increased again the next quarter despite being banned in Russia.

Historically, commentators have offered predictions of Facebook's decline or end, based on causes such as a declining user base; the legal difficulties of being a closed platform, inability to generate revenue, inability to offer user privacy, inability to adapt to mobile platforms, or Facebook ending itself to present a next generation replacement; or Facebook's role in Russian interference in the 2016 United States elections.

The highest number of Facebook users as of October 2018 are from India and the United States, followed by Indonesia, Brazil and Mexico. Region-wise, the highest number of users are from Asia-Pacific (947 million) followed by Europe (381 million) and US-Canada (242 million). The rest of the world has 750 million users.

Over the 2008–2018 period, the percentage of users under 34 declined to less than half of the total.

In many countries the social networking sites and mobile apps have been blocked temporarily or permanently, including China, Iran, Vietnam, Pakistan, Syria, and North Korea. In May 2018, the government of Papua New Guinea announced that it would ban Facebook for a month while it considered the impact of the website on the country, though no ban has since occurred. In 2019, Facebook announced it would start enforcing its ban on users, including influencers, promoting any vape, tobacco products, or weapons on its platforms.

3.1.2 Instagram

Instagram is a photo and video sharing social networking service owned by Meta Platforms. It allows users to upload media that can be edited with filters, be organized by hashtags, and be associated with a location via geographical tagging. Posts can be shared publicly or with preapproved followers. Users can browse other users' content by tags and locations, view trending content, like photos, and follow other users to add their content to a personal feed. A Meta-operated image-centric social media platform, it is available on iOS, Android, Windows 10, and the web. Users can take photos and edit them using built-in filters and other tools, then share them on other social media platforms like Facebook. It supports 32 languages including English, Spanish, French, Korean, and Japanese.

Instagram was originally distinguished by allowing content to be framed only in a square (1:1) aspect ratio of 640 pixels to match the display width of the iPhone at the time. In 2015, this restriction was eased with an increase to 1080 pixels. It also added messaging features, the ability to include multiple images or videos in a single post, and a Stories feature—similar to its main competitor Snapchat—which allowed users to post their content to a sequential feed, with each post accessible to others for 24 hours. As of January 2019, Stories is used by 500 million people daily.

Originally launched for iOS in October 2010 by Kevin Systrom and Mike Krieger, Instagram rapidly gained popularity, with one million registered users in two months, 10 million in a year, and 1 billion by June 2018. In April 2012, Facebook Inc. acquired the service for approximately US$1 billion in cash and stock. The Android version of Instagram was released in April 2012, followed by a feature-limited desktop interface in November 2012, a Fire OS app in June 2014, and an app for Windows 10 in October 2016. As of October 2015, over 40 billion photos had been uploaded. Although often admired for its success and influence, Instagram has also been criticized for negatively affecting teens' mental health, its policy and interface changes, its alleged censorship, and illegal and inappropriate content uploaded by users.

History

Instagram began development in San Francisco as Burbn, a mobile check-in app created by Kevin Systrom and Mike Krieger. On March 5, 2010, Systrom closed a $500,000 (equivalent to $682,200 in 2023) seed funding round with Baseline Ventures and Andreessen Horowitz while working on Burbn. Realizing that it was too similar to Foursquare, they refocused their app on photo-sharing, which had become a popular feature among its users. They renamed it Instagram, a portmanteau of instant camera and telegram.

Josh Riedel joined the company in October as Community Manager, Shayne Sweeney joined in November as an engineer, and Jessica Zollman joined as a Community Evangelist in August 2011. The first Instagram post was a photo of South Beach Harbor at Pier 38, posted by Mike Krieger at 5:26 p.m. on July 16, 2010. On October 6, 2010, the Instagram iOS app was officially released through the

App Store. In February 2011, it was reported that Instagram had raised $7 million (equivalent to $9,357,057 in 2023) in Series A funding from a variety of investors, including Benchmark Capital, Jack Dorsey, Chris Sacca (through Capital fund), and Adam D'Angelo. The deal valued Instagram at around $20 million. In April 2012, Instagram raised $50 million (equivalent to $65,610,000 in 2023) from venture capitalists with a valuation of $500 million (equivalent to $656,100,000 in 2023). Joshua Kushner was the second largest investor in Instagram's Series B fundraising round, leading his investment firm, Thrive Capital, to double its money after the sale to Facebook.

On April 3, 2012, Instagram released a version of its app for Android phones, and it was downloaded more than one million times in less than one day. The Android app has since received two significant updates: first, in March 2014, which cut the file size of the app by half and added performance improvements; then in April 2017, to add an offline mode that allows users to view and interact with content without an Internet connection. At the time of the announcement, it was reported that 80% of Instagram's 600 million users were located outside the U.S., and while the aforementioned functionality was live at its announcement, Instagram also announced its intention to make more features available offline, and that they were "exploring an iOS version". On April 9, 2012, Facebook, Inc. (now Meta Platforms) bought Instagram for $1 billion (equivalent to $1,312,000,000 in 2023) in cash and stock, with a plan to keep the company independently managed. Britain's Office of Fair Trading approved the deal on August 14, 2012, and on August 22, 2012, the Federal Trade Commission in the U.S. closed its investigation, allowing the deal to proceed. On September 6, 2012, the deal between Instagram and Facebook officially closed with a purchase price of $300 million in cash and 23 million shares of stock.

The deal closed just before Facebook's scheduled initial public offering according to CNN. The deal price was compared to the $35 million Yahoo! paid for Flickr in 2005. Mark Zuckerberg said Facebook was "committed to building and growing Instagram independently." According to *Wired*, the deal netted Systrom $400 million.

In November 2012, Instagram launched website profiles, allowing anyone to see user feeds from a web browser with limited functionality, as well as a selection of *badges*, and web widget buttons to link to profiles.

Since the app's launch it had used the Foursquare API technology to provide named location tagging. In March 2014, Instagram started to test and switch the technology to use Facebook Places.

In June 2015, the desktop website user interface was redesigned to become more flat and minimalistic, but with more screen space for each photo and to resemble the layout of Instagram's mobile website. Furthermore, one row of pictures only has three instead of five photos to match the mobile layout. The *slideshow banner* on the top of profile pages, which simultaneously slide-showed seven picture tiles of pictures posted by the user, alternating at different times in a random order, has been removed. In addition, the formerly angular profile pictures became circular.

In April 2016, Instagram released a Windows 10 Mobile app, after years of demand from Microsoft and the public to release an app for the platform. The platform previously had a beta version of Instagram, first released on November 21, 2013, for Windows Phone 8. The new app added support for videos (viewing and creating posts or stories, and viewing live streams), album posts and direct messages. Similarly, an app for Windows 10 personal computers and tablets was released in October 2016. In May, Instagram updated its mobile website to allow users to upload photos, and to add a "lightweight" version of the Explore tab.

On May 11, 2016, Instagram revamped its design, adding a black-and-white flat design theme for the app's user interface, and a less skeuomorphistic, more abstract, "modern" and colorful icon. Rumors of a redesign first started circulating in April, when *The Verge* received a screenshot from a tipster, but at the time, an Instagram spokesperson simply told the publication that it was only a concept.

On December 6, 2016, Instagram introduced comment liking. However, unlike post likes, the user who posted a comment does not receive notifications about comment likes in their notification inbox. Uploaders can optionally decide to deactivate comments on a post.

The mobile website allows uploading pictures since May 4, 2017. Image filters and the ability to upload videos were not introduced then.

On April 30, 2019, the Windows 10 Mobile app was discontinued, though the mobile website remains available as a progressive web application (PWA) with limited functionality. The app remains available on Windows 10 computers and tablets, also updated to a PWA in 2020.

To comply with the GDPR regulations regarding data portability, Instagram introduced the ability for users to download an archive of their user data in April 2018.

IGTV launched on June 20, 2018, as a standalone video application. The application was shut down and removed from app stores in March 2022, citing low usage and a shift to short-form video content.

On September 24, 2018, Krieger and Systrom announced in a statement they would be stepping down from Instagram. On October 1, 2018, it was announced that Adam Mosseri would be the new head of Instagram.

During Facebook F8, it was announced that Instagram would, beginning in Canada, pilot the removal of publicly displayed "like" counts for content posted by other users. Like counts would only be visible to the user who originally posted the content. Mosseri stated that this was intended to have users "worry a little bit less about how many likes they're getting on Instagram and spend a bit more time connecting with the people that they care about." It has been argued that low numbers of likes in relativity to others could contribute to a lower self-esteem in users. The pilot began in May 2019, and was extended to 6 other markets in July. The pilot was expanded worldwide in November 2019. Also in July 2019, Instagram announced that it would implement new features designed to reduce harassment and negative comments on the service.

In August 2019, Instagram also began to pilot the removal of the "Following" tab from the app, which had allowed users to view a feed of the likes and comments made by users they follow. The change was made official in October, with head of product Vishal Shah stating that the feature was underused and that some users were "surprised" when they realized their activity was being surfaced in this manner. In October 2019, Instagram introduced a limit on the number of posts visible in page scrolling mode unless logged in. Until this point, public profiles had been available to all users, even when not logged in. Following the change, after viewing a number of posts a pop-up requires the user to log in to continue viewing content.

That month, Instagram launched a separate app known as Threads. Similar to Snapchat, the app allowed users to communicate through messaging and video chats. It was integrated with Instagram's "Close friends" feature, so that users could send images, photos, and texts privately to others, and also had Instagram's photo editing system embedded into the app. However, Instagram discontinued this version of Threads in December 2021, mainly due to most of its features being rolled out on Instagram itself, as well as low usage compared to other social media applications. Threads was not well-received among Instagram's user base. Since its launch, only approximately 220,000 users globally downloaded the app, which represented less than 0.1% of Instagram's monthly active users, indicating a lack of success in driving adoption.

In March 2020, Instagram launched a new feature called "Co-Watching". The new feature allows users to share posts with each other over video calls. According to Instagram, they pushed forward the launch of Co-Watching in order to meet the demand for virtually connecting with friends and family due to social distancing as a result of the COVID-19 pandemic. In August 2020, Instagram began a pivot to video, introducing a new feature called "Reels". The intent was to compete with the video-sharing site TikTok. Instagram also added suggested posts in August 2020. After scrolling through posts from the past 48 hours, Instagram displays posts related to their interests from accounts they do not follow.

In February 2021, Instagram began testing a new feature called Vertical Stories, said by some sources to be inspired by TikTok. The same month, they also began testing the removal of ability to share feed posts to stories.

In March 2021, Instagram launched a new feature in which four people can go live at once. Instagram also announced that adults would not be allowed to message teens who don't follow them as part of a series of new child safety policies.

In May 2021, Instagram began allowing users in some regions to add pronouns to their profile page.

On October 4, 2021, Meta services suffered their worst outage since 2008, bringing down Instagram, Facebook, and WhatsApp. Security experts identified the problem as possibly being DNS-related.

On March 17, 2022, Zuckerberg confirmed plans to add non-fungible tokens (NFTs) to the platform.

In September 2022, Ireland's Data Protection Commission fined the company $402 million under privacy laws recently adopted by the European Union over how it handled the privacy data of minors.

After being trialled in mid-2022, Instagram introduced Notes in December 2022. This feature allows users to share updates as short text posts of up to 60 characters with certain people, who can then reply to them using messaging on Instagram.

In February 2023, Instagram introduced a new feature allowing users to browse and post GIFs in their comments. That same month, Zuckerberg announced that Meta would start selling blue "verified" badges on Instagram and Facebook.

On July 5, 2023, Meta launched Threads, a social network platform connected to Instagram that allows users to make public shortform blog posts comprising text, photos, and videos, as well as to converse with other users and reblog other users' posts. Threads aims to compete with Twitter.

In April 2022, Instagram began testing the removal of the ability to see "recent" posts from various hashtags. This change became permanent and system wide a year later, and now hashtags can only be used to see a selection of curated content from "top" users. These changes are ostensibly an attempt to hinder the spread of misinformation, while Instagram has also repeatedly stated that hashtags do not help posts get views. In April 2024, Instagram announced that they would start testing new tools "within weeks" to fight sextortion, a form of blackmail involving intimate pictures sent online.

Features and Tools

Users can upload photographs and short videos, follow other users' feeds, and geotag images with the name of a location. Users can set their account as "private", thereby requiring that they approve any new follower requests. Users can connect their Instagram account to other social networking sites, enabling them to share uploaded photos to those sites. In September 2011, a new version of the app included new and live filters, instant tilt–shift, high-resolution photographs, optional borders, one-click rotation, and an updated icon. Photos were initially restricted to a square, 1:1 aspect ratio; since August 2015, the app supports portrait and widescreen aspect ratios as well. Users could formerly view a map of a user's geotagged photos. The feature was removed in September 2016, citing low usage.

Since December 2016, posts can be "saved" into a private area of the app. The feature was updated in April 2017 to let users organize saved posts into named collections. Users can also "archive" their posts in a private storage area, out of visibility for the public and other users. The move was seen as a way to prevent users from deleting photos that don't garner a desired number of "likes" or are deemed boring, but also as a way to limit the "emergent behavior" of deleting photos, which deprives the service of content. In August, Instagram announced that it would start organizing comments into threads, letting users more easily interact with replies.

Since February 2017, up to ten pictures or videos can be included in a single post, with the content appearing as a swipeable carousel. The feature originally limited photos to the square format, but received an update in August to enable portrait and landscape photos instead.

In April 2018, Instagram launched its version of a portrait mode called "focus mode", which gently blurs the background of a photo or video while keeping the subject in focus when selected. In November, Instagram began to support Alt text to add descriptions of photos for the visually impaired. They are either generated automatically using object recognition (using existing Facebook technology) or manually specified by the uploader.

On March 1, 2021, Instagram launched a new feature named Instagram Live "Rooms" Let Four People Go Live Together.

In May 2021, Instagram announced a new accessibility feature for videos on Instagram Reels and Stories to allow creators to place closed captions on their content.

In January 2011, Instagram introduced hashtags to help users discover both photos and each other. Instagram encourages users to make tags both specific and relevant, rather than tagging generic words like "photo", to make photographs stand out and to attract like-minded Instagram users.

Users on Instagram have created "trends" through hashtags. The trends deemed the most popular on the platform often highlight a specific day of the week to post the material on. Examples of popular trends include #SelfieSunday, in which users post a photo of their faces on Sundays; #MotivationMonday, in which users post motivational photos on Mondays; #TransformationTuesday, in which users post photos highlighting differences from the past to the present; #WomanCrushWednesday, in which users post photos of women they have a romantic interest in or view favorably, as well as its #ManCrushMonday counterpart centered on men; and #ThrowbackThursday, in which users post a photo from their past, highlighting a particular moment.

In December 2017, Instagram began to allow users to follow hashtags, which display relevant highlights of the topic in their feeds. The ability to search "Recent" hashtags was temporarily disabled during the 2020 U.S. elections, to prevent the spread of misinformation. In 2022 this was again tested on some users, and in April 2023 the ability to search recent hashtags was removed entirely. Now, users are only able to see a curated selection of "popular" posts using a given hashtag. Instagram said that this is to prevent abuse and so that hashtags do not help users gain views, but it has been noted that using hashtags is the only free method for a user to reach past their existing followers.

In June 2012, Instagram introduced "Explore", a tab inside the app that displays popular photos, photos taken at nearby locations, and search. The tab was updated in June 2015 to feature trending tags and places, curated content, and the ability to search for locations. In April 2016, Instagram added a "Videos You Might Like" channel to the tab, followed by an "Events" channel in August, featuring videos from concerts, sports games, and other live events, followed by the addition of Instagram Stories in October. The tab was later expanded again in November 2016 after Instagram Live launched to display an algorithmically curated page of the "best" Instagram Live videos currently airing. In May 2017, Instagram once again updated the Explore tab to promote public Stories content from nearby places.

Instagram offers a number of photographic filters that users can apply to their images. In February 2012, Instagram added a "Lux" filter, an effect that "lightens shadows, darkens highlights and increases contrast". In December 2014, Slumber, Crema, Ludwig, Aden, and Perpetua were five new filters added to the Instagram filter family.

Initially a purely photo-sharing service, Instagram incorporated 15-second video sharing in June 2013. The addition was seen by some in the technology media as Facebook's attempt at competing with the then-popular video-sharing application Vine. In August 2015, Instagram added support for widescreen videos. In March 2016, Instagram increased the 15-second video limit to one minute. Albums were introduced in February 2017, which allow up to 10 minutes of video to be shared in one post.

IGTV was a vertical video application launched by Instagram in June 2018. Basic functionality is also available within the Instagram app and website. IGTV allows uploads of up to 10 minutes in length with a file size of up to 650 MB, with verified and popular users allowed to upload videos of up to one hour in length with a file size of up to 5.4 GB. The app automatically begins playing videos as soon as it is launched, which CEO Kevin Systrom contrasted to video hosts where one must first locate a video. In March 2022, the application was shut down.

In November 2019, it was reported that Instagram had begun to pilot a new video feature known as “Reels” in Brazil, expanding to France and Germany afterwards. It is similar in functionality to the Chinese video-sharing service TikTok, with a focus on allowing users to record short videos set to pre-existing sound clips from other posts. Users could make up to 15 (later 30) second videos using this feature. Reels also integrates with existing Instagram filters and editing tools.

In July 2020, Instagram rolled out Reels to India after TikTok was banned in the country. The following month, Reels officially launched in 50 countries including the United States, Canada and United Kingdom. Instagram introduced a reels button on the home page.

On June 17, 2021, Instagram launched full-screen advertisements in Reels. The ads are similar to regular reels and can run up to 30 seconds. They are distinguished from regular content by the “sponsored” tag under the account name.

Despite the “TikTokification” of Reels and the parent company Meta spending millions on courting content creators, user engagement continued to lag far behind TikTok as of 2022.

In December 2013, Instagram announced Instagram Direct, a feature that lets users interact through private messaging (colloquially called “DM” OR “DMs”; in some regions, the messages may be known simply as “direct”/”directs”). Users who follow each other can send private messages with photos and videos, in contrast to the public-only requirement that was previously in place. When users receive a private message from someone they don’t follow, the message is marked as pending and the user must accept to see it. Users can send a photo to a maximum of 15 people. The feature received a major update in September 2015, adding conversation threading and making it possible for users to share locations, hashtag pages, and profiles through private messages directly from the news feed. Additionally, users can now reply to private messages with text, emoji or by clicking on a heart icon. A camera inside Direct lets users take a photo and send it to the recipient without leaving the conversation. A new update in November 2016 let users make their private messages “disappear” after being viewed by the recipient, with the sender receiving a notification if the recipient takes a screenshot.

In April 2017, Instagram redesigned Direct to combine all private messages, both permanent and ephemeral, into the same message threads. In May, Instagram made it possible to send website links in messages, and also added support for sending photos in their original portrait or landscape orientation without cropping.

In April 2020, Direct became accessible from the Instagram website, allowing users to send direct messages from a web version using WebSocket technology.

In August 2020, Facebook started merging Instagram Direct into Facebook Messenger. After the update (which is rolled out to a segment of the user base) the Instagram Direct icon transforms into Facebook Messenger icon.

In March 2021, a feature was added that prevents adults from messaging users under 18 who do not follow them as part of a series of new child safety policies.

In August 2023, Instagram introduced new adjustments to protect user privacy and prevent harassment and spam. Users can now only receive one direct message from accounts that they do not follow, and must approve the message request before further messages can be sent. This setting can be changed to allow unlimited messages from other accounts that the user does not follow.

In August 2016, Instagram launched Instagram Stories, a feature that allows users to take photos, add effects and layers, and add them to their Instagram story. Images uploaded to a user's story expire after 24 hours. The media noted the feature's similarities to Snapchat. In response to criticism that it copied functionality from Snapchat, CEO Kevin Systrom told *Recode* that "Day One: Instagram was a combination of Hipstamatic, Twitter [and] some stuff from Facebook like the 'Like' button. You can trace the roots of every feature anyone has in their app, somewhere in the history of technology". Although Systrom acknowledged the criticism as "fair", *Recode* wrote that "he likened the two social apps' common features to the auto industry: Multiple car companies can coexist, with enough differences among them that they serve different consumer audiences". Systrom further stated that "When we adopted [Stories], we decided that one of the really annoying things about the format is that it just kept going and you couldn't pause it to look at something, you couldn't rewind. We did all that, we implemented that." He also told the publication that Snapchat "didn't have filters, originally. They adopted filters because Instagram had filters and a lot of others were trying to adopt filters as well."

In November, Instagram added live video functionality to Instagram Stories, allowing users to broadcast themselves live, with the video disappearing immediately after ending.

In January 2017, Instagram launched skippable ads, where five-second photo and 15-second video ads appear in-between different stories.

In April 2017, Instagram Stories incorporated augmented reality stickers, a "clone" of Snapchat's functionality.

In May 2017, Instagram expanded the augmented reality sticker feature to support face filters, letting users add specific visual features onto their faces.

Later in May, *TechCrunch* reported about tests of a Location Stories feature in Instagram Stories, where public Stories content at a certain location are compiled and displayed on a business, landmark or place's Instagram page. A few days later, Instagram announced "Story Search", in which users can search for geographic locations or hashtags and the app displays relevant public Stories content featuring the search term.

In June 2017, Instagram revised its live-video functionality to allow users to add their live broadcast to their story for availability in the next 24 hours, or discard the broadcast immediately. In July, Instagram started allowing users to respond to Stories content by sending photos and videos, complete with Instagram effects such as filters, stickers, and hashtags.

Stories were made available for viewing on Instagram's mobile and desktop websites in late August 2017.

On December 5, 2017, Instagram introduced "Story Highlights", also known as "Permanent Stories", which are similar to Instagram Stories, but don't expire.

In June 2018, the daily active story users of Instagram had reached 400 million users, and monthly active users had reached 1 billion active users.

Instagram introduced the verification feature, known as the blue verified badge, in December 2014. This feature allows users to verify their accounts to confirm their authenticity. Instagram began allowing users to request verification for their accounts in August 2018. This marked a significant shift from the previous system where verification was typically initiated by Instagram itself for accounts it deemed to be of public interest or high-profile. With the introduction of this feature, eligible users could apply for verification directly through the Instagram app. The Instagram blue verified badge is a symbol displayed next to an account's name to signify that the account is authentic, credible, and belongs to a public figure, celebrity, brand, or entity of significant public interest. It helps users easily identify legitimate accounts amidst the vast number of profiles on the platform. The badge appears as a blue checkmark located next to the account's username in search results, profile pages, and comments. Obtaining the blue verified badge typically requires meeting certain criteria set by Instagram, such as being notable, authentic, unique, complete, and adhering to the platform's terms of service and community guidelines. Instagram verifies accounts based on its own discretion, and not all accounts meeting the criteria may be verified. Users can apply for verification through Instagram's settings, but the decision to grant verification ultimately rests with Instagram's team. Meta (formerly Facebook) launched paid verification on Instagram in 2021. This allowed eligible Instagram users to request verification for their accounts by paying a fee, rather than relying solely on meeting the platform's traditional criteria for verification.

Emily White joined Instagram as Director of Business Operations in April 2013. She said in an interview with *The Wall Street Journal* in September 2013 that the company should be ready to begin selling advertising by September 2014 as a way to generate business from a popular entity that had not yet created profit for its parent company. White left Instagram in December 2013 to join Snapchat. In August 2014, James Quarles became Instagram's Global Head of Business and Brand Development, tasked with overseeing advertisement, sales efforts, and developing new "monetization products", according to a spokesperson.

In October 2013, Instagram announced that video and image ads would soon appear in feeds for users in the United States, with the first image advertisements displaying on November 1, 2013. Video ads followed nearly a year later on October 30, 2014. In June 2014, Instagram announced the rollout of ads in the United Kingdom, Canada and Australia, with ads starting to roll out that autumn.

In March 2015, Instagram announced it would implement "carousel ads", allowing advertisers to display multiple images with options for linking to additional content. The company launched carousel image ads in October 2015, and video carousel ads in March 2016.

In February 2016, Instagram announced that it had 200,000 advertisers on the platform. This number increased to 500,000 by September 2016, and 1 million in March 2017.

In May 2016, Instagram launched new tools for business accounts, including business profiles, analytics and the ability to promote posts as ads. To access the tools, businesses had to link a corresponding Facebook page. The new analytics page, known as Instagram Insights, allowed business accounts to view top posts, reach, impressions, engagement and demographic data. Insights rolled out first in the United States, Australia, and New Zealand, and expanded to the rest of the world later in 2016.

In November 2018, Instagram added the ability for business accounts to add product links directing users to a purchase page or to save them to a "shopping list". In April 2019, Instagram added the option to "Checkout on Instagram", which allows merchants to sell products directly through the Instagram app.

In March 2020, via a blog post, Instagram announced that they are making major moderation changes in order to decrease the flow of disinformation, hoaxes and fake news regarding COVID-19 on its platform, "We'll remove COVID-19 accounts from account recommendations, and we are working to remove some COVID-19 related content from Explore unless posted by a credible health organization. We will also start to downrank content in feed and Stories that has been rated false by third-party fact-checkers."

In June 2021, Instagram launched a native affiliate marketing tool creators can use to earn commissions based on sales. Commission-enabled posts are labeled "Eligible for Commission" on the user side to identify them as affiliate posts. Launch partners included Sephora, MAC, and Kopari.

Instagram has developed and released three stand-alone apps with specialized functionality. In July 2014, it released Bolt, a messaging app where users click on a friend's profile photo to quickly send an image, with the content disappearing after being seen. It was followed by the release of Hyperlapse in August, an iOS-exclusive app that uses "clever algorithm processing" to create tracking shots and fast time-lapse videos. Microsoft launched a Hyperlapse app for Android and Windows in May 2015, but there has been no official Hyperlapse app from Instagram for either of these platforms to date. In October 2015, it released Boomerang, a video app that combines photos into short, one-second videos that play back-and-forth in a loop.

The popularity of Instagram has led to a variety of third-party services designed to integrate with it, including services for creating content to post on the service and generating content from Instagram photos (including physical print-outs), analytics, and alternative clients for platforms with insufficient or no official support from Instagram (such as in the past, iPads).

In November 2015, Instagram announced that effective June 1, 2016, it would end "feed" API access to its platform in order to "maintain control for the community and provide a clear roadmap for developers" and "set up a more sustainable environment built around authentic experiences on the platform", including those oriented towards content creation, publishers, and advertisers. Additionally, third-party clients have been prohibited from using the text strings "insta" or "gram" in their name. It was reported that these changes were primarily intended to discourage third-party clients replicating the entire Instagram experience (due to increasing monetization of the service), and security reasons (such as preventing abuse by automated click farms, and the hijacking of accounts). In the wake of the Cambridge Analytica scandal, Instagram began to impose further restrictions on its API in 2018.

Third-party services can be used for unlimited browsing of public Instagram profiles without having to create an account, as well as for anonymous browsing of someone else's Stories. Stories are more authentic than typical photos posted as posts because users know that in 24 hours their Stories will disappear if they don't add them as highlighted (however users can check who saw their Story for 48 hours after it was published). For this reason, they are very valuable for market research.

On December 16, 2019, Facebook announced it would expand its fact-checking programs towards Instagram, by using third-party fact-checkers organizations false information is able to be identified, reviewed and labeled as false information. Content when rated as false or partly false is removed from the explore page and hashtag pages, additionally content rated as false or partly false are labeled as such. With the addition of Facebook fact-checking program came the use of image matching technology to find further instances of misinformation. If a piece of content is labeled false or partly false on Facebook or Instagram then duplicates of such content will also be labeled as false.

In April 2016, Instagram began rolling out a change to the order of photos visible in a user's timeline, shifting from a strictly chronological order to one determined by an algorithm. Instagram said the algorithm was designed so that users would see more of the photos by users that they liked, but there was significant negative feedback, with many users asking their followers to turn on post notifications in order to make sure they see updates. The company wrote a tweet to users upset at the prospect of the change, but did not back down, nor provide a way to change it back, which they reaffirmed in 2020. However, in December 2021, Adam Mosseri, in a Senate hearing on child safety issues, stated that the company is developing a version of the feed that would show user posts in chronological order.

Since 2017, Instagram has employed the ability to reduce the prominence of accounts ("shadowbanning") it believes may be generating non-genuine engagement and spam (including excessive use of unneeded hashtags), preventing posts from appearing in search results and in the app's Explore section. In a now-deleted Facebook post, Instagram wrote that "When developing content, we recommend focusing on your business objective or goal rather than hashtags". Instagram has since been accused of extending the practice to censor posts under vague and inconsistent circumstances, particularly in regards to sexually suggestive material.

Instagram caused the userbase to fall into outrage with the December 2018 update. They found an attempt to alter the flow of the feed from the traditional vertical scroll to emulate and piggy-back the popularity of their Instagram Stories with a horizontal scroll, by swiping left. Various backtracking statements were released explaining it as a bug, or as a test release that had been accidentally deployed to too large an audience.

In November 2020, Instagram replaced the activity feed tab with a new "Shop" tab, moving the activity feed to the top. The "new post" button was also relocated to the top and replaced with a Reels tab The company states that "the Shop tab gives you a better way to connect with brands and creators and discover products you love" and the Reels tab "makes it easier for you to discover short, fun videos from creators all over the world and people just like you." However, users have not responded well to the change, taking their complaints to Twitter and Reddit, and *The New York Times* has shunned Reels in particular, saying "Not only does Reels fail in every way as a TikTok clone, but it's confusing, frustrating and impossible to navigate".

Also in 2020, Instagram rolled out a feature titled "suggested posts", which adds posts from accounts Instagram thinks a user would like to such user's feed. The feature was met with controversy from *The Verge*, which reported that suggested posts would keep users glued to their feed, give Instagram more advertising space, and ultimately harm the mental health of users, while Instagram executive Julian Gutman rebutted, stating the feature was not intended to keep users glued to their screens. Suggested posts received more controversy after Fast Company stated that the feature would be impossible to turn off.

On June 23, 2021, Instagram announced a test change to the "suggested posts" feature. The company will put suggested posts ahead of posts from people who the user is following in the Instagram feed, citing positive reception as the reason for this change.

User Characteristics and Behavior

Following the release in October 2010, Instagram had one million registered users in December 2010. In June 2011, it announced that it had 5 million users, which increased to 10 million in September. This growth continued to 30 million users in April 2012, 80 million in July 2012, 100 million in February 2013, 130 million in June 2013, 150 million in September 2013, 300 million in December 2014, 400 million in September 2015, 500 million in June 2016, 600 million in December 2016, 700 million in April 2017, and 800 million in September 2017.

In June 2011, Instagram passed 100 million photos uploaded to the service. This grew to 150 million in August 2011, and by June 2023, there were over 50 billion photos uploaded to the service.

In October 2016, Instagram Stories reached 100 million active users, two months after launch. This increased to 150 million in January 2017, 200 million in April, surpassing Snapchat's user growth, and 250 million active users in June 2017.

In April 2017, Instagram Direct had 375 million monthly users.

As of 2014 Instagram's users are divided equally, with 50% iPhone owners and 50% Android owners. While Instagram has a neutral gender-bias format, 68% of Instagram users are female and 32% are male. Instagram's geographical use is shown to favor urban areas, as 17% of US adults who live in urban areas use

Instagram, while only 11% of adults in suburban and rural areas do so. While Instagram may appear to be one of the most widely used sites for photo sharing, only 7% of daily photo uploads, among the top four photo-sharing platforms, come from Instagram. Instagram has been proven to attract the younger generation, with 90% of its 150 million users under the age of 35. From June 2012 to June 2013, Instagram approximately doubled their number of users. With regards to income, 15% of US Internet users who make less than $30,000 per year use Instagram, while 14% of those making $30,000 to $50,000 and 12% of users who make more than $50,000 per year do so. With respect to the education demographic, respondents with some college education proved to be the most active on Instagram, with 23%. Following behind, college graduates consist of 18% and users with a high school diploma or less make up 15%. Among these Instagram users, 24% say they use the app several times a day.

Ongoing research continues to explore how media content on the platform affects user engagement. Past research has found that media which show people's faces receive more 'likes' and comments and that using filters that increase warmth, exposure, and contrast also boosts engagement. Users are more likely to engage with images that depict fewer individuals compared to groups and they are also more likely to engage with content that has not been watermarked, as they view this content as less original and reliable compared to user-generated content. Recently Instagram has come up with an option for users to apply for a verified account badge; however, this does not guarantee every user who applies will get the verified blue tick.

The motives for using Instagram among young people are mainly to look at posts, particularly for the sake of social interactions and recreation. In contrast, the level of agreement expressed in creating Instagram posts was lower, which demonstrates that Instagram's emphasis on visual communication is widely accepted by young people in social communication.

In June 2020, because of the Black Lives Matter movement, Instagram became more widely used as a social justice platform. Instagram-based activism (as well as other social media) has been criticized and dismissed for being performative, reductionist, and overly focused on aesthetics.

3.1.3 Twitter

Twitter was a social networking service that was rebranded in 2023 to create the social networking service X. Founded in 2006, it was purchased by Elon Musk in 2022 before its rebrand. At its peak popularity, the service was one of the world's largest social media websites and the fifth-most visited website in the world. The service was created in March 2006 and launched in July of that year. Its creators, Jack Dorsey, Noah Glass, Biz Stone, and Evan Williams, then founded Twitter, Inc. in

San Francisco, California, as a managing company for it in April 2007. A signature characteristic of the service was that posts were required to be brief (originally limited to 140 characters, later expanded to 280 in 2017). Users could share short text messages, images, and videos in posts called "tweets", and like or "retweet" other users' content. Twitter also included direct messaging, bookmarks, and lists. Features added late in the service's history included groups ("communities") and the ability to annotate tweets by other users to add context, known as Community Notes.

By 2012 more than 100 million users were producing 340 million tweets per day. The majority of tweets were produced by a minority of users. In 2020, it was estimated that approximately 48 million accounts (15%) were bots rather than genuine users.

In October 2022, the billionaire businessman Elon Musk acquired Twitter for US$44 billion, and became its chief executive officer (CEO). He stated that his aim was to promote free speech. Since his acquisition, the platform has been criticized for enabling the increased spread of disinformation and hate speech. Linda Yaccarino succeeded Musk as CEO on June 5, 2023, with Musk remaining as the chairman and the chief technology officer. In July 2023, Musk announced that Twitter would be rebranded to X and the bird logo would be retired.

History

"Twitter all began with status-sharing service TXTMob," explains an article on TNW. Tad Hirsch, a student and activist associated with the Ruckus Society, the Institute for Applied Autonomy, and later the MIT Media Lab, built the basic first application to help activists organize protests at the 2004 Republican National Convention. Inspired by TXTmob and other SMS sharing applications of the day, members of the podcasting company Odeo had an "all-day brainstorming session" to decide on building a new application. Jack Dorsey, then an undergraduate student, claims to have introduced the group to the idea of an individual using an SMS service to communicate with a small group.

The original project code name for the service was *twttr*, an idea that Williams later ascribed to Noah Glass, inspired by Flickr and the five-character length of American SMS short codes. The decision was also partly due to the fact that the domain twitter.com was already in use, and it was six months after the launch of twttr that the crew purchased the domain and changed the name of the service to *Twitter*.

The developers initially considered "10958" as the service's short code for SMS text messaging, but later changed it to "40404" for "ease of use and memorability". Work on the project started in February 2006. Dorsey published the first Twitter message on March 21, 2006:

Dorsey explained the origin of the "Twitter" title as:

- ...we came across the word "twitter", and it was just perfect. The definition was "a short burst of inconsequential information", and "chirps from birds". And that's exactly what the product was.

The first Twitter prototype, developed by Dorsey and contractor Florian Weber, was used as an internal service for Odeo employees. The full version was introduced publicly on July 15, 2006. In October 2006, Biz Stone, Evan Williams, Dorsey, and other members of Odeo formed Obvious Corporation and acquired Odeo, together with its assets—including Odeo.com and Twitter.com—from the investors and shareholders. Williams fired Glass, who was silent about his part in Twitter's startup until 2011. Twitter spun off into its own company in April 2007. Williams provided insight into the ambiguity that defined this early period in a 2013 interview:

- With Twitter, it wasn't clear what it was. They called it a social network, they called it microblogging, but it was hard to define, because it didn't replace anything. There was this path of discovery with something like that, where over time you figure out what it is. Twitter actually changed from what we thought it was in the beginning, which we described as status updates and a social utility. It is that, in part, but the insight we eventually came to was Twitter was really more of an information network than it is a social network.

The tipping point for Twitter's popularity was the 2007 South by Southwest Interactive (SXSWi) conference. During the event, Twitter usage increased from 20,000 tweets per day to 60,000. "The Twitter people cleverly placed two 60-inch plasma screens in the conference hallways, exclusively streaming Twitter messages," remarked *Newsweek*'s Steven Levy. "Hundreds of conference-goers kept tabs on each other via constant twitters. Panelists and speakers mentioned the service, and the bloggers in attendance touted it." Reaction at the conference was highly positive. Twitter staff received the festival's Web Award prize with the remark "we'd like to thank you in 140 characters or less. And we just did!"

The company experienced rapid initial growth. In 2009, Twitter won the "Breakout of the Year" Webby Award. On November 29, 2009, Twitter was named the Word of the Year by the Global Language Monitor, declaring it "a new form of social interaction". In February 2010, Twitter users were sending 50 million tweets per day. By March 2010, the company recorded over 70,000 registered applications. As of June 2010, about 65 million tweets were posted each day, equaling about 750 tweets sent each second, according to Twitter. As of March 2011, that was about 140 million tweets posted daily. As noted on Compete.com, Twitter moved up to the third-highest-ranking social networking site in January 2009 from its previous rank of twenty-second.

Twitter's usage spikes during prominent events. For example, a record was set during the 2010 FIFA World Cup when fans wrote 2,940 tweets per second in the thirty-second period after Japan scored against Cameroon on June 14, 2010. The record was broken again when 3,085 tweets per second were posted after the Los Angeles Lakers' victory in the 2010 NBA Finals on June 17, 2010, and then again at the close of Japan's victory over Denmark in the World Cup when users published 3,283 tweets per second. The record was set again during the 2011 FIFA Women's World Cup Final between Japan and the United States, when 7,196 tweets per second were published. When American singer Michael Jackson died on June 25, 2009, Twitter servers crashed after users were updating their status to include the words "Michael Jackson" at a rate of 100,000 tweets per hour. The current record as of August 3, 2013, was set in Japan, with 143,199 tweets per second during a television screening of the movie *Castle in the Sky* (beating the previous record of 33,388, also set by Japan for the television screening of the same movie).

The first unassisted off-Earth Twitter message was posted from the International Space Station by NASA astronaut T. J. Creamer on January 22, 2010. By late November 2010, an average of a dozen updates per day were posted on the astronauts' communal account, @NASA_Astronauts. NASA has also hosted over 25 "tweetups", events that provide guests with VIP access to NASA facilities and speakers with the goal of leveraging participants' social networks to further the outreach goals of NASA.

Twitter acquired application developer Atebits on April 11, 2010. Atebits had developed the Apple Design Award-winning Twitter client Tweetie for the Mac and iPhone. The application became the official Twitter client for the iPhone, iPad and Mac.

From September through October 2010, the company began rolling out "New Twitter", an entirely revamped edition of twitter.com. Changes included the ability to see pictures and videos without leaving Twitter itself by clicking on individual tweets which contain links to images and clips from a variety of supported websites, including YouTube and Flickr, and a complete overhaul of the interface, which shifted links such as '@mentions' and 'Retweets' above the Twitter stream, while 'Messages' and 'Log Out' became accessible via a black bar at the very top of twitter.com. As of November 1, 2010, the company confirmed that the "New Twitter experience" had been rolled out to all users. In 2019, Twitter was announced to be the 10th most downloaded mobile app of the decade, from 2010 to 2019.

On April 5, 2011, Twitter tested a new homepage and phased out the "Old Twitter". However, a glitch came about after the page was launched, so the previous "retro" homepage was still in use until the issues were resolved; the new homepage was reintroduced on April 20. On December 8, 2011, Twitter overhauled its website once more to feature the "Fly" design, which the service says is easier for new users to follow and promotes advertising. In addition to the *Home* tab, the *Connect* and *Discover* tabs were introduced along with a redesigned profile and timeline of Tweets. The site's layout has been compared to that of Facebook. On February 21, 2012, it was announced that Twitter and Yandex agreed to a partnership. Yandex, a Russian search engine, finds value within the partnership due to Twitter's real-time news feeds. Twitter's director of business development explained that it is important to have Twitter content where Twitter users go. On March 21, 2012, Twitter celebrated its sixth birthday by announcing that it had 140 million users, a 40% rise from September 2011, who were sending 340 million tweets per day.

On June 5, 2012, a modified logo was unveiled through the company blog, removing the text to showcase the slightly redesigned bird as the sole symbol of Twitter. On December 18, 2012, Twitter announced it had surpassed 200 million monthly active users.

On January 28, 2013, Twitter acquired Crashlytics in order to build out its mobile developer products. On April 18, 2013, Twitter launched a music app called Twitter Music for the iPhone. On August 28, 2013, Twitter acquired Trendrr, followed by the acquisition of MoPub on September 9, 2013. As of September 2013, the company's data showed that 200 million users sent over 400 million tweets daily, with nearly 60% of tweets sent from mobile devices.

During Super Bowl XLVII on February 3, 2013, when the power went out in the Mercedes-Benz Superdome, Mondelez International vice president Lisa Mann was asked to tweet "You can still dunk in the dark", referring to Oreo cookies. She approved and later told *Ad Age* in 2020, "Literally the world [had] changed when I woke up the next morning." This became a milestone in the development of commenting daily on culture.

In April 2014, Twitter underwent a redesign that made the site resemble Facebook somewhat, with a profile picture and biography in a column left to the timeline, and a full-width header image with parallax scrolling effect. That layout was used as the main for the desktop front end until July 2019, undergoing changes over time such as having rounded profile pictures since June 2017.

In April 2015, the Twitter.com desktop homepage changed. Later in the year it became apparent that growth had slowed, according to Fortune, Business Insider, Marketing Land and other news websites including Quartz (in 2016).

On April 29, 2018, the first commercial tweet from space was sent by a private company Solstar utilizing solely commercial infrastructure during the New Shepard flight. Since May 2018, tweet replies deemed by an algorithm to be detractive from the conversation are initially hidden and only loaded by actuating a "Show more replies" element at the bottom. In 2019, Twitter released another redesign of its user interface. By the start of 2019, Twitter had more than 330 million monthly active users.

Twitter experienced considerable growth during the COVID-19 pandemic in 2020. The platform also was increasingly used for misinformation related to the pandemic. Twitter started marking tweets which contained misleading information, and adding links to fact-checks. In May 2020, Twitter moderators marked two tweets from U.S. President Donald Trump as "potentially misleading" and linked to a fact-check. Trump responded by signing an executive order to weaken Section 230 of the Communications Decency Act, which limits social media sites' liability for content moderation decisions. Twitter later banned Trump, claiming that he violated "the glorification of violence policy". The ban drew criticism from conservatives and European leaders, who saw it as an interference on freedom of speech.

On June 5, 2021, the Nigerian government issued an indefinite ban on Twitter usage in the country, citing "misinformation and fake news spread through it have had real world violent consequences", after the platform removed tweets made by the Nigerian President Muhammadu Buhari. Nigeria's ban was criticized by Amnesty International.

In 2021, Twitter began the research phase of Bluesky, an open source decentralized social media protocol where users can choose which algorithmic curation they want. The same year, Twitter also released Twitter Spaces, a social audio feature; "super follows", a way to subscribe to creators for exclusive content; and a beta of "ticketed Spaces", which makes access to certain audio rooms paid. Twitter unveiled a redesign in August 2021, with adjusted colors and a new Chirp font, which improves the left-alignment of most Western languages.

In June 2022, Twitter announced a partnership with e-commerce giant Shopify, and its plans to launch a sales channel app for U.S. Shopify merchants.

On August 23, 2022, the contents of a whistleblower complaint by former information security head Peiter Zatko to the United States Congress were published. Zatko had been fired by Twitter in January 2022. The complaint alleges that Twitter failed to disclose several data breaches, had negligent security measures, violated United States securities regulations, and broke the terms of a previous settlement with the Federal Trade Commission over the safeguarding of user data. The report also claims that the Indian government forced Twitter to hire one of its agents to gain direct access to user data.

Following Twitter's change in ownership, Musk began referring to the platform as "X/Twitter" and "X (Twitter)", and renamed several features to remove references to bird-oriented terminology, including Birdwatch to Community Notes and Quote

Tweets to Quotes. On July 23, 2023, Musk confirmed the rebrand, which started when the X.com domain (formerly associated with PayPal) began redirecting to Twitter; the logo was changed from the bird to the X the next day, and the platform's official main and associated accounts also began using the letter X within their handles. The @x handle was originally owned by photographer Gene X Hwang, who registered it in 2007. Hwang had expressed willingness to sell the handle, but received an email on July 25, 2023, stating that the company was taking it. He was offered some X merchandise and a meeting with the company's leaders, but no financial benefits. The Android app's name and icon were changed to X on Google Play by July 27; the same change went live on the App Store on July 31 after Apple granted an exception to its minimum character length of 2. Around that time, some more elements of the Twitter branding were removed from the web version, including tweets being renamed to "posts".

The rebrand was described as unusual, given that Twitter's brand was already strong internationally, with words like "tweet" having entered common language. The rebranding has been criticized on the basis that the trademarkability of the name and logo is weak: there are almost 900 companies in the U.S. that own an X trademark, including an existing social media-related logo owned by Meta Platforms. The X logo uses a blackboard bold X, a character that has appeared in mathematical textbooks since the 1970s and that is included in Unicode as U+1D54F 𝕏 MATHEMATICAL DOUBLE-STRUCK CAPITAL X.

A few days after the rebrand took effect, an AP Stylebook update recommended that journalists refer to the platform as "X, formerly known as Twitter". In September 2023, *Ad Age*, citing *The Harris Poll*, noted that the rebranding had not publicly caught on, with the majority of users as well as notable brands still referring to X as "Twitter". In December 2023, Fidelity estimated the value of the company to be down 71.5 percent from its purchase price. Since Musk's takeover, data from app-tracking firms has shown that global usage of X has declined by approximately 15%, compared to a decline of 5–10% in some other social media sites. X has disputed that usage has dropped at all. On May 17, 2024, the URL was officially changed from twitter.com to x.com.

Appearance and Features

Tweets were publicly visible by default, but senders can restrict message delivery to only their followers. Users can mute users they do not wish to interact with, block accounts from viewing their posts, and remove accounts from their followers list. Users can post via the Twitter website, compatible external applications (such as for smartphones), or by Short Message Service (SMS) available in certain countries. Users may subscribe to other users' posts—this is known as "following" and subscribers are known as "followers" or "tweeps", a portmanteau of Twitter and peeps. Individual posts can be forwarded by other users to their own feed, a process known as a "repost" or "retweet". In 2015, Twitter launched "quote tweet" (originally called "retweet with comment"), a feature that allows users to add a comment to their post, imbedding one post in the other. Users can also "like" (formerly "favorite") individual tweets.

The counters for "likes", "retweets/reposts", and replies appear next to the respective buttons in timelines such as on profile pages and search results. Counters for likes and reposts exist on a post's standalone page too. Since September 2020, quote tweets, formerly known as "retweet with comment", have their own counter on their post page. Until the legacy desktop front end that was discontinued in 2020, a row with miniature profile pictures of up to ten liking or retweeting users was displayed (earliest documented implementation in December 2011 overhaul), as well as a tweet reply counter next to the according button on a tweet's page.

Twitter allows users to update their profile via their mobile phones either by text messaging or by apps released for certain smartphones and tablets. Twitter has been compared to a web-based Internet Relay Chat (IRC) client. Twitter announced in a tweet on September 1, 2022, that the ability to edit a tweet was being tested for select users. The company said the feature was being tested first to determine whether it could be abused. Editing would be allowed for 30 minutes, and previous versions of an edited post would be available. Eventually, all Twitter Blue subscribers would be able to use the feature.

Users can group posts together by topic or type by use of hashtags – words or phrases prefixed with a "#" sign. Similarly, the "@" sign followed by a username is used for mentioning or replying to other users. In 2014, Twitter introduced hashflags, special hashtags that automatically generate a custom emoji next to them for a certain period of time. Hashflags may be generated by Twitter themselves or be purchased by corporations. To repost a message from another X user and share it with one's own followers, a user can click the repost button within the post. Users can reply to other accounts' replies. Users can hide replies to their messages and select who can reply to each of their tweets before sending them: anyone, accounts who follow the poster, specific accounts, or none.

The original, strict 140 character limit was gradually relaxed. In 2016, Twitter announced that attachments, links, and media such as photos, videos, and the person's handle, would no longer count; a user photo post used to count for around 24 characters. In 2017, Twitter handles were similarly excluded. The same year, Twitter doubled its historical 140-character-limitation to 280. Under the new limit, glyphs are counted as a variable number of characters, depending upon the script they are from. In 2023, Twitter announced that Twitter Blue users could create posts with up to 4,000 characters in length.

t.co is a URL shortening service created by Twitter. It is only available for links posted to Twitter and not available for general use. All links posted to Twitter use a t.co wrapper. Twitter intended the service to protect users from malicious sites, and to use it to track clicks on links within tweets. Twitter had previously used the services of third parties TinyURL and bit.ly.

In June 2011, Twitter announced its own integrated photo-sharing service that enables users to upload a photo and attach it to a Tweet right from Twitter.com. Users now also have the ability to add pictures to Twitter's search by adding hashtags to the tweet. Twitter also plans to provide photo galleries designed to gather and syndicate all photos that a user has uploaded on Twitter and third-party services such as TwitPic. On March 29, 2016, Twitter introduced the ability to add a caption of up to 480 characters to each image attached to a tweet, accessible via screen reading software or by hovering the mouse above a picture inside TweetDeck. In April 2022, Twitter made the ability to add and view captions globally available. Descriptions can be added to any uploaded image with a limit of 1000 characters. Images that have a description will feature a badge that says *ALT* in the bottom left corner, which will bring up the description when clicked.

In 2015, Twitter began to roll out the ability to attach poll questions to tweets. Polls are open for up to 7 days, and voters are not personally identified. In Twitter's early years, users could communicate with Twitter using SMS. Twitter discontinued this feature in most countries in April 2023, after hackers had exposed vulnerabilities in the feature.

In 2016, Twitter began to place a larger focus on live streaming video programming, hosting various events including streams of the Republican and Democratic conventions during the U.S. presidential campaign, and winning a bid for non-exclusive streaming rights to ten NFL games in 2016. During an event in New York in May 2017, Twitter announced that it planned to construct a 24-hour streaming video channel hosted within the service, featuring content from various partners. Twitter announced a number of new and expanded partnerships for its streaming video services at the event, including Bloomberg, BuzzFeed, Cheddar, IMG Fashion, Live Nation Entertainment, Major League Baseball, MTV and BET, NFL Network, the PGA Tour, *The Players' Tribune*, Ben Silverman and Howard T. Owens' Propagate, *The Verge*, Stadium and the WNBA. as of the first quarter of 2017, Twitter had over 200 content partners, who streamed over 800 hours of video over 450 events.

Twitter Spaces is a social audio feature that enables users to host or participate in a live-audio virtual environment called *space* for conversation. A maximum of 13 people are allowed onstage. The feature was initially limited to users with at least 600 followers, but since October 2021, any Twitter user can create a Space. In March 2020, Twitter began to test a stories feature known as "fleets" in some markets, which officially launched on November 17, 2020. Fleets could contain text and media, are only accessible for 24 hours after they are posted, and are accessed within the Twitter app; Twitter announced it would start implementing advertising into fleets in June 2021. Fleets were removed in August 2021; Twitter had intended for fleets to encourage more users to tweet regularly, but instead they were generally used by already-active users.

A word, phrase, or topic that is mentioned at a greater rate than others is said to be a "trending topic". A topic can "trend" because of an event that naturally prompts tweets, or through a concerted effort by users. These topics help Twitter and its users understand world events and the public's opinion on them. The Twitter web interface displays a list of trending topics on a sidebar on the home page, along with sponsored content.

Trending topics are sometimes the result of concerted efforts and manipulations by fans of certain celebrities or cultural phenomena, particularly musicians like Lady Gaga, Justin Bieber, Rihanna and One Direction, and novel series *Twilight* and *Harry Potter*. Twitter has altered the trend algorithm in the past to prevent manipulation of this type with limited success. Twitter also censors trending hashtags that are claimed to be abusive or offensive. Twitter censored the #thatsafrican and #thingsdarkiessay hashtags after users complained that they found the hashtags offensive.

In late 2009, the "Twitter Lists" feature was added, making it possible for users to follow a curated list of accounts all at once, rather than following individual users. Currently, lists can be set to either public or private. Public lists may be recommended to users via the general Lists interface and appear in search results. If a users follows a public list, it will appear in the "View Lists" section of their profile, so that other users may quickly find it and follow it as well. Private lists can only be followed if the creator shares a specific link to their list. Lists add a separate tab to the Twitter interface with the title of the list, such as "News" or "Economics".

In October 2015, Twitter introduced "Moments"—a feature that allows users to curate tweets from other users into a larger collection. Twitter initially intended the feature to be used by its in-house editorial team and other partners; they populated a dedicated tab in Twitter's apps, chronicling news headlines, sporting events, and other content. In September 2016, creation of moments became available to all Twitter users.

On October 21, 2021, report based on a "long-running, massive-scale randomized experiment" that analyzed "millions of tweets sent between 1 April and 15 August 2020", found that Twitter's machine learning recommendation algorithm amplified right-leaning politics on personalized user Home timelines. The report compared seven countries with active Twitter users where data was available—Germany, Canada, the United Kingdom, Japan, France, and Spain—and examined Tweets "from major political groups and politicians". Researchers used the 2019 Chapel Hill Expert Survey (CHESDATA) to position parties on political ideology within each country. The "machine learning algorithms"—introduced by Twitter in 2016—personalized 99% of users' feeds by displaying Tweets—even older Tweets and Retweets from accounts the user had not directly followed—but that the algorithm had "deemed relevant" to the users' past preferences. Twitter randomly chose 1% of users whose Home timelines displayed content in reverse-chronological order from users they directly followed.

Twitter had mobile apps for iPhone, iPad, and Android. In April 2017, Twitter introduced *Twitter Lite*, a progressive web app designed for regions with unreliable and slow Internet connections, with a size of less than one megabyte, designed for devices with limited storage capacity.

On June 3, 2021, Twitter announced a paid subscription service called Twitter Blue. Following Twitter's ongoing "X" name change, the subscription was rebranded to X Blue (or simply Blue), and, on August 5, 2023, was rebranded to X Premium (or simply Premium). The subscription provides additional premium features to the service. In November 2023 a "Premium+" subscription was launched, with a higher monthly fee giving benefits such as the omission of adverts.

In November 2022, Musk announced plans to add account verification and the ability to upload longer audio and video to Twitter Blue. A previous perk offering advertising-free news articles from participating publishers was dropped, but Musk stated that Twitter did want to work with publishers on a similar "paywall bypass" perk. Musk had pushed for a more expensive version of Twitter Blue following his takeover, arguing that it would be needed to offset a decline in advertising revenue. Twitter states that paid verification is required to help reduce fraudulent accounts.

The verification marker was included in a premium tier of Twitter Blue introduced on November 9, 2022, priced at US$7.99. On November 11, 2022, after the introduction of this feature led to prominent issues involving accounts using the feature to impersonate public figures and companies, Twitter Blue with verification was temporarily suspended. After about a month, Twitter Blue was relaunched on December 12, 2022, though for those purchasing the service through the iOS app store, the cost will be $10.99 a month as to offset the 30% revenue split that Apple takes.

Twitter initially grandfathered users and entities that had gained verification due to their status as public figures, referring to them as "legacy verified accounts" that "may or may not be notable". On March 25, 2023, it was announced that "legacy" verification status would be removed; a subscription will be required to retain verified status, costing $1,000 per-month for organizations (which are designated with a gold verified symbol), plus an additional $50 for each "affiliate". The change was originally scheduled for April 1, 2023, but was delayed to April 20, 2023, following criticism of the changes. Musk also announced plans for the "For You" timeline to prioritize verified accounts and user followers only beginning April 15, 2023, and threatened to only allow verified users to participate in polls (although the latter change has yet to occur).

Effective April 21, 2023, Twitter requires companies to participate in the verified organizations program in order to purchase advertising on the platform, although companies that spend at least $1,000 on advertising per-month automatically receive membership in the program at no additional cost.

From April 25, 2023, verified users are now prioritized in replies to tweets.

In June 2021, the company opened applications for its premium subscription options called Super Follows. This lets eligible accounts charge $2.99, $4.99 or $9.99 per month to subscribe to the account. The launch only generated about $6,000 in its first two weeks. In 2023, the Super Follows feature was rebranded as simply "subscriptions", allowing users to publish exclusive long-form posts and videos for their subscribers; the pivot in marketing was reportedly intended to help compete with Substack.

In May 2021, Twitter began testing a Tip Jar feature on its iOS and Android clients. The feature allows users to send monetary tips to certain accounts, providing a financial incentive for content creators on the platform. The Tip Jar is optional and users can choose whether or not to enable tips for their account. On September 23, 2021, Twitter announced that it will allow users to tip users on the social network with bitcoin. The feature will be available for iOS users. Previously, users could tip with fiat currency using services such as Square's Cash App and PayPal's Venmo. Twitter will integrate the Strike bitcoin lightning wallet service. It was noted that at this current time, Twitter will not take a cut of any money sent through the tips feature.

On August 27, 2021, Twitter rolled out Ticketed Spaces, which let Twitter Spaces hosts charge between $1 and $999 for access to their rooms. In April 2022, Twitter announced that it will partner with Stripe, Inc. for piloting cryptocurrency payouts for limited users in the platform. Eligible users of Ticketed Spaces and Super Follows will be able to receive their earnings in the form of USD coin, a stablecoin whose value is that of the U.S. dollar. Users can also hold their earnings in crypto wallets, and then exchange them into other cryptocurrencies. From 2014 to 2017, Twitter offered a "Buy button" feature, allowing tweets to embed products that could be purchased from within the service. Users could also add their billing and shipping information directly to their accounts. The buy button's platform partners at launch included Stripe, Gumroad, Musictoday, and The Fancy,

In July 2021, Twitter began testing a "Shop module" for iOS users in the United States, allowing accounts associated with brands to display a carousel of cards on their profiles showcasing products. Unlike the Buy button, where order fulfillment was handed from within Twitter, these cards are external links to online storefronts from which the products may be purchased. In March 2022, Twitter expanded the test to allow companies to showcase up to 50 products on their profiles.

In November 2021, Twitter introduced support for "shoppable" live streams, in which brands can hold streaming events that similarly display banners and pages highlighting products that are featured in the presentation.

Usage

Daily user estimates vary as the company does not publish statistics on active accounts. A February 2009 Compete.com blog entry ranked Twitter as the third most used social network based on their count of 6 million unique monthly visitors and 55 million monthly visits. An April 2017 a statista.com blog entry ranked Twitter as the tenth most used social network based on their count of 319 million monthly visitors. Its global user base in 2017 was 328 million.

In 2009, Twitter was mainly used by older adults who might not have used other social sites before Twitter. According to comScore only 11% of Twitter's users were aged 12 to 17. According to a study by Sysomos in June 2009, women made up a slightly larger Twitter demographic than men—53% over 47%. It also stated that 5% of users accounted for 75% of all activity. According to Quancast, 27 million people in the US used Twitter in September 2009; 63% of Twitter users were under 35 years old; 60% of Twitter users were Caucasian, but a higher than average (compared to other Internet properties) were African American/black (16%) and Hispanic (11%); 58% of Twitter users have a total household income of at least US$60,000. The prevalence of African American Twitter usage and in many popular hashtags has been the subject of research studies.

Twitter grew from 100 million monthly active users (MAUs) in September 2011, to 255 million in March 2014, and more than 330 million in early 2019. In 2013, there were over 100 million users actively using Twitter daily and about 500 million tweets every day. A 2016 Pew research poll found that Twitter is used by 24% of all online US adults. It was equally popular with men and women (24% and 25% of online Americans respectively), but more popular with younger generations (36% of 18–29 year olds). A 2019 survey conducted by the Pew Foundation found that Twitter users are three times as likely to be younger than 50 years old, with the median age of adult U.S. users being 40. The survey found that 10% of users who are most active on Twitter are responsible for 80% of all tweets. San Antonio-based market-research firm Pear Analytics analyzed 2,000 tweets (originating from the United States and in English) over a two-week period in August 2009 from 11:00 am to 5:00 pm (CST) and separated them into six categories. Pointless babble made up 40%, with 38% being conversational. Pass-along value had 9%, self-promotion 6% with spam and news each making 4%.

Despite Jack Dorsey's own open contention that a message on Twitter is "a short burst of inconsequential information", social networking researcher danah boyd responded to the Pear Analytics survey by arguing that what the Pear researchers labeled "pointless babble" is better characterized as "social grooming" or "peripheral awareness" (which she justifies as persons "want[ing] to know what the people around them are thinking and doing and feeling, even when co-presence isn't viable"). Similarly, a survey of Twitter users found that a more specific social role of passing along messages that include a hyperlink is an expectation of reciprocal linking by followers.

According to research published in April 2014, around 44% of user accounts have never tweeted. About 22% of Americans say they have used Twitter, according to a 2019 Pew Research Center survey. In 2009, Nielsen Online reported that Twitter had a user-retention rate of forty percent. Many people stop using the service after a month; therefore the site may potentially reach only about ten percent of all Internet users. Noting how demographics of Twitter users differ from the average Americans, commentators have cautioned against media narratives that treat Twitter as representative of the population, adding that only 10% of users Tweet actively, and that 90% of Twitter users have Tweeted no more than twice. In 2016, shareholders sued Twitter, alleging it "artificially inflated its stock price by misleading them about user engagement". The company announced on September 20, 2021, that it would pay $809.5 million to settle this class-action lawsuit.

User engagement is usually measured by the number of likes, replies and reposts. A 2023 study showed that retweets are more likely to contain positive content and address larger audiences using the first-person pronoun "we". Replies, on the other hand, are more likely to contain negative content and address individuals using the second-person pronoun "you" and the third-person pronouns "he" or "she". While influencers with many followers tend to post positive messages, often using the word "love" when addressing larger audiences, users with less followers tend to engage in interpersonal conversations to provoke user engagement.

Branding

When it was known as Twitter, X was internationally identifiable by its signature bird logo, or the Twitter Bird. The original logo, which was simply the word *Twitter*, was in use from its launch in March 2006. It was accompanied by an image of a bird which was later discovered to be a piece of clip art created by the British graphic designer Simon Oxley. A new logo had to be redesigned by founder Biz Stone with help from designer Philip Pascuzzo, which resulted in a more cartoon-like bird in 2009. This version had been named “Larry the Bird” after Larry Bird of the NBA’s Boston Celtics fame.

Within a year, the Larry the Bird logo underwent a redesign by Stone and Pascuzzo to eliminate the cartoon features, leaving a solid silhouette of Larry the Bird that was used from 2010 through 2012. In 2012, Douglas Bowman created a further simplified version of Larry the Bird, keeping the solid silhouette but making it more similar to a mountain bluebird. This logo was simply called the “Twitter Bird” and was used until July 2023.

On July 22, 2023, Elon Musk announced that the service would be re-branded to “X”, in his pursuit of creating an “everything app”. Musk’s X profile picture, along with the official X accounts, and the icons when browsing/signing up for the platform, were updated to reflect the new logo. The logo (𝕏) is a Unicode mathematical alphanumeric symbol for the letter “X” styled in double-strike bold.

Mike Proulx of *The New York Times* was critical of this change, saying the brand value has been “wiped out”. Mike Carr says the new logo gives a “’Big Brother’ tech overlord vibe” in contrast to the “cuddly” nature of the previous bird logo. Users review bombed the newly rebranded “X” app on the iOS App Store on the day it was revealed, and *Rolling Stone*’s Miles Klee said that the rebrand “reeks of desperation”.

Technology

Twitter relies on open-source software. The Twitter Web interface uses the Ruby on Rails framework, deployed on a performance enhanced Ruby Enterprise Edition implementation of Ruby.

In the early days of Twitter, tweets were stored in MySQL databases that were temporally sharded (large databases were split based on time of posting). After the huge volume of tweets coming in caused problems reading from and writing to these databases, the company decided that the system needed re-engineering.

From Spring 2007 to 2008, the messages were handled by a Ruby persistent queue server called Starling. Since 2009, implementation has been gradually replaced with software written in Scala. The switch from Ruby to Scala and the JVM has given Twitter a performance boost from 200 to 300 requests per second per host to around 10,000–20,000 requests per second per host. This boost was greater than the 10x improvement that Twitter’s engineers envisioned when starting the switch. The continued development of Twitter has also involved a switch from monolithic development of a single app to an architecture where different services are built independently and joined through remote procedure calls.

As of April 6, 2011, Twitter engineers confirmed that they had switched away from their Ruby on Rails search stack to a Java server they call Blender.

Individual tweets are registered under unique IDs called snowflakes, and geolocation data is added using 'Rockdove'. The URL shortener *t.co* then checks for a spam link and shortens the URL. Next, the tweets are stored in a MySQL database using Gizzard, and the user receives an acknowledgement that the tweets were sent. Tweets are then sent to search engines via the Firehose API. The process is managed by FlockDB and takes an average of 350 ms.

On August 16, 2013, Raffi Krikorian, Twitter's vice president of platform engineering, shared in a blog post that the company's infrastructure handled almost 143,000 tweets per second during that week, setting a new record. Krikorian explained that Twitter achieved this record by blending its homegrown and open source technologies.

Twitter was recognized for having one of the most open and powerful developer APIs of any major technology company. The service's API allows other web services and applications to integrate with Twitter. Developer interest in Twitter began immediately following its launch, prompting the company to release the first version of its public API in September 2006. The API quickly became iconic as a reference implementation for public REST APIs and is widely cited in programming tutorials.

From 2006 until 2010, Twitter's developer platform experienced strong growth and a highly favorable reputation. Developers built upon the public API to create the first Twitter mobile phone clients as well as the first URL shortener. Between 2010 and 2012, however, Twitter made a number of decisions that were received unfavorably by the developer community. In 2010, Twitter mandated that all developers adopt OAuth authentication with just 9 weeks of notice. Later that year, Twitter launched its own URL shortener, in direct competition with some of its most well-known third-party developers. And in 2012, Twitter introduced stricter usage limits for its API, "completely crippling" some developers. While these moves successfully increased the stability and security of the service, they were broadly perceived as hostile to developers, causing them to lose trust in the platform.

In July 2020, Twitter released version 2.0 of the public API and began showcasing Twitter apps made by third-party developers on its Twitter Toolbox section in April 2022.

In January 2023, Twitter ended third-party access to its APIs, forcing all third-party Twitter clients to shut down. This was controversial among the developer community, as many third-party apps predated the company's official apps, and the change was not announced beforehand. Twitterrific's Sean Heber confirmed in a blog post that the 16-year-old app has been discontinued. "We are sorry to say that the app's sudden and undignified demise is due to an unannounced and undocumented policy change by an increasingly capricious Twitter – a Twitter that we no longer recognize as trustworthy nor want to work with any longer."

In February 2023, Twitter announced it would be ending free access to Twitter API, and began offering paid tier plans with a more limited access.

On April 17, 2012, Twitter announced it would implement an "Innovators Patent Agreement" which would obligate Twitter to only use its patents for defensive purposes.

Twitter has a history of both using and releasing open-source software while overcoming technical challenges of their service. A page in their developer documentation thanks dozens of open-source projects which they have used, from revision control software like Git to programming languages such as Ruby and Scala. Software released as open source by the company includes the Gizzard Scala framework for creating distributed datastores, the distributed graph database FlockDB, the Finagle library for building asynchronous RPC servers and clients, the TwUI user interface framework for iOS, and the Bower client-side package manager. The popular Bootstrap frontend framework was also started at Twitter and is 10th most popular repository on GitHub.

On March 31, 2023, Twitter released the source code for Twitter's recommendation algorithm, which determines what tweets show up on the user's personal timeline, to GitHub. According to Twitter's blog post: "We believe that we have a responsibility, as the town square of the internet, to make our platform transparent. So today we are taking the first step in a new era of transparency and opening much of our source code to the global community." Elon Musk, the CEO at the time, had been promising the move for a while — on March 24, 2022, before he owned the site, he polled his followers about whether Twitter's algorithm should be open source, and around 83 percent of the responses said "yes". In February, he promised it would happen within a week before pushing back the deadline to March 31 earlier this month.

Also in March 2023, Twitter suffered a security attack which resulted in proprietary code being released. Twitter then had the source code removed.

Twitter introduced the first major redesign of its user interface in September 2010, adopting a dual-pane layout with a navigation bar along the top of the screen, and an increased focus on the inline embedding of multimedia content. Critics considered the redesign an attempt to emulate features and experiences found in mobile apps and third-party Twitter clients. The new layout was revised in 2011 with a focus on continuity with the web and mobile versions, introducing "Connect" (interactions with other users such as replies) and "Discover" tabs, an updated profile design, and moving all content to the right pane (leaving the left pane dedicated to functions and the trending topics list). In March 2012, Twitter became available in Arabic, Farsi, Hebrew and Urdu, the first right-to-left language versions of the site. In 2023 the Twitter Web site listed 34 languages supported by Twitter.com.

In September 2012, a new layout for profiles was introduced, with larger "covers" that could be customized with a custom header image, and a display of the user's recent photos posted. The "Discover" tab was discontinued in April 2015, and was succeeded on the mobile app by an "Explore" tab—which features trending topics and moments.

In September 2018, Twitter began to migrate selected web users to its progressive web app (based on its Twitter Lite experience for mobile web), reducing the interface to two columns. Migrations to this iteration of Twitter increased in April 2019, with some users receiving it with a modified layout.

In July 2019, Twitter officially released this redesign, with no further option to opt-out while logged in. It is designed to further-unify Twitter's user experience between the web and mobile application versions, adopting a three-column layout with a sidebar containing links to common areas (including "Explore" that has been merged with the search page) which previously appeared in a horizontal top bar, profile elements such as picture and header images and biography texts merged into the same column as the timeline, and features from the mobile version (such as multi-account support, and an opt-out for the "top tweets" mode on the timeline).

In response to early Twitter security breaches, the United States Federal Trade Commission (FTC) brought charges against the service; the charges were settled on June 24, 2010. This was the first time the FTC had taken action against a social network for security lapses. The settlement requires Twitter to take a number of steps to secure users' private information, including maintenance of a "comprehensive information security program" to be independently audited biannually.

After a number of high-profile hacks of official accounts, including those of the Associated Press and *The Guardian*, in April 2013, Twitter announced a two-factor login verification as an added measure against hacking.

On July 15, 2020, a major hack of Twitter affected 130 high-profile accounts, both verified and unverified ones such as Barack Obama, Bill Gates, and Elon Musk; the hack allowed bitcoin scammers to send tweets via the compromised accounts that asked the followers to send bitcoin to a given public address, with the promise to double their money. Within a few hours, Twitter disabled tweeting and reset passwords from all verified accounts. Analysis of the event revealed that the scammers had used social engineering to obtain credentials from Twitter employees to access an administration tool used by Twitter to view and change these accounts' personal details as to gain access as part of a "smash and grab" attempt to make money quickly, with an estimated US$120,000 in bitcoin deposited in various accounts before Twitter intervened. Several law enforcement entities including the FBI launched investigations into the attack.

On August 5, 2022, Twitter disclosed that a bug introduced in a June 2021 update to the service allowed threat actors to link email addresses and phone numbers to twitter user's accounts. The bug was reported through Twitter's bug bounty program in January 2022 and subsequently fixed. While Twitter originally believed no one had taken advantage of the vulnerability, it was later revealed that a user on the online hacking forum Breach Forums had used the vulnerability to compile a list of over 5.4 million user profiles, which they offered to sell for $30,000. The information compiled by the hacker includes user's screen names, location and email addresses which could be utilised in phishing attacks or used to deanonymize accounts running under pseudonyms.

During an outage, Twitter users were at one time shown the "fail whale" error message image created by Yiying Lu, illustrating eight orange birds using a net to hoist a whale from the ocean captioned "Too many tweets! Please wait a moment and try again." Web designer and Twitter user Jen Simmons was the first to coin the term "fail whale" in a September 2007 tweet.

In a November 2013 *Wired* interview Chris Fry, VP of Engineering at that time, noted that the company had taken the "fail whale" out of production as the platform was now more stable. Twitter had approximately ninety-eight percent uptime in 2007 (or about six full days of downtime). The downtime was particularly noticeable during events popular with the technology industry such as the 2008 Macworld Conference & Expo keynote address.

3.1.4 LinkedIn

LinkedIn is a business and employment-focused social media platform that works through websites and mobile apps. It was launched on May 5, 2003 by Reid Hoffman and Eric Ly. Since December 2016, LinkedIn has been a wholly owned subsidiary of Microsoft. The platform is primarily used for professional networking and career development, and allows jobseekers to post their CVs and employers to post jobs. From 2015, most of the company's revenue came from selling access to information about its members to recruiters and sales professionals. LinkedIn has more than 1 billion registered members from over 200 countries and territories.

LinkedIn allows members (both workers and employers) to create profiles and connect with each other in an online social network which may represent real-world professional relationships. Members can invite anyone (whether an existing member or not) to become a connection. LinkedIn can also be used to organize offline events, join groups, write articles, publish job postings, post photos and videos, and more.

History

The company was founded in December 2002 by Reid Hoffman and the founding team members from PayPal and Socialnet.com (Allen Blue, Eric Ly, Jean-Luc Vaillant, Lee Hower, Konstantin Guericke, Stephen Beitzel, David Eves, Ian McNish, Yan Pujante, Chris Saccheri). In late 2003, Sequoia Capital led the Series A investment in the company. In August 2004, LinkedIn reached 1 million users. In March 2006, LinkedIn achieved its first month of profitability. In April 2007, LinkedIn reached 10 million users. In February 2008, LinkedIn launched a mobile version of the site.

In June 2008, Sequoia Capital, Greylock Partners, and other venture capital firms purchased a 5% stake in the company for $53 million, giving the company a post-money valuation of approximately $1 billion. In November 2009, LinkedIn opened its office in Mumbai and soon thereafter in Sydney, as it started its Asia-Pacific team expansion. In 2010, LinkedIn opened an International Headquarters in Dublin, Ireland, received a $20 million investment from Tiger Global Management LLC at a valuation of approximately $2 billion, announced its first acquisition, Mspoke, and improved its 1% premium subscription ratio. In October of that year, Silicon Valley Insider ranked the company No. 10 on its Top 100 List of most valuable startups. By December, the company was valued at $1.575 billion in private markets. LinkedIn started its India operations in 2009 and a major part of the first year was dedicated to understanding professionals in India and educating members to leverage LinkedIn for career development.

LinkedIn filed for an initial public offering in January 2011. The company traded its first shares on May 19, 2011, under the NYSE symbol "LNKD", at $45 (~$60.00 in 2023) per share. Shares of LinkedIn rose as much as 171% on their first day of trade on the New York Stock Exchange and closed at $94.25, more than 109% above IPO price. Shortly after the IPO, the site's underlying infrastructure was revised to allow accelerated revision-release cycles.

In 2011, LinkedIn earned $154.6 million in advertising revenue alone, surpassing Twitter, which earned $139.5 million. LinkedIn's fourth-quarter 2011, earnings soared because of the company's increase in success in the social media world. By this point, LinkedIn had about 2,100 full-time employees compared to the 500 that it had in 2010.

In April 2014, LinkedIn announced that it had leased 222 Second Street, a 26-story building under construction in San Francisco's SoMa district, to accommodate up to 2,500 of its employees, with the lease covering 10 years. The goal was to join all San Francisco-based staff (1,250 as of January 2016) in one building, bringing sales and marketing employees together with the research and development team. In March 2016 they started to move in. In February 2016 following an earnings report, LinkedIn's shares dropped 43.6% within a single day, down to $108.38 per share. LinkedIn lost $10 billion of its market capitalization that day.

In 2016, access to LinkedIn was blocked by Russian authorities for non-compliance with the 2015 national legislation that requires social media networks to store citizens' personal data on servers located in Russia.

In June 2016, Microsoft announced that it would acquire LinkedIn for $196 a share, a total value of $26.2 billion. It was the largest acquisition made by Microsoft, until the acquisition of Activision Blizzard in 2022. The acquisition would be an all-cash, debt-financed transaction. Microsoft would allow LinkedIn to "retain its distinct brand, culture and independence", with Weiner to remain as CEO, who would then report to Microsoft CEO Satya Nadella. Analysts believed Microsoft saw the opportunity to integrate LinkedIn with its Office product suite to help better integrate the professional network system with its products. The deal was completed on December 8, 2016.

In late 2016, LinkedIn announced a planned increase of 200 new positions in its Dublin office, which would bring the total employee count to 1,200. Since 2017 94% of B2B marketers use LinkedIn to distribute content.

Soon after LinkedIn's acquisition by Microsoft, LinkedIn's new desktop version was introduced. The new version was meant to make the user experience seamless across mobile and desktop. Some changes were made according to the feedback received from the previously launched mobile app. Features that were not heavily used were removed. For example, the contact tagging and filtering features are not supported anymore.

Following the launch of the new user interface (UI), some users complained about the missing features which were there in the older version, slowness, and bugs in it. The issues were faced by free and premium users and with both the desktop and mobile versions of the site.

In 2019, LinkedIn launched globally the feature Open for Business that enables freelancers to be discovered on the platform. LinkedIn Events was launched in the same year.

In June 2020, Jeff Weiner stepped down as CEO and become executive chairman after 11 years in the role. Ryan Roslansky stepped up as CEO from his previous position as the senior vice president of product. In late July 2020, LinkedIn announced it laid off 960 employees, about 6 percent of the total workforce, from the talent acquisition and global sales teams. In an email to all employees, CEO Ryan Roslansky said the cuts were due to effects of the global COVID-19 pandemic. In April 2021, CyberNews claimed that 500 million LinkedIn's accounts have leaked online. However, LinkedIn stated that "We have investigated an alleged set of LinkedIn data that has been posted for sale and have determined that it is actually an aggregation of data from a number of websites and companies".

In June 2021, PrivacySharks claimed that more than 700 million LinkedIn records were on sale on a hacker forum. LinkedIn later stated that this is not a breach, but scraped data which is also a violation of their Terms of Service.

Microsoft ended LinkedIn operations in China in October 2021. In 2022, LinkedIn earned $13.8 billion in revenue, compared to $10.3 billion in 2021.

In May 2023, LinkedIn cut 716 positions from its 20,000 workforce. The move, according to a letter from the company's CEO Ryan Roslansky, was made to streamline the business's operations. Roslansky further stated that this decision would result in the creation of 250 job opportunities. Additionally, LinkedIn also announced the discontinuance of its China local job apps.

In 2013, a class action lawsuit entitled *Perkins vs. LinkedIn Corp* was filed against the company, accusing it of automatically sending invitations to contacts in a member's email address book without permission. The court agreed with LinkedIn that permission had in fact been given for invitations to be sent, but not for the two further reminder emails. LinkedIn settled the lawsuit in 2015 for $13 million (~$16.3 million in 2023). Many members should have received a notice in their email with the subject line "Legal Notice of Settlement of Class Action". The Case No. is 13-CV-04303-LHK.

In May 2017, LinkedIn sent a Cease-And-Desist letter to hiQ Labs, a Silicon Valley startup that collects data from public profiles and provides analysis of this data to its customers. The letter demanded that hiQ immediately cease "scraping" data from LinkedIn's servers, claiming violations of the CFAA (Computer Fraud and Abuse Act) and the DMCA (Digital Millennium Copyright Act). In response hiQ sued LinkedIn in the Northern District of California in San Francisco, asking the court to prohibit LinkedIn from blocking its access to public profiles while the court considered the merits of its request. The court served a preliminary injunction against LinkedIn, which was then forced to allow hiQ to continue to collect public data. LinkedIn appealed this ruling; in September 2019, the appeals court rejected LinkedIn's arguments and the preliminary injunction was upheld. The dispute is ongoing.

Membership

As of 2015, LinkedIn had more than 400 million members in over 200 countries and territories. It is significantly ahead of Viadeo (50 million as of 2013.) In 2011, its membership grew by approximately two new members every second. In 2020, LinkedIn's membership grew to over 690 million LinkedIn members. As of September 2021, LinkedIn has 774+ million registered members from over 200 countries and territories.

Platform and Features

The basic functionality of LinkedIn allows users to create profiles, which for employees typically consist of a curriculum vitae describing their work experience, education and training, skills, and a personal photo. Employers can list jobs and search for potential candidates. Users can find jobs, people and business opportunities recommended by someone in one's contact network. Users can save jobs that they would like to apply for. Users also have the ability to follow different companies.

The site also enables members to make "connections" to each other in an online social network which may represent real-world professional relationships. Members can invite anyone to become a connection. Users can obtain introductions to the connections of connections (termed *second-degree connections*) and connections of second-degree connections (termed *third-degree connections*).

A member's list of connections can be used in a number of ways. For example, users can search for second-degree connections who work at a company they are interested in, and then ask a specific first-degree connection in common for an introduction. The "gated-access approach" (where contact with any professional requires either an existing relationship, or the intervention of a contact of theirs) is intended to build trust among the service's users. LinkedIn participated in the EU's International Safe Harbor Privacy Principles.

Users can interact with each other in a variety of ways:

- Connections can interact by choosing to "like" posts and "congratulate" others on updates such as birthdays, anniversaries and new positions, as well as by direct messaging.
- Users can share video with text and filters with the introduction of LinkedIn Video.
- Users can write posts and articles within the LinkedIn platform to share with their network.

Since September 2012, LinkedIn has enabled users to "endorse" each other's skills. However, there is no way of flagging anything other than positive content. LinkedIn solicits endorsements using algorithms that generate skills members might have. Members cannot opt out of such solicitations, with the result that it sometimes appears that a member is soliciting an endorsement for a non-existent skill.

LinkedIn 'applications' often refer to external third-party applications that interact with LinkedIn's developer API. However, in some cases, it could refer to sanctioned applications featured on a user's profile page.

In February 2015, LinkedIn released an updated terms of use for their developer API. The developer API allows both companies and individuals the ability to interact with LinkedIn's data through creation of managed third-party applications. Applications must go through a review process and request permission from the user before accessing a user's data.

Normal use of the API is outlined in LinkedIn's developer documents, including:

- Sign into external services using LinkedIn.
- Add items or attributes to a user profile.
- Share items or articles to user's timeline.

In October 2008, LinkedIn enabled an "applications platform" which allows external online services to be embedded within a member's profile page. Among the initial applications were an Amazon Reading List that allows LinkedIn members to display books they are reading, a connection to Tripit, and a Six Apart, WordPress and TypePad application that allows members to display their latest blog postings within their LinkedIn profile. In November 2010, LinkedIn allowed businesses to list products and services on company profile pages; it also permitted LinkedIn members to "recommend" products and services and write reviews. Shortly after, some of the external services were no longer supported, including Amazon's Reading List.

A mobile version of the site was launched in February 2008 and made available in six languages: Chinese, English, French, German, Japanese and Spanish. In January 2011, LinkedIn acquired CardMunch, a mobile app maker that scans business cards and converts into contacts. In June 2013, CardMunch was noted as an available LinkedIn app. In October 2013, LinkedIn announced a service for iPhone users called "Intro", which inserts a thumbnail of a person's LinkedIn profile in correspondence with that person when reading mail messages in the native iOS Mail program. This is accomplished by re-routing all emails from and to the iPhone through LinkedIn servers, which security firm Bishop Fox asserts has serious privacy implications, violates many organizations' security policies, and resembles a man-in-the-middle attack.

LinkedIn also supports daily the formation of interest groups. In 2012, there were 1,248,019 such groups whose membership varies from 1 to 744,662. Groups support a limited form of discussion area, moderated by the group owners and managers. Groups may be private, accessible to members only or may be open to Internet users in general to read, though they must join in order to post messages. Since groups offer the functionality to reach a wide audience without so easily falling foul of anti-spam solutions, there is a constant stream of spam postings, and there now exists a range of firms who offer a spamming service for this very purpose. LinkedIn has devised a few mechanisms to reduce the volume of spam, but recently decided to remove the ability of group owners to inspect the email address of new members in order to determine if they were spammers. Groups also keep their members informed through emails with updates to the group, including most talked about discussions within your professional circles.

In December 2011, LinkedIn announced that they are rolling out polls to groups. In November 2013, LinkedIn announced the addition of Showcase Pages to the platform. In 2014, LinkedIn announced they were going to be removing Product and Services Pages paving the way for a greater focus on Showcase Pages.

LinkedIn maintains an internal knowledge graph of entities (people, organizations, groups) that helps it connect everyone working in a field or at an organization or network. This can be used to query the neighborhood around each entity to find updates that might be related to it.

In January 2013, LinkedIn dropped support for LinkedIn Answers and cited a new 'focus on development of new and more engaging ways to share and discuss professional topics across LinkedIn' as the reason for the retirement of the feature. The feature had been launched in 2007 and allowed users to post questions to their network and allowed users to rank answers.

In 2014, LinkedIn retired InMaps, a feature which allowed you to visualize your professional network. The feature had been in use since January 2011. According to the company's website, LinkedIn Referrals will no longer be available after May 2018. In September 2021, LinkedIn discontinued LinkedIn stories, a feature that was rolled out worldwide in October 2020.

Usage

LinkedIn is particularly well-suited for personal branding, which, according to Sandra Long, entails "actively managing one's image and unique value" to position oneself for career opportunities. LinkedIn has evolved from being a mere platform for job searchers into a social network which allows users a chance to create a personal brand. Career coach Pamela Green describes a personal brand as the "emotional experience you want people to have as a result of interacting with you," and a LinkedIn profile is an aspect of that. A contrasting report suggests that a personal brand is "a public-facing persona, exhibited on LinkedIn, Twitter and other networks, that showcases expertise and fosters new connections." LinkedIn allows professionals to build exposure for their brand within the site itself and on the World Wide Web as a whole. With a tool that LinkedIn dubs a *Profile Strength Meter*, the site encourages users to offer enough information in their profile to optimize visibility by search engines. It can strengthen a user's LinkedIn presence if they belong to professional groups on the site. The site enables users to add a video to their profiles. Some users hire a professional photographer for their profile photo. Video presentations can be added to one's profile. LinkedIn's capabilities have been expanding so rapidly that a cottage industry of outside consultants has grown up to help users navigate the system. A particular emphasis is helping users with their LinkedIn profiles.

- There's no hiding in the long grass on LinkedIn... The number one mistake people make on the profile is to not have a photo.—Sandra Long of Post Road Consulting, 2017

In October 2012, LinkedIn launched the LinkedIn Influencers program, which features global thought leaders who share their professional insights with LinkedIn's members. As of May 2016, there are 750+ Influencers. The program is invite-only and features leaders from a range of industries, including Richard Branson, Narendra Modi, Arianna Huffington, Greg McKeown, Rahm Emanuel, Jamie Dimon, Martha Stewart, Deepak Chopra, Jack Welch, and Bill Gates.

Job seekers and employers widely use LinkedIn. According to Jack Meyer, the site has become the "premier digital platform" for professionals to network online. In Australia, which has approximately twelve million working professionals, ten million of them are on LinkedIn, according to Anastasia Santoreneos, suggesting that the probability was high that one's "future employer is probably on the site." According to one estimate based on worldwide figures, 122 million users got job interviews via LinkedIn and 35 million were hired by a LinkedIn online connection.

LinkedIn also allows users to research companies, non-profit organizations, and governments they may be interested in working for. Typing the name of a company or organization in the search box causes pop-up data about the company or organization to appear. Such data may include the ratio of female to male employees, the percentage of the most common titles/positions held within the company, the location of the company's headquarters and offices, and a list of present and former employees. In July 2011, LinkedIn launched a new feature allowing companies to include an "Apply with LinkedIn" button on job listing pages. The new plugin allowed potential employees to apply for positions using their LinkedIn profiles as resumes.

LinkedIn can help small businesses connect with customers. In the site's parlance, two users have a "first-degree connection" when one accepts an invitation from another. People connected to each of them are "second-degree connections" and persons connected to the second-degree connections are "third-degree connections." This forms a user's internal LinkedIn network, making the user's profile more likely to appear in searches.

LinkedIn's Profinder is a marketplace where freelancers can (for a monthly subscription fee) bid for project proposals submitted by individuals and small businesses. In 2017, it had around 60,000 freelancers in more than 140 service areas, such as headshot photography, bookkeeping or tax filing.

The premise for connecting with someone has shifted significantly in recent years. Before the 2017 new interface was launched, LinkedIn encouraged connections between people who'd already worked, studied, done business, or the like. Since 2017, that step has been removed from the connection request process - and users are allowed to connect with up to 30,000 people. This change means LinkedIn is a more proactive networking site for job applicants trying to secure a career move or for salespeople wanting to generate new client leads.

LinkedIn Top Companies is a series of lists published by LinkedIn, identifying companies in the United States, Australia, Brazil, Canada, China, France, Germany, India, Italy, Japan, Mexico, Spain, and the United Kingdom that are attracting the most intense interest from job candidates. The 2019 lists identified Google's parent company, Alphabet, as the most sought-after U.S. company, with Facebook ranked second and Amazon ranked third.

The lists are based on more than one billion actions by LinkedIn members worldwide. The Top Companies lists were started in 2016 and are published annually. The 2021 top list identified Amazon as the top company, with Alphabet ranked second and JPMorgan & Chase Co. ranked third.

Since 2015, LinkedIn has published annual rankings of Top Voices on the platform, recognizing "members that generated the most engagement and interaction with their posts." The 2020 lists included 14 industry categories, ranging from data science to sports, as well as 14 country lists, extending from Australia to Italy.

LinkedIn also publishes data-driven annual rankings of the Top Startups in more than a dozen countries, based on "employment growth, job interest from potential candidates, engagement, and attraction of top talent."

In 2008, LinkedIn launched LinkedIn DirectAds as a form of sponsored advertising. In October 2008, LinkedIn revealed plans to open its social network of 30 million professionals globally as a potential sample for business-to-business research. It is testing a potential social network revenue model – research that, to some, appears more promising than advertising. On July 23, 2013, LinkedIn announced its Sponsored Updates ad service. Individuals and companies can now pay a fee to have

LinkedIn sponsor their content and spread it to their user base. This is a common way for social media sites such as LinkedIn to generate revenue. LinkedIn launched its carousel ads feature in 2018, making it the newest addition to the platform's advertising options. With carousel ads, businesses can showcase their products or services through a series of swipeable cards, each with its unique image, headline, and description.

They can be used for various marketing objectives, such as promoting a new product launch, driving website traffic, generating leads, or building brand awareness.

LinkedIn today announced the creation of Business Manager. The new Business Manager is a centralized platform designed to make it easier for large companies and agencies to manage people, ad accounts, and business pages.

In 2015, LinkedIn added an analytics tool to its publishing platform. The tool allows authors to better track the traffic that their posts receive. In relation to this functionality, LinkedIn has gained more users over the years in the interest of clearly monitoring users' posts through post-performance analytics

Role in Networking

LinkedIn has been described by online trade publication *TechRepublic* as having "become the de facto tool for professional networking". LinkedIn has also been praised for its usefulness in fostering business relationships. "LinkedIn is, far and away, the most advantageous social networking tool available to job seekers and business professionals today," according to *Forbes*.

LinkedIn has inspired the creation of specialised professional networking opportunities, such as co-founder Eddie Lou's Chicago startup, Shiftgig (released in 2012 as a platform for hourly workers).

3.1.5 YouTube

YouTube is the largest video-sharing platform with over 2 billion logged-in monthly users. It serves as both a social media platform and a search engine for video content.

Key Features:

- **Channels:** Businesses and individuals can create channels to upload and organize video content.
- **Playlists:** Curate groups of videos on specific topics.
- **YouTube Ads:** Various ad formats, including skippable ads, non-skippable ads, and bumper ads.
- **Live Streaming:** Broadcast live events and interact with viewers in real time.

Best Practices:

- **Quality Production:** Invest in high-quality video production to attract and retain viewers.
- **SEO Optimization:** Use keywords in titles, descriptions, and tags to improve search visibility.
- **Consistent Posting:** Regularly upload new content to keep the audience engaged.
- **Engage with Comments:** Respond to comments to build a community and foster engagement.

3.1.6 Pinterest

Pinterest is an American image sharing and social media service designed to enable saving and discovery of information (specifically "ideas") like recipes, home, style, motivation, and inspiration on the internet using images and, on a smaller scale, animated GIFs and videos, in the form of pinboards. Created by Ben Silbermann, Paul Sciarra, and Evan Sharp, Pinterest, Inc. is headquartered in San Francisco.

History

Pinterest emerged from an earlier app created by Ben Silbermann and Paul Sciarra called *Tote* which served as a virtual replacement for paper catalogs. *Tote* struggled as a business, significantly due to difficulties with mobile payments. At the time, mobile payment technology was not sophisticated enough to enable easy on-the-go transactions, inhibiting users from making many purchases via the app. *Tote* users however were amassing large collections of favorite items and sharing them with other users. The behavior struck a chord with Silbermann, and he shifted the company to building Pinterest, which allowed users to create collections of a variety of items and share them with each other.

The development of Pinterest began in December 2009, and the site launched the prototype as a closed beta in March 2010. Nine months after the launch, the website had 10,000 users. Silbermann said he wrote to the first 5,000 users, offering his phone number and even meeting with some of them. The launch of an iPhone app in early March 2011 brought in more downloads than expected. This was followed by an iPad app and Pinterest Mobile, a version of the website for non-iPhone users. Silbermann and a few programmers operated the site out of a small apartment until the summer of 2011.

Pinterest grew rapidly during this period. On August 10, 2011, *Time* magazine listed Pinterest in its "50 Best Websites of 2011" article. In December 2011, the site became one of the top 10 largest social network services, according to Hitwise data, with 11 million total visits per week. Pinterest won the Best New Startup of 2011 at the

TechCrunch Crunchies Awards. For January 2012, comScore reported the site had 11.7 million unique U.S. visitors, making it the fastest site ever to break through the 10 million unique visitor mark. At the 2012 Webby Awards, Pinterest won Best Social Media App and People's Voice Award for best functioning visual design.

On March 23, 2012, Pinterest unveiled updated terms of service that eliminated the policy that gave it the right to sell its users' content. On August 10, 2012, Pinterest altered their policy so that a request or an invitation was no longer required to join the site. In October 2012, Pinterest launched business accounts allowing businesses to either convert their existing personal accounts into business accounts or start from scratch.

In April 2017, Pinterest removed their post "liking" feature as it seemed redundant to "boards", which are user collections of posts. Users' existing indexes of liked posts were converted into a collection ("board") named as such.

Although starting out as a "social network" with boards, in later years the company has put increasing emphasis in visual search and e-commerce, such as shopping catalogs. In February 2019, *The Wall Street Journal* stated that Pinterest secretly filed for an initial public offering (IPO) of stock. The total valuation of the company at the time reached $12 billion. They went public on April 18, 2019, at $19 per share, closing the day at $24.40 per share.

For 2020, Pinterest reported advertising revenue of $1.7 billion, an increase of 48% from 2019. On March 3, 2021, Pinterest announced "Pinterest Premiere", a video ads product "which will appear in people's feeds, targeted to their interests and other characteristics." Later in April, chief financial officer Todd Morgenfeld announced plans to spend more money on marketing in order to offset a potential slowdown in activity as the United States economy reopened with more people getting vaccinated for COVID-19.

On October 20, 2021, Bloomberg reported that PayPal is interested in acquiring Pinterest, with a potential price of around $70 a share. PayPal's board and management decided later that same week to back away from a potential deal.

In December 2021, Pinterest acquired the editing and video creation app Vochi. Following this, In May 2022, it was announced that Pinterest released a new video streaming app "Pinterest TV studio". The app is aimed at allowing users to live-stream on its platform and use different devices for different angles while live-streaming on the Pinterest platform.

On June 28, 2022, Pinterest announced that co-founder, CEO and President, Ben Silbermann would transition to the newly created role of Executive Chairman, and online commerce expert Bill Ready will become Chief Executive Officer and a member of the Board of Directors.

In January 2023 at CES, Pinterest announced its partnership with LiveRamp, a data enablement platform to create data 'clean rooms' for selected advertisers on the platform. These 'clean rooms' will allow Pinterest's ad partners to utilize first-party data for personalized ads without having to share the data with Pinterest. With data privacy a large concern for online platforms and their users, this partnership is an effort to stimulate ad business on the platform while keeping its user's data safe and in compliance with new data collection regulations. The first advertiser to pilot this feature will be grocery retailer, Albertsons with a winter healthy eating campaign.

Features and Content

The creators behind Pinterest summarized the service as a "catalogue of ideas" that inspires users to "go out and do that thing", although that it is not an image-based "social network". It also has a very large fashion profile. In later years, Pinterest has also been described as a "visual search engine".

Pinterest consists mainly of "pins" and "boards". A pin is an image that has been linked from a website or uploaded. Pins saved from one user's board can be saved to someone else's board, a process known as "repinning". Boards are collections of pins dedicated to a theme. Boards with multiple ideas can have different sections that further contain multiple pins. Users can follow and unfollow other users as well as boards, which would fill the "home feed".

Content can also be found outside Pinterest and similarly uploaded to a board via the "Save" button, which can be downloaded to the bookmark bar on a web browser, or be implemented by a webmaster directly on the website. It was originally called the "Pin it" button, but it was renamed in 2016 to "Save" to try to make the site more intuitive to new users.

In August 2016, Pinterest launched a video player that lets users and brands upload and store clips of any length straight to the site.

The home feed is a collection of Pins from the users, boards, and topics followed, as well as a few promoted pins and pins Pinterest has picked. On the main Pinterest page, a "pin feed" appears, displaying the chronological activity from the Pinterest boards that a user follows.

In October 2013, Pinterest began displaying advertisements in the form of "Promoted Pins". Promoted Pins are based on an individual user's interests, things done on Pinterest, or a result of visiting an advertiser's site or app.

In 2015, Pinterest implemented a feature that allows users to search with images instead of words.

In March 2020, Pinterest introduced the "Today" tab on the home feed which shows trending pins.

In October 2022, Pinterest announced that its video-focused "Idea Pins" feature has included the ability to add popular tracks from top artists from licensing deals with Warner Music Group, Warner Chappell Music, Merlin, and BMG.

In 2017, Pinterest introduced a "visual search" function that allows users to search for elements in images (existing pins, existing parts of a photo, or new photos) and guide users to suggested similar content within Pinterest's database. The tools powered by artificial intelligence are called Pinterest Lens, Shop the Look, and Instant Ideas.

The platform has drawn businesses, especially retailers, to create pages aimed at promoting their companies online as a "virtual storefront".

In 2013, Pinterest introduced a new tool called "Rich Pins", to enhance the customer experience when browsing through pins made by companies. Business pages can include various data, topics, and information such as prices of products, ratings of movies or ingredients for recipes.

In June 2015, Pinterest unveiled "buyable pins" that allows users to purchase things directly from Pinterest. In October 2018, the buyable pins feature was replaced by "Product Pins"

In March 2019, Pinterest added product catalogs and personalized shopping recommendations with the "more from [brand]" option, showcasing a range of product Pins from the same business.

Pinterest Analytics is a service that generates comprehensive statistics on a specific website's traffic, commonly used by marketers. *Impressions*, *Engagements*, *Pin clicks*, *Outbound clicks*, and *Saves* are some aspects of user data that Pinterest Analytics provides. It also collects data that depicts the percentage of change within a specific time to determine if a product is more popular on a specific day during the week or is slowly becoming unpopular. This data can help marketing agencies. The "Most Clicked" tab in Pinterest Analytics demonstrates products that are more likely to sell. Through the access of Pinterest Analytics, companies receive data via API.

Pinterest has the conception of creating a digital and visual bookmarking platform for displaying personal identities and tastes. The Pinterest interface emphasizes the content of pins and links while the users are the media through which the content is communicated, spreading among users through pinning and repinning. The individualized formulation of the app makes it not very social; instead, it serves its pursuit to discover, develop, and refine personal interests. Pinterest faces a decline in the period of platforms like TikTok.

In 2021, the site announced its new Creator Fund, with the stated aim of trying to support creators and their ability to monetize their efforts to preserve engagement and interactions on the platform. The program's initial launch increased creators' overall monthly views by 72%. Pinterest will invest $1.2 million in underrepresented creators via cash grants, ad credits, and equipment.

Pinterest profiles that claimed to be aged 16 and under were defaulted to private, and all of their followers were removed. Moreover, new affordances have been created surrounding group board invites and messaging within the application, restricting these functions to mutual followers. This rollout is following the review by NBC News by Stephen Sauer of the nonprofit Canadian centre for Child Protection, who found that "his homepage 'almost immediately' filled with images of children often dressed in similarly revealing attire, several of which had received sexually suggestive comments". In order to further the agenda of protecting young users, Pinterest has added more affordances for reporting 'spam', 'inappropriate cover images', and options to 'call-out when content may involve a minor'.

Usage

Pinterest is a free website that requires registration to use. The service is currently accessible through a web browser, and apps for iOS, Android, and Windows 10 PCs.

In February 2013, Reuters and ComScore stated that Pinterest had 48.7 million users globally, and a study released in July 2013 by French social media agency Semiocast revealed the website had 70 million users worldwide. In October 2016, the company had 150 million monthly active users (70 million in the U.S. and 80 million outside it), rising to 175 million monthly active users by April 2017 and 250 million in September 2018. As of July 2020, there were over 400 million monthly active users. In April 2023, Pinterest reported 463 million monthly active users, which suggests that 7.4% of the world's population over age 13 use Pinterest.

Around 2020, Pinterest was thought to flood search results in Google Images. In 2022 Google claimed to have performed changes to increase "diversity" in the search results. Pinterest claimed that, as a consequence of Google's changes of November 2021, "U.S. monthly active users coming to Pinterest from the web, desktop and mobile web declined around 30% year over year".

Pinterest has largely appealed to women, especially with its early user base. A 2020 report found that over 60% of the global users are women. Although men have not been a primary audience on Pinterest, it's been found that their usage has increased 48%. In terms of age distribution, users between the ages of 18 and 25 have grown twice as fast as those over the age of 25. However, both users between the ages of 18 and 25 and users between the ages of 25 and 40 have been driving the growth of Pinterest.

Data from Pinterest has been used for research in different areas. For example, it is possible to find patterns of activity that attract the attention of audience and content reposting, including the extent to which users specialize in particular topics, and homophily among users. Another work focused on studying the characteristics, manifestations and overall effects of user behaviors from various aspects, as well as correlations between neighboring users and the topology of the network structure. There is also a study that was based on Pinterest and proposed a novel pinboard recommendation system for Twitter users.

3.1.7 TikTok

TikTok, whose mainland Chinese counterpart is Douyin, is a short-form video hosting service owned by Chinese internet company ByteDance. It hosts user-submitted videos, which can range in duration from three seconds to 60 minutes. It can be accessed with a smart phone app.

Since its launch, TikTok has become one of the world's most popular social media platforms, using recommendation algorithms that were better than alternative apps at connecting content creators with new audiences. Many of its users are young and part of Generation Z. In April 2020, TikTok surpassed two billion mobile downloads worldwide. Cloudflare ranked TikTok the most popular website of 2021, surpassing Google. The popularity of TikTok has allowed viral trends in food and music to take off and increase the platform's cultural impact worldwide.

TikTok has come under scrutiny due to data privacy violations, mental health concerns, misinformation, offensive content, and its role during the Israel–Hamas war. Countries have fined, banned, or attempted to restrict TikTok to protect children or out of national security concerns over possible user data collection by the Chinese government through ByteDance.

Corporate Structure

TikTok Ltd was incorporated in the Cayman Islands and is based in both Singapore and Los Angeles. It owns four entities that are based respectively in the United States, Australia (which also runs the New Zealand business), United Kingdom (also owns subsidiaries in the European Union), and Singapore (owns operations in Southeast Asia and India).

Its parent company, Beijing-based ByteDance, is owned by founders and Chinese investors, other global investors, and employees. One of ByteDance's main domestic subsidiaries is owned by Chinese state funds and entities through a 1% golden share. Employees have reported that multiple overlaps exist between TikTok and ByteDance in terms of personnel management and product development. TikTok says that since 2020, its US based CEO is responsible for making important decisions and has downplayed its China connection.

History

ByteDance planned on Douyin expanding overseas. The founder of ByteDance,

Zhang Yiming, stated that "China is home to only one-fifth of Internet users globally. If we don't expand on a global scale, we are bound to lose to peers eyeing the four-fifths. So, going global is a must."

ByteDance created TikTok as a global version of Douyin. TikTok was launched in the international market in September 2017. On 9 November 2017, ByteDance spent nearly $1 billion to purchase Musical.ly, a startup headquartered in Shanghai with an overseas office in Santa Monica, California. Musical.ly was a social media video platform that allowed users to create short lip-sync and comedy videos, initially released in August 2014. TikTok merged with Musical.ly on 2 August 2018 with existing accounts and data consolidated into one app, keeping the title TikTok.

On 23 January 2018, the TikTok app ranked first among free application downloads on app stores in Thailand and other countries. TikTok has been downloaded more than 130 million times in the United States and has reached 2 billion downloads worldwide, according to data from mobile research firm Sensor Tower (those numbers exclude Android users in China).

In the United States, celebrities, including Jimmy Fallon and Tony Hawk, began using the app in 2018. Other celebrities, including Jennifer Lopez, Jessica Alba, Will Smith, and Justin Bieber joined TikTok as well as many others. In January 2019, TikTok allowed creators to embed merchandise sale links into their videos.

On 3 September 2019, TikTok and the U.S. National Football League (NFL) announced a multi-year partnership. The agreement occurred just two days before the NFL's 100th season kick-off at Soldier Field, where TikTok hosted activities for fans in honor of the deal. The partnership entails the launch of an official NFL TikTok account, which is to bring about new marketing opportunities such as sponsored videos and hashtag challenges. In July 2020, TikTok, excluding Douyin, reported close to 800 million monthly active users worldwide after less than four years of existence.

In May 2021, TikTok appointed Shou Zi Chew as their new CEO who assumed the position from interim CEO Vanessa Pappas, following the resignation of Kevin A. Mayer on 27 August 2020. In September 2021, TikTok reported that it had reached 1 billion users. In 2021, TikTok earned $4 billion in advertising revenue.

In October 2022, TikTok was reported to be planning an expansion into the e-commerce market in the US, following the launch of TikTok Shop in the United Kingdom. The company posted job listings for staff for a series of order fulfillment centers in the US and is reportedly planning to start the new live shopping business before the end of the year. The *Financial Times* reported that TikTok will launch a video gaming channel, but the report was denied in a statement to Digiday, with TikTok instead aiming to be a social hub for the gaming community.

According to data from app analytics group Sensor Tower, advertising on TikTok in the US grew by 11% in March 2023, with companies including Pepsi, DoorDash, Amazon and Apple among the top spenders. According to estimates from research group Insider Intelligence, TikTok is projected to generate $14.15 billion in revenue in 2023, up from $9.89 billion in 2022. In March 2024, *The Wall Street Journal* reported that TikTok's growth in the U.S. had stagnated.

Since at least 2020, following calls to ban TikTok in the country, the Committee on Foreign Investment in the United States (CFIUS) has been investigating the company's 2017 merger with Musical.ly but has not finalized any of its negotiations with TikTok, such as the Project Texas proposal, waiting instead for Congress to act.

TikTok was downloaded over 104 million times on Apple's App Store during the first half of 2018, according to data provided to CNBC by Sensor Tower.

After merging with musical.ly in August, downloads increased and TikTok became the most downloaded app in the U.S. in October 2018, which musical.ly had done once before. In February 2019, TikTok, together with Douyin, hit one billion downloads globally, excluding Android installs in China. In 2019, media outlets cited TikTok as the 7th-most-downloaded mobile app of the decade, from 2010 to 2019. It was also the most-downloaded app on Apple's App Store in 2018 and 2019, surpassing Facebook, YouTube and Instagram. In September 2020, a deal was confirmed between ByteDance and Oracle in which the latter will serve as a partner to provide cloud hosting. In November 2020, TikTok signed a licensing deal with Sony Music. In December 2020, Warner Music Group signed a licensing deal with TikTok.

The advertising revenue of short video clips is lower than other social media: while users spend more time, American audience is monetized at a rate of $0.31 per hour, a third the rate of Facebook and a fifth the rate of Instagram, $67 per year while Instagram will make more than $200.

In July 2023, Iranian Mehr News Agency reported "experts from Douyin" will meet Iranian business in Tehran to enable Iranian exports to China.

In 2023, several high-level executives transferred from ByteDance to TikTok to focus on moneymaking operations. Some moved from Beijing to the US. According to sources for the *Wall Street Journal*, the personnel move led to concerns from some TikTok employees and was reported to the office of US Senator Ted Cruz for further investigation. In December 2023, TikTok invested $1.5 billion in GoTo's Indonesian e-commerce business, Tokopedia. In March 2024, *The Information* reported that it is an open secret among investors that TikTok loses billions of dollar annually. Although the size of its user base falls short of that of Facebook, Instagram, or YouTube, TikTok reached 1 billion active monthly users faster than any of them.

Competition from TikTok prompted Instagram, which is owned by Facebook, to spend $120 million as of 2022 to entice more content creators to its Reels service, although engagement level remained low. Snapchat had likewise paid out $250 million in 2021 to its creators. Many platforms and services, including YouTube Shorts, began to imitate TikTok's format and recommendation page. Those changes caused a backlash from users of Instagram, Spotify, and Twitter.

In March 2022, *The Washington Post* reported that Facebook's owner Meta Platforms paid Targeted Victory—a consulting firm backed by supporters of the U.S. Republican Party—to coordinate lobbying and media campaigns against TikTok and portray it as "a danger to American children and society". Its efforts included asking local reporters to serve as "back channels" of anti-TikTok messages, writing opinion articles and letters to the editor, including one in the name of a concerned parent, amplifying stories about TikTok trends, such as "devious licks" and "Slap a Teacher", that actually originated on Facebook, and promoting Facebook's own corporate initiatives. Ties to Meta were not disclosed to the other parties involved. Targeted Victory said that it is "proud of the work". A Meta spokesperson said that all platforms, including TikTok, should face scrutiny.

The Wall Street Journal reported that Silicon Valley executives met with US lawmakers to build an "anti-China alliance" before TikTok CEO's congressional hearing in March 2023.

In April 2024, TikTok users started receiving notifications that their current and future picture posts would be shown on a new app called TikTok Notes. The app is not released yet but TikTok confirmed it is working on it. TikTok Notes will be a direct competitor to Instagram for photo sharing. Jasmine Enberg, a principal social media analyst at eMarketer, observes that launching Notes as a separate app, instead of as a new feature in TikTok, may be done in response to regulatory and consumer scrutiny. On April 18, Notes first released to users in Canada and Australia for limited testing.

Features

The mobile app allows users to create short videos, which often feature music in the background and can be sped up, slowed down, or edited with a filter. They can also add their own sound on top of the background music. To create a music video with the app, users can choose background music from a wide variety of music genres, edit with a filter and record a 15-second video with speed adjustments before uploading it to share with others on TikTok or other social platforms.

The "For You" page on TikTok is a feed of videos that are recommended to users based on their activity on the app. Content is curated by TikTok's artificial intelligence depending on the content a user liked, interacted with, or searched.

This helps users find new content and creators reach new audiences, in contrast to other social networks that base recommendations on the interactions and relationships between users.

TikTok's algorithm, recognized by *The New York Times* in 2020 as one of the most advanced for shaping user experiences and social interactions, stands out from traditional social media. While typical platforms focus on active user actions like likes, clicks, or follows, TikTok monitors a wider array of behaviors during video viewing. This comprehensive observation is then used to refine its algorithms, as noted by *Wired* in 2020. Furthermore, *The Wall Street Journal* in 2021 highlighted its superiority over other social media platforms in understanding users' preferences and emotions. TikTok's algorithm leverages this insight to present similar content, creating an environment that users often find hard to disengage from.

The app's "react" feature allows users to film their reaction to a specific video, over which it is placed in a small window that is movable around the screen. Its "duet" feature allows users to film a video aside from another video. The "duet" feature was another trademark of musical.ly. The duet feature is also only able to be used if both parties adjust the privacy settings.

Videos that users do not want to post yet can be stored in their "drafts". The user is allowed to see their "drafts" and post when they find it fitting. The app allows users to set their accounts as "private". When first downloading the app, the user's account is public by default. The user can change to private in their settings. Private content remains visible to TikTok but is blocked from TikTok users who the account holder has not authorized to view their content. Users can choose whether any other user, or only their "friends", may interact with them through the app via comments, messages, or "react" or "duet" videos. Users also can set specific videos to either "public", "friends only", or "private" regardless if the account is private or not.

Users can also send their friends videos, emojis, and messages with direct messaging. TikTok has also included a feature to create a video based on the user's comments. Influencers often use the "live" feature. This feature is only available for those who have at least 1,000 followers and are over 16 years old. If over 18, the user's followers can send virtual "gifts" that can be later exchanged for money.

TikTok announced a "family safety mode" in February 2020 for parents to be able to control their children's presence on the app. There is a screen time management option, restricted mode, and the option to put a limit on direct messages. The app expanded its parental controls feature called "Family Pairing" in September 2020 to provide parents and guardians with educational resources to understand what children on TikTok are exposed to. Content for the feature was created in partnership with online safety nonprofit, Internet Matters. In October 2021, TikTok launched a test feature that allows users to directly tip certain creators. Accounts of users that are of age, have at least 100,000 followers and agree to the terms can activate a "Tip" button on their profile, which allows followers to tip any amount, starting from $1.

In December 2021, TikTok started beta-testing Live Studio, a streaming software that would let users broadcast applications open on their computers, including games. The software also launched with support for mobile and PC streaming. However, a few days later, users on Twitter discovered that the software uses code from the open-source OBS Studio. OBS made a statement saying that, under the GNU GPL version 2, TikTok has to make the code of Live Studio publicly available if it wants to use any code from OBS.

In May 2022, TikTok announced TikTok Pulse, an ad revenue-sharing program. It covers the "top 4% of all videos on TikTok" and is only available to creators with more than 100,000 followers. If an eligible creator's video reaches the top 4%, they will receive a 50% share of the revenue from ads displayed with the video.

In July 2023, TikTok launched a new streaming service called TikTok Music, currently available only in Brazil and Indonesia. This service allows users to listen to, download and share songs. It is reported that TikTok Music features songs from major record companies like Universal Music Group, Sony Music and Warner Music Group. On 19 July 2023, TikTok Music was expanded for select users in Australia, Mexico and Singapore.

Following a dispute with TikTok regarding payouts for artists and regulation of AI-generated music content on the platform, Universal Music Group decided not to renew its licensing agreement with TikTok, causing its catalogue of 3 million recordings to become unavailable for usage after 31 January 2024. This marked the company's first instance of withdrawing its music from a major platform, in contrast to Warner Music, which had recently renewed its own licensing deal with TikTok. In March 2024, Universal Music Publishing Group removed its catalogue of 4 million compositions from TikTok. In April 2024, Taylor Swift's music returned to the platform.

3.1.8 Choosing the Right Platform

Selecting the right social media platforms for your marketing strategy depends on several factors:

- **Target Audience:** Understand where your audience spends their time. Different platforms attract different demographics and interests.
- **Content Type:** Consider the type of content you create and which platforms are best suited for it. For example, Instagram and Pinterest are ideal for visual content, while LinkedIn is better for professional articles and insights.

- **Business Goals:** Align your platform choice with your business objectives. If you aim to build brand awareness, platforms with large user bases like Facebook and Instagram may be beneficial. For B2B marketing, LinkedIn could be more effective.
- **Resources:** Evaluate your resources and capacity to manage multiple platforms. It's better to have a strong presence on a few platforms than a weak presence on many.

3.1.9 Measuring Success

To gauge the effectiveness of your social media strategy, track key performance indicators (KPIs) such as:

- **Engagement:** Likes, comments, shares, and interaction rates.
- **Reach:** Number of unique users who see your content.
- **Traffic:** Visits to your website generated from social media.
- **Follower Growth:** Increase in the number of followers or subscribers.

Tools like Google Analytics, social media analytics, and third-party tools like Hootsuite and Sprout Social can help track and analyze these metrics.

3.2 BUILDING A SOCIAL MEDIA STRATEGY

A well-crafted social media strategy is crucial for any business looking to leverage the power of social media to achieve its marketing objectives. With billions of active users across various platforms, social media offers a unique opportunity to connect with audiences, build brand awareness, and drive business growth.

Building a successful social media strategy requires a comprehensive approach that includes setting clear goals, conducting thorough audience research, creating engaging content, selecting the right platforms, maintaining a content calendar, engaging with your audience, and regularly measuring and optimizing performance.

By following these steps, businesses can effectively leverage social media to connect with their audience, build brand awareness, and drive business growth. As the social media landscape continues to evolve, staying adaptable and continuously refining your strategy will be key to sustained success.

3.2.1 Setting Clear Goals

The foundation of any effective social media strategy is clear, measurable goals. These goals should align with your overall business objectives and provide a roadmap for your social media efforts. Common goals for social media marketing include:

- **Increasing Brand Awareness:** Expanding your reach and making more people aware of your brand.
- **Driving Website Traffic:** Attracting visitors to your website through social media content and links.
- **Boosting Sales:** Encouraging conversions and purchases through social media promotions and advertisements.
- **Enhancing Customer Engagement:** Building a community of followers who interact with your content.
- **Improving Customer Service:** Using social media as a platform to respond to customer inquiries and resolve issues.

Setting SMART goals (Specific, Measurable, Achievable, Relevant, Time-bound) ensures clarity and focus, enabling you to track progress and measure success effectively.

3.2.2 Conducting Audience Research

Understanding your target audience is crucial for crafting a social media strategy that resonates with them. Audience research involves identifying who your customers are, what they care about, and where they spend their time online. Key steps in audience research include:

- **Demographic Analysis:** Identify the age, gender, location, income level, and other demographic characteristics of your audience.
- **Psychographic Analysis:** Understand your audience's interests, values, lifestyles, and behaviors.
- **Platform Preferences:** Determine which social media platforms your audience prefers and how they use them.
- **Pain Points and Needs:** Identify the challenges and needs of your audience that your products or services can address.

Tools like social media analytics, surveys, and customer feedback can provide valuable insights into your audience. Creating detailed buyer personas based on this research helps tailor your content and messaging to meet their preferences and needs.

3.2.3 Creating Engaging Content

Content is the heart of your social media strategy. Engaging, high-quality content attracts and retains followers, encourages interaction, and drives conversions. Key aspects of content creation include:

Content Types

Different types of content serve various purposes and appeal to different audience segments. Common content types include:

- **Posts and Updates:** Regular updates on products, services, company news, and industry trends.
- **Images and Infographics:** Visually appealing content that conveys information quickly and effectively.
- **Videos:** Engaging video content, including tutorials, behind-the-scenes looks, interviews, and product demonstrations.
- **Blog Articles:** In-depth articles on topics relevant to your audience, providing valuable information and insights.
- **User-Generated Content:** Content created by your customers, such as reviews, testimonials, and social media posts.
- **Interactive Content:** Quizzes, polls, and surveys that encourage audience participation.

Content Themes

Developing content themes helps maintain consistency and align your content with your brand message. Themes can be based on your business objectives, audience interests, or seasonal events. Examples include:

- **Educational Content:** Providing tips, tutorials, and how-to guides that offer value to your audience.
- **Inspirational Content:** Sharing stories, quotes, and achievements that inspire and motivate your audience.
- **Promotional Content:** Highlighting special offers, discounts, and product launches to drive sales.
- **Entertaining Content:** Posting humorous, light-hearted content that entertains and engages your audience.

3.2.4 Selecting the Right Platforms

Not all social media platforms are suitable for every business. Selecting the right platforms involves considering where your audience is most active and which platforms best support your content types. Major platforms include:

- **Facebook:** Versatile for various content types and demographics, ideal for building a community and running targeted ads.
- **Instagram:** Focuses on visual content and is popular among younger audiences. Great for brands with strong visual elements.

- **Twitter:** Best for real-time updates, news, and engaging in public conversations.
- **LinkedIn:** Ideal for B2B marketing, professional networking, and sharing industry insights.
- **YouTube:** Perfect for video content, tutorials, and vlogs.
- **Pinterest:** Effective for visual discovery and ideas, particularly in fashion, home decor, and food.
- **TikTok:** Popular for short-form videos and trends, especially among younger audiences.

3.2.5 Creating a Content Calendar

A content calendar helps organize and schedule your social media posts, ensuring consistency and strategic planning.

- **Planning Ahead:** Outline your content themes and types for each month, aligning them with your marketing goals and seasonal events.
- **Scheduling:** Determine the best times to post on each platform based on audience activity and engagement patterns.
- **Consistency:** Maintain a consistent posting frequency to keep your audience engaged and build a reliable presence.
- **Flexibility:** Allow room for spontaneous posts and real-time engagement, adapting to trending topics and audience feedback.

3.2.6 Engaging with Your Audience

Engagement is a crucial component of a successful social media strategy. Building relationships with your audience fosters loyalty and trust.

- **Responding to Comments:** Acknowledge and respond to comments on your posts to show appreciation and foster dialogue.
- **Encouraging Interaction:** Ask questions, run polls, and encourage user-generated content to promote active participation.
- **Monitoring Mentions:** Keep track of brand mentions and respond to user-generated content that features your products or services.
- **Customer Support:** Use social media as a platform for addressing customer inquiries and resolving issues promptly.

3.2.7 Measuring and Analyzing Performance

Regularly measuring and analyzing your social media performance helps optimize your strategy and achieve better results. Key metrics to track include:

- **Reach:** The number of unique users who see your content.
- **Engagement:** Likes, comments, shares, and other interactions with your content.
- **Traffic:** The number of visitors driven to your website from social media.
- **Conversions:** Actions taken by users, such as sign-ups, downloads, or purchases.
- **Follower Growth:** The increase in the number of followers or subscribers.

Tools like Google Analytics, social media analytics platforms, and third-party tools like Hootsuite and Sprout Social can provide valuable data on these metrics. Regularly reviewing this data helps identify trends, strengths, and areas for improvement.

3.2.8 Optimizing Your Strategy

Based on your performance analysis, continuously optimize your social media strategy to achieve better results. Key optimization tactics include:

- **A/B Testing:** Experiment with different types of content, headlines, and posting times to see what resonates best with your audience.
- **Content Refresh:** Update and repurpose high-performing content to maintain its relevance and reach new audiences.
- **Trend Adaptation:** Stay current with social media trends and incorporate them into your strategy to keep your content fresh and engaging.
- **Feedback Integration:** Use audience feedback to refine your content and engagement tactics.

3.3 CONTENT CREATION FOR SOCIAL MEDIA

Content creation for social media is an essential component of any successful digital marketing strategy. It involves crafting engaging, relevant, and valuable content tailored to specific social media platforms to connect with your audience, drive engagement, and achieve marketing objectives.

Content creation for social media is a dynamic and essential part of any digital marketing strategy. By understanding the importance of engaging content, leveraging various content types, and following best practices, businesses can effectively connect with their audience, build brand awareness, and drive growth. Utilizing tools and developing a strategic approach to content creation ensures consistency, quality, and optimization. As the social media landscape continues to evolve, staying adaptable and innovative in your content creation efforts will be key to achieving sustained success.

3.3.1 Importance of Content Creation for Social Media

Content creation is vital for several reasons:

- **Engagement:** High-quality content captures attention and encourages interactions, such as likes, comments, and shares, which help build a community around your brand.
- **Brand Awareness:** Regularly posting relevant content increases visibility and helps more people become aware of your brand.
- **Customer Trust:** Providing valuable content establishes your brand as a trusted source of information, which can build credibility and trust with your audience.
- **Conversions:** Engaging content can drive traffic to your website, generate leads, and convert followers into customers.
- **SEO Benefits:** Consistently producing and sharing quality content can improve your search engine rankings, making it easier for potential customers to find you online.

3.3.2 Types of Content for Social Media

Different types of content serve various purposes and can be more effective on specific platforms.

Text-Based Posts

Text-based posts are straightforward and easy to create. They are effective for sharing updates, asking questions, or making announcements.

Best Practices:

- Keep the message clear and concise.
- Use a conversational tone.
- Include a call-to-action (CTA) to encourage engagement.
- Use emojis to add personality and convey emotions.

Platform Examples:

- **Twitter:** Ideal for short, timely updates and interactions.
- **Facebook:** Effective for sharing longer posts, updates, and discussions.

Images

Visual content is highly engaging and can convey messages quickly. High-quality images can capture attention and drive higher engagement rates.

Best Practices:

- Use high-resolution, eye-catching images.
- Ensure the images are relevant to your brand and message.
- Add text overlays or captions to provide context.
- Maintain a consistent visual style to reinforce brand identity.

Platform Examples:

- **Instagram**: Primarily image-focused, perfect for sharing visually appealing content.
- **Pinterest**: Great for sharing inspirational and aspirational images.

Videos

Videos are one of the most engaging content types and can effectively convey complex messages. They are ideal for tutorials, product demos, behind-the-scenes looks, and storytelling.

Best Practices:

- Keep videos short and to the point.
- Focus on storytelling to make the content more relatable.
- Include subtitles for accessibility and to cater to viewers who watch without sound.
- Use a strong opening to capture attention within the first few seconds.

Platform Examples:

- **YouTube:** The go-to platform for longer video content, such as tutorials and vlogs.
- **Instagram and Facebook:** Effective for shorter videos, stories, and live streams.

Stories

Stories are short, ephemeral content that disappears after 24 hours. They are ideal for sharing real-time updates, behind-the-scenes looks, and engaging directly with followers.

Best Practices:

- Use interactive features like polls, questions, and quizzes to engage viewers.
- Post regularly to keep your audience coming back.
- Highlight important stories to keep them accessible beyond 24 hours.

- Use storytelling techniques to make the content more compelling.

Platform Examples:

- **Instagram Stories:** Popular for real-time updates and interactive content.
- **Facebook Stories:** Effective for reaching a broader audience with similar features to Instagram Stories.

Infographics

Infographics are visually appealing representations of data, statistics, or information. They are highly shareable and can simplify complex information.

Best Practices:

- Focus on clear and concise information.
- Use engaging visuals and color schemes to make the infographic attractive.
- Ensure the information is accurate and well-researched.
- Include your brand logo and website for attribution.

Platform Examples:

- **Pinterest:** Ideal for sharing infographics due to its visual nature.
- **LinkedIn:** Effective for sharing professional and informative infographics.

User-Generated Content (UGC)

UGC is content created by your followers or customers. It includes reviews, testimonials, photos, and videos featuring your products or services.

Best Practices:

- Encourage customers to share their experiences with your brand.
- Run contests or campaigns to incentivize UGC creation.
- Always credit the original creator when sharing UGC.

Platform Examples:

- **Instagram:** Great for sharing customer photos and testimonials.
- **Twitter:** Effective for retweeting customer feedback and reviews.

3.3.3 Best Practices for Social Media Content Creation

Creating successful social media content involves more than just posting regularly. Here are some best practices to consider:

Understand Your Audience

- Conduct audience research to identify their preferences, interests, and behaviors.
- Create content that resonates with your audience and addresses their needs and pain points.
- Use social media analytics to gain insights into what content performs best.

Maintain Consistency

- Establish a consistent posting schedule to keep your audience engaged.
- Maintain a consistent brand voice and visual style across all content.
- Use a content calendar to plan and organize your posts.

Focus on Quality Over Quantity

- Prioritize creating high-quality, valuable content rather than posting frequently.
- Ensure all content is well-crafted, error-free, and professionally designed.
- Use high-quality visuals and engaging copy to capture attention.

Leverage Trends and Hashtags

- Stay up-to-date with current trends and incorporate them into your content when relevant.
- Use trending hashtags to increase the discoverability of your posts.
- Participate in social media challenges and events to engage with a broader audience.

Encourage Engagement

- Include CTAs in your posts to encourage likes, comments, and shares.
- Respond to comments and messages to build relationships with your followers.
- Run contests, polls, and quizzes to foster interaction.

Analyze and Optimize

- Regularly review social media analytics to measure the performance of your content.
- Identify which types of content perform best and replicate their success.
- Use insights to refine your content strategy and optimize future posts.

3.3.4 Tools for Content Creation

Several tools can streamline the content creation process and enhance the quality of your social media posts:

- **Canva:** A graphic design tool that allows you to create stunning visuals, including images, infographics, and social media graphics.
- **Adobe Spark:** A content creation tool for designing graphics, videos, and web pages.
- **Hootsuite:** A social media management platform that includes scheduling, analytics, and content creation features.
- **Lumen5:** A video creation tool that converts blog posts and articles into engaging videos.
- **Buffer:** A social media management tool that helps schedule posts, analyze performance, and create content.

3.3.5 Strategies for Effective Content Creation

Developing a robust content creation strategy involves several key steps:

Set Clear Objectives

- Define what you want to achieve with your social media content, such as increasing brand awareness, driving traffic, or generating leads.
- Set specific, measurable goals to track progress and measure success.

Create a Content Calendar

- Plan your content in advance to ensure consistency and organization.
- Schedule posts to maintain a regular posting frequency and avoid last-minute content creation.

Incorporate a Variety of Content Types

- Use a mix of content types, such as text posts, images, videos, and infographics, to keep your audience engaged.
- Experiment with different formats to see what resonates best with your followers.

Collaborate with Influencers and Partners

- Partner with influencers and other brands to expand your reach and credibility.
- Collaborate on content creation, such as co-hosted events, joint videos, and guest blog posts.

Encourage User-Generated Content

- Run campaigns and contests that encourage your followers to create and share content related to your brand.
- Feature UGC on your social media profiles to build trust and authenticity.

3.4 COMMUNITY MANAGEMENT AND ENGAGEMENT

Community management and engagement are critical components of a successful digital marketing strategy. They involve building, nurturing, and maintaining relationships with a brand's audience to create a loyal, active community. Effective community management and engagement can lead to increased brand loyalty, customer satisfaction, and positive word-of-mouth marketing.

Community management and engagement are integral to building a loyal, active audience that supports and advocates for your brand. By understanding the importance of community management, employing effective strategies, and following best practices, businesses can create strong, engaged communities that drive long-term success.

Utilizing the right tools and measuring key metrics ensures continuous improvement and optimization of community management efforts. As the digital landscape evolves, staying authentic, responsive, and value-driven in your community management approach will be essential for maintaining a thriving, engaged community.

3.4.1 Importance of Community Management and Engagement

Community management and engagement offer several key benefits to businesses:

- **Customer Loyalty**: Engaging with your audience fosters a sense of belonging and loyalty. When customers feel valued and heard, they are more likely to stay loyal to your brand.
- **Brand Advocacy**: A strong, engaged community can become brand advocates, spreading positive word-of-mouth and attracting new customers.
- **Customer Feedback**: Communities provide valuable insights into customer preferences, needs, and pain points, allowing businesses to improve products and services.
- **Crisis Management**: An engaged community can help mitigate the impact of negative feedback or crises by providing a platform for transparent communication and quick resolution.
- **Increased Engagement**: Active community management encourages more interactions, leading to higher engagement rates and a stronger online presence.

3.4.2 Strategies for Building and Maintaining a Community

Building and maintaining a community requires a strategic approach that focuses on genuine engagement and value creation. Here are some key strategies:

Identify Your Audience

Understanding your target audience is the first step in building a community. Conduct thorough research to identify their demographics, interests, behaviors, and preferences.

This knowledge will help you create content and interactions that resonate with your audience.

Create Valuable Content

Content is the foundation of community engagement. Provide valuable, relevant, and engaging content that addresses your audience's needs and interests. This could include blog posts, videos, infographics, tutorials, and more. Consistently delivering high-quality content keeps your community engaged and coming back for more.

Leverage Social Media

Social media platforms are ideal for community building and engagement. Each platform has unique features and user demographics, so choose the ones that align with your audience. Regularly post content, respond to comments, and participate in conversations to foster a sense of community.

Foster Two-Way Communication

Encourage open, two-way communication between your brand and your audience. Respond to comments, messages, and feedback promptly and genuinely. Show appreciation for positive feedback and address concerns or complaints professionally.

Host Events and Activities

Organize online events, webinars, live streams, and Q&A sessions to engage with your community in real-time. These events provide opportunities for direct interaction and build stronger relationships with your audience.

Encourage User-Generated Content

User-generated content (UGC) is a powerful tool for community engagement. Encourage your audience to create and share content related to your brand, such as reviews, testimonials, photos, and videos. Feature UGC on your social media profiles and website to show appreciation and build trust.

Create Exclusive Groups

Exclusive groups, such as Facebook Groups or LinkedIn Groups, provide a more intimate space for community members to connect and engage. These groups can be used to share exclusive content, host discussions, and provide special offers.

3.4.3 Best Practices for Community Management

Effective community management requires consistency, authenticity, and strategic planning. Here are some best practices:

Set Clear Objectives

Define clear objectives for your community management efforts. These could include increasing engagement, gathering feedback, or building brand loyalty. Having specific goals helps you measure success and adjust your strategies accordingly.

Be Authentic

Authenticity is key to building trust and credibility with your community. Be genuine in your interactions, show empathy, and stay true to your brand values. Avoid overly promotional content and focus on providing value to your audience.

Monitor and Moderate

Regularly monitor your community for discussions, comments, and feedback. Moderate discussions to ensure a positive and respectful environment. Address any inappropriate behavior or content promptly to maintain a safe and welcoming community.

Provide Consistent Value

Consistently provide value to your community through informative, entertaining, or inspiring content. Stay up-to-date with industry trends and audience preferences to ensure your content remains relevant and engaging.

Empower Your Community

Empower your community members by giving them a voice and involving them in decision-making processes. Ask for their opinions, conduct polls, and feature their content. This sense of involvement and ownership strengthens their connection to your brand.

Measure and Analyze

Regularly measure and analyze your community management efforts to understand what's working and what's not. Use analytics tools to track engagement metrics, such as likes, comments, shares, and sentiment. Use these insights to refine your strategies and improve your community management efforts.

3.4.4 Tools for Community Management

Several tools can help streamline community management and engagement efforts:

- **Hootsuite:** A social media management platform that allows you to schedule posts, monitor conversations, and analyze engagement metrics.
- **Sprout Social:** A comprehensive tool for social media management, including engagement, publishing, analytics, and listening features.
- **Buffer:** A social media scheduling and analytics tool that helps manage multiple accounts and track performance.
- **Facebook Groups:** A platform for creating and managing exclusive communities where members can interact and engage.
- **Discord:** A communication platform ideal for creating communities with features like voice, video, and text channels.
- **Slack:** A collaboration tool that can be used to create and manage community channels for discussions and interactions.

3.4.5 Metrics for Measuring Community Management Success

Measuring the success of your community management efforts involves tracking various metrics to understand engagement levels and community growth. Key metrics include:

- **Engagement Rate:** The number of interactions (likes, comments, shares) divided by the total number of followers. A higher engagement rate indicates a more active and involved community.
- **Sentiment Analysis:** Analyzing the tone and sentiment of comments, mentions, and discussions to gauge overall community sentiment towards your brand.
- **Response Time:** The average time it takes for you to respond to comments and messages. Faster response times indicate better community management and customer service.
- **User-Generated Content:** The volume and quality of content created by your community members. High levels of UGC indicate strong engagement and loyalty.
- **Community Growth:** The increase in the number of community members or followers over time. Steady growth suggests effective community management and engagement strategies.
- **Event Participation:** The number of attendees and the level of engagement in your online events, webinars, or live streams.

- **Feedback and Reviews:** The quantity and quality of feedback, reviews, and testimonials provided by your community members.

3.5 SOCIAL MEDIA ANALYTICS AND REPORTING

Social media analytics and reporting are essential components of any effective social media strategy. They provide insights into how well your social media efforts are performing, help identify areas for improvement, and guide future strategies. By leveraging analytics, businesses can understand their audience better, measure the impact of their campaigns, and make data-driven decisions.

Social media analytics and reporting are crucial for understanding the effectiveness of your social media efforts, optimizing your strategy, and achieving your business goals. By focusing on key metrics, utilizing the right tools, and following best practices for reporting, businesses can gain valuable insights into their audience, content performance, and overall social media impact. Regular analysis and data-driven decision-making ensure that social media strategies remain effective, relevant, and aligned with the evolving digital landscape. As social media continues to grow in importance, mastering analytics and reporting will be essential for sustained success and competitive advantage.

3.5.1 Importance of Social Media Analytics and Reporting

Measuring Success

Social media analytics enable businesses to measure the success of their campaigns and strategies. By tracking key performance indicators (KPIs), marketers can determine what's working and what isn't, allowing for adjustments to improve outcomes.

Understanding Audience Behavior

Analytics provide insights into audience demographics, preferences, and behaviors. This information helps businesses tailor their content and engagement strategies to better meet the needs and interests of their audience.

Optimizing Content

Analyzing performance data helps identify which types of content resonate most with your audience. This allows you to focus on creating more of what works and less of what doesn't, optimizing your content strategy for better engagement.

Improving ROI

By understanding which campaigns and strategies deliver the best results, businesses can allocate resources more effectively, ensuring a higher return on investment (ROI) for their social media efforts.

Competitive Analysis

Social media analytics can also be used to monitor competitors. By analyzing their performance, businesses can identify trends, benchmark their efforts, and find opportunities to differentiate themselves.

3.5.2 Key Metrics to Track

When it comes to social media analytics, there are numerous metrics available. The key is to focus on the ones that align with your business goals. Here are some of the most important metrics to track:

Engagement Metrics

- **Likes/Reactions:** Indicates how many people appreciate your content.
- **Comments:** Shows how many people are engaging in conversations around your posts.
- **Shares/Retweets:** Measures how often your content is shared, extending its reach.
- **Engagement Rate:** The total number of engagements (likes, comments, shares) divided by the number of impressions or followers. This metric indicates how engaging your content is.

Reach and Impressions

- **Reach:** The total number of unique users who have seen your content. Reach helps gauge the size of your audience.
- **Impressions:** The total number of times your content is displayed, regardless of whether it was clicked. Impressions indicate how often your content is being viewed.

Follower Metrics

- **Follower Growth:** The increase or decrease in the number of followers over a specific period. This metric shows how well you are attracting and retaining followers.
- **Audience Demographics:** Information about your followers' age, gender, location, and interests. Understanding your audience demographics helps tailor your content to their preferences.

Website Traffic

- **Referral Traffic:** The number of visitors to your website that came from your social media channels. This metric shows how effective your social media efforts are at driving traffic to your site.

- **Click-Through Rate (CTR):** The number of clicks on your social media posts divided by the number of impressions. A higher CTR indicates that your content is compelling enough to drive action.

Conversion Metrics

- **Conversion Rate:** The percentage of users who take a desired action (such as making a purchase or signing up for a newsletter) after clicking through from a social media post. This metric measures the effectiveness of your social media efforts in driving conversions.
- **Cost Per Conversion:** The total cost of your social media efforts divided by the number of conversions. This metric helps evaluate the efficiency of your campaigns.

Customer Service Metrics

- **Response Time:** The average time it takes to respond to comments or messages. Faster response times indicate better customer service.
- **Resolution Rate:** The percentage of customer service issues resolved through social media. A higher resolution rate indicates effective social media support.

3.5.3 Tools for Social Media Analytics

There are various tools available to help businesses track and analyze their social media performance.

Native Analytics Tools

- **Facebook Insights:** Provides detailed analytics on page performance, including reach, engagement, and audience demographics.
- **Twitter Analytics:** Offers insights into tweet performance, including impressions, engagements, and follower growth.
- **Instagram Insights:** Tracks metrics such as reach, impressions, engagement, and follower demographics.
- **LinkedIn Analytics:** Provides data on post performance, follower growth, and audience demographics.

Third-Party Tools

- **Google Analytics:** Tracks website traffic from social media channels, providing insights into referral traffic, conversions, and user behavior.
- **Hootsuite:** A social media management platform that includes analytics and reporting features for multiple social media accounts.
- **Sprout Social:** Offers comprehensive analytics and reporting tools,

including engagement metrics, audience demographics, and content performance.

- **Buffer**: Provides analytics on post performance, engagement, and follower growth across various social media platforms.

Advanced Analytics Tools

- **Socialbakers:** An AI-powered platform that offers advanced analytics, competitive benchmarking, and content optimization insights.
- **Brandwatch:** Provides in-depth social media listening and analytics, helping businesses track brand sentiment, monitor competitors, and identify trends.

3.5.4 Best Practices for Effective Reporting

Effective reporting involves more than just tracking metrics; it requires analyzing the data to gain actionable insights. Here are some best practices for social media reporting:

- **Align Metrics with Goals:** Ensure that the metrics you track and report on align with your overall business and marketing goals. This alignment helps demonstrate the impact of your social media efforts on achieving these objectives.
- **Regular Reporting:** Set a regular reporting schedule, such as weekly, monthly, or quarterly. Consistent reporting allows you to track progress over time and make timely adjustments to your strategy.
- **Visualize Data:** Use visual aids like charts, graphs, and infographics to present data in a clear and engaging manner. Visualizations make it easier to identify trends, patterns, and outliers.
- **Focus on Insights:** Rather than just presenting raw data, focus on providing insights and actionable recommendations. Explain what the data means, why it matters, and how it can inform future strategies.
- **Benchmarking:** Compare your performance against industry benchmarks and competitors. Benchmarking helps identify areas where you are excelling and areas that need improvement.
- **Segment Reporting:** Segment your reports by different aspects such as platform, campaign, or content type.
- **Track Trends Over Time:** Monitor long-term trends to understand how your social media performance evolves. This analysis helps identify consistent growth patterns and areas that may need long-term strategy adjustments.

CHAPTER 4
SEARCH ENGINE OPTIMIZATION (SEO)

4.1 FUNDAMENTALS OF SEO

Search engine optimization (SEO) is the process of improving the quality and quantity of website traffic to a website or a web page from search engines. SEO targets unpaid traffic (known as "natural" or "organic" results) rather than direct traffic or paid traffic. Unpaid traffic may originate from different kinds of searches, including image search, video search, academic search, news search, and industry-specific vertical search engines.

As an Internet marketing strategy, SEO considers how search engines work, the computer-programmed algorithms that dictate search engine behavior, what people search for, the actual search terms or keywords typed into search engines, and which search engines are preferred by their targeted audience. SEO is performed because a website will receive more visitors from a search engine when websites rank higher on the search engine results page (SERP). These visitors can then potentially be converted into customers.

4.1.1 History

Webmasters and content providers began optimizing websites for search engines in the mid-1990s, as the first search engines were cataloging the early Web. Initially, all webmasters only needed to submit the address of a page, or URL, to the various engines, which would send a web crawler to *crawl* that page, extract links to other pages from it, and return information found on the page to be indexed. The process involves a search engine spider downloading a page and storing it on the search engine's own server.

A second program, known as an indexer, extracts information about the page, such as the words it contains, where they are located, and any weight for specific words, as well as all links the page contains. All of this information is then placed into a scheduler for crawling at a later date.

Website owners recognized the value of a high ranking and visibility in search engine results, creating an opportunity for both white hat and black hat SEO practitioners. According to industry analyst Danny Sullivan, the phrase "search engine optimization" probably came into use in 1997. Sullivan credits Bruce Clay as one of the first people to popularize the term.

Early versions of search algorithms relied on webmaster-provided information such as the keyword meta tag or index files in engines like ALIWEB. Meta tags provide a guide to each page's content. Using metadata to index pages was found to be less than reliable, however, because the webmaster's choice of keywords in the meta tag could potentially be an inaccurate representation of the site's actual content. Flawed data in meta tags, such as those that were inaccurate or incomplete, created the potential for pages to be mischaracterized in irrelevant searches. Web content providers also manipulated some attributes within the HTML source of a page in an attempt to rank well in search engines. By 1997, search engine designers recognized that webmasters were making efforts to rank well in their search engine and that some webmasters were even manipulating their rankings in search results by stuffing pages with excessive or irrelevant keywords. Early search engines, such as Altavista and Infoseek, adjusted their algorithms to prevent webmasters from manipulating rankings.

By heavily relying on factors such as keyword density, which were exclusively within a webmaster's control, early search engines suffered from abuse and ranking manipulation. To provide better results to their users, search engines had to adapt to ensure their results pages showed the most relevant search results, rather than unrelated pages stuffed with numerous keywords by unscrupulous webmasters. This meant moving away from heavy reliance on term density to a more holistic process for scoring semantic signals. Since the success and popularity of a search engine are determined by its ability to produce the most relevant results to any given search, poor quality or irrelevant search results could lead users to find other search sources. Search engines responded by developing more complex ranking algorithms, taking into account additional factors that were more difficult for webmasters to manipulate.

Companies that employ overly aggressive techniques can get their client websites banned from the search results. In 2005, the *Wall Street Journal* reported on a company, Traffic Power, which allegedly used high-risk techniques and failed to disclose those risks to its clients. *Wired* magazine reported that the same company sued blogger and SEO Aaron Wall for writing about the ban. Google's Matt Cutts later confirmed that Google did in fact ban Traffic Power and some of its clients.

Some search engines have also reached out to the SEO industry and are frequent sponsors and guests at SEO conferences, webchats, and seminars. Major search engines provide information and guidelines to help with website optimization. Google has a Sitemaps program to help webmasters learn if Google is having any problems indexing their website and also provides data on Google traffic to the website. Bing Webmaster Tools provides a way for webmasters to submit a sitemap and web feeds, allows users to determine the "crawl rate", and track the web pages index status.

In 2015, it was reported that Google was developing and promoting mobile search as a key feature within future products. In response, many brands began to take a different approach to their Internet marketing strategies.

Relationship with Google

In 1998, two graduate students at Stanford University, Larry Page and Sergey Brin, developed "Backrub", a search engine that relied on a mathematical algorithm to rate the prominence of web pages. The number calculated by the algorithm, PageRank, is a function of the quantity and strength of inbound links. PageRank estimates the likelihood that a given page will be reached by a web user who randomly surfs the web and follows links from one page to another. In effect, this means that some links are stronger than others, as a higher PageRank page is more likely to be reached by the random web surfer.

Page and Brin founded Google in 1998. Google attracted a loyal following among the growing number of Internet users, who liked its simple design. Off-page factors (such as PageRank and hyperlink analysis) were considered as well as on-page factors (such as keyword frequency, meta tags, headings, links and site structure) to enable Google to avoid the kind of manipulation seen in search engines that only considered on-page factors for their rankings. Although PageRank was more difficult to game, webmasters had already developed link-building tools and schemes to influence the Inktomi search engine, and these methods proved similarly applicable to gaming PageRank. Many sites focus on exchanging, buying, and selling links, often on a massive scale. Some of these schemes, or link farms, involved the creation of thousands of sites for the sole purpose of link spamming.

By 2004, search engines had incorporated a wide range of undisclosed factors in their ranking algorithms to reduce the impact of link manipulation. The leading search engines, Google, Bing, and Yahoo, do not disclose the algorithms they use to rank pages. Some SEO practitioners have studied different approaches to search engine optimization and have shared their personal opinions. Patents related to search engines can provide information to better understand search engines. In 2005, Google began personalizing search results for each user. Depending on their history of previous searches, Google crafted results for logged in users.

In 2007, Google announced a campaign against paid links that transfer PageRank. On June 15, 2009, Google disclosed that they had taken measures to mitigate the effects of PageRank sculpting by use of the nofollow attribute on links. Matt Cutts, a well-known software engineer at Google, announced that Google Bot would no longer treat any no follow links, in the same way, to prevent SEO service providers from using nofollow for PageRank sculpting. As a result of this change, the usage of nofollow led to evaporation of PageRank. In order to avoid the above, SEO engineers developed alternative techniques that replace nofollowed tags with obfuscated JavaScript and thus permit PageRank sculpting. Additionally, several solutions have been suggested that include the usage of iframes, Flash, and JavaScript.

In December 2009, Google announced it would be using the web search history of all its users in order to populate search results. On June 8, 2010 a new web indexing system called Google Caffeine was announced. Designed to allow users to find news results, forum posts, and other content much sooner after publishing than before, Google Caffeine was a change to the way Google updated its index in order to make things show up quicker on Google than before. According to Carrie Grimes, the software engineer who announced Caffeine for Google, "Caffeine provides 50 percent fresher results for web searches than our last index..." Google Instant, real-time-search, was introduced in late 2010 in an attempt to make search results more timely and relevant. Historically site administrators have spent months or even years optimizing a website to increase search rankings. With the growth in popularity of social media sites and blogs, the leading engines made changes to their algorithms to allow fresh content to rank quickly within the search results.

In February 2011, Google announced the Panda update, which penalizes websites containing content duplicated from other websites and sources. Historically websites have copied content from one another and benefited in search engine rankings by engaging in this practice. However, Google implemented a new system that punishes sites whose content is not unique. The 2012 Google Penguin attempted to penalize websites that used manipulative techniques to improve their rankings on the search engine. Although Google Penguin has been presented as an algorithm aimed at fighting web spam, it really focuses on spammy links by gauging the quality of the sites the links are coming from. The 2013 Google Hummingbird update featured an algorithm change designed to improve Google's natural language processing and semantic understanding of web pages. Hummingbird's language processing system falls under the newly recognized term of "conversational search", where the system pays more attention to each word in the query in order to better match the pages to the meaning of the query rather than a few words. With regards to the changes made to search engine optimization, for content publishers and writers, Hummingbird is intended to resolve issues by getting rid of irrelevant content and spam, allowing Google to produce high-quality content and rely on them to be 'trusted' authors.

In October 2019, Google announced they would start applying BERT models for English language search queries in the US. Bidirectional Encoder Representations from Transformers (BERT) was another attempt by Google to improve their natural language processing, but this time in order to better understand the search queries of their users. In terms of search engine optimization, BERT intended to connect users more easily to relevant content and increase the quality of traffic coming to websites that are ranking in the Search Engine Results Page.

4.1.2 Methods

Getting Indexed

The leading search engines, such as Google, Bing, and Yahoo!, use crawlers to find pages for their algorithmic search results. Pages that are linked from other search engine-indexed pages do not need to be submitted because they are found automatically. The Yahoo! Directory and DMOZ, two major directories which closed in 2014 and 2017 respectively, both required manual submission and human editorial review. Google offers Google Search Console, for which an XML Sitemap feed can be created and submitted for free to ensure that all pages are found, especially pages that are not discoverable by automatically following links in addition to their URL submission console. Yahoo! formerly operated a paid submission service that guaranteed to crawl for a cost per click; however, this practice was discontinued in 2009.

Search engine crawlers may look at a number of different factors when crawling a site. Not every page is indexed by search engines. The distance of pages from the root directory of a site may also be a factor in whether or not pages get crawled.

Mobile devices are used for the majority of Google searches. In November 2016, Google announced a major change to the way they are crawling websites and started to make their index mobile-first, which means the mobile version of a given website becomes the starting point for what Google includes in their index. In May 2019, Google updated the rendering engine of their crawler to be the latest version of Chromium (74 at the time of the announcement). Google indicated that they would regularly update the Chromium rendering engine to the latest version. In December 2019, Google began updating the User-Agent string of their crawler to reflect the latest Chrome version used by their rendering service. The delay was to allow webmasters time to update their code that responded to particular bot User-Agent strings. Google ran evaluations and felt confident the impact would be minor.

Preventing Crawling

To avoid undesirable content in the search indexes, webmasters can instruct spiders not to crawl certain files or directories through the standard robots.txt file in the root directory of the domain. Additionally, a page can be explicitly excluded from a search engine's database by using a meta tag specific to robots (usually <meta name="robots" content="noindex">). When a search engine visits a site, the robots.txt located in the root directory is the first file crawled. The robots.txt file is then parsed and will instruct the robot as to which pages are not to be crawled. As a search engine crawler may keep a cached copy of this file, it may on occasion crawl pages a webmaster does not wish to crawl. Pages typically prevented from being crawled include login-specific pages such as shopping carts and user-specific content such as search results from internal searches. In March 2007, Google warned webmasters that they should prevent indexing of internal search results because those pages are considered search spam. In 2020, Google sunsetted the standard (and open-sourced their code) and now treats it as a hint not a directive. To adequately ensure that pages are not indexed, a page-level robot's meta tag should be included.

Increasing Prominence

A variety of methods can increase the prominence of a webpage within the search results. Cross linking between pages of the same website to provide more links to important pages may improve its visibility. Page design makes users trust a site and want to stay once they find it. When people bounce off a site, it counts against the site and affects its credibility. Writing content that includes frequently searched keyword phrases so as to be relevant to a wide variety of search queries will tend to increase traffic. Updating content so as to keep search engines crawling back frequently can give additional weight to a site. Adding relevant keywords to a web page's metadata, including the title tag and meta description, will tend to improve the relevancy of a site's search listings, thus increasing traffic. URL canonicalization of web pages accessible via multiple URLs, using the canonical link element or via 301 redirects can help make sure links to different versions of the URL all count towards the page's link popularity score. These are known as incoming links, which point to the URL and can count towards the page link's popularity score, impacting the credibility of a website.

White Hat versus Black Hat Techniques

SEO techniques can be classified into two broad categories: techniques that search engine companies recommend as part of good design ("white hat"), and those techniques of which search engines do not approve ("black hat"). Search engines attempt to minimize the effect of the latter, among them spamdexing. Industry commentators have classified these methods and the practitioners who employ them as either white hat SEO or black hat SEO. White hats tend to produce results that last a long time, whereas black hats anticipate that their sites may eventually be banned either temporarily or permanently once the search engines discover what they are doing.

An SEO technique is considered a white hat if it conforms to the search engines' guidelines and involves no deception. As the search engine guidelines are not written as a series of rules or commandments, this is an important distinction to note. White hat SEO is not just about following guidelines but is about ensuring that the content a search engine indexes and subsequently ranks is the same content a user will see. White hat advice is generally summed up as creating content for users, not for search engines, and then making that content easily accessible to the online "spider" algorithms, rather than attempting to trick the algorithm from its intended purpose. White hat SEO is in many ways similar to web development that promotes accessibility, although the two are not identical.

Black hat SEO attempts to improve rankings in ways that are disapproved of by the search engines or involve deception. One black hat technique uses hidden text, either as text colored similar to the background, in an invisible div, or positioned off-screen. Another method gives a different page depending on whether the page is being requested by a human visitor or a search engine, a technique known as cloaking. Another category sometimes used is grey hat SEO. This is in between the black hat and white hat approaches, where the methods employed avoid the site being penalized but do not act in producing the best content for users. Grey hat SEO is entirely focused on improving search engine rankings.

Search engines may penalize sites they discover using black or grey hat methods, either by reducing their rankings or eliminating their listings from their databases altogether. Such penalties can be applied either automatically by the search engines' algorithms or by a manual site review. One example was the February 2006 Google removal of both BMW Germany and Ricoh Germany for the use of deceptive practices. Both companies, however, quickly apologized, fixed the offending pages, and were restored to Google's search engine results page.

4.1.3 As Marketing Strategy

SEO is not an appropriate strategy for every website, and other Internet marketing strategies can be more effective, such as paid advertising through pay-per-click (PPC) campaigns, depending on the site operator's goals. Search engine marketing (SEM) is the practice of designing, running, and optimizing search engine ad campaigns. Its difference from SEO is most simply depicted as the difference between paid and unpaid priority ranking in search results. SEM focuses on prominence more so than relevance; website developers should regard SEM with the utmost importance with consideration to visibility as most navigate to the primary listings of their search. A successful Internet marketing campaign may also depend upon building high-quality web pages to engage and persuade internet users, setting up analytics programs to enable site owners to measure results, and improving a site's conversion rate. In November 2015, Google released a full 160-page version of its Search Quality Rating Guidelines to the public, which revealed a shift in their focus towards "usefulness" and mobile local search. In recent years the mobile market has exploded, overtaking the use of desktops, as shown in by StatCounter in October 2016, where they analyzed 2.5 million websites and found that 51.3% of the pages were loaded by a mobile device. Google has been one of the companies that are utilizing the popularity of mobile usage by encouraging websites to use their Google Search Console, the Mobile-Friendly Test, which allows companies to measure up their website to the search engine results and determine how user-friendly their websites are. The closer the keywords are together their ranking will improve based on key terms.

SEO may generate an adequate return on investment. However, search engines are not paid for organic search traffic, their algorithms change, and there are no guarantees of continued referrals. Due to this lack of guarantee and uncertainty, a business that relies heavily on search engine traffic can suffer major losses if the search engines stop sending visitors. Search engines can change their algorithms, impacting a website's search engine ranking, possibly resulting in a serious loss of traffic. According to Google's CEO, Eric Schmidt, in 2010, Google made over 500 algorithm changes – almost 1.5 per day. It is considered a wise business practice for website operators to liberate themselves from dependence on search engine traffic. In addition to accessibility in terms of web crawlers user web accessibility has become increasingly important for SEO.

4.1.4 International Markets

Optimization techniques are highly tuned to the dominant search engines in the target market. The search engines' market shares vary from market to market, as does competition. In 2003, Danny Sullivan stated that Google represented about 75% of all searches. In markets outside the United States, Google's share is often larger, and Google remains the dominant search engine worldwide as of 2007. As of 2006, Google had an 85–90% market share in Germany. While there were hundreds of SEO firms in the US at that time, there were only about five in Germany. As of June 2008, the market share of Google in the UK was close to 90% according to Hitwise. That market share is achieved in a number of countries.

As of 2009, there are only a few large markets where Google is not the leading search engine. In most cases, when Google is not leading in a given market, it is lagging behind a local player. The most notable example markets are China, Japan, South Korea, Russia, and the Czech Republic, where respectively Baidu, Yahoo! Japan, Naver, Yandex and Seznam are market leaders.

Successful search optimization for international markets may require professional translation of web pages, registration of a domain name with a top level domain in the target market, and web hosting that provides a local IP address. Otherwise, the fundamental elements of search optimization are essentially the same, regardless of language.

4.1.5 Legal Precedents

On October 17, 2002, SearchKing filed suit in the United States District Court, Western District of Oklahoma, against the search engine Google. SearchKing's claim was that Google's tactics to prevent spamdexing constituted a tortious interference with contractual relations. On May 27, 2003, the court granted Google's motion to dismiss the complaint because SearchKing "failed to state a claim upon which relief may be granted."

In March 2006, KinderStart filed a lawsuit against Google over search engine rankings. KinderStart's website was removed from Google's index prior to the lawsuit, and the amount of traffic to the site dropped by 70%. On March 16, 2007, the United States District Court for the Northern District of California (San Jose Division) dismissed KinderStart's complaint without leave to amend and partially granted Google's motion for Rule 11 sanctions against KinderStart's attorney, requiring him to pay part of Google's legal expenses.

4.2 KEYWORD RESEARCH AND STRATEGY

Keyword research and strategy are foundational elements of effective search engine optimization (SEO). By identifying and targeting the right keywords, businesses can enhance their online visibility, attract relevant traffic, and improve their search engine rankings.

Keyword research and strategy are essential components of successful SEO. By understanding user intent, targeting relevant keywords, and implementing best practices, businesses can improve their search engine rankings, drive targeted traffic, and achieve their marketing objectives. Continuous monitoring and adjustment of keyword strategy ensure sustained success in the ever-evolving landscape of search engine optimization. As SEO continues to play a critical role in digital marketing, mastering keyword research and strategy will be key to maintaining a competitive edge.

4.2.1 Importance of Keyword Research in SEO

Understanding User Intent

Keyword research helps businesses understand what users are searching for and why. By analyzing search terms, businesses can gain insights into user intent, which is crucial for creating content that meets the needs and expectations of their audience.

Improving Search Rankings

Identifying relevant keywords and strategically incorporating them into website content can significantly improve search engine rankings. Higher rankings increase the likelihood of attracting organic traffic from search engines.

Driving Targeted Traffic

By targeting specific keywords related to their products or services, businesses can attract highly relevant traffic. This targeted traffic is more likely to convert into leads or customers, enhancing the overall effectiveness of SEO efforts.

Competitive Advantage

Conducting thorough keyword research allows businesses to identify opportunities that competitors might be missing. By targeting less competitive keywords, businesses can carve out a niche and gain a competitive edge.

4.2.2 The Process of Conducting Keyword Research

Conducting effective keyword research involves several steps:

Brainstorming and Initial List Creation

Start by brainstorming a list of potential keywords related to your business, products, or services. Consider the terms and phrases your target audience might use when searching for information related to your industry.

Using Keyword Research Tools

Several tools can help expand and refine your initial keyword list:

- **Google Keyword Planner:** A free tool that provides keyword ideas, search volume data, and competition levels.
- **SEMrush:** A comprehensive SEO tool that offers keyword research, competitor analysis, and search volume data.
- **Ahrefs:** Another powerful SEO tool that provides keyword suggestions, search volume, and keyword difficulty scores.
- **Moz Keyword Explorer:** Offers keyword suggestions, search volume, and difficulty metrics.
- **Ubersuggest:** A free tool that provides keyword ideas, search volume, and competition data.

Analyzing Search Volume and Competition

Evaluate the search volume and competition for each keyword. Keywords with high search volume and low competition are ideal, as they offer the potential for significant traffic with less competition.

Understanding Keyword Difficulty

Keyword difficulty scores indicate how challenging it is to rank for a specific keyword. Tools like Ahrefs and Moz provide difficulty scores, helping you prioritize keywords that offer the best balance between search volume and competition.

Considering Long-Tail Keywords

Long-tail keywords are longer, more specific phrases that typically have lower search volume but higher conversion rates. These keywords often represent more specific user intent and can be easier to rank for.

Analyzing Competitor Keywords

Examine the keywords your competitors are targeting. Tools like SEMrush and Ahrefs allow you to analyze competitor websites and identify the keywords they are ranking for. This analysis can reveal keyword opportunities and gaps in your own strategy.

4.2.3 Developing a Keyword Strategy

Once you have conducted thorough keyword research, the next step is to develop a keyword strategy that aligns with your business goals and SEO objectives.

Categorizing Keywords

Organize your keywords into categories based on themes or topics. This categorization helps you create targeted content clusters and ensures that your website covers a broad range of relevant topics.

Prioritizing Keywords

Prioritize your keywords based on factors such as search volume, competition, relevance, and business goals. Focus on high-priority keywords that offer the best opportunities for driving traffic and achieving your objectives.

Mapping Keywords to Content

Map your keywords to specific pages or pieces of content on your website. Ensure that each page targets a primary keyword and includes relevant secondary keywords to support the main topic.

Creating Content Around Keywords

Develop high-quality content that incorporates your target keywords naturally. Focus on providing value to your audience by addressing their needs and answering their questions.

Avoid keyword stuffing, as this can negatively impact user experience and search rankings.

4.2.4 Best Practices for Implementing and Optimizing Keywords

On-Page SEO

On-page SEO involves optimizing individual web pages to rank higher in search engine results. Key elements of on-page SEO include:

- **Title Tags:** Include your primary keyword in the title tag, preferably near the beginning. Keep the title tag under 60 characters to ensure it displays fully in search results.
- **Meta Descriptions:** Write compelling meta descriptions that include your primary keyword and encourage users to click through to your site. Keep meta descriptions under 160 characters.
- **Header Tags:** Use header tags (H1, H2, H3, etc.) to structure your content and include keywords in your headers. The H1 tag should contain the primary keyword, while H2 and H3 tags can include secondary keywords.
- **URL Structure:** Include keywords in your URLs to make them more descriptive and SEO-friendly. Keep URLs short and relevant.
- **Content Optimization:** Incorporate keywords naturally throughout your content, including in the first paragraph, subheadings, and body text. Aim for a keyword density of around 1-2%.

Technical SEO

Technical SEO involves optimizing the technical aspects of your website to improve search engine crawling and indexing. Key elements of technical SEO include:

- **Site Speed:** Ensure your website loads quickly, as site speed is a ranking factor for search engines. Use tools like Google PageSpeed Insights to identify and fix speed issues.
- **Mobile-Friendliness:** Ensure your website is mobile-friendly, as search engines prioritize mobile-optimized sites. Use responsive design to provide a seamless experience across devices.
- **XML Sitemaps:** Create and submit an XML sitemap to search engines to help them crawl and index your site more effectively.
- **Robots.txt:** Use the robots.txt file to control which pages search engines can and cannot crawl. Ensure important pages are accessible to search engines.

Off-Page SEO

Off-page SEO involves activities outside your website that can impact your search rankings. Key elements of off-page SEO include:

- **Backlinks:** Acquire high-quality backlinks from reputable websites. Backlinks act as votes of confidence and can significantly improve your search rankings.
- **Social Signals:** Promote your content on social media to increase visibility and drive traffic. While social signals are not direct ranking factors, they can indirectly impact SEO.
- **Guest Blogging:** Contribute guest posts to authoritative websites in your industry. Include links back to your site to build backlinks and increase exposure.

4.2.5 Measuring and Adjusting Your Keyword Strategy

Effective keyword strategy requires continuous monitoring and adjustment. Use analytics tools to track the performance of your keywords and make data-driven decisions. Key metrics to monitor include:

- **Organic Traffic:** The number of visitors coming to your site from organic search results.
- **Keyword Rankings:** The position of your keywords in search engine results pages (SERPs).
- **Click-Through Rate (CTR):** The percentage of users who click on your search result after seeing it in the SERPs.
- **Bounce Rate:** The percentage of visitors who leave your site after viewing only one page. A high bounce rate may indicate that your content is not meeting user expectations.

Regularly review your keyword performance and adjust your strategy as needed. Stay up-to-date with SEO best practices and algorithm updates to maintain and improve your search rankings.

4.3 ON-PAGE AND OFF-PAGE SEO

Search Engine Optimization (SEO) is the practice of enhancing a website's visibility on search engine results pages (SERPs). SEO is typically divided into two main categories: on-page SEO and off-page SEO. Both are crucial for achieving a high ranking and driving organic traffic to your website.

On-page and off-page SEO are two sides of the same coin, both essential for achieving higher search engine rankings and driving organic traffic. On-page SEO focuses on optimizing the elements within your control on your website, such as content, HTML elements, and site structure. Off-page SEO involves activities outside your website, such as acquiring high-quality backlinks, engaging on social media, and building your online reputation. By integrating both strategies and continuously monitoring performance, businesses can enhance their online visibility, attract targeted traffic, and achieve long-term SEO success.

4.3.1 On-Page SEO

On-page SEO refers to the optimization techniques applied directly on the website to improve its position in the search rankings.

It involves tweaking various elements of the site to make it more search engine friendly and enhance user experience.

Key Components of On-Page SEO

- **Content Quality and Relevance**
  - **Keywords**: Use relevant keywords that match user intent. Place them naturally in titles, headers, and body text.
  - **Originality**: Ensure content is unique and valuable. Plagiarism can hurt your rankings.
  - **Depth**: Provide comprehensive information that fully addresses the topic.
- **HTML Elements:**
  - **Title Tags**: Include primary keywords and keep titles under 60 characters to ensure they display correctly in SERPs.
  - **Meta Descriptions**: Write compelling meta descriptions with keywords to increase click-through rates. Keep them under 160 characters.
  - **Header Tags (H1, H2, H3, etc.)**: Use header tags to structure content and include keywords. H1 should be unique and descriptive.
- **URL Structure:**
  - Use clear, descriptive URLs that include keywords. Avoid long, complex URLs.
- **Internal Linking:**
  - Link to other relevant pages within your website to improve navigation and spread link equity.
- **Image Optimization:**
  - Use descriptive file names and alt tags with keywords for images. Compress images to enhance loading speed.
- **Mobile-Friendliness:**
  - Ensure your website is responsive and offers a good user experience on mobile devices. Google uses mobile-first indexing.
- **Page Speed:**
  - Optimize loading times by compressing files, leveraging browser caching, and improving server response times.
- **User Experience (UX):**

  - Focus on a clean design, easy navigation, and fast load times to keep users engaged and reduce bounce rates.

Best Practices for On-Page SEO

- **Keyword Research:** Conduct thorough keyword research to identify terms your target audience uses. Use tools like Google Keyword Planner, Ahrefs, or SEMrush.
- **Content Strategy:** Develop a content strategy that aligns with user needs and search intent. Regularly update and refresh content.
- **Schema Markup:** Implement schema markup to help search engines understand your content and improve rich snippet visibility.
- **Analytics and Monitoring:** Use tools like Google Analytics and Google Search Console to monitor performance and make data-driven adjustments.

4.3.2 Off-Page SEO

Off-page SEO refers to activities conducted outside your website to improve its search engine rankings. It involves building relationships, promoting your content, and increasing your site's authority and trustworthiness.

Key Components of Off-Page SEO

- **Backlinks:**
  - **Quality over Quantity**: Focus on acquiring high-quality backlinks from authoritative and relevant sites.
  - **Diversity**: Gain links from various sources such as blogs, news sites, forums, and directories.
  - **Anchor Text**: Use varied and natural anchor text to avoid appearing manipulative.
- **Social Media Engagement:**
  - **Content Promotion**: Share your content on social media platforms to increase visibility and attract backlinks.
  - **Engagement**: Interact with your audience through comments, shares, and likes to boost brand awareness and trust.
- **Guest Blogging:**
  - Write guest posts for reputable websites in your industry. Include a link back to your site to build backlinks and increase exposure.
- **Influencer Outreach:**
  - Collaborate with influencers to promote your content or brand. Influencers can drive traffic and generate high-quality backlinks.
- **Online Reputation Management:**

- Monitor and manage your online reputation by responding to reviews and addressing any negative feedback. Positive reviews can enhance your credibility.

- **Content Marketing:**
  - Create shareable and link-worthy content such as infographics, videos, and in-depth articles. Promote this content to attract backlinks.

Best Practices for Off-Page SEO

- **Link Building**: Develop a strategic approach to link building, focusing on quality and relevance. Avoid black-hat techniques like buying links.
- **Content Syndication:** Distribute your content on platforms like Medium, LinkedIn, and industry-specific sites to reach a broader audience.
- **Community Participation**: Engage in online communities, forums, and Q&A sites related to your industry. Provide valuable insights and link back to your content where relevant.
- **Monitoring and Analysis:** Use tools like Ahrefs, Moz, and SEMrush to monitor your backlink profile, track mentions, and analyze the effectiveness of your off-page efforts.

4.3.3 Integrating On-Page and Off-Page SEO

A successful SEO strategy requires a balanced approach, integrating both on-page and off-page tactics. Here's how to combine them effectively:

- **Keyword Consistency:** Ensure the keywords you target in your on-page SEO are reflected in your off-page efforts. Use them in anchor text and content promotion.
- **Content Creation and Promotion:** Create high-quality, optimized content (on-page) and promote it through various channels (off-page) to attract backlinks and social shares.
- **Link Building and Internal Linking:** While acquiring external backlinks, also focus on internal linking to distribute link equity across your site and improve navigation.
- **Monitoring and Adjusting:** Regularly monitor both on-page and off-page metrics using SEO tools. Analyze the data to identify what's working and make necessary adjustments.
- **Brand Building:** Use off-page strategies like social media engagement and influencer collaborations to build your brand, which in turn supports on-page SEO by increasing direct traffic and brand searches.

4.4 TECHNICAL SEO AND WEBSITE OPTIMIZATION

Technical SEO and website optimization are critical components of a comprehensive SEO strategy. They involve optimizing the technical aspects of a website to improve its visibility and ranking on search engine results pages (SERPs).

Technical SEO and website optimization are essential for ensuring that search engines can effectively crawl, index, and understand your website. By focusing on key elements such as site speed, mobile-friendliness, URL structure, security, and structured data, you can improve your website's visibility and ranking in SERPs. Utilizing tools like Google Search Console, Screaming Frog, and GTmetrix can help you identify and fix technical issues. Adhering to best practices and conducting regular audits will ensure your website remains optimized and competitive in the ever-evolving landscape of search engine optimization.

4.4.1 Importance of Technical SEO

Technical SEO focuses on improving the infrastructure of a website to ensure that search engines can crawl, index, and understand its content effectively. Here are some reasons why technical SEO is important:

- **Enhanced Crawlability and Indexability**: Proper technical SEO ensures that search engine bots can easily crawl and index your website. If search engines can't access your pages, they won't appear in search results.
- **Improved User Experience (UX)**: A technically sound website offers a better user experience. This includes fast loading times, mobile-friendliness, and easy navigation, which can reduce bounce rates and increase user engagement.
- **Higher Search Rankings**: Technical issues can negatively impact your search rankings. By addressing these issues, you can improve your website's performance in SERPs.
- **Increased Security**: Technical SEO includes measures to secure your website, such as implementing HTTPS. A secure website is trusted more by both users and search engines.

4.4.2 Key Elements of Technical SEO

- **Site Speed and Performance:**
  - **Page Load Speed**: Optimize images, leverage browser caching, and minimize CSS and JavaScript files to improve page load times.
  - **Server Response Time**: Ensure your server responds quickly to requests. Use a reliable hosting service and consider using a Content Delivery Network (CDN).

- **Mobile-Friendliness:**
  - **Responsive Design**: Ensure your website adapts to different screen sizes and devices.
  - **Mobile Usability**: Check for mobile usability issues such as clickable elements being too close together or text being too small to read.
- **URL Structure:**
  - **Clean URLs**: Use clear, descriptive URLs that include relevant keywords. Avoid using long, complex URLs with unnecessary parameters.
  - **Canonicalization**: Implement canonical tags to prevent duplicate content issues and indicate the preferred version of a page.
- **XML Sitemaps:**
  - **Creating Sitemaps**: Generate an XML sitemap to help search engines discover and index your pages. Submit the sitemap to Google Search Console and Bing Webmaster Tools.
  - **Sitemap Updates**: Regularly update your sitemap to reflect any changes to your website's structure or content.
- **Robots.txt File:**
  - **Configuring Robots.txt**: Use the robots.txt file to control which pages search engine bots can crawl. Ensure important pages are accessible while preventing the indexing of irrelevant or sensitive pages.
- **HTTPS and Website Security:**
  - **SSL Certificates**: Implement HTTPS to secure data transferred between the server and users. HTTPS is also a ranking factor for Google.
  - **Security Measures**: Use security plugins, firewalls, and regular software updates to protect your website from attacks.
- **Structured Data Markup:**
  - **Schema.org**: Implement structured data markup to help search engines understand your content better and provide rich results in SERPs.
  - **Testing and Validation**: Use tools like Google's Structured Data Testing Tool to validate your markup and ensure it's implemented correctly.
- **Website Architecture:**
  - **Hierarchy**: Design a clear and logical website architecture with a hierarchical structure. Use categories and subcategories to organize content.
  - **Internal Linking**: Use internal links to connect related content and distribute link equity throughout your site.

4.4.3 Tools for Technical SEO

Several tools can help you identify and fix technical SEO issues. Here are some popular options:

- **Google Search Console:**
  - **Performance Reports**: Monitor your website's performance, including clicks, impressions, and average position in SERPs.
  - **Crawl Errors**: Identify and fix crawl errors to ensure all important pages are indexed.
  - **Sitemaps and Robots.txt**: Submit sitemaps and test robots.txt files.
- **Google PageSpeed Insights**
  - **Speed Scores**: Analyze your website's speed on both mobile and desktop devices. Get suggestions for improving page load times.
- **Screaming Frog SEO Spider**
  - **Site Audits**: Crawl your website to identify technical issues such as broken links, duplicate content, and missing metadata.
- **GTmetrix**
  - **Performance Analysis**: Get detailed reports on your website's speed and performance, along with actionable recommendations.
- **Ahrefs:**
  - **Site Audit Tool**: Conduct comprehensive site audits to identify technical SEO issues and monitor your website's health.
- **Moz Pro:**
  - **Crawl Diagnostics**: Use the crawl diagnostics tool to find and fix technical issues that could affect your search rankings.
- **SEMrush:**
  - **Site Audit**: Run site audits to uncover technical SEO problems and get recommendations for improvements.

4.4.4 Best Practices for Website Optimization

- **Regular Audits:** Perform regular technical SEO audits to identify and fix issues promptly. Use tools like Screaming Frog, Ahrefs, and SEMrush for comprehensive site audits.
- **Optimizing Images:** Compress and resize images to reduce load times. Use descriptive file names and alt tags to improve accessibility and SEO.
- **Enhancing Mobile Experience:** Ensure your website is fully responsive and provides an excellent user experience on mobile devices. Test your site using Google's Mobile-Friendly Test.
- **Improving Page Load Times:** Minimize HTTP requests, enable browser caching, and use a CDN to deliver content faster. Optimize CSS, JavaScript, and HTML files.

- **Ensuring Site Security:** Implement HTTPS and regularly update your SSL certificate. Use security plugins, conduct regular security scans, and stay updated with the latest security practices.
- **Implementing Structured Data:** Use Schema.org markup to provide search engines with more context about your content. Test your structured data with Google's Structured Data Testing Tool.
- **Fixing Broken Links:** Regularly check for and fix broken links to maintain a seamless user experience and prevent negative impacts on SEO.
- **Maintaining a Clean URL Structure:** Use short, descriptive URLs that include relevant keywords. Avoid using complex parameters and ensure consistency across your site.
- **Optimizing Internal Linking:** Use internal links to guide users and search engines through your site. Ensure each page is linked from at least one other page.
- **Monitoring Performance:** Use tools like Google Analytics and Google Search Console to monitor your website's performance. Track key metrics and make data-driven decisions to optimize your site further.

4.5 LOCAL SEO AND MOBILE OPTIMIZATION

4.5.1 Local SEO (Search Engine Optimization)

- **Google My Business:** Claim and optimize your Google My Business listing. Ensure that your business information, such as name, address, phone number (NAP), and hours of operation, are accurate and consistent across all online platforms.
- **Local Keywords:** Target keywords that include geographic locations relevant to your business. For example, if you're a bakery in San Francisco, use keywords like "best bakery in San Francisco" or "San Francisco pastry shop."
- **Local Citations:** Ensure your business is listed accurately on various online directories and citation sites such as Yelp, Yellow Pages, and industry-specific directories.
- **Customer Reviews:** Encourage satisfied customers to leave positive reviews on platforms like Google, Yelp, and Facebook. Respond to reviews, both positive and negative, to show engagement and build trust.
- **Localized Content:** Create content tailored to your local audience. This could include blog posts about local events, news, or tips related to your industry in your area.

4.5.2 Mobile Optimization

- **Responsive Design:** Ensure your website is mobile-friendly and responsive, meaning it adapts to different screen sizes and devices seamlessly. Google prioritizes mobile-friendly websites in its search rankings.
- **Page Speed:** Optimize your website's loading speed for mobile devices. Users expect fast-loading pages, and Google considers page speed as a ranking factor.
- **Mobile-Friendly Content:** Format your content for easy readability on mobile devices. Use shorter paragraphs, bullet points, and larger fonts to enhance the mobile user experience.
- **Mobile SEO:** Optimize your website's content and metadata for mobile search. Focus on concise, relevant titles and meta descriptions that display effectively on mobile search results.
- **Local Mobile Optimization:** Incorporate local keywords in your mobile content and metadata to target users searching for local businesses on their mobile devices.
- **Mobile App (if Applicable):** If your business has a mobile app, ensure it provides a seamless user experience and integrates with other mobile optimization efforts.

CHAPTER 5

PAY-PER-CLICK (PPC) ADVERTISING

5.1 INTRODUCTION TO PPC

Pay-per-click (PPC) is an internet advertising model used to drive traffic to websites, in which an advertiser pays a publisher (typically a search engine, website owner, or a network of websites) when the ad is clicked.

Pay-per-click is usually associated with first-tier search engines (such as Google Ads, Amazon Advertising, and Microsoft Advertising). With search engines, advertisers typically bid on keyword phrases relevant to their target market and pay when ads (text-based search ads or shopping ads that are a combination of images and text) are clicked. In contrast, content sites commonly charge a fixed price per click rather than use a bidding system.

PPC display advertisements, also known as banner ads, are shown on websites with related content that have agreed to show ads and are typically not pay-per-click advertising, but instead, usually charge on a cost per thousand impressions (CPM).

Social networks such as Facebook, Instagram, LinkedIn, Reddit, Pinterest, TikTok, and Twitter have also adopted pay-per-click as one of their advertising models. The amount advertisers pay depends on the publisher and is usually driven by two major factors: the quality of the ad, and the maximum bid the advertiser is willing to pay per click measured against its competitors' bids. In general, the higher the quality of the ad, the lower the cost per click is charged, and vice versa.

However, websites can offer PPC ads. Websites that utilize PPC ads will display an advertisement when a query (keyword or phrase) matches an advertiser's keyword list that has been added in different ad groups, or when a content site displays relevant content.

Such advertisements are called *sponsored links* or *sponsored ads*, or beneath organic results on search engine results pages (SERPs), or anywhere a web developer chooses on a content site.

The PPC advertising model is open to abuse through click fraud, although Google and others have implemented automated systems to guard against abusive clicks by competitors or corrupt web developers.

5.1.1 Purpose

Pay-per-click, along with cost per impression (CPM) and cost per order, is used to assess the cost-effectiveness and profitability of internet marketing and drive the cost of running an advertisement campaign as low as possible while retaining set goals. In Cost Per Thousand Impressions (CPM), the advertiser only pays for every 1000 impressions of the ad. Pay-per-click (PPC) has an advantage over cost-per-impression in that it conveys information about how effective the advertising was. Clicks are a way to measure attention and interest. If the main purpose of an ad is to generate a click, or more specifically drive traffic to a destination, then pay-per-click is the preferred metric. The quality and placement of the advertisement will affect click through rates and the resulting total pay-per-click cost.

5.1.2 Construction

Cost-per-click (CPC) is calculated by dividing the advertising cost by the number of clicks generated by an advertisement. The basic formula is:

Cost-per-click ($) = Advertising cost ($) / Ads clicked (#)

There are two primary models for determining pay-per-click: flat-rate and bid-based. In both cases, the advertiser must consider the potential value of a click from a given source. This value is based on the type of individual the advertiser is expecting to receive as a visitor to their website, and what the advertiser can gain from that visit, which is usually short-term or long-term revenue. As with other forms of advertising, targeting is key, and factors that often play into PPC campaigns include the target's interest (often defined by a search term they have entered into a search engine or the content of a page that they are browsing), intent (e.g., to purchase or not), location (for geo targeting), a device used (e.g. whether the user is searching from a desktop device or mobile) and the day and time that they are browsing.

Flat-Rate PPC

In the flat-rate model, the advertiser and publisher agree upon a fixed amount that will be paid for each click. In many cases, the publisher has a rate card that lists the pay-per-click (PPC) within different areas of their website or network. These various amounts are often related to the content on pages, with content that generally attracts more valuable visitors having a higher cost per click than content that attracts less valuable visitors. However, in many cases, advertisers can negotiate lower rates, especially when committing to a long-term or high-value contract. The flat-rate model is particularly common on comparison shopping engines, which typically publish rate cards. However, these rates are sometimes minimal, and advertisers can pay more for greater visibility. These sites are usually neatly compartmentalized into product or service categories, allowing a high degree of targeting by advertisers. In many cases, the entire core content of these sites is paid ads.

Bid-Based PPC

The advertiser signs a contract that allows them to compete against other advertisers in a private auction hosted by a publisher or, more commonly, an advertising network. Each advertiser informs the host of the maximum amount that he or she is willing to pay for a given ad spot (often based on a keyword), usually using online tools to do so. The auction plays out in an automated fashion every time a visitor triggers the ad spot.

When the ad spot is part of a search engine results page (SERP), the automated auction takes place whenever a search for the keyword that is being bid upon occurs. All bids for the keyword that targets the searcher's Geo-location, the day and time of the search, etc. are then compared, and the winner is determined. All this happens in real-time, therefore this is called real-time-bidding or RTB, and in a fraction of a second. In situations where there are multiple ad spots, a common occurrence on SERPs, there can be multiple winners whose positions on the page are influenced by the amount each has bid and the quality of their ad. The bid and Quality Score are used to give each advertiser's advert an ad rank. The ad with the highest ad rank shows up first. The predominant three match types for both Google and Bing are Broad, Exact, and Phrase Match. Google Ads and Bing Ads also offer the Broad Match Modifier type (although Google retired it in July 2021) which differs from broad match in that the keyword must contain the actual keyword terms in any order and doesn't include relevant variations of the terms.

In addition to ad spots on SERPs, the major advertising networks allow for contextual ads to be placed on the properties of 3rd-parties with whom they have partnered. These publishers sign up to host ads on behalf of the network. In return, they receive a portion of the ad revenue that the network generates, which can be anywhere from 50% to over 80% of the gross revenue paid by advertisers. These properties are often referred to as a *content network* and the ads on them as *contextual ads* because the ad spots are associated with keywords based on the context of the page on which they are found. In general, ads on content networks have a much lower click-through rate (CTR) and conversion rate (CR) than ads found on SERPs and consequently are less highly valued. Content network properties can include websites, newsletters, and e-mails.

Advertisers pay for every single click they receive, with the actual amount paid based on the amount of bid. It is common practice amongst auction hosts to charge a winning bidder just slightly more (e.g. one penny) than the next highest bidder or the actual amount bid, whichever is lower. This avoids situations where bidders are constantly adjusting their bids by very small amounts to see if they can still win the auction while paying just a little bit less per click.

In order to maximize success and achieve scale, automated bid management systems can be deployed. These systems can be used directly by the advertiser, though they are more commonly used by advertising agencies that offer PPC bid management as a service. These tools generally allow for bid management at scale, with thousands or even millions of PPC bids controlled by a highly automated system. The system generally sets each bid based on the goal that has been set for it, such as maximizing profit, maximizing traffic, getting the very targeted customer at break even, and so forth.

The system is usually tied into the advertiser's website and fed the results of each click, which then allows it to set bids. The effectiveness of these systems is directly related to the quality and quantity of the performance data that they have to work with — low-traffic ads can lead to a scarcity of data problem that renders many bid management tools useless at worst, or inefficient at best. As a rule, the contextual advertising system (Google Ads, Yandex.Direct, etc.) uses an auction approach as the advertising payment system.

5.1.3 History

There are several sites that claim to be the first PPC model on the web, with many appearing in the mid-1990s. For example, in 1996, the first known and documented version of a PPC was included in a web directory called Planet Oasis. This was a desktop application featuring links to informational and commercial websites, and it was developed by Ark Interface II, a division of Packard Bell NEC Computers. The initial reactions from commercial companies to Ark Interface II's "pay-per-visit" model were skeptical, however. By the end of 1997, over 400 major brands were paying between $.005 to $.25 per click plus a placement fee.

In February 1998 Jeffrey Brewer of Goto.com, a 25-employee startup company (later Overture, now part of Yahoo!), presented a pay per click search engine proof-of-concept to the TED conference in California. This presentation and the events that followed created the PPC advertising system. Credit for the concept of the PPC model is generally given to Idealab and Goto.com founder Bill Gross.

Google started search engine advertising in December 1999. It was not until October 2000 that the AdWords system was introduced, allowing advertisers to create text ads for placement on the Google search engine. However, PPC was only introduced in 2002; until then, advertisements were charged at cost-per-thousand impressions or Cost per mille (CPM). Overture has filed a patent infringement lawsuit against Google, saying the rival search service overstepped its bounds with its ad-placement tools.

Although GoTo.com started PPC in 1998, Yahoo! did not start syndicating GoTo.com (later Overture) advertisers until November 2001. Prior to this, Yahoo's primary source of SERPs advertising included contextual IAB advertising units (mainly 468x60 display ads). When the syndication contract with Yahoo! was up for renewal in July 2003, Yahoo! announced its intent to acquire Overture for $1.63 billion. Today, companies such as adMarketplace, ValueClick and acknowledge offering PPC services, as an alternative to AdWords and AdCenter.

Among PPC providers, Google Ads (formerly Google AdWords), Microsoft adCenter and Yahoo! Search Marketing had been the three largest network operators, all three operating under a bid-based model. For example, in the year 2014, PPC(AdWords) or online advertising attributed approximately US$45 billion of the total US$66 billion of Google's annual revenue In 2010, Yahoo and Microsoft launched their combined effort against Google, and Microsoft's Bing began to be the search engine that Yahoo used to provide its search results. Since they joined forces, their PPC platform was renamed AdCenter. Their combined network of third-party sites that allow AdCenter ads to populate banner and text ads on their site is called BingAds.

5.1.4 PPC Statistics

- Customers are 50% more likely to purchase something after clicking a paid ad.
- SMEs spend $108,000 to $120,000 annually on PPC ads.
- 57.5% of users don't recognize paid ads when they see them.
- Click bots and fake traffic cost online advertisers $35 Billion.

5.1.5 Legal

In 2012, Google was initially ruled to have engaged in misleading and deceptive conduct by the Australian Competition & Consumer Commission (ACCC) in possibly the first legal case of its kind. The ACCC ruled that Google was responsible for the content of its sponsored AdWords ads that had shown links to a car sales website Carsales. The ads had been shown by Google in response to a search for Honda Australia. The ACCC said the ads were deceptive, as they suggested Carsales was connected to the Honda company. The ruling was later overturned when Google appealed to the High Court of Australia. Google was found not liable for the misleading advertisements run through AdWords despite the fact that the ads were served up by Google and created using the company's tools.

5.1.6 Click Fraud

A common concern amongst advertisers is the practice known as "click fraud". This takes two forms:

- Publishers who illegitimately click on or fraudulently arrange for clicks to be generated on adverts, in order to increase their own publisher revenues. In 2018, the FBI, in partnership with Google and other major industry ad platforms, cracked down on an illegal ad fraud scheme known as "3ve", which was estimated to have defrauded advertisers several millions of dollars in combined ad costs. The case highlighted the extent of ad fraud; as of 2018, ad fraud annual revenue was on track to be worth more than the illicit drug trade, with over $19 billion estimated to have been stolen by click fraudsters.
- Advertisers who attempt to derail competitors' adverts, by clicking on them in an effort to raise their competitors' costs in order to give themselves an unfair advantage in the advertising space. The Google Ads platforms claim to be able to identify such clicks, and label such traffic as "invalid clicks".

5.2 CRAFTING EFFECTIVE PPC CAMPAIGNS

Crafting effective PPC (Pay-Per-Click) campaigns is both an art and a science. It involves strategic planning, meticulous execution, and continuous optimization to achieve desired results. Crafting effective PPC campaigns requires a combination of strategic planning, creative execution, and continuous optimization. By understanding the key components of PPC advertising and implementing best practices and strategies, businesses can drive targeted traffic, generate leads, and achieve their marketing objectives efficiently and cost-effectively. With the right approach and ongoing refinement, PPC advertising can be a powerful tool for growing your business and maximizing ROI in the digital landscape.

5.2.1 Understanding PPC Campaigns

PPC advertising allows businesses to bid on keywords relevant to their products or services and display ads to users who search for those terms on search engines or browse relevant websites. When a user clicks on the ad, the advertiser pays a fee, hence the name "pay-per-click."

5.2.2 Key Components of Effective PPC Campaigns

Keyword Research

- Conduct thorough keyword research to identify relevant search terms that your target audience is likely to use.
- Use tools like Google Keyword Planner, SEMrush, or Ahrefs to discover keywords with high search volume and moderate competition.
- Group keywords into themed ad groups to create targeted campaigns and ad sets.

Compelling Ad Copy

- Write persuasive ad copy that grabs attention, highlights unique selling propositions (USPs), and includes a clear call-to-action (CTA).
- Use ad extensions such as site links, callouts, and structured snippets to provide additional information and improve ad visibility.
- Test different variations of ad copy to identify which messages resonate best with your audience.

Landing Page Optimization

- Ensure that your landing pages are relevant to the ad copy and provide a seamless user experience.
- Optimize landing page elements such as headlines, images, and CTAs to align with the intent of the PPC campaign.
- Implement A/B testing to refine landing page design and messaging for better conversion rates.

Targeting Options

- Utilize targeting options such as location targeting, device targeting, and audience targeting to reach your ideal customers.
- Experiment with different targeting settings to find the most effective combination for your campaign objectives.
- Refine targeting based on performance data and adjust bid adjustments accordingly.

Bid Management

- Set appropriate bids for your keywords based on their estimated value and competition level.
- Monitor bid performance and adjust bids to maintain a competitive position while maximizing ROI.
- Consider using automated bidding strategies like target CPA or ROAS (Return on Ad Spend) to streamline bid management and optimize performance.

Ad Testing and Optimization

- Continuously test different ad variations, including headlines, descriptions, and display URLs, to improve click-through rates (CTRs) and conversion rates.

- Analyze performance metrics such as CTR, conversion rate, and cost per conversion to identify underperforming ads and make data-driven optimizations.
- Implement ad scheduling to show ads at times when your target audience is most likely to be active and engaged.

Tracking and Measurement

- Implement conversion tracking to measure the effectiveness of your PPC campaigns in driving desired actions, such as form submissions, purchases, or phone calls.
- Use Google Analytics or other tracking tools to analyze campaign performance, identify trends, and make informed decisions.
- Set up custom tracking parameters to track the performance of specific campaigns, ad groups, or keywords more accurately.

5.2.3 Strategies for Success

Start with Clear Objectives

- Clearly define your campaign objectives, whether it's driving website traffic, generating leads, or increasing sales.
- Align your PPC campaign strategy with your broader marketing goals to ensure consistency and effectiveness.

Know Your Audience

- Develop detailed buyer personas to understand your target audience's demographics, interests, and pain points.
- Tailor your PPC campaigns to address the needs and preferences of your target audience effectively.

Focus on Quality Score

- Improve Quality Score by optimizing ad relevance, landing page experience, and expected click-through rate.
- Higher Quality Scores can lead to lower costs per click (CPC) and better ad positions, resulting in improved campaign performance.

Budget Management

- Allocate your PPC budget strategically based on the potential ROI of different keywords and campaigns.
- Monitor budget utilization regularly and reallocate funds to high-performing campaigns or opportunities for growth.

Continuous Optimization

- PPC campaign optimization is an ongoing process that requires regular monitoring and adjustment.
- Analyze performance data regularly to identify areas for improvement and implement optimization tactics accordingly.
- Stay updated on industry trends, algorithm changes, and best practices to stay ahead of the competition.

Integration with Other Marketing Channels

- Integrate your PPC campaigns with other marketing channels, such as social media, email, and content marketing, to create a cohesive and synergistic marketing strategy.
- Leverage cross-channel data and insights to optimize campaign targeting, messaging, and performance across multiple touchpoints.

Monitor Competitors

- Keep an eye on your competitors' PPC activities, including their ad copy, keywords, and bidding strategies.
- Identify opportunities to differentiate your brand and capitalize on gaps or weaknesses in your competitors' campaigns.

5.3 AD PLATFORMS: GOOGLE ADS, BING ADS, AND BEYOND

Ad platforms like Google Ads and Bing Ads have revolutionized the way businesses advertise online, offering powerful tools and targeting options to reach potential customers across search engines, websites, and mobile apps.

Ad platforms like Google Ads, Bing Ads, Facebook Ads, and others offer powerful tools and targeting options to reach potential customers across search engines, social media, and websites. By understanding the features, benefits, and best practices of each platform, businesses can create effective advertising campaigns that drive traffic, conversions, and ROI in the competitive digital landscape. Whether you're looking to increase visibility on search engines, engage users on social media, or reach professionals on professional networks, there's an ad platform to suit your needs and objectives.

5.3.1 Google Ads

Google Ads is an online advertising platform developed by Google, where advertisers bid to display brief advertisements, service offerings, product listings, and videos to web users. It can place ads in the results of search engines like Google Search (the Google Search Network), mobile apps, videos, and on non-search websites.

Services are offered under a pay-per-click (PPC) pricing model. Google Ads is the main source of revenue for Alphabet Inc., contributing US$224.47 billion in revenue in 2022.

History

Google launched AdWords in the year 2000. Initially, Google itself would set up and manage advertisers' campaigns. Google then introduced a self-service AdWords portal for small businesses that wanted to manage their own campaigns. In 2005, Google started a campaign management service known as "Jumpstart". In 2007, Google acquired DoubleClick for $3.1 billion. The acquisition was strategically important for Google, providing access to DoubleClick's advanced ad-serving technology and established industry relationships.

This deal, while "transforming Google into a powerhouse", later attracted antitrust scrutiny, raising questions about its impact on market competition and digital advertising dominance. In 2008, Google launched the Google Online Marketing Challenge, an in-class academic exercise for tertiary students. Google retired the DoubleClick and AdWords brands in 2018 to simplify entry points for advertisers and ad sellers. The core product was renamed Google Ads, providing access to inventory on Google Search, its YouTube video service, the Google Play app store, and AdSense website publisher partners.

Functionality

Google Ads' system is based partly on cookies and partly on keywords determined by advertisers. Google uses these characteristics to place advertising copy on pages that they think might be relevant. In 2023, Google introduced Topics API, which allows targeting ads based on browsing history stored in browser, to Google Chrome. Advertisers pay when users divert their browsing to click on the advertising copy. Adverts can be implemented locally, nationally, or internationally. Google's text advertisements mimic what the average search result looks like on Google. Offering text-only search ads initially, Google unveiled "Showcase Shopping" ads in 2016.

With this format, retailers can choose to have a series of product images that appear in search results related to various search queries and keywords. In May 2016, Google announced Expanded Text Ads, allowing 23% more text. Image ads in the display network can be one of the several different standardized sizes as designated by the Interactive Advertising Bureau (IAB). Besides the Google search engine, advertisers also have the option of enabling their ads to show on Google's partner network, members of which receive a portion of the generated income.

Restrictions on Ad Content

The "Family status" of an ad ("family safe", "non-family safe", or "adult") is set by a Google reviewer and indicates what "audiences the ad and website are appropriate for". This will change at what time, on which page, and in which country an ad can appear.

As of December 2010, Google AdWords decreased restrictions on sales of hard alcohol. It now allows ads that promote the sale of hard alcohol and liquor. This is an extension of a policy change that was made in December 2008, which permitted ads that promote the branding of hard alcohol and liquor.

Some keywords, such as those related to hacking, are not allowed at all. From June 2007, Google banned AdWords adverts for student essay-writing services, a move which received positive feedback from universities. Google has a variety of specific keywords and categories that it prohibits that vary by type and country. For example, use of keywords for alcohol related products are prohibited in Thailand and Turkey; keywords for gambling and casinos are prohibited in Poland; keywords for abortion services are prohibited in Russia and Ukraine; and keywords for adult related services or products are prohibited worldwide as of June 2014.

In March 2020, at the beginning of the Coronavirus crisis, Google blocked all face masks keywords from being eligible for ad targeting as part of a policy to prevent companies from attempting to capitalize on the pandemic.

Cost

Every time a user conducts a search on Google, Google Ads runs an auction in real time determines which search ads are displayed on the search results page as well as the ad's position. The cost of a Google Ads campaign therefore depends on a variety of factors, including the maximum amount an advertiser is willing to pay-per-click of the keyword, and the quality score of the ad (based on its relevance and click frequency and ad extensions). Although an advanced bidding strategy can be used to automatically reach a predefined Cost per action (CPA), this should not be confused with a fixed CPA pricing model.

Conversion Tracking

In addition to tracking clicks, Google Ads provides advertisers an ability to track and report other conversions that happen after the click such as purchases, sign ups or calls. Conversion tracking is implemented by sending an identifier to the advertiser's website as a URL parameter, which is then used by advertiser to send conversions to Google Ads, allowing Google Ads to trace conversion back to the original click for reporting. Google also allows advertisers to install a pixel on their website that sends conversions to the Adwords account. This allows advertisers to target their ads to drive conversions more effectively. For most traffic, Google sends a unique identifier for each click (in a *gclid* parameter), allowing to determine source of conversion precisely. To comply with tracking restrictions on Apple devices, anonymized identifiers that aren't associated with specific person are used (called *wbraid* and *gbraid*). Google Ads provides ability to report many of such anonymous conversions by using "modeled conversions" that combine additional customer details to deduce, which user to attribute the conversion to.

Google Ads can be integrated with Google Analytics 4 (GA4), which can improve conversion tracking effectiveness. This integration allows for a more comprehensive understanding of user interactions across different platforms and devices.

Google Ads introduced enhanced conversions to make conversion measurement more accurate. In 2018, *Bloomberg News* reported that Google had paid millions of dollars to Mastercard for its users' credit card data for offline conversion tracking purposes. The deal had not been publicly announced.

Google Consent Mode

The introduction of Google Consent Mode in 2020 represents an effort by Google to navigate the complex intersection of aggressive digital advertising strategies and the stringent global data privacy standards that regulate them. This feature, which allows advertisers on the Google Ads platform to adjust how cookies are utilized based on user consent, is a response to heightened privacy expectations and legal frameworks such as the European Union's General Data Protection Regulation (GDPR).

While Google presents Consent Mode as a tool that enables advertisers to maintain compliance with privacy laws while minimizing disruption to targeted advertising, its effectiveness and genuineness in protecting user privacy have been subjects of debate. Critics argue that while the tool ostensibly supports compliance, it also allows Google to maintain its dominant position in the digital advertising market by providing a mechanism that superficially addresses privacy concerns without significantly altering the underlying data collection practices.

Moreover, the introduction of advanced features in Consent Mode V2 in late 2023, which includes more granular controls over data usage and conversion modeling based on artificial intelligence, raises further questions. These enhancements aim to mitigate data loss from users who opt out of tracking, thus preserving the efficacy of Google Ads. However, they also underscore the ongoing tension between user privacy and the business imperatives of digital advertising, highlighting the challenges in achieving a true balance between the two.

In this context, Google Consent Mode can be seen both as a strategic adaptation to regulatory pressures and as part of a broader industry trend towards more nuanced data handling practices. Nonetheless, the extent to which these changes genuinely benefit users, as opposed to primarily aiding advertisers and platforms like Google, remains a critical area for scrutiny.

Technology

The AdWords system was initially implemented on top of the MySQL database engine. After the system had been launched, management decided to use Oracle instead but was eventually reverted to MySQL after the system became much slower. Eventually, Google developed a custom distributed Relational database (RD) known as Google Spanner specifically for the needs of the ad business. The interface offers Spreadsheet Editing, Search Query Reports, and conversion metrics.

Lawsuits

Google Ads have been the subject of lawsuits relating to Trademark Law (*Google, Inc. v. American Blind & Wallpaper Factory, Inc.* and *Rescuecom Corp. v. Google Inc.*), fraud (*Goddard v. Google, Inc.*), and click fraud.

Overture Services, Inc. sued Google for patent infringement in April 2002 in relation to the AdWords service. The suit was settled in 2004 after Yahoo! acquired Overture; Google agreed to issue 2.7 million shares of common stock to Yahoo! in exchange for a perpetual license under the patent.

In 2006, Google settled a click fraud lawsuit for US$90 million. In May 2011, Google cancelled the AdWords advertisement purchased by a Dublin sex worker rights group named "Turn Off the Blue Light" (TOBL), claiming that it represented an "egregious violation" of company ad policy by "selling adult sexual services". However, TOBL is a nonprofit campaign for sex worker rights and is not advertising or selling adult sexual services. After TOBL members held a protest outside Google's European headquarters in Dublin and sent in written complaints, Google reviewed the group's website. Google found the website content to be advocating a political position and restored the AdWords advertisement.

In June 2012, Google rejected the Australian Sex Party's ads for AdWords and sponsored search results for the July 12 by-election for the state seat of Melbourne, saying the Australian Sex Party breached its rules which prevent solicitation of donations by a website that did not display tax exempt status. Although the Australian Sex Party amended its website to display tax deductibility information, Google continued to ban the ads. The ads were reinstated on election eve after it was reported in the media that the Australian Sex Party was considering suing Google. On September 13, 2012, the Australian Sex Party lodged formal complaints against Google with the US Department of Justice and the Australian competition watchdog, accusing Google of "unlawful interference in the conduct of a state election in Victoria with corrupt intent" in violation of the Foreign Corrupt Practices Act.

In December 2019, France fined Google €150 million for advertiser suspensions on Google Ads, arguing it had "abused its dominant position by adopting opaque and difficult to understand rules" which it was then free to "interpret and modify" at its own discretion.

In early 2022, Google suspended all ad sales in Russia in response to the ongoing invasion of Ukraine. Over 1,000 Russian businesses that had purchased pre-paid ads, which were neither delivered nor refunded, joined the bankruptcy proceedings of the Russian Google subsidiary.

Controversies

Trademarked Keywords

Google has come under fire for allowing AdWords advertisers to bid on trademarked keywords. In 2004, Google started allowing advertisers to bid on a wide variety of search terms in the US and Canada, including trademarks of their competitors and in May 2008 expanded this policy to the UK and Ireland. Until 2023, advertisers were restricted from using other companies' trademarks in their advertisement text if the trademark has been registered with Advertising Legal Support team.

In March 2010, Google was involved with a trademark infringement case involving three French companies that own Louis Vuitton trademarks. The lawsuit concerned if Google was responsible for advertisers purchasing keywords that violate trademark infringement. Ultimately, the Court of Justice of the European Union ruled that Google AdWords were "not a breach of EU trademark law, but that the content of some advertisements that are linked by Google keywords may well be in breach depending upon the particular facts of the case." Additionally, in some American jurisdictions, the use of a person's name as a keyword for advertising or trade purposes without the person's consent has raised Right to Privacy concerns.

In 2013, the Tenth Circuit Court of Appeals held in *1-800 Contacts, Inc. v. Lens.com, Inc.* that online contact lens seller Lens.com did not commit trademark infringement when it purchased AdWords and other search advertisements using competitor 1-800 Contacts' federally registered 1800 CONTACTS trademark as a keyword. In August 2016, the Federal Trade Commission filed an administrative complaint against 1-800 Contacts alleging that its search advertising trademark enforcement practices have unreasonably restrained competition in violation of the FTC Act. 1-800 Contacts has denied all wrongdoing and is scheduled to appear before an FTC administrative law judge in April 2017.

IT Support Ban

In 2018, Google implemented a policy change that restricts the advertising of consumer technical support, including services related to troubleshooting, security, virus removal, internet connectivity, online accounts (such as password resets or login support), or software installation", Google's Director of Global Product Policy, David Graff stated that the policy was intended to "address abuse" and "fraudulent activity" from third-party technical support providers, and that a verification program for legitimate providers would be rolled out "in the coming months". This is yet to manifest, resulting in an effective ban on all IT support and repair related services on the Google Ads platform. Commentators have expressed concerns that this is an attempt by Google to stifle consumers' right to repair electronic devices.

Use by Fossil Fuel Companies for Greenwashing

Fossil fuel companies, funders and public relations agencies including ExxonMobil, Shell, Aramco, McKinsey, and Goldman Sachs are among the largest customers of Google Ads. One in five Google Ads for climate-related terms (e.g. net zero, carbon storage, carbon capture and energy transition) were paid by fossil fuel companies. A study by *The Guardian* and InfluenceMap found that Shell's ads appeared on 86% of searches for "net zero". Over half of users in a 2020 survey could not tell the difference between a normal Google result and a Google Ad. One of the study's authors, InfluenceMap stated "Google is letting groups with a vested interest in the continued use of fossil fuels pay to influence the resources people receive when they are trying to educate themselves. The oil and gas sector has moved away from contesting the science of climate change and now instead seeks to influence public discussions about decarbonization in its favor."

Anti-Abortion Clinics

A report conducted by the Tech Transparency Project found that women from low-income areas in US cities are more likely to be targeted by anti-abortion crisis pregnancy centers than women in wealthier areas of the city. Many of these crisis centers have portrayed themselves as abortion clinics while advocating anti-abortion measures for pregnant women. The research was conducted in Atlanta, Miami, and Phoenix with women from three different income brackets, using the phrases "abortion clinic near me" and "I want an abortion." According to the results, Phoenix showed a 16% increase in crisis center recommendations from low to middle income, while there was a 49% difference when compared to high-income areas.

5.3.2 Bing Ads

Microsoft Advertising (formerly Bing Ads) is an online advertising platform developed by Microsoft, where advertisers bid to display brief ads, service offers, product listings and videos to web users. It provides pay per click advertising on search engines Bing, Yahoo! and DuckDuckGo, as well as on other websites, mobile apps, and videos. In 2021, Microsoft Advertising surpassed US$10 billion in annual revenue.

History

Microsoft was the last of the "big three" search engines (which also includes Google and Yahoo!) to develop its own system for delivering pay per click (PPC) ads. Until the beginning of 2006, all of the ads displayed on the MSN Search engine were supplied by Overture (and later Yahoo!). MSN collected a portion of the ad revenue in return for displaying Yahoo!'s ads on its search engine.

As search marketing grew, Microsoft began developing its own system, MSN adCenter, for selling PPC advertisements directly to advertisers. As the system was phased in, MSN Search (now Bing) showed Yahoo! and adCenter advertising in its search results. Microsoft effort to create AdCenter was led by Tarek Najm, then general manager of the MSN division of Microsoft. In June 2006, the contract between Yahoo! and Microsoft had expired and Microsoft was displaying only ads from adCenter until 2010.

In November 2006 Microsoft acquired Deep Metrix, a company situated in Gatineau, Canada, that created web-analytics software. Microsoft has built a new product adCenter Analytics based on the acquired technology. In October, 2007 the beta version of Microsoft Project Gatineau was released to a limited number of participants.

In May 2007, Microsoft agreed to purchase the digital marketing solutions parent company, aQuantive, for roughly $6 billion. Microsoft later resold Atlas, a key piece of the aQuantive acquisition, to Facebook in 2013.

Microsoft acquired ScreenTonic on May 3, 2007, AdECN on July 26, 2007, and YaData on February 27, 2008, and merged their technologies into adCenter.

On February 23, 2009, the Publisher Leadership Council was created under the umbrella of Microsoft Advertising. The council was responsible for delivering the next-generation advertising platform for the publishers of digital media resulting in the formation of Microsoft pubCenter.

In January 2010, Microsoft announced a deal in which it would take over the functional operation of Yahoo! Search, and set up a joint venture to sell advertising on both Yahoo! Search and Bing known as the Microsoft Search Alliance. A complete transition of all Yahoo! sponsored ad clients to Microsoft adCenter occurred in October 2010.

On September 10, 2012, adCenter was renamed to Bing Ads, and the Search Alliance was renamed the Yahoo! Bing Network.

In April 2015, the Yahoo! partnership was modified; Yahoo! Search will only have to feature Bing results on the "majority" of desktop traffic, leaving the company open to "enhance the search experience" non-exclusively on both desktop and mobile. Additionally, Microsoft will take over as the exclusive seller of ads delivered through Bing; Yahoo! will sell its own ads through its new in-house Gemini platform.

On June 29, 2015, AOL Inc. announced a deal and partnership to take over the majority of Microsoft's ad sales business. Under the pact, AOL will take over the sale of display, video, and mobile ads on various Microsoft platforms in nine countries, including Brazil, Canada, the United States, and the United Kingdom. As many as 1200 Microsoft employees involved with the business will be transferred to AOL. In turn, AOL's properties will replace Google Search with Bing, and display Bing Ads sold by Microsoft.

In May 2018, Bing Ads released additional productivity and time-saving tools for users managing their campaigns via Bing Ads Editor. On April 30, 2019, Bing Ads was re-branded to Microsoft Ads. On August 5, 2019, Microsoft acquired PromoteIQ, a leading provider of vendor marketing technology to online retailers and brands. On December 21, 2021, Microsoft announced its plans to acquire Xandr from AT&T. Six months later, Microsoft disclosed that the acquisition had been completed.

Technology

Similar to Google Ads, Microsoft Ads uses both the maximum amount an advertiser is willing to pay per click (PPC) on their ad and the advertisement's click-through rate (CTR) to determine how frequently an advertisement is shown. This system encourages advertisers to write effective ads and to advertise only on searches which are relevant to their advertisement.

In 2021, Microsoft Ads began rolling out LinkedIn audience observation and bid management targeting, allowing advertisers to monitor and bid against common LinkedIn Ads audiences, including company size, industry, job function, as well as lists of individual companies.

Similar to Google Ads Editor, Microsoft Ads provides a desktop tool to manage campaigns offline, called Microsoft Ads Editor. Using this editor you can make offline changes to your campaigns and later sync it online. Microsoft Ads also provides APIs that can be used to manage advertising campaigns.

5.3.3 Beyond Google Ads and Bing Ads

While Google Ads and Bing Ads dominate the online advertising landscape, several other ad platforms offer unique targeting options and advertising opportunities for businesses looking to diversify their ad spend and reach new audiences.

Facebook Ads

- Reach over 2.8 billion monthly active users on Facebook and Instagram with targeted ads based on demographics, interests, and behavior.

- Leverage advanced targeting options such as custom audiences, lookalike audiences, and retargeting to reach specific audience segments and drive conversions.
- Experiment with various ad formats, including image ads, video ads, carousel ads, and lead ads, to engage users and achieve your campaign objectives.

LinkedIn Ads

- Target professionals and businesses on LinkedIn with ads tailored to their industry, job title, company size, and other professional attributes.
- Utilize LinkedIn's robust targeting options to reach decision-makers and influencers within your target industries and drive high-quality leads and conversions.
- Leverage sponsored content, sponsored InMail, and text ads to engage users across LinkedIn's platform and achieve your marketing goals.

Twitter Ads

- Promote your tweets, accounts, or trends on Twitter to reach users based on their interests, keywords, and demographics.
- Utilize Twitter's targeting options, including keyword targeting, interest targeting, and follower targeting, to reach relevant audiences and drive engagement.
- Experiment with different ad formats, such as promoted tweets, promoted accounts, and promoted trends, to maximize reach and engagement on the platform.

5.4 CONVERSIONS RATE OPTIMIZATION FOR PPC

Crafting a Pay-Per-Click (PPC) campaign isn't solely about getting clicks—it's about converting those clicks into valuable actions, whether it's a purchase, a sign-up, or any other desired outcome. That's where Conversion Rate Optimization (CRO) comes into play.

Conversion Rate Optimization (CRO) is essential for maximizing the effectiveness and ROI of your PPC campaigns. By focusing on key components such as landing page optimization, ad messaging, user experience, and continuous testing, you can improve conversion rates and drive meaningful results for your business. With a data-driven approach and a commitment to ongoing optimization, you can unlock the full potential of your PPC campaigns and achieve your conversion goals efficiently and effectively in the competitive digital landscape.

5.4.1 Understanding Conversion Rate Optimization (CRO) for PPC

Conversion Rate Optimization (CRO) refers to the process of enhancing your PPC campaigns to improve the percentage of visitors who complete a desired action, often referred to as a conversion. These actions can vary depending on your campaign objectives, ranging from making a purchase to filling out a contact form or downloading an eBook.

5.4.2 Key Components of Conversion Rate Optimization for PPC

Clear Conversion Goals

- Define specific and measurable conversion goals for your PPC campaigns. Whether it's sales, leads, or sign-ups, clarity on your objectives is crucial for effective optimization.
- Align your conversion goals with your overall business objectives to ensure consistency and relevance.

Optimized Landing Pages

- Design landing pages that are tailored to the intent of your PPC ads and provide a seamless user experience.
- Keep landing pages focused and clutter-free, with a clear headline, compelling copy, prominent call-to-action (CTA), and relevant imagery.
- Implement A/B testing to experiment with different landing page elements and layouts to identify the most effective variations.

Relevant Ad Messaging

- Ensure that your ad copy aligns with the content and messaging of your landing pages to maintain a consistent user experience.
- Highlight the unique value proposition (UVP) of your offer in your ad copy to entice users to click through and convert.
- Test different ad variations to identify the most compelling messaging that resonates with your target audience.

User-Friendly Forms

- Streamline your conversion process by optimizing the forms on your landing pages.
- Keep forms short and simple, only asking for essential information required to complete the conversion.
- Use form validation and inline error messages to guide users and reduce friction in form submission.

Compelling CTAs

- Use clear and compelling CTAs that encourage users to take the desired action, whether it's "Buy Now," "Sign Up," or "Download Now."
- Experiment with different CTA styles, colors, and placement to optimize click-through and conversion rates.
- Create a sense of urgency or scarcity in your CTAs to prompt immediate action from users.

Mobile Optimization

- Ensure that your landing pages are optimized for mobile devices to cater to the growing number of mobile users.
- Use responsive design to adapt your landing pages to various screen sizes and resolutions.
- Optimize page load times and minimize friction in the conversion process on mobile devices.

Personalization and Targeting

- Leverage audience segmentation and targeting to deliver personalized experiences to different user segments.
- Create tailored landing pages and ad messaging for specific audience segments based on demographics, interests, or behavior.
- Use dynamic keyword insertion (DKI) to customize ad copy based on the search query, increasing relevance and click-through rates.

5.4.3 Strategies for Success

Data-Driven Optimization

- Use data analytics and tracking tools to monitor key metrics such as conversion rate, bounce rate, and average session duration.
- Conduct thorough A/B testing and multivariate testing to identify optimization opportunities and validate hypotheses.
- Continuously analyze performance data and iterate on your PPC campaigns to improve conversion rates over time.

Conversion Funnel Analysis

- Analyze the conversion funnel to identify potential bottlenecks or points of friction that may be hindering conversion.
- Identify areas for optimization at each stage of the funnel, from ad impression to post-conversion follow-up.

- Implement targeted strategies to address specific pain points and improve overall funnel performance.

Remarketing and Retargeting

- Implement remarketing campaigns to re-engage users who have previously interacted with your website or shown interest in your products or services.
- Tailor your remarketing ads and messaging based on users' previous interactions to encourage them to complete the desired action.
- Use dynamic remarketing to display personalized ads featuring products or services that users have previously viewed or shown interest in.

Continuous Testing and Iteration

- Adopt a culture of continuous testing and iteration to uncover insights and optimize performance.
- Test different elements of your PPC campaigns, including ad copy, landing page design, and targeting options, to identify what resonates best with your audience.
- Regularly review and update your conversion goals and KPIs based on changing business objectives and market conditions.

Cross-Channel Optimization

- Integrate your PPC campaigns with other marketing channels, such as email marketing, social media, and content marketing, to create a cohesive and integrated customer experience.
- Leverage cross-channel data and insights to optimize messaging, targeting, and conversion strategies across multiple touchpoints.
- Implement cross-channel attribution models to accurately measure the impact of each channel on overall conversion performance.

Competitive Analysis

- Monitor competitors' PPC activities and performance to identify potential opportunities and areas for improvement.
- Benchmark your conversion rates against industry averages and top competitors to set realistic goals and performance targets.
- Identify gaps or weaknesses in competitors' conversion strategies and capitalize on them to gain a competitive advantage.

5.5 PPC ANALYTICS AND OPTIMIZATION

PPC (Pay-Per-Click) advertising is a dynamic and data-driven marketing channel that requires continuous monitoring and optimization to maximize ROI (Return on Investment). PPC analytics and optimization are essential components of a successful digital advertising strategy. By tracking key performance metrics, analyzing campaign data, and implementing optimization strategies, advertisers can improve ad effectiveness, increase conversion rates, and maximize ROI. With continuous monitoring, testing, and iteration, advertisers can stay ahead of the competition and achieve their marketing objectives efficiently and effectively in the ever-evolving digital landscape.

5.5.1 Importance of PPC Analytics

PPC analytics play a crucial role in understanding campaign performance, identifying areas for improvement, and making data-driven decisions to optimize ad spend and maximize ROI. By analyzing PPC data, advertisers can gain insights into audience behavior, ad effectiveness, and conversion trends, enabling them to refine targeting, messaging, and bidding strategies for better results.

Key Benefits of PPC Analytics

- **Performance Evaluation:** Track key performance metrics such as click-through rate (CTR), conversion rate, cost per acquisition (CPA), and return on ad spend (ROAS) to evaluate the effectiveness of PPC campaigns.
- **Audience Insights:** Gain insights into audience demographics, interests, and behavior to better understand target audiences and tailor ad messaging and targeting accordingly.
- **Ad Testing:** Conduct A/B testing and multivariate testing to experiment with different ad creatives, landing pages, and targeting options and identify what resonates best with your audience.
- **Budget Allocation:** Monitor budget utilization and performance metrics to allocate ad spend effectively across campaigns, ad groups, and keywords, maximizing ROI and minimizing wasted spend.
- **Competitive Analysis:** Analyze competitors' PPC activities and performance to identify opportunities and threats, benchmark performance against industry averages, and gain a competitive edge.

5.5.2 Key Metrics to Track

Click-Through Rate (CTR)

- CTR measures the percentage of users who click on your ads after seeing them.

- A high CTR indicates that your ads are relevant and compelling to your target audience.

Conversion Rate

- Conversion rate measures the percentage of users who complete a desired action, such as making a purchase or filling out a form, after clicking on your ads.
- A high conversion rate indicates that your ads and landing pages are effectively converting clicks into actions.

Cost Per Click (CPC)

- CPC measures the average cost you pay each time a user clicks on your ads.
- Monitoring CPC helps you optimize bidding strategies and maximize ROI by ensuring you're not overpaying for clicks.

Cost Per Acquisition (CPA)

- CPA measures the average cost you pay to acquire a new customer or lead through your PPC campaigns.
- Lowering CPA through optimization tactics like improved ad targeting and landing page optimization can increase campaign profitability.

Quality Score

- Quality Score is a metric used by search engines to evaluate the relevance and quality of your ads and landing pages.
- A higher Quality Score can lead to lower CPCs and better ad positions, resulting in improved campaign performance and ROI.

Return on Ad Spend (ROAS)

- ROAS measures the revenue generated for every dollar spent on advertising.
- A ROAS of 3:1, for example, means you're generating $3 in revenue for every $1 spent on ads.

5.5.3 Strategies for PPC Optimization

Keyword Optimization

- Conduct keyword research to identify relevant and high-performing keywords for your campaigns.
- Continuously monitor keyword performance and adjust bids, match types, and negative keywords to improve relevancy and efficiency.

Ad Copy Optimization

- Write compelling ad copy that highlights unique selling points, benefits, and calls-to-action.
- Test different ad variations to identify what resonates best with your audience and drives higher CTRs and conversion rates.

Landing Page Optimization

- Optimize landing pages for relevance, clarity, and conversion.
- Ensure landing pages align with ad messaging, load quickly, and provide a seamless user experience across devices.

Ad Extensions

- Use ad extensions such as site links, callouts, and structured snippets to provide additional information and improve ad visibility and CTRs.

Device Targeting

- Segment campaigns by device (desktop, mobile, tablet) and adjust bids and messaging based on device performance and user behavior.

Ad Scheduling

- Schedule ads to display at times when your target audience is most active and likely to convert.
- Use ad scheduling to allocate budget more efficiently and maximize ROI during peak times.

Remarketing and Retargeting

- Implement remarketing campaigns to re-engage users who have previously visited your website or interacted with your ads.
- Tailor ad messaging and offers based on users' previous interactions to encourage them to complete the desired action.

5.5.4 Continuous Monitoring and Optimization

PPC optimization is an ongoing process that requires continuous monitoring, testing, and iteration to achieve optimal results.

By regularly analyzing performance data, testing different strategies, and making data-driven adjustments, advertisers can improve campaign efficiency, increase conversion rates, and maximize ROI over time.

Key Optimization Practices

- **Regular Monitoring**: Monitor campaign performance metrics regularly to identify trends, anomalies, and areas for improvement.
- **A/B Testing**: Test different ad variations, landing page designs, and targeting options to identify what resonates best with your audience.
- **Data Analysis:** Use data analytics tools and reports to analyze campaign performance, identify optimization opportunities, and make informed decisions.
- **Optimization Tools**: Utilize PPC management tools and automation features to streamline campaign management and optimization processes.
- **Adaptation:** Stay updated on industry trends, algorithm changes, and best practices to adapt your strategies and tactics accordingly.

CHAPTER 6
EMAIL MARKETING

6.1 THE POWER OF EMAIL IN DIGITAL MARKETING

Email remains one of the most powerful and effective tools in digital marketing, providing businesses with a direct and cost-effective way to engage with their audience, nurture leads, and drive conversions. Email marketing remains a powerful and effective tool for businesses to engage with their audience, nurture leads, and drive conversions.

By following best practices, implementing targeted strategies, and leveraging automation tools, businesses can maximize the impact of their email campaigns and achieve their marketing objectives efficiently and effectively in today's competitive digital landscape.

With its ability to deliver personalized, timely, and relevant messages to subscribers, email marketing continues to be a valuable asset for businesses looking to grow and succeed online.

6.1.1 The Importance of Email Marketing

Email marketing continues to be a cornerstone of digital marketing strategies for businesses of all sizes and industries. Its enduring popularity is due to several key factors:

- **Direct Communication:** Email allows businesses to communicate directly with their audience, delivering targeted messages to subscribers' inboxes.
- **Cost-Effective:** Compared to other marketing channels, email marketing is highly cost-effective, offering an impressive return on investment (ROI).
- **Personalization:** Email enables businesses to personalize messages based on subscriber preferences, behaviors, and demographics, increasing engagement and relevance.
- **Automation:** Automation tools allow businesses to send targeted emails based on triggers such as user actions or specific time intervals, streamlining the marketing process.

- **Measurable Results:** Email marketing platforms provide detailed analytics and reporting, allowing businesses to track metrics such as open rates, click-through rates, and conversions, and optimize campaigns accordingly.

6.1.2 Key Benefits of Email Marketing

- **Audience Engagement:** Email marketing allows businesses to engage with their audience on a one-to-one basis, fostering relationships and building trust over time.
- **Lead Nurturing:** Email campaigns can be used to nurture leads through the sales funnel, providing valuable content and offers to move prospects closer to conversion.
- **Customer Retention:** Email is an effective tool for retaining customers and encouraging repeat purchases through targeted offers, promotions, and loyalty programs.
- **Brand Awareness:** Regular email communication keeps your brand top-of-mind with subscribers, increasing brand awareness and recognition.
- **Drive Conversions:** Email campaigns can drive immediate action from subscribers, whether it's making a purchase, signing up for a webinar, or downloading a resource.

6.1.3 Best Practices for Email Marketing

- **Build a Quality Email List:** Focus on growing an engaged and opt-in email list by offering valuable incentives such as discounts, content, or exclusive access.
- **Segmentation:** Segment your email list based on factors such as demographics, purchase history, or engagement level to deliver more targeted and relevant messages.
- **Personalization:** Use subscriber data to personalize email content, including recipient's name, past purchases, or preferences, to increase engagement and response rates.
- **Compelling Subject Lines:** Craft attention-grabbing subject lines that entice recipients to open your emails, avoiding spammy language and excessive punctuation.
- **Mobile Optimization:** Optimize email templates and designs for mobile devices to ensure a seamless user experience for subscribers on smartphones and tablets.

- **Clear Call-to-Action (CTA):** Include a clear and compelling call-to-action (CTA) in your emails to prompt recipients to take the desired action, whether it's clicking through to your website or making a purchase.
- **Testing and Optimization:** A/B test different elements of your emails, including subject lines, content, images, and CTAs, to identify what resonates best with your audience and optimize performance.
- **Provide Value:** Focus on providing value to subscribers with informative content, helpful tips, exclusive offers, and relevant promotions, rather than solely promoting products or services.
- **Monitor and Analyze:** Track key metrics such as open rates, click-through rates, conversion rates, and unsubscribe rates to measure the effectiveness of your email campaigns and make data-driven decisions for improvement.

6.1.4 Strategies for Success

- **Welcome Series:** Create a series of automated welcome emails to introduce new subscribers to your brand, provide valuable information, and encourage engagement.
- **Drip Campaigns:** Develop automated drip campaigns that deliver a series of targeted emails over time based on subscriber actions or interests, guiding them through the buyer's journey.
- **Cart Abandonment Emails:** Send targeted emails to users who abandon their carts on your website, reminding them of items left behind and incentivizing them to complete their purchase.
- **Re-engagement Campaigns:** Re-engage inactive subscribers with targeted emails designed to win back their interest and encourage them to re-engage with your brand.
- **Promotional Campaigns:** Use email to promote sales, discounts, and special offers to drive immediate action and boost revenue.
- **Educational Content:** Provide educational content such as how-to guides, tutorials, and industry insights to position your brand as a trusted resource and build credibility with subscribers.
- **Customer Feedback:** Solicit feedback from customers through surveys or feedback forms sent via email, demonstrating that you value their input and are committed to improving their experience.

6.2 DEVELOPING AN EMAIL MARKETING STRATEGY

Developing an effective email marketing strategy is essential for businesses looking to engage with their audience, nurture leads, and drive conversions. Developing an email marketing strategy requires careful planning, audience segmentation, content creation, automation, and ongoing optimization. By setting clear goals, understanding your audience, choosing the right tools, planning your content, implementing automation, designing engaging emails, and measuring performance, you can create effective email campaigns that drive results and contribute to the success of your business. With the power of email marketing, businesses can engage with their audience, nurture leads, and build lasting relationships that drive growth and revenue over time.

6.2.1 Define Your Goals

Before diving into email marketing, it's essential to define clear and measurable goals for your campaigns. Common objectives include:

- Increasing sales or revenue.
- Generating leads or sign-ups.
- Building brand awareness.
- Driving website traffic.
- Improving customer retention or loyalty.

Having well-defined goals will guide your strategy and help you measure the success of your email campaigns.

6.2.2 Understand Your Audience

Understanding your audience is crucial for creating targeted and relevant email campaigns. Conduct market research and gather data on your audience's demographics, preferences, behaviors, and pain points. Segment your email list based on factors such as:

- Demographics (age, gender, location).
- Purchase history.
- Engagement level.
- Interests or preferences.

Segmentation allows you to tailor your email content to different audience segments, increasing relevance and engagement.

6.2.3 Choose the Right Email Marketing Platform

Selecting the right email marketing platform is essential for managing your campaigns efficiently and effectively. Consider factors such as ease of use, automation capabilities, reporting and analytics features, and integration with other tools and platforms. Popular email marketing platforms include:

- Mailchimp.
- Constant Contact.
- Campaign Monitor.
- HubSpot.
- ActiveCampaign.

Choose a platform that aligns with your budget, goals, and technical requirements.

6.2.4 Plan Your Content

Develop a content plan that aligns with your goals, audience, and brand messaging. Create a content calendar to schedule your email campaigns and ensure a consistent and timely delivery of content.

Types of email content to consider include:

- Welcome emails for new subscribers.
- Educational or informative content.
- Promotional offers or discounts.
- Product updates or announcements.
- Customer testimonials or case studies.
- Newsletters with curated content or industry insights.

Tailor your content to each audience segment and stage of the buyer's journey, providing value and relevance to recipients.

6.2.5 Implement Automation

Utilize automation to streamline your email marketing processes and deliver personalized experiences to subscribers. Set up automated workflows triggered by user actions or specific time intervals, such as:

- Welcome series for new subscribers.
- Abandoned cart recovery emails.
- Birthday or anniversary emails.
- Re-engagement campaigns for inactive subscribers.
- Lead nurturing sequences based on user behavior.

Automation allows you to deliver timely and targeted messages without manual intervention, increasing efficiency and scalability.

6.2.6 Design Engaging Emails

Design visually appealing and mobile-responsive email templates that reflect your brand identity and messaging. Pay attention to elements such as:

- Eye-catching subject lines to entice recipients to open your emails.
- Clear and compelling calls-to-action (CTAs) to prompt action.
- Consistent branding and design elements for brand recognition.
- Personalization elements such as dynamic content or merge tags.
- Mobile optimization for a seamless user experience on smartphones and tablets.

Test your email templates across different devices and email clients to ensure compatibility and usability.

6.2.7 Measure and Optimize

Track key metrics and performance indicators to evaluate the effectiveness of your email campaigns. Common metrics to monitor include:

- **Open Rate:** The percentage of recipients who open your emails
- **Click-Through Rate (CTR):** The percentage of recipients who click on links within your emails
- **Conversion Rate:** The percentage of recipients who complete a desired action, such as making a purchase or signing up
- **Bounce Rate:** The percentage of emails that are returned as undeliverable
- **Unsubscribe Rate:** The percentage of recipients who opt out of receiving future emails

Use A/B testing to experiment with different subject lines, content, CTAs, and sending times to identify what resonates best with your audience. Analyze the data to uncover insights and trends, and use this information to optimize your email marketing strategy over time.

6.3 EMAIL DESIGN AND CONTENT BEST PRACTICES

6.3.1 Email Design

Email design plays a critical role in the success of email marketing campaigns. A well-designed email not only captures the recipient's attention but also encourages engagement, clicks, and conversions. Effective email design is essential for capturing the recipient's attention, driving engagement, and achieving your marketing goals. By following key principles, best practices, and leveraging design tools and templates, you can create visually appealing and impactful email campaigns that resonate with your audience and deliver results. With a well-designed email strategy in place, businesses can effectively communicate with subscribers, build brand loyalty, and drive conversions in today's competitive digital landscape.

Importance of Email Design

Email design is more than just aesthetics; it's about creating a user experience that resonates with your audience and drives desired actions. Here's why email design matters:

- **First Impression**: The design of your email is the first thing recipients see when they open it, influencing their initial perception of your brand and message.
- **Brand Identity**: Consistent branding elements such as colors, fonts, and imagery help reinforce your brand identity and build brand recognition among subscribers.
- **Engagement**: Well-designed emails are visually appealing and capture the recipient's attention, increasing the likelihood of engagement with your content and CTAs.
- **Mobile Optimization**: With a growing number of users accessing emails on mobile devices, responsive design is crucial for ensuring a seamless user experience across devices and screen sizes.

Key Principles of Email Design

- **Clarity and Simplicity**: Keep your email design clean and clutter-free, with a clear hierarchy of information and a single focused message.
- **Consistency**: Maintain consistent branding elements throughout your email, including colors, fonts, logos, and imagery, to reinforce brand identity and recognition.
- **Visual Hierarchy**: Use visual cues such as size, color, and placement to guide the recipient's attention and highlight important elements such as CTAs and key messages.
- **Whitespace**: Use whitespace effectively to create breathing room between elements and improve readability, ensuring your content is easy to digest and understand.
- **Accessibility**: Design your emails with accessibility in mind, ensuring they are readable and usable for all recipients, including those with disabilities.

Best Practices for Email Design

- **Responsive Design:** Ensure your emails are optimized for mobile devices with responsive design techniques, including fluid layouts, scalable images, and mobile-friendly CTAs.
- **Eye-Catching Subject Line:** Pair your well-designed email with an attention-grabbing subject line that entices recipients to open and engage with your content.
- **Clear Call-to-Action (CTA):** Use a prominent and compelling CTA button that stands out from the rest of the email and clearly communicates the desired action.
- **Imagery:** Incorporate high-quality images and graphics that support your message and enhance visual appeal, but avoid overloading your email with excessive imagery.
- **Typography:** Choose web-safe fonts that are easy to read and render well across different email clients and devices, and use font sizes and styles to create hierarchy and emphasis.
- **Whitespace and Layout:** Use whitespace strategically to create a sense of balance and organization in your email design, and experiment with different layout options to find what works best for your content.
- **Preview Text:** Optimize your preview text to provide additional context and incentive for recipients to open your email, complementing the subject line and driving engagement.

Examples of Effective Email Designs

- **Promotional Emails:** A well-designed promotional email from an e-commerce retailer may feature striking product imagery, clear pricing information, and a compelling CTA button.
- **Newsletter Emails:** Newsletter emails often use a clean and structured layout, with clear section headers, concise summaries, and visually appealing imagery or graphics.
- **Welcome Emails:** Welcome emails typically have a friendly and inviting design, with a personalized greeting, an introduction to the brand or service, and a clear call-to-action to get started.
- **Event or Announcement Emails:** Emails announcing upcoming events or new product launches may feature bold headlines, eye-catching visuals, and a sense of urgency to encourage immediate action.

Tools for Email Design

- **Email Marketing Platforms:** Popular email marketing platforms such as Mailchimp, Constant Contact, and Campaign Monitor offer built-in email design tools and templates to help you create professional-looking emails with ease.
- **Graphic Design Software:** Design tools like Adobe Photoshop, Illustrator, or Canva allow you to create custom graphics and imagery for your emails, giving you full control over the design process.
- **HTML/CSS Templates:** HTML email templates provide a starting point for designing custom email layouts, allowing you to customize colors, fonts, and styles to match your brand identity.

6.3.2 Content Best Practices

Content marketing has become a cornerstone of digital strategy for businesses across industries. From improving search engine rankings to building brand authority and engaging with target audiences, content plays a pivotal role in achieving various marketing objectives.

Content marketing is a powerful tool for businesses to attract, engage, and retain customers in today's digital landscape. By following these best practices and focusing on delivering valuable, relevant, and compelling content to your audience, you can create meaningful connections, build brand authority, and drive tangible results for your business. With a strategic approach to content creation and distribution, businesses can leverage the power of content marketing to achieve their marketing goals and stay ahead of the competition.

Know Your Audience

Understanding your audience is paramount to crafting content that resonates with them. Conduct market research, analyze customer data, and develop buyer personas to gain insights into their demographics, preferences, pain points, and behaviors. Tailor your content to address their needs and interests, ensuring it's relevant and valuable to them.

Set Clear Goals

Before creating content, define clear and measurable goals that align with your overall marketing objectives. Whether it's increasing brand awareness, generating leads, driving website traffic, or boosting sales, having specific goals will guide your content strategy and help you measure success effectively.

Provide Value

Focus on creating content that provides genuine value to your audience. Whether it's educational resources, helpful tips, entertaining stories, or practical solutions to their problems, aim to inform, inspire, or entertain your audience with every piece of content you create.

Quality Over Quantity

While consistency is important in content marketing, quality should always take precedence over quantity. Focus on producing high-quality, well-researched, and engaging content that delivers real value to your audience, rather than churning out content for the sake of it.

Variety of Formats

Experiment with a variety of content formats to cater to different preferences and consumption habits. From blog posts, articles, and ebooks to videos, infographics, podcasts, and interactive content, diversifying your content formats can help you reach a wider audience and keep them engaged.

Search Engine Optimization (SEO)

Optimize your content for search engines to improve visibility and attract organic traffic. Conduct keyword research to identify relevant keywords and incorporate them naturally into your content, including titles, headings, meta descriptions, and body copy. Focus on creating valuable, relevant, and user-friendly content that addresses search intent and provides a positive user experience.

Compelling Headlines

Craft attention-grabbing headlines that entice readers to click and engage with your content. Use power words, numbers, questions, and emotional triggers to pique curiosity and spark interest. Experiment with different headline formulas and analyze performance to identify what resonates best with your audience.

Engaging Visuals

Incorporate compelling visuals such as images, videos, infographics, and illustrations to enhance your content and make it more engaging and shareable. Visual content not only captures attention but also conveys information more effectively and leaves a lasting impression on your audience.

Authenticity and Transparency

Be authentic and transparent in your content to build trust and credibility with your audience. Share behind-the-scenes insights, customer stories, and personal anecdotes to humanize your brand and connect with your audience on a deeper level.

Consistent Branding

Maintain consistent branding across all your content to reinforce brand identity and recognition. Use brand colors, fonts, logos, and messaging consistently across different channels and content formats to create a cohesive and memorable brand experience.

Call-to-Action (CTA)

Include clear and compelling calls-to-action (CTAs) in your content to prompt desired actions from your audience. Whether it's signing up for a newsletter, downloading a resource, or making a purchase, guide your audience towards the next step in their journey with persuasive CTAs that drive action.

Audience Engagement

Encourage audience engagement and interaction with your content by inviting comments, questions, and feedback. Respond promptly to comments and messages, and actively participate in conversations to foster a sense of community and build relationships with your audience.

Measure and Iterate

Track key performance metrics such as website traffic, engagement, conversions, and ROI to evaluate the effectiveness of your content marketing efforts. Use analytics tools and performance data to identify what's working well and what needs improvement, and iterate on your content strategy accordingly.

6.4 SEGMENTATION, PERSONALIZATION AND AUTOMATION

Segmentation, personalization, and automation are integral components of effective email marketing strategies. By leveraging these techniques, businesses can deliver targeted, relevant, and timely messages to their subscribers, leading to higher engagement, increased conversions, and improved overall performance of email campaigns.

Segmentation, personalization, and automation are essential strategies for optimizing email marketing campaigns and driving results. By segmenting your email list, personalizing your content, and automating your workflows, businesses can deliver targeted, relevant, and timely messages to their audience, leading to higher engagement, increased conversions, and improved ROI. With the right tools, tactics, and best practices in place, businesses can leverage segmentation, personalization, and automation to create more effective and efficient email marketing campaigns that deliver tangible results and contribute to their overall marketing success.

6.4.1 Segmentation in Email Marketing

Segmentation involves dividing your email list into smaller, more targeted segments based on specific criteria such as demographics, behaviors, preferences, or purchase history. Segmentation allows businesses to tailor their email campaigns to different audience segments, ensuring that the content is relevant and valuable to each group of recipients.

Benefits of Segmentation

- **Improved Relevance**: Segmented emails are more relevant to recipients' interests and needs, leading to higher engagement rates and lower unsubscribe rates.
- **Higher Conversion Rates**: By delivering targeted messages to segmented audiences, businesses can increase the likelihood of recipients taking desired actions, such as making a purchase or signing up for a webinar.
- **Better Email Deliverability**: Segmented email lists often result in higher engagement metrics, which can positively impact email deliverability and inbox placement rates.
- **Optimized Resources**: Segmenting your email list allows you to allocate resources more efficiently by focusing on high-priority segments that are most likely to generate results.

Best Practices for Segmentation

- **Collect Relevant Data:** Gather data on your subscribers' demographics, behaviors, preferences, and purchase history to inform your segmentation strategy.
- **Define Segmentation Criteria:** Determine the criteria you'll use to segment your email list, such as age, gender, location, past purchases, or engagement level.
- **Create Targeted Content**: Develop tailored content for each segment based on their interests, needs, and preferences, ensuring that the messaging resonates with recipients.
- **Test and Iterate**: Continuously test different segmentation strategies and iterate based on performance metrics to optimize your email campaigns over time.

6.4.2 Personalization in Email Marketing

Personalization involves customizing email content and messaging to individual recipients based on their preferences, behaviors, or past interactions with your brand. Personalized emails go beyond simply addressing recipients by name; they deliver relevant content and offers that speak directly to each recipient's unique needs and interests.

Benefits of Personalization

- **Increased Engagement**: Personalized emails are more likely to capture recipients' attention and elicit a response, leading to higher open rates, click-through rates, and conversion rates.
- **Improved Customer Experience**: Personalized emails demonstrate that you understand and care about your subscribers' preferences, enhancing their overall experience with your brand.
- **Enhanced Brand Loyalty**: By delivering personalized content and offers, businesses can strengthen relationships with their subscribers and foster long-term loyalty.
- **Higher ROI**: Personalized emails have been shown to generate higher returns on investment compared to non-personalized emails, making personalization a valuable investment for businesses.

Best Practices for Personalization

- **Use Dynamic Content**: Incorporate dynamic content blocks in your emails to personalize messaging, product recommendations, or offers based on recipients' past behavior or preferences.
- **Segmentation-Based Personalization**: Combine segmentation with personalization to deliver highly targeted emails that address specific audience segments' needs and interests.
- **Behavioral Triggers**: Implement automated triggers based on recipients' actions or behaviors, such as abandoned cart emails, re-engagement campaigns, or post-purchase follow-ups.
- **A/B Testing**: Test different personalization tactics, such as subject lines, content, or offers, to identify what resonates best with your audience and drives the highest engagement and conversions.

6.4.3 Automation in Email Marketing

Automation involves using technology to automate repetitive tasks and workflows, such as sending welcome emails, nurturing leads, or re-engaging inactive subscribers.

Email automation allows businesses to deliver timely and relevant messages to their audience without manual intervention, saving time and resources while maximizing efficiency and effectiveness.

Benefits of Automation

- **Increased Efficiency:** Automation streamlines the email marketing process, allowing businesses to send targeted messages at scale without manual effort.
- **Timely Communication:** Automated emails can be triggered based on specific actions or events, ensuring that recipients receive timely and relevant messages when they're most likely to engage.
- **Consistent Messaging:** Automation ensures consistency in messaging and branding across all stages of the customer journey, providing a seamless experience for subscribers.
- **Scalability:** Automation allows businesses to scale their email marketing efforts as their subscriber base grows, without compromising on the quality or relevance of their communications.

Best Practices for Automation

- **Map Out Customer Journeys:** Identify key touchpoints and interactions in the customer journey where automated emails can provide value and drive engagement.
- **Set Up Triggered Campaigns:** Implement automated campaigns triggered by specific actions or events, such as welcome emails, abandoned cart reminders, or post-purchase follow-ups.
- **Segmentation and Personalization:** Combine automation with segmentation and personalization to deliver highly targeted and relevant emails that resonate with individual recipients.
- **Monitor and Optimize:** Regularly monitor the performance of your automated campaigns and make data-driven optimizations to improve results over time.

6.5 MEASURING EMAIL MARKETING EFFECTIVENESS

Measuring email marketing effectiveness is crucial for understanding the performance of your campaigns, optimizing strategies, and maximizing ROI. By tracking key metrics and analyzing performance data, businesses can gain insights into how their emails are performing, identify areas for improvement, and make data-driven decisions to drive better results.

Measuring email marketing effectiveness is essential for optimizing campaign performance, driving better results, and maximizing ROI. By tracking key metrics, analyzing performance data, and making data-driven decisions, businesses can gain valuable insights into their audience, campaign effectiveness, and areas for improvement. With a strategic approach to measuring effectiveness and continuous optimization efforts, businesses can enhance the impact of their email marketing campaigns and achieve their marketing objectives more effectively in today's competitive digital landscape.

6.5.1 Importance of Measuring Email Marketing Effectiveness

Measuring email marketing effectiveness provides businesses with valuable insights into the impact of their campaigns and helps them make informed decisions to improve performance. Here are some reasons why measuring effectiveness is important:

ROI Tracking

Measuring effectiveness allows businesses to track the return on investment (ROI) of their email marketing efforts, helping them understand the cost-effectiveness of their campaigns and justify their marketing spend.

Performance Evaluation

By analyzing key metrics, businesses can evaluate the performance of their email campaigns, identify what's working well and what's not, and make data-driven optimizations to improve results.

Audience Insights

Measuring effectiveness provides valuable insights into audience behavior, preferences, and engagement patterns, allowing businesses to better understand their target audience and tailor future campaigns accordingly.

Optimization Opportunities

Analyzing performance data uncovers optimization opportunities, such as improving subject lines, tweaking content, or adjusting sending times, to enhance campaign effectiveness and drive better results.

6.5.2 Key Metrics to Track

To measure email marketing effectiveness, businesses should track a range of key metrics that provide insights into different aspects of campaign performance. Here are some essential metrics to monitor:

Open Rate

The percentage of recipients who open your emails. A high open rate indicates that your subject lines are compelling and your emails are getting noticed.

Click-Through Rate (CTR)

The percentage of recipients who click on links within your emails. CTR measures the effectiveness of your email content and calls-to-action in driving engagement.

Conversion Rate

The percentage of recipients who complete a desired action, such as making a purchase or filling out a form, after clicking on a link in your email. Conversion rate measures the effectiveness of your emails in driving conversions and achieving your campaign objectives.

Bounce Rate

The percentage of emails that are returned as undeliverable. A high bounce rate may indicate issues with your email list quality or deliverability.

Unsubscribe Rate

The percentage of recipients who unsubscribe from your email list after receiving your emails. Monitoring unsubscribe rate helps you understand the level of engagement and satisfaction among your subscribers.

Revenue Generated

The total revenue generated from your email marketing campaigns. Tracking revenue allows you to measure the direct impact of your emails on sales and revenue generation.

6.5.3 Strategies for Measuring Effectiveness

Set Clear Objectives

Define clear and measurable objectives for your email marketing campaigns, such as increasing sales, driving website traffic, or boosting brand awareness. Align your metrics with these objectives to ensure you're tracking the right KPIs.

Use Email Marketing Software

Utilize email marketing software with built-in analytics and reporting capabilities to track key metrics, analyze performance data, and generate actionable insights. Popular email marketing platforms such as Mailchimp, Constant Contact, and Campaign Monitor offer robust analytics features.

A/B Testing

Conduct A/B tests on different elements of your emails, such as subject lines, content, CTAs, and sending times, to identify what resonates best with your audience and drives higher engagement and conversions.

Segmentation and Personalization

Segment your email list based on relevant criteria such as demographics, behaviors, or preferences, and personalize your emails accordingly. Monitor performance metrics for each segment to understand how different audience groups are responding to your campaigns.

Monitor Trends Over Time

Track key metrics over time to identify trends, patterns, and fluctuations in performance. Look for correlations between different metrics and campaign variables to uncover insights and opportunities for improvement.

Integrate with CRM and E-commerce Platforms

Integrate your email marketing software with your customer relationship management (CRM) system and e-commerce platform to track email interactions, sales data, and customer behavior across different touchpoints. This holistic view of customer data enables you to measure the full impact of your email marketing efforts on customer acquisition, retention, and lifetime value.

Benchmark Against Industry Standards

Compare your email marketing performance metrics against industry benchmarks to gauge how well you're performing relative to your peers. Use industry benchmarks as a reference point for setting goals and identifying areas for improvement.

CHAPTER 7
MOBILE MARKETING

7.1 THE RISE OF MOBILE MARKETING

The rise of mobile marketing has transformed the way businesses connect with their audience, engage with consumers, and drive growth in the digital age. With the increasing prevalence of smartphones and mobile devices, mobile marketing has become an essential strategy for reaching consumers anytime, anywhere. Mobile marketing has become an essential strategy for businesses looking to connect with consumers in today's mobile-first world. By leveraging mobile channels, technologies, and tactics, businesses can reach their target audience, engage with customers, drive conversions, and stay ahead of the competition. With the right strategies and investments in mobile marketing, businesses can unlock new opportunities for growth, enhance the customer experience, and achieve success in the digital age.

7.1.1 Evolution of Mobile Marketing

Mobile marketing has evolved significantly since the advent of smartphones and mobile internet. Initially, mobile marketing primarily consisted of SMS marketing and basic mobile websites. However, advancements in technology and changes in consumer behavior have led to the emergence of more sophisticated mobile marketing strategies and tactics. Today, mobile marketing encompasses a wide range of channels and techniques, including mobile apps, mobile-optimized websites, social media advertising, mobile search, location-based marketing, and mobile messaging platforms.

7.1.2 Key Trends in Mobile Marketing

Mobile Apps

The popularity of mobile apps continues to grow, with consumers spending a significant amount of time on their smartphones using various apps for social networking, entertainment, shopping, and productivity. Businesses are leveraging mobile apps to provide personalized experiences, drive engagement, and facilitate transactions with their customers.

Mobile Optimization

With the majority of internet traffic coming from mobile devices, optimizing websites and digital assets for mobile users is essential. Mobile optimization ensures that websites are responsive, load quickly, and provide a seamless user experience across different screen sizes and devices.

Location-Based Marketing

Location-based marketing utilizes the GPS capabilities of mobile devices to deliver targeted messages, offers, and promotions to consumers based on their geographic location.

Businesses can use location-based marketing to drive foot traffic to physical stores, target users in specific areas, and deliver personalized experiences based on their whereabouts.

Mobile Advertising

Mobile advertising has become a significant revenue driver for businesses, with platforms such as Google Ads and Facebook Ads offering sophisticated targeting options for reaching mobile users. Mobile ads can appear within mobile apps, social media feeds, search results, and other mobile content, allowing businesses to reach their target audience with relevant messaging.

Mobile Payments

The adoption of mobile payment solutions such as Apple Pay, Google Pay, and mobile wallets has transformed the way consumers make purchases. Businesses are integrating mobile payment options into their checkout processes to provide convenient and secure payment experiences for customers.

Mobile Messaging

Mobile messaging platforms such as SMS, MMS, and chat apps are powerful tools for reaching consumers directly on their smartphones. Businesses use mobile messaging for customer service, notifications, promotions, and personalized communication with their audience.

7.1.3 Strategies for Mobile Marketing Success

Create Mobile-Optimized Experiences

Ensure that your website, landing pages, and digital assets are optimized for mobile users, with fast load times, responsive design, and intuitive navigation.

Develop Mobile Apps

If feasible for your business, consider developing a mobile app to provide a seamless and personalized experience for your customers. Mobile apps can offer features such as loyalty programs, in-app purchases, push notifications, and exclusive content.

Utilize Location-Based Targeting

Leverage location-based marketing tactics to target consumers based on their geographic location and deliver relevant messages or offers that are tailored to their surroundings.

Implement Mobile Advertising

Invest in mobile advertising campaigns to reach your target audience across various mobile channels and platforms. Use advanced targeting options to ensure that your ads are seen by the right people at the right time.

Optimize for Mobile Search

Optimize your website and content for mobile search to improve visibility and rankings in mobile search results. Focus on mobile-friendly design, page speed, and local SEO to enhance your mobile search presence.

Engage with Mobile Messaging

Leverage mobile messaging platforms such as SMS, MMS, and chat apps to engage with your audience in real-time, deliver personalized messages, and provide customer support.

Track and Analyze Performance

Monitor key metrics such as mobile traffic, engagement, conversions, and ROI to measure the effectiveness of your mobile marketing efforts. Use analytics tools to gain insights into user behavior and optimize your strategies accordingly.

7.1.4 Impact of Mobile Marketing on Businesses

The rise of mobile marketing has had a profound impact on businesses across industries:

Increased Reach

Mobile marketing enables businesses to reach consumers anytime, anywhere, tapping into a larger audience and expanding their market reach.

Improved Engagement

Mobile devices are personal and highly interactive, allowing businesses to engage with consumers in meaningful ways through personalized messages, targeted offers, and interactive content.

Enhanced Customer Experience

Mobile marketing allows businesses to provide seamless and convenient experiences for their customers, whether through mobile apps, mobile-optimized websites, or mobile messaging platforms.

Better Data Insights

Mobile marketing provides businesses with valuable data and insights into consumer behavior, preferences, and interactions, enabling them to make informed decisions and optimize their strategies for better results.

Competitive Advantage

Businesses that embrace mobile marketing and adapt to the mobile-first mindset gain a competitive advantage in today's digital landscape, positioning themselves as innovative, customer-centric, and forward-thinking brands.

7.2 MOBILE-FRIENDLY WEBSITES AND SEO

Mobile-friendly websites and SEO are essential components of a successful digital strategy in today's mobile-centric world. With the majority of internet users accessing content on mobile devices, having a website optimized for mobile is no longer optional—it's a necessity. Mobile-friendly websites and SEO are critical for attracting, engaging, and retaining mobile users in today's digital landscape. By prioritizing mobile optimization, businesses can improve user experience, increase visibility in mobile search results, and drive organic traffic and conversions. With responsive design, fast page load times, optimized content, and mobile-specific SEO strategies, businesses can create a seamless and enjoyable mobile experience for their audience while maximizing their presence and performance in mobile search.

7.2.1 Importance of Mobile-Friendly Websites for SEO

User Experience (UX)

A mobile-friendly website provides a positive user experience for visitors accessing your site on smartphones and tablets. Google considers UX as a ranking factor, so a poor mobile experience can negatively impact your search rankings.

Mobile-First Indexing

Google primarily uses the mobile version of a website's content for indexing and ranking purposes. If your site is not mobile-friendly, it may not perform well in mobile search results, leading to a loss of visibility and traffic.

Page Load Speed

Mobile users expect fast-loading pages. Mobile-friendly design optimizes page load times, which is crucial for both user satisfaction and SEO performance. Google's Page Experience update emphasizes the importance of fast-loading pages for ranking purposes.

Reduced Bounce Rates

Mobile users are more likely to bounce from a website if it's not optimized for their devices. High bounce rates can signal to search engines that your content may not be relevant or useful to users, potentially impacting your rankings.

Local SEO

Mobile searches often have local intent, such as "near me" queries. Having a mobile-friendly website is essential for local SEO, as it increases the chances of appearing in local search results and attracting nearby customers.

7.2.2 Key Considerations for Mobile-Friendly Websites

Responsive Design

Use responsive web design to create a single website that adapts seamlessly to different screen sizes and devices. Responsive design ensures that your site looks and functions well on mobile, tablet, and desktop devices.

Mobile-Friendly Layout

Optimize your website's layout for mobile devices, with easy-to-navigate menus, clear calls-to-action (CTAs), and touch-friendly buttons. Keep content concise and prioritize the most important information for mobile users.

Fast Page Load Times

Improve page load times by optimizing images, minimizing server response times, and reducing unnecessary scripts and resources. Tools like Google's PageSpeed Insights can help identify performance issues and provide recommendations for improvement.

Optimized Content

Ensure that your content is easy to read and interact with on mobile devices. Use legible fonts, adequate spacing, and appropriately sized text and images. Break up content into short paragraphs and use headings to improve readability.

Mobile SEO Best Practices

Implement mobile-specific SEO best practices, such as optimizing meta tags, titles, and descriptions for mobile search. Use structured data markup to provide context and enhance visibility in mobile search results.

7.2.3 Best Practices for Mobile SEO

Optimize for Local Search

Claim and optimize your Google My Business listing, ensure NAP (name, address, phone number) consistency across online directories, and optimize website content for local keywords to improve visibility in local search results.

Mobile-First Indexing

Ensure that your website's mobile version is equivalent in content and functionality to the desktop version. Prioritize mobile optimization when creating new content, updating existing pages, and implementing site changes.

Voice Search Optimization

With the increasing popularity of voice search, optimize your website for conversational queries and natural language patterns. Use long-tail keywords and FAQ-style content to address common voice search queries.

Structured Data Markup

Implement structured data markup to provide search engines with additional context about your content, such as product details, reviews, events, and FAQs. Structured data can enhance visibility in mobile search results and enable rich snippets and other enhanced features.

Mobile-Friendly Testing

Regularly test your website's mobile-friendliness using tools like Google's Mobile-Friendly Test. Address any issues or errors identified during testing to ensure a smooth user experience on mobile devices.

7.2.4 Mobile-Friendly Website Maintenance

Regular Audits and Updates

Conduct regular audits of your website's mobile performance, including page load times, mobile usability, and mobile SEO. Make necessary updates and optimizations to keep your site competitive in mobile search.

Monitor Analytics

Use web analytics tools to monitor mobile traffic, user engagement, and conversion rates. Analyze mobile-specific metrics to identify trends, opportunities, and areas for improvement.

User Feedback

Gather feedback from mobile users through surveys, user testing, and customer support channels. Use this feedback to identify pain points, address usability issues, and enhance the overall mobile experience.

Stay Current with Mobile Trends

Stay informed about mobile technology trends, updates to search engine algorithms, and changes in user behavior. Adapt your mobile strategy accordingly to remain competitive in the ever-evolving mobile landscape.

7.3 SMS AND MESSAGING APPS IN MARKETING

SMS (Short Message Service) and messaging apps have emerged as powerful tools for marketers to connect with their audience, deliver personalized messages, and drive engagement in today's digital landscape.

With billions of active users worldwide, messaging platforms offer unparalleled reach and accessibility, making them an integral part of modern marketing strategies. SMS and messaging apps play a crucial role in modern marketing, offering businesses a direct and effective way to communicate with their audience, deliver personalized messages, and drive engagement.

With high open rates, instant delivery, and two-way communication capabilities, SMS and messaging apps enable businesses to reach their audience anytime, anywhere, and foster meaningful relationships with their customers.

By following best practices, segmenting their audience, and delivering targeted and relevant messages, businesses can leverage the power of SMS and messaging app marketing to achieve their marketing goals and drive business growth in today's mobile-first world.

7.3.1 Role of SMS and Messaging Apps in Marketing

Direct Communication

SMS and messaging apps provide a direct and instant communication channel between businesses and consumers. Marketers can reach their audience directly on their mobile devices, delivering timely messages, promotions, and updates.

Personalization

SMS and messaging apps enable personalized communication, allowing marketers to tailor messages based on user preferences, behaviors, and past interactions. Personalized messages resonate with recipients and can lead to higher engagement and conversion rates.

Real-Time Engagement

Messaging platforms facilitate real-time engagement with consumers, enabling instant communication, feedback, and support. Businesses can quickly respond to inquiries, address customer concerns, and provide assistance, fostering positive relationships with their audience.

Automation

Many messaging platforms offer automation capabilities, allowing businesses to automate routine tasks, such as sending automated responses, drip campaigns, and transactional messages. Automation saves time and resources while ensuring consistent and timely communication with customers.

Rich Media Content

Messaging apps support various types of rich media content, including images, videos, GIFs, and interactive elements. Marketers can use multimedia content to create engaging and visually appealing messages that capture attention and drive interaction.

7.3.2 Benefits of SMS and Messaging Apps in Marketing

- **High Open Rates**: SMS boasts high open rates, with the majority of messages being read within minutes of delivery. Messaging apps also have high engagement rates, as users frequently check their messages throughout the day.
- **Instant Delivery**: Messages sent via SMS and messaging apps are delivered instantly to recipients' devices, ensuring timely communication and immediate visibility.
- **Two-Way Communication**: SMS and messaging apps facilitate two-way communication between businesses and consumers, allowing for interactive conversations, feedback, and engagement.
- **Cost-Effective**: SMS and messaging apps offer cost-effective marketing solutions compared to traditional channels like print or TV advertising. With minimal costs per message, businesses can reach a large audience at a fraction of the cost.
- **Opt-In Audience**: Users typically opt-in to receive SMS messages or join messaging app groups, indicating their interest in hearing from businesses. This opt-in audience is more receptive to marketing messages and more likely to engage with content.

7.3.3 Best Practices for SMS and Messaging App Marketing

- **Obtain Consent**: Always obtain consent from users before sending them SMS messages or adding them to messaging app groups. Respect user preferences and provide clear opt-in and opt-out mechanisms.
- **Segmentation**: Segment your audience based on demographics, preferences, and behavior to deliver targeted and relevant messages. Tailor your content to different audience segments to maximize engagement and effectiveness.
- **Personalization**: Personalize your messages with recipients' names, past purchase history, or other relevant information to make messages more relevant and engaging. Personalization increases the likelihood of recipients taking action on your messages.

- **Timing**: Send messages at optimal times when recipients are most likely to be receptive and engaged. Avoid sending messages late at night or during busy times when they may be less likely to see or respond to them.
- **Clear Call-to-Action (CTA)**: Include a clear and compelling call-to-action (CTA) in your messages, prompting recipients to take the desired action, such as making a purchase, visiting a website, or contacting your business.
- **Monitor Performance**: Track key metrics such as open rates, click-through rates, conversion rates, and unsubscribe rates to measure the effectiveness of your SMS and messaging app campaigns. Use analytics to analyze performance data and optimize your strategies for better results.

7.3.4 Examples of SMS and Messaging App Marketing

- **Promotions and Offers**: Businesses can use SMS to send exclusive promotions, discounts, and special offers to their subscribers, encouraging them to make a purchase or visit a store.
- **Customer Service and Support**: Messaging apps enable businesses to provide customer service and support in real-time, addressing inquiries, resolving issues, and providing assistance to customers whenever and wherever they need it.
- **Appointment Reminders**: Service-based businesses such as salons, clinics, and restaurants can use SMS to send appointment reminders and confirmations to their customers, reducing no-shows and improving efficiency.
- **Event Invitations**: Businesses can use SMS and messaging apps to send invitations, RSVP reminders, and event updates to attendees, keeping them informed and engaged before, during, and after the event.
- **Product Updates and Announcements**: Companies can use messaging apps to announce new product launches, updates, or releases to their customers, generating excitement and anticipation around their offerings.

7.4 MOBILE APPS AND LOCATION-BASED MARKETING

Mobile apps and location-based marketing have revolutionized the way businesses engage with consumers, providing opportunities for personalized, contextually relevant interactions based on users' real-time locations. With the widespread adoption of smartphones and the increasing availability of location-based services, businesses can leverage mobile apps to deliver targeted messages, promotions, and experiences tailored to users' geographical proximity.

7.4.1 Role of Mobile Apps in Location-Based Marketing

Location Awareness

Mobile apps can leverage GPS, Wi-Fi, and beacon technology to determine users' precise locations. This location data enables businesses to deliver targeted messages and promotions based on users' proximity to physical locations.

Personalized Experiences

By combining location data with user profiles and preferences, businesses can deliver personalized experiences within their mobile apps. This may include location-based recommendations, offers, or content tailored to users' interests and behaviors.

Geofencing

Geofencing allows businesses to create virtual boundaries around specific geographic areas. When users enter or exit these geofenced areas, businesses can trigger location-based notifications, reminders, or promotions within their mobile apps.

In-Store Engagement

Mobile apps can enhance in-store engagement by providing users with relevant information, promotions, or loyalty rewards based on their current location within a physical store.

This encourages users to explore products, make purchases, and interact with the brand while in-store.

Analytics and Insights

Location data collected from mobile apps can provide valuable insights into user behavior, foot traffic patterns, and engagement metrics. Businesses can use this data to optimize marketing strategies, improve customer experiences, and make data-driven decisions.

7.4.2 Benefits of Location-Based Marketing for Businesses

Increased Relevance

Location-based marketing allows businesses to deliver highly relevant and contextual messages to users based on their real-time locations. This increases the likelihood of engagement and conversion by offering users timely and personalized experiences.

Improved Targeting

Location data enables businesses to target users based on their physical proximity to specific locations, such as stores, events, or points of interest. This precise targeting increases the effectiveness of marketing campaigns and enhances ROI.

Enhanced Customer Engagement

Location-based marketing facilitates interactive and engaging experiences that encourage users to interact with the brand both online and offline. By delivering relevant content and promotions based on users' locations, businesses can drive increased engagement and loyalty.

Drive Foot Traffic

Location-based promotions and incentives can incentivize users to visit physical store locations, driving foot traffic and increasing sales. By offering exclusive discounts or rewards to users who are nearby, businesses can attract customers and boost revenue.

Data-Driven Insights

Location data provides businesses with valuable insights into user behavior and preferences, allowing for more informed decision-making and targeted marketing strategies. By analyzing location-based data, businesses can identify trends, optimize campaigns, and refine their offerings to better meet customer needs.

7.4.3 Best Practices for Location-Based Marketing in Mobile Apps

- **Obtain Consent**: Obtain explicit consent from users before collecting and using their location data. Clearly communicate how and why location data will be used and provide users with the option to opt-in or opt-out of location-based services within the app.
- **Provide Value**: Deliver valuable and relevant content or promotions to users based on their real-time locations. Ensure that location-based messages are timely, contextually relevant, and offer clear benefits or incentives to users.
- **Segmentation**: Segment users based on their location, preferences, and behaviors to deliver targeted messages and promotions. Tailor content and offers to different user segments to maximize relevance and engagement.
- **Geofencing Optimization**: Optimize geofencing parameters to ensure accuracy and effectiveness. Set appropriate geofence sizes and shapes, adjust trigger distances, and refine targeting criteria based on user feedback and performance metrics.

- **Measure and Analyze**: Track and analyze key metrics such as engagement rates, conversion rates, and foot traffic attribution to evaluate the effectiveness of location-based marketing efforts. Use insights from analytics to optimize campaigns, refine targeting strategies, and improve ROI.

7.4.4 Examples of Location-Based Marketing in Mobile Apps

Retail

Retailers can use mobile apps to deliver location-based promotions, discounts, and recommendations to users when they are near physical store locations. For example, sending a push notification with a special offer when a user is within a certain distance of a store.

Food and Beverage

Restaurants and cafes can use mobile apps to offer location-based promotions, such as happy hour deals or discounts on nearby food orders. Geofencing can also be used to send notifications to users attending nearby events or festivals.

Travel and Hospitality

Hotels and travel companies can use mobile apps to provide guests with personalized recommendations, local attractions, and exclusive offers based on their current location. Geofencing can be used to send notifications about nearby amenities or events.

Entertainment and Events

Event organizers can use mobile apps to provide attendees with real-time updates, directions, and exclusive offers based on their location within the event venue. Geofencing can be used to send notifications about nearby attractions or activities.

Health and Fitness

Health and fitness apps can use location data to provide users with personalized workout recommendations, outdoor activity suggestions, and nearby fitness classes or facilities. Geofencing can be used to remind users to exercise when they are near a designated workout area.

7.5 MOBILE ANALYTICS AND TRENDS

Mobile analytics and trends play a crucial role in shaping the strategies of businesses across industries, as the world continues to shift towards mobile-first experiences. With the exponential growth in mobile device usage, coupled with advancements in technology, mobile analytics provide valuable insights into user behavior, preferences, and trends.

Mobile analytics play a vital role in helping businesses understand user behavior, optimize user experiences, and drive business growth in today's mobile-centric world.

By leveraging mobile analytics tools and strategies, businesses can gain valuable insights into user interactions, track key metrics, and make data-driven decisions to improve app performance, increase user engagement, and achieve their business objectives. As mobile technology continues to evolve, staying abreast of emerging trends in mobile analytics will be essential for businesses to remain competitive and effectively meet the needs of their mobile users.

7.5.1 Importance of Mobile Analytics

Understanding User Behavior

Mobile analytics help businesses gain insights into how users interact with their mobile apps and websites. By tracking metrics such as session duration, screen views, and user interactions, businesses can understand user behavior and identify areas for improvement.

Optimizing User Experience

Mobile analytics enable businesses to optimize the user experience (UX) of their mobile apps and websites. By analyzing user feedback, navigation patterns, and performance metrics, businesses can make data-driven decisions to enhance usability and engagement.

Measuring Performance

Mobile analytics provide businesses with quantitative data on the performance of their mobile apps and websites. Metrics such as app downloads, active users, and conversion rates help businesses measure the success of their mobile initiatives and identify areas for growth.

Personalization and Targeting

Mobile analytics enable businesses to personalize experiences and target users with relevant content and offers. By analyzing user demographics, preferences, and behavior, businesses can deliver personalized recommendations and marketing messages to drive engagement and conversions.

Iterative Improvement

Mobile analytics facilitate iterative improvement by enabling businesses to test, measure, and optimize their mobile strategies. By monitoring key metrics and analyzing performance data, businesses can make incremental changes to their mobile apps and websites to achieve better results over time.

7.5.2 Key Trends in Mobile Analytics

App Analytics

With the proliferation of mobile apps, app analytics has become increasingly important for businesses.

App analytics tools provide insights into app usage, user engagement, retention, and conversion metrics, helping businesses optimize their apps for success.

In-App Events Tracking

In-app events tracking allows businesses to monitor user interactions within their apps, such as clicks, swipes, purchases, and form submissions. By tracking in-app events, businesses can understand how users engage with different features and content within the app.

Cross-Device Tracking

As users interact with brands across multiple devices, cross-device tracking has become essential for understanding the customer journey.

Mobile analytics tools that offer cross-device tracking capabilities enable businesses to gain a holistic view of user behavior and engagement across devices.

Location Analytics

Location analytics provide insights into users' geographic locations and movements, enabling businesses to deliver location-based experiences and targeted marketing campaigns. Location analytics help businesses understand where their users are located, how they move between locations, and how location influences their behavior.

Machine Learning and Predictive Analytics

Machine learning and predictive analytics are transforming mobile analytics by enabling businesses to forecast user behavior and trends. By leveraging machine learning algorithms, businesses can predict user preferences, identify patterns, and personalize experiences in real-time.

7.5.3 Strategies for Leveraging Mobile Analytics

Define Key Performance Indicators (KPIs)

Identify key metrics and KPIs that align with your business goals and objectives. Common KPIs for mobile analytics include app downloads, active users, retention rates, engagement metrics, and conversion rates.

Implement Tracking and Measurement

Implement mobile analytics tools and tracking mechanisms to collect data on user interactions, app usage, and performance metrics. Ensure that tracking is implemented accurately and consistently across all touchpoints.

Segmentation and User Profiling

Segment users based on demographics, behaviors, and preferences to gain insights into different audience segments. Use user profiling to understand the needs, preferences, and motivations of different user groups and tailor experiences accordingly.

A/B Testing and Experimentation

Conduct A/B tests and experiments to test different variations of your mobile apps and websites.

Experiment with different features, designs, and messaging to identify what resonates best with your audience and drives desired outcomes.

Continuous Monitoring and Optimization

Continuously monitor key metrics and performance data to identify trends, patterns, and areas for improvement. Use insights from mobile analytics to optimize user experiences, refine marketing strategies, and drive business growth.

7.5.4 Emerging Trends in Mobile Analytics

Augmented Reality (AR) Analytics

With the rise of augmented reality (AR) experiences in mobile apps, AR analytics are becoming increasingly important for businesses. AR analytics tools provide insights into user interactions with AR content, such as interactions with virtual objects and environments.

Voice Analytics

Voice analytics enable businesses to track and analyze user interactions with voice-enabled devices and applications. Voice analytics tools provide insights into voice search queries, voice commands, and user engagement with voice-based interfaces.

Privacy-First Analytics

With growing concerns around data privacy and security, privacy-first analytics solutions are gaining traction. Privacy-first analytics tools prioritize user privacy and data protection while still providing valuable insights into user behavior and engagement.

Real-Time Analytics

Real-time analytics enable businesses to monitor user interactions and app performance in real-time. Real-time analytics tools provide immediate insights into user behavior, enabling businesses to respond quickly to changing trends and events.

Predictive Analytics

Predictive analytics leverage machine learning algorithms to forecast user behavior and trends. Predictive analytics tools analyze historical data to identify patterns and make predictions about future user actions, enabling businesses to anticipate user needs and personalize experiences proactively.

CHAPTER 8
INFLUENCER MARKETING

8.1 UNDERSTANDING IN INFLUENCER MARKETING

Influencer marketing (also known as influence marketing) is a form of social media marketing involving endorsements and product placement from influencers, people and organizations who have a purported expert level of knowledge or social influence in their field. Influencers are someone (or something) with the power to affect the buying habits or quantifiable actions of others by uploading some form of original—often sponsored—content to social media platforms like Instagram, YouTube, Snapchat, TikTok or other online channels. Influencer marketing is when a brand enrolls influencers who have an established credibility and audience on social media platforms to discuss or mention the brand in a social media post. Influencer content may be framed as testimonial advertising.

8.1.1 Social Influence

Most discussions of social influence focus on social persuasion and compliance. In the context of influencer marketing, influence is less about arguing for a point of view or product than about loose interactions between parties in a community (often with the aim of encouraging purchasing or behavior). Although influence is often equated with advocacy, it may also be negative. The two-step flow of communication model was introduced in *The People's Choice* (Paul Lazarsfeld, Bernard Berelson, and Hazel Gaudet's 1940 study of voters' decision-making processes), and developed in *Personal Influence* and *The Effects of Mass Communication.*

Influencer marketing is also important through social comparison theory. As psychologist Chae reports, influencers serve as a comparison tool. Consumers may compare influencer lifestyles with their imperfections. Meanwhile, followers may view influencers as people with perfect lifestyles, interests, and dressing style. As such, the promoted products may serve as a shortcut towards a complete lifestyle. Chae's study finds women with low self-esteem compare themselves to the influencers. When using an influencer, a brand may use consumer insecurities to its benefits. For this reason, influencer marketing may lead to faulty advertising.

8.1.2 Influencers

There is a lack of consensus about what an influencer is. One writer defines them as "a range of third parties who exercise influence over the organization and its potential customers." Another defines an influencer as a "third party who significantly shapes the customer's purchasing decision but may never be accountable for it." According to another, influencers are "well-connected, create an impact, have active minds, and are trendsetters". And just because an individual has many followers does not necessarily mean they have much influence over those individuals, only that they have many followers. A 1% increase in influencer marketing spending can lead to a 0.5% increase in audience engagement.

Identifying Influencers

Market-research techniques can be used to identify influencers, using predefined criteria to determine the extent and type of influence. "Activists" get involved with organizations such as their communities, political movements, and charities. "Connected influencers" have large social networks. "Authoritative influencers" are trusted by others. "Active minds" have a diverse range of interests. "Trendsetters" are the early adopters (or leavers) of markets. According to Malcolm Gladwell, "The success of any kind of social epidemic is heavily dependent on the involvement of people with a particular and rare set of social gifts". He has identified three types of influencers who are responsible for the "generation, communication and adoption" of messages:

- Connectors network with a variety of people, have a wide reach, and are essential to word-of-mouth communication.
- Mavens use information, share it with others, and are insightful about trends.
- Salesmen are "charismatic persuaders". Their influence is the tendency of others to imitate their behavior.

Influencer Categories

Influencers are categorized by the number of followers they have on social media. They include celebrity endorsements from those with large followings, to niche content creators with a loyal following on social-media platforms such as YouTube, Instagram, Facebook, and Twitter. Their followers range in number from hundreds of millions to 1,000.

- **Nano-Influencers:** These are influencers that have a following ranging from 1k to 10k.
- **Micro-Influencers:** These are the influencers with followers in the range of 10K to 100k
- **Macro-Influencers:** These are the influencers with followers from the range of 100K to 500k

- **Mega/Celeb-Influencers:** These are the influencers with more than 500k followers

Businesses pursue people who aim to lessen their consumption of advertisements, and are willing to pay their influencers more. Targeting influencers is seen as increasing marketing's reach, counteracting a growing tendency by prospective customers to ignore marketing.

Marketing researchers Kapitan and Silvera find that influencer selection extends into product personality. This product and benefit matching is key. For a shampoo, it should use an influencer with good hair. Likewise, a flashy product may use bold colors to convey its brand. If an influencer is not flashy, they will clash with the brand. Matching an influencer with the product's purpose and mood is important.

B2B Influencers

For most business-to-consumer (B2C) campaigns, influencers may include everyday consumers who influence their audience. In high-value business-to-business (B2B) transactions, influencers may be diverse and might include consultants, government-backed regulators, financiers, and user communities. Forrester Research analyst Michael Speyer notes that for small and medium-sized businesses, "IT sales are influenced by several parties, including peers, consultants, bloggers, and technology resellers." According to Speyer, "Vendors need to identify and characterize influencers inside their market. This requires a comprehensive influencer identification program and the establishment of criteria for ranking influencer impact on the decision process." Influencers can play a variety of roles at different times in a decision-making process, an idea developed by Brown and Hayes.

Payment

Most influencers are paid before the start of a marketing campaign, and others are paid after it ends. Consensus exists about how much an influencer should be paid. Compensation may vary by how many people an influencer can reach, the extent to which they will endorse the product (a deliverable), and the success of their past endorsements have performed. Top-tier influencers and celebrities may receive a six- or seven-figure fee for a single social-media post. In addition to (or in lieu of) a fee, payment may include free products or services. For influencers with smaller followings, free products or services may be the only form of compensation.

8.1.3 Social Media

Online activity can play a central role in offline decision-making, allowing consumers to research products. Social media have created new opportunities for marketers to expand their strategy beyond traditional mass-media channels.

Many use influencers to increase the reach of their marketing messages. Online influencers who curate personal brands have become marketing assets because of their relationship with their followers. Social-media influencers establish themselves as opinion-leaders with their followers and may have persuasive strengths such as attractiveness, likeability, niche expertise, and perceived good taste. The interactive and personal nature of social media allows parasocial relationships to form between influencers and their followers, which impacts purchase behavior. Influencer marketing on social media reaches consumers who use ad-blockers.

Critics of an online-intensive approach say that by researching exclusively online, consumers can overlook input from other influential individuals. Early-2000s research suggested that 80 to 92 percent of influential consumer exchanges occurred face-to-face with word-of-mouth (WOM), compared to seven to 10 percent in an online environment. Scholars and marketers distinguish WOM from electronic word-of-mouth (eWOM).

2017 Controversies

YouTuber PewDiePie's antisemitic and racist comments led to cancelled deals with the Walt Disney Company and a "widespread backlash". Celebrity influencer Kendall Jenner and other media personalities failed to disclose their paid endorsements of the fraudulent Fyre Festival, as required by the Federal Trade Commission. YouTuber Logan Paul posted a video containing a dead body in Japan's Suicide Forest, sparking a backlash and accusations of insensitivity.

Use by Governments

A wide range of global population, particularly generation Z, has been relying on social media influencers for all sorts of information. With millions of followers on their accounts, including Instagram, Snapchat, Facebook and others, influencers have not just been working with brands, but also governments. Countries like Egypt and the United Arab Emirates have been using these influencers to spread a positive image of them and cover the bad press over human rights. In Dubai, many such influencers have been working to promote the city's tourism by acquiring an expensive license or through agencies. It has become a full-time business in Dubai's post-oil economy. The Emirati authorities follow rigid plans and strategies to hit the correct spots. A strict check is maintained over the content of the influencers to make sure that everything is being depicted in a positive light. Dubai authorities also restrict these influencers from speaking anything against the regime, religion, or politics. A report in October 2022 revealed that the influencers, who promote a glistening Dubai on their social media, sell sex to pay their lifestyle. These influencers are paid thousands of pounds a night. The amount also depends on the number of followers, where more followers means more money. Apart from cash, these influencers are paid with jewellery, flights, bags, etc. While prostitution is illegal in Dubai, it has always been there. Increase in influencers selling sex was believed to be due to the rise in number of ultra-rich expatriates in the Dubai, including the Russian oligarchs moving to the emirate to escape the US sanctions.

8.1.4 Applications

Marketers use influencer marketing to establish credibility in a market, to create social conversations about brands, and to focus on driving online or in-store sales. Marketers leverage credibility gained over time to promote a variety of products or services. Success in influencer marketing is measured through earned media value, impressions, and cost per action.

A social media influencer's personal brand and product relation with marketers are important concepts. As social learning theory suggests, influencers serve as informed consumers and authenticity matters. When credible influencers match up with the product, consumers will consider the promoted recommendations. A study found that respondents see influencers as a neutral authority pitch for a product. Compared to CEO spokespeople, influencers are more approachable and trustworthy. Consumers are more likely to respond to influencers if both parties share certain characteristics and beliefs.

A 2015 article depicts that attributions drive endorsers and that globally 77% of shoppers would or may take action following what family, friends, and online reviews endorse. It shows that word of mouth marketing and digital media have changed the impact and reach of endorsements.

8.1.5 Regulation

In the United States, the Federal Trade Commission (FTC) treats influencer marketing as a form of paid endorsement. It is governed by the rules for native advertising, which include compliance with established truth-in-advertising standards and disclosure by endorsers (influencers) and is known as the Endorsement Guides. The FTC compiled an easy-to-read guide on disclosure for influencers, specifying rules and tips on how to make good disclosures on social media. The guidelines include reminders of disclosing sponsored products in easily visible places so it is hard to miss, using easy-to-understand language, and giving honest reviews about sponsored products.

In 2017, the FTC sent more than 90 educational letters to celebrity and athlete influencers with the reminder of the obligation to clearly disclose business relationships while sponsoring and promoting products. The same year, in response to YouTubers Trevor Martin and Thomas Cassell deceptively endorsing an online gambling site they owned, the FTC took three separate actions to catch the attention of influencers. By using law enforcement, warning letters, and updating the Endorsement Guidelines, the FTC provided influencers with endorsement questions or involved in misleading endorsements and disclosures with clear procedures of how to follow the laws.

Media-regulating bodies in other countries – such as Australia – followed the FTC in creating influencer-marketing guidelines. The United Kingdom's Competition and Markets Authority adopted similar laws and tips for influencers to follow.

Branded Content on Social Media Platforms

Facebook and Instagram

Facebook and Instagram have a set of brand content policies for influencer marketing and endorsements. Branded content may only be posted through Instagram and Facebook, and require the business relationships between influencers and endorsers to be tagged when promoting branded content. The branded tool provided in the business layout of Facebook and Instagram is to be used whenever promoting products and endorsers.

YouTube

As of August 2020, YouTube has updated the branded content policies. YouTube and Google's ad policies require influencers to check a box titled *paid promotion* when publishing sponsored videos and provides instructions on how to set it up. The policies require disclosure messages for the viewers to indicate that the content is promoted.

8.1.6 Abuse

All criteria used to determine the veracity of an influencer account can be fabricated. Third-party sites and apps sell services to individual accounts which include falsely increasing followers, likes, and comments. Instagram has failed to shut down all such websites. One marketing agency, Mediakix tested whether fake accounts could be profitable. The company created two fictitious accounts, built their online presence through paid followers and engagement (likes and comments), and applied for work in marketing campaigns on popular influencer marketing platforms. They published their results, an explanation of how the false accounts were created, and which brands had sponsored them.

An analysis of over 7,000 influencers in the UK indicated that about half of their followers have up to 20,000 "low-quality" followers themselves, consisting of internet bots and other suspicious accounts. Over four in 10 engagements with this group of influencers are considered "non-authentic". A study of UK influencers which looked at almost 700,000 posts from the first half of 2018 found that 12 percent of UK influencers had bought fake followers. Twenty-four percent of influencers were found to have abnormal growth patterns in another study, indicating that they had manipulated their likes or followers.

Influencer fraud (including fake followers) was estimated to cost businesses up to $1.3 billion, about 15 percent of global influencer-marketing spending. Research in 2019 accounted only for the calculable cost of fake followers.

8.1.7 Virtual Influencers

Virtual influencers are virtual characters, intentionally designed by 3D artists to look like real people in real situations. Although most of the characters can be easily identified as computer graphics, some are very realistic and can fool users. The characters are usually identified as models, singers, or other celebrities. Their creators write their biographies, conduct interviews on their behalf, and act like the characters themselves. Lil Miquela was a realistic virtual influencer which prompted curiosity and speculation until it was learned that she was created by advertisers.

8.2 SELECTION THE RIGHT INFLUENCERS

Selecting the right influencers is crucial for the success of influencer marketing campaigns. With the rise of social media platforms, influencers have become powerful voices that can impact consumer behavior, shape brand perceptions, and drive engagement. However, not all influencers are created equal, and choosing the right ones requires careful consideration of various factors.

Selecting the right influencers is essential for the success of influencer marketing campaigns. By considering factors such as audience alignment, engagement, authenticity, and relevance to your brand, you can identify influencers who are well-positioned to amplify your message, drive engagement, and achieve your campaign objectives.

By leveraging influencer marketing effectively, businesses can tap into the power of social influence, connect with their target audience authentically, and achieve tangible results in today's competitive digital landscape.

8.2.1 Importance of Selecting the Right Influencers

Audience Alignment

The right influencers have an audience that aligns with your target demographic and interests. By choosing influencers whose followers match your target audience, you can ensure that your message resonates with the right people and drives meaningful engagement.

Credibility and Authenticity

Authenticity is essential in influencer marketing. Selecting influencers who are genuine, credible, and trustworthy helps build credibility for your brand and fosters authentic connections with their followers.

Relevance to Your Brand

The best influencers are those whose content and values align with your brand identity and messaging. By partnering with influencers who share your brand values and beliefs, you can ensure that their endorsements feel natural and authentic to their audience.

Engagement and Influence

Look for influencers who have a track record of high engagement rates and genuine influence over their audience. Influencers with high engagement rates are more likely to drive meaningful interactions and action from their followers.

Campaign Objectives

Different influencers excel in different areas, whether it's driving awareness, generating leads, or driving sales. Choose influencers whose strengths align with your campaign objectives and desired outcomes.

8.2.2 Key Criteria for Selecting Influencers

- **Reach and Audience Size:** Consider the size of the influencer's audience and their reach on social media platforms. While macro-influencers with large followings can reach a broad audience, micro-influencers with smaller followings often have higher engagement rates and more niche audiences.
- **Engagement Rate:** Look beyond follower count and examine the influencer's engagement rate, including likes, comments, shares, and saves. A high engagement rate indicates that the influencer has an active and engaged audience that values their content.
- **Relevance and Niche:** Evaluate the influencer's content, interests, and niche to ensure alignment with your brand and campaign objectives. Choose influencers whose content resonates with your target audience and complements your brand's values and messaging.
- **Authenticity and Trustworthiness:** Assess the influencer's authenticity, credibility, and trustworthiness by reviewing their content, interactions with followers, and brand partnerships. Look for influencers who are genuine, transparent, and have built trust with their audience over time.
- **Past Collaborations and Successes:** Research the influencer's past collaborations and campaigns to understand their track record and

effectiveness. Look for influencers who have successfully partnered with brands in your industry and delivered tangible results.

- **Content Quality and Style:** Evaluate the quality, style, and tone of the influencer's content to ensure that it aligns with your brand's aesthetic and messaging. Choose influencers who produce high-quality content that resonates with their audience and showcases your brand in a positive light.

8.2.3 Best Practices for Selecting Influencers

Conduct Thorough Research

Take the time to research potential influencers thoroughly, including reviewing their social media profiles, content, engagement metrics, and audience demographics. Look for influencers who are active, consistent, and have a genuine connection with their audience.

Utilize Influencer Marketing Platforms

Consider using influencer marketing platforms and tools to streamline the influencer selection process. These platforms provide access to a database of influencers, audience insights, and campaign management tools to help you find the right influencers for your brand.

Engage with Influencers Authentically

Build relationships with potential influencers by engaging with their content, commenting, sharing, and expressing genuine interest in their work. Authentic engagement helps establish rapport and lays the foundation for successful collaborations.

Set Clear Expectations and Guidelines

Clearly communicate your campaign objectives, expectations, and guidelines to influencers upfront. Provide detailed briefs outlining the campaign scope, deliverables, messaging, and any specific requirements or restrictions.

Negotiate Fair Compensation

Discuss compensation with influencers openly and transparently, taking into account factors such as reach, engagement, content quality, and exclusivity. Negotiate fair compensation that aligns with the influencer's value and the scope of the campaign.

Monitor and Measure Performance

Continuously monitor the performance of influencer marketing campaigns and track key metrics such as reach, engagement, click-through rates, and conversions.

Use data and analytics to evaluate the effectiveness of influencer partnerships and optimize future campaigns.

8.2.4 Case Studies and Examples

Daniel Wellington

The watch brand Daniel Wellington has successfully leveraged influencer marketing to build brand awareness and drive sales. By partnering with lifestyle influencers on Instagram, Daniel Wellington has created a cohesive brand image and cultivated a loyal following of brand advocates.

Fashion Nova

Fashion Nova, a popular fashion retailer, has built its brand primarily through influencer marketing on social media. By collaborating with influencers across various platforms, Fashion Nova has generated buzz, sparked trends, and attracted a diverse audience of fashion enthusiasts.

Sephora

Sephora, a leading beauty retailer, has effectively utilized influencer marketing to promote its products and engage with beauty enthusiasts. Sephora partners with beauty influencers to create engaging content, share product reviews, and showcase new launches, driving excitement and engagement among its audience.

8.3 CRAFTING COLLABORATIVE CONTENTS

Crafting collaborative content in influencer marketing involves leveraging the creativity, expertise, and influence of both brands and influencers to create engaging, authentic, and mutually beneficial content that resonates with audiences. Collaborative content allows brands to tap into the unique perspectives and creative talents of influencers while providing influencers with the opportunity to align with brands they believe in and create content that authentically reflects their personal brand. Collaborative content is a powerful strategy in influencer marketing, enabling brands to leverage the creativity, authenticity, and influence of influencers to connect with their audience in a meaningful way. By collaborating with influencers on content creation, brands can tap into new audiences, drive engagement, and build credibility and trust with their target audience. By following key strategies for crafting successful collaborations and drawing inspiration from examples of effective collaborative content campaigns, brands can harness the power of influencer marketing to achieve their marketing objectives and drive business growth in today's digital landscape.

8.3.1 Importance of Collaborative Content in Influencer Marketing

- **Authenticity and Credibility**: Collaborative content allows brands to leverage the authenticity and credibility of influencers to connect with their audience in a genuine and meaningful way. When influencers authentically endorse and create content for a brand, it resonates more strongly with their followers, leading to increased trust and credibility.

- **Creativity and Innovation**: Collaborating with influencers brings fresh perspectives and creative ideas to brand campaigns. Influencers often have a deep understanding of their audience and can offer unique insights and creative concepts that resonate with their followers and drive engagement.
- **Audience Reach and Engagement**: By partnering with influencers, brands can extend their reach and access new audiences that they may not be able to reach through traditional marketing channels. Collaborative content leverages the influencer's existing audience and engagement to amplify brand messaging and drive meaningful interactions.
- **Content Variety and Diversity**: Collaborative content allows brands to diversify their content strategy and experiment with different formats, styles, and platforms. Influencers bring their own unique voice, style, and perspective to collaborations, resulting in a diverse range of content that appeals to a broader audience.
- **Relationship Building**: Collaborative content fosters meaningful relationships between brands and influencers, built on trust, mutual respect, and shared values. By working together on content creation, brands and influencers can strengthen their partnership and create a foundation for future collaborations.

8.3.2 Strategies for Crafting Collaborative Content

- **Define Clear Objectives and Goals**: Start by defining the objectives and goals of the collaboration, including what you hope to achieve and how success will be measured. Align on key performance indicators (KPIs) such as reach, engagement, conversions, and brand sentiment.
- **Identify the Right Influencers**: Choose influencers whose audience, content style, and values align with your brand and campaign objectives. Look for influencers who have a genuine connection with their audience and a track record of creating high-quality, engaging content.
- **Collaborate on Content Ideation**: Collaborate with influencers on content ideation to brainstorm creative concepts and ideas that resonate with their audience and align with your brand messaging.

Encourage influencers to share their creative input and contribute ideas for content themes, formats, and delivery.

- **Co-Create Content:** Work closely with influencers to co-create content that authentically integrates your brand messaging and resonates with their audience. Provide influencers with creative freedom to interpret the brief and express their unique voice and style while ensuring alignment with brand guidelines and objectives.
- **Amplify Content Across Channels:** Once the collaborative content is created, amplify it across multiple channels to maximize reach and engagement. Share the content on social media platforms, brand websites, email newsletters, and other relevant channels to extend its reach and visibility.
- **Engage and Interact with Audiences:** Encourage engagement and interaction with the collaborative content by responding to comments, questions, and feedback from audiences. Foster meaningful conversations and connections with followers to deepen engagement and build brand loyalty.

8.3.3 Examples of Effective Collaborative Content Campaigns

Nike x Serena Williams

Nike collaborated with tennis champion Serena Williams to create a series of collaborative content campaigns celebrating female empowerment and athleticism. The campaigns featured powerful imagery, inspiring stories, and authentic endorsements from Serena Williams, resonating with Nike's audience and driving engagement.

Dove x Real Beauty Influencers

Dove partnered with a diverse group of real beauty influencers to create collaborative content campaigns promoting body positivity and self-confidence. The campaigns featured authentic testimonials, personal stories, and empowering messages that resonated with Dove's audience and sparked meaningful conversations around beauty standards.

GoPro x Adventure Influencers

GoPro collaborated with adventure influencers to create collaborative content showcasing epic adventures and outdoor experiences captured with GoPro cameras. The campaigns featured stunning photography, breathtaking videos, and firsthand accounts of adrenaline-pumping adventures, inspiring GoPro enthusiasts and driving brand engagement.

Starbucks x Coffee Influencers

Starbucks partnered with coffee influencers to create collaborative content campaigns highlighting unique coffee recipes, brewing techniques, and coffee culture around the world. The campaigns featured visually appealing imagery, informative videos, and engaging storytelling that resonated with coffee enthusiasts and drove traffic to Starbucks locations.

Sephora x Beauty Influencers

Sephora collaborated with beauty influencers to create collaborative content campaigns showcasing the latest beauty trends, makeup tutorials, and product reviews. The campaigns featured product demonstrations, honest reviews, and expert tips from beauty influencers, driving awareness and sales for Sephora's beauty products.

8.4 LEGAL CONSIDERATIONS AND ETHICS

Legal considerations and ethics play a vital role in influencer marketing, ensuring transparency, compliance with regulations, and ethical practices in partnerships between brands and influencers. As influencer marketing continues to evolve and grow in popularity, it's essential for brands and influencers to understand and adhere to legal requirements and ethical guidelines to maintain trust with their audiences and mitigate potential risks.

Legal considerations and ethics are essential aspects of influencer marketing, ensuring transparency, compliance, and ethical conduct in partnerships between brands and influencers. By adhering to legal requirements, such as FTC guidelines, ASA guidelines, and GDPR regulations, and upholding ethical standards, brands and influencers can build trust with their audiences, protect their interests, and mitigate risks associated with influencer marketing. By following best practices for legal compliance and ethical conduct, brands and influencers can create authentic, transparent, and mutually beneficial partnerships that deliver value to both parties and maintain credibility in the eyes of consumers.

8.4.1 Importance of Legal Considerations and Ethics in Influencer Marketing

- **Transparency and Disclosure:** Legal considerations and ethics require transparency and disclosure in influencer marketing partnerships. Audiences have the right to know when content is sponsored or paid for by a brand, and failure to disclose sponsored content can damage trust and credibility with followers.
- **Consumer Protection:** Legal regulations such as truth-in-advertising laws and consumer protection regulations aim to protect consumers

from deceptive or misleading advertising practices. Adhering to legal requirements ensures that consumers are not misled by sponsored content and have accurate information to make informed purchasing decisions.

- **Compliance with Regulations:** Influencer marketing is subject to various regulations and guidelines, including advertising laws, disclosure requirements, data privacy regulations, and industry-specific guidelines. Compliance with these regulations is essential to avoid legal consequences, fines, or penalties for non-compliance.
- **Brand Reputation and Trust:** Ethical considerations in influencer marketing are critical for maintaining brand reputation and trust with audiences. Brands and influencers who engage in transparent, ethical practices build credibility and trust with their followers, leading to stronger relationships and brand loyalty.
- **Risk Mitigation:** Legal considerations and ethics help mitigate risks associated with influencer marketing, including potential legal disputes, negative publicity, and damage to brand reputation. By following legal requirements and ethical guidelines, brands and influencers can minimize risks and protect their interests.

8.4.2 Key Legal Considerations and Regulations in Influencer Marketing

FTC Guidelines

The Federal Trade Commission (FTC) in the United States provides guidelines for influencer marketing disclosure and transparency. The FTC requires influencers to disclose material connections with brands and provide clear and conspicuous disclosures in sponsored content.

ASA Guidelines

The Advertising Standards Authority (ASA) in the United Kingdom regulates advertising practices and sets guidelines for influencer marketing disclosure and transparency. The ASA requires influencers to clearly disclose paid partnerships and distinguish between editorial content and advertising.

EU GDPR

The General Data Protection Regulation (GDPR) in the European Union governs the collection, processing, and protection of personal data. Influencer marketing campaigns that involve the collection or processing of personal data must comply with GDPR requirements, including obtaining consent from individuals and ensuring data security and privacy.

Truth-in-Advertising Laws

Truth-in-advertising laws require influencers to ensure that their content is accurate, truthful, and not deceptive or misleading.

Influencers must disclose any material connections with brands and avoid making false or exaggerated claims about products or services.

Endorsement Guidelines

Endorsement guidelines provide rules and requirements for influencer endorsements and testimonials. Influencers must disclose any material connections with brands and ensure that their endorsements are truthful, honest, and based on genuine experiences.

8.4.3 Best Practices for Legal Compliance and Ethical Conduct

Disclose Sponsorships Clearly

Clearly disclose sponsored content and paid partnerships in influencer marketing campaigns. Use clear and conspicuous disclosure language such as "#ad," "Paid partnership with [brand]," or "Sponsored by [brand]" to ensure transparency with audiences.

Use Disclosures Across Platforms

Ensure that disclosures are visible and prominent across all platforms where influencer content is published, including social media posts, videos, blog posts, and other digital channels.

Educate Influencers

Provide influencers with guidance and training on legal requirements, disclosure best practices, and ethical considerations in influencer marketing.

Educated influencers are better equipped to comply with regulations and uphold ethical standards in their content.

Review and Approve Content

Review influencer content before it is published to ensure compliance with legal requirements, brand guidelines, and ethical standards.

Provide feedback and guidance to influencers to address any issues or concerns proactively.

Monitor and Enforce Compliance

Monitor influencer campaigns and enforce compliance with legal requirements and ethical guidelines. Take prompt action to address any violations or discrepancies and ensure that influencer content meets regulatory and ethical standards.

8.4.4 Case Studies and Examples

Lord & Taylor Instagram Campaign

In 2015, Lord & Taylor faced legal scrutiny from the FTC for failing to disclose paid sponsorships in an Instagram campaign. The FTC alleged that Lord & Taylor had deceived consumers by paying influencers to post sponsored content without disclosing the sponsorship. Lord & Taylor settled with the FTC and agreed to disclose paid sponsorships in future campaigns.

Kylie Jenner and Instagram Posts

In 2018, Kylie Jenner faced criticism for promoting a detox tea brand on Instagram without disclosing that the posts were paid advertisements. The posts received backlash from followers and raised concerns about transparency and disclosure in influencer marketing. Kylie Jenner later edited the captions to include disclosure language.

8.5 MEASURING INFLUENCER CAMPAIGN SUCCESS

Measuring the success of influencer campaigns is essential for evaluating their impact, optimizing strategies, and maximizing return on investment (ROI) in influencer marketing. With the growing popularity of influencer collaborations, brands need effective methods to assess the performance and effectiveness of their campaigns accurately.

Measuring the success of influencer campaigns is essential for evaluating performance, optimizing strategies, and maximizing ROI in influencer marketing. By tracking key metrics such as engagement, reach, conversions, and brand sentiment, brands can assess the impact of influencer collaborations on marketing objectives and business outcomes. Utilizing tracking methods, analytics tools, and optimization strategies enables brands to measure influencer campaign success accurately, drive meaningful results, and build stronger, more effective influencer partnerships in today's digital landscape.

8.5.1 Importance of Measuring Influencer Campaign Success

Performance Evaluation

Measuring campaign success allows brands to evaluate the performance of influencer collaborations against predefined objectives and key performance indicators (KPIs). By assessing campaign metrics and outcomes, brands can determine whether their investment in influencer marketing has generated the desired results.

ROI Analysis

Measuring campaign success enables brands to calculate the return on investment

(ROI) of influencer marketing initiatives. By comparing the costs of the campaign to the achieved outcomes, such as sales, conversions, or brand awareness, brands can determine the efficiency and profitability of their influencer partnerships.

Optimization Opportunities

Analyzing campaign performance provides insights into what worked well and what areas need improvement. By identifying strengths and weaknesses in influencer campaigns, brands can optimize future strategies, refine targeting, and allocate resources more effectively to achieve better results.

Budget Allocation

Measuring campaign success helps brands make informed decisions about budget allocation and resource allocation for future influencer marketing initiatives. By understanding which campaigns deliver the highest ROI and impact, brands can allocate budgets strategically to maximize returns and achieve marketing objectives.

Building Long-Term Relationships

Measuring the success of influencer campaigns fosters transparency, accountability, and trust between brands and influencers. By demonstrating the value of influencer collaborations through tangible results, brands can build stronger, more sustainable relationships with influencers and foster long-term partnerships.

8.5.2 Key Metrics for Measuring Influencer Campaign Success

Engagement Metrics

Engagement metrics such as likes, comments, shares, and saves indicate how audiences interacted with influencer content. High engagement rates suggest that the content resonated well with the audience and drove meaningful interactions.

Reach and Impressions

Reach and impressions metrics quantify the size and visibility of influencer content across social media platforms. Higher reach and impressions indicate broader exposure and potential reach to a larger audience.

Follower Growth

Follower growth metrics track the increase in followers gained by the brand's social media accounts or website as a result of influencer campaigns. Positive follower growth suggests that the campaign successfully attracted new followers and expanded the brand's audience.

Click-Through Rate (CTR)

CTR measures the percentage of users who clicked on a link or call-to-action (CTA) included in influencer content. A higher CTR indicates that the content effectively drove traffic to the brand's website, landing page, or product page.

Conversion Metrics

Conversion metrics, such as sales, leads, sign-ups, or downloads, measure the number of desired actions taken by users as a result of influencer campaigns. Tracking conversions allows brands to assess the direct impact of influencer collaborations on business objectives.

Brand Sentiment

Brand sentiment metrics evaluate the overall sentiment and perception of the brand among consumers following influencer campaigns. Positive sentiment indicates that the campaign positively influenced brand perception and reputation.

8.5.3 Methods for Tracking and Measuring Influencer Campaign Success

- **Tracking Links and UTMs:** Use tracking links and unique tracking parameters (UTMs) to monitor traffic, clicks, and conversions generated by influencer content. UTMs allow brands to attribute website visits and conversions directly to influencer campaigns accurately.
- **Social Media Analytics Tools:** Utilize social media analytics tools provided by platforms such as Instagram Insights, Facebook Analytics, and Twitter Analytics to track engagement, reach, impressions, and audience demographics of influencer content.
- **Google Analytics:** Integrate Google Analytics with influencer campaigns to track website traffic, referral sources, and conversion events. Set up goals and conversion tracking to monitor specific actions taken by users who interact with influencer content.
- **Influencer Marketing Platforms:** Leverage influencer marketing platforms and tools that offer campaign tracking, performance analytics, and reporting features. These platforms provide insights into influencer reach, engagement, and audience demographics, streamlining the measurement process.
- **Surveys and Feedback:** Collect feedback from audiences through surveys, polls, or comments to gauge their perception and sentiment towards influencer campaigns. Qualitative feedback provides valuable insights into audience preferences, interests, and reactions to influencer content.

8.5.4 Strategies for Optimizing Influencer Campaign Outcomes

- **Set Clear Objectives and KPIs:** Define clear objectives and key performance indicators (KPIs) for influencer campaigns aligned with marketing goals and business objectives. Establish measurable targets to track progress and evaluate campaign success effectively.
- **Collaborate with the Right Influencers**: Choose influencers whose audience, content style, and values align with your brand and campaign objectives. Collaborate with influencers who have a genuine connection with their audience and a track record of driving engagement and conversions.
- **Provide Clear Guidelines and Briefs**: Communicate clear guidelines, expectations, and creative briefs to influencers to ensure alignment with brand messaging, values, and visual aesthetics. Provide examples and references to guide influencer content creation and maintain brand consistency.
- **Monitor Performance in Real-Time**: Monitor influencer campaign performance in real-time and adjust strategies and tactics as needed based on emerging insights and data. Continuously track key metrics and KPIs to identify trends, patterns, and areas for optimization.
- **Engage with Audiences**: Engage with audiences actively by responding to comments, questions, and feedback generated by influencer content. Foster meaningful interactions and conversations with followers to strengthen brand relationships and drive engagement.

8.5.5 Case Studies and Examples

Daniel Wellington Influencer Campaign

Daniel Wellington, a watch brand, collaborated with influencers on Instagram to promote its products. By tracking engagement metrics and referral traffic, Daniel Wellington measured the success of influencer campaigns and achieved significant sales growth.

ASOS Influencer Campaign

ASOS, an online fashion retailer, partnered with influencers to create collaborative content showcasing its latest fashion collections. By monitoring reach, engagement, and conversions, ASOS measured the impact of influencer campaigns on brand awareness and sales.

CHAPTER 9
VIDEO MARKETING

9.1 THE IMPACT OF VIDEO CONTENT

Video content has revolutionized the landscape of digital marketing, offering brands an unparalleled opportunity to engage, educate, and entertain audiences in a dynamic and immersive format. With the rise of video-sharing platforms such as YouTube, TikTok, and Instagram, video marketing has become an indispensable tool for businesses to reach and connect with consumers effectively.

Video content has transformed the landscape of digital marketing, offering brands a powerful tool to engage, entertain, and educate audiences in a dynamic and immersive format. With its visual appeal, emotional impact, and versatility, video content has become an indispensable component of successful marketing strategies across industries. By understanding the impact of video content in video marketing, leveraging key benefits, and implementing effective strategies for creating compelling video content, brands can harness the power of video to reach and connect with audiences, drive engagement, and achieve their marketing objectives in today's digital age.

9.1.1 Importance of Video Content in Video Marketing

- **Enhanced Engagement**: Video content captures attention and engages audiences more effectively than other forms of media. The combination of visuals, audio, and storytelling creates an immersive experience that resonates with viewers and encourages interaction and sharing.
- **Increased Brand Awareness**: Video content is highly shareable and has the potential to reach a vast audience across various platforms. By creating compelling and share-worthy videos, brands can increase brand awareness and visibility, reaching new audiences and expanding their reach.
- **Improved Communication**: Video content enables brands to communicate complex ideas, messages, and stories in a concise and digestible format. Through visual storytelling, brands can convey emotions, evoke empathy, and connect with audiences on a deeper level, fostering stronger relationships and brand loyalty.

- **Higher Conversion Rates:** Video content has been shown to drive higher conversion rates and sales compared to other forms of content. Video testimonials, product demonstrations, and explainer videos help educate and persuade consumers, leading to increased purchase intent and conversion.
- **SEO Benefits:** Video content can improve search engine optimization (SEO) and drive organic traffic to websites and landing pages. Video-rich content enhances user experience, increases dwell time on web pages, and improves search engine rankings, resulting in more visibility and traffic.

9.1.2 Key Benefits of Video Content in Video Marketing

- **Visual Appeal**: Video content captivates audiences with stunning visuals, vibrant colors, and dynamic animations, creating an engaging and memorable viewing experience.
- **Emotional Connection**: Video content evokes emotions and triggers human connections, fostering empathy, trust, and loyalty towards brands.
- **Versatility**: Video content is versatile and can be adapted to various formats, including how-to tutorials, product reviews, behind-the-scenes footage, interviews, and storytelling.
- **Accessibility**: Video content is accessible to a wide range of audiences, including visual learners, non-native speakers, and individuals with disabilities, making it an inclusive and effective communication tool.
- **Measurability**: Video content can be easily tracked and measured using analytics tools to monitor performance, engagement, and ROI, allowing brands to optimize strategies and improve results over time.

9.1.3 Strategies for Creating Compelling Video Content

- **Know Your Audience**: Understand your target audience's preferences, interests, and pain points to create video content that resonates with their needs and desires.
- **Tell a Story**: Craft compelling narratives and storytelling arcs that capture attention, evoke emotions, and convey brand messages effectively.
- **Keep it Short and Sweet**: Maintain brevity and conciseness in video content to keep viewers engaged and prevent drop-off. Aim for shorter videos that deliver key messages efficiently and effectively.

- **Focus on Quality**: Invest in high-quality production values, including video resolution, audio quality, lighting, and editing, to create professional-looking videos that reflect positively on your brand.
- **Be Authentic and Transparent**: Maintain authenticity and transparency in video content by showcasing real people, real experiences, and real stories. Authenticity builds trust and credibility with audiences and strengthens brand relationships.
- **Optimize for Mobile**: Ensure that video content is optimized for mobile viewing, with responsive designs, fast loading times, and vertical formats suitable for mobile devices.

9.1.4 Impact of Video Content on Social Media Platforms

- **YouTube**: YouTube is the second-largest search engine globally, with over two billion logged-in monthly users. Video content on YouTube can reach a massive audience and drive engagement through channels, playlists, and video recommendations.
- **Instagram**: Instagram has emerged as a popular platform for short-form video content, with features such as Stories, Reels, and IGTV. Video content on Instagram allows brands to showcase products, share behind-the-scenes footage, and connect with audiences in authentic and interactive ways.
- **TikTok**: TikTok has experienced explosive growth, particularly among younger demographics, with its short-form, user-generated video content. Brands can leverage TikTok to create viral video challenges, influencer partnerships, and branded content campaigns that resonate with Gen Z and millennial audiences.
- **LinkedIn**: LinkedIn has introduced native video content features, allowing brands to share thought leadership, industry insights, and behind-the-scenes content with a professional audience. Video content on LinkedIn can enhance brand visibility, showcase expertise, and foster connections within the business community.

9.1.5 Examples of Effective Video Marketing Campaigns

- **Dollar Shave Club**: Dollar Shave Club revolutionized the razor industry with its viral video campaign "Our Blades Are F***ing Great." The humorous and irreverent video went viral on social media, attracting millions of views and driving subscriptions to the brand's razor subscription service.

- **Nike:** Nike's "Dream Crazy" campaign featuring Colin Kaepernick sparked controversy and conversation with its powerful video ad advocating for social justice and equality. The video received widespread attention and praise for its bold messaging and inspirational storytelling.
- **Apple:** Apple's "Shot on iPhone" campaign showcases the capabilities of iPhone cameras through user-generated video content. The campaign features stunning visuals, creative storytelling, and diverse perspectives captured by iPhone users worldwide.

9.2 STRATEGIES FOR VIDEO MARKETING

Video marketing has emerged as a potent tool for businesses to engage with their target audience, drive brand awareness, and boost conversion rates. With the proliferation of online platforms and the increasing consumption of video content, businesses are leveraging video marketing to convey their message effectively and stand out in a crowded digital landscape.

Video marketing offers businesses a powerful platform to engage with their audience, drive brand awareness, and achieve marketing objectives effectively. By implementing strategic content creation, distribution, optimization, and measurement strategies, businesses can maximize the impact of their video marketing efforts and connect with consumers in meaningful ways. With the right strategies in place, businesses can leverage the storytelling power of video content to captivate audiences, drive engagement, and ultimately, drive business growth in today's digital age.

9.2.1 Content Creation Strategies

- **Understand Your Audience:** Start by understanding your target audience's demographics, preferences, and pain points. Tailor your video content to resonate with their interests and needs, ensuring maximum relevance and engagement.
- **Define Clear Objectives:** Clearly define the goals and objectives of your video marketing campaigns. Whether it's increasing brand awareness, driving website traffic, or boosting sales, align your content creation efforts with your overarching business objectives.
- **Tell Compelling Stories:** Storytelling is a powerful tool in video marketing. Craft compelling narratives that resonate with your audience emotionally, evoke empathy, and leave a lasting impression. Incorporate elements such as character development, conflict resolution, and emotional arcs to captivate viewers' attention.

- **Showcase Your Brand:** Use video content to showcase your brand's unique value proposition, personality, and values. Highlight what sets your brand apart from the competition and why consumers should choose your products or services.
- **Educate and Inform:** Provide value to your audience by creating educational and informative video content. Address common pain points, answer frequently asked questions, and offer practical tips and advice related to your industry or niche.

9.2.2 Distribution Strategies

- **Choose the Right Platforms:** Select platforms that align with your target audience's preferences and behavior. Whether it's YouTube, Facebook, Instagram, LinkedIn, or TikTok, choose platforms where your audience is most active and engaged.
- **Optimize for Each Platform:** Tailor your video content to each platform's unique specifications and best practices. Optimize video length, format, aspect ratio, and captions to maximize visibility, engagement, and shareability on each platform.
- **Leverage Paid Advertising:** Supplement organic reach with paid advertising to amplify the reach and impact of your video content. Use targeting options such as demographics, interests, and behavior to reach specific audience segments and drive desired actions.
- **Collaborate with Influencers:** Partner with influencers and content creators in your industry to expand your reach and leverage their existing audience. Collaborative video content can help introduce your brand to new audiences and build credibility through endorsements and recommendations.
- **Embed Videos on Your Website:** Incorporate video content into your website to enhance user experience, increase dwell time, and boost conversion rates. Embed videos on landing pages, product pages, and blog posts to provide additional context and information to visitors.

9.2.3 Optimization Strategies

- **Optimize for Search Engines:** Enhance the discoverability of your video content by optimizing for search engines. Use relevant keywords, tags, and descriptions in video titles and metadata to improve search rankings and visibility on platforms like YouTube and Google.
- **Create Attention-Grabbing Thumbnails:** Design eye-catching thumbnails that entice viewers to click and watch your videos. Use

high-quality images, bold text, and contrasting colors to make your thumbnails stand out in search results and recommendations.

- **Engage Viewers Early**: Capture viewers' attention within the first few seconds of your video to prevent them from scrolling or clicking away. Use engaging visuals, compelling hooks, and intriguing questions to pique curiosity and encourage viewers to continue watching.
- **Include Calls-to-Action (CTAs)**: Encourage viewers to take action after watching your video by including clear and compelling calls-to-action (CTAs). Prompt viewers to subscribe to your channel, visit your website, download a resource, or make a purchase to drive desired outcomes.
- **Monitor Performance Metrics**: Track key performance metrics such as views, watch time, engagement, and conversion rates to assess the effectiveness of your video marketing efforts. Use analytics tools and dashboards to monitor performance in real-time and make data-driven decisions for optimization.

9.2.4 Measurement Strategies

- **Set Measurable Goals**: Establish specific, measurable, achievable, relevant, and time-bound (SMART) goals for your video marketing campaigns. Define KPIs such as views, engagement, click-through rates, and conversions to track progress and evaluate success.
- **Track Performance Metrics**: Use analytics tools and platforms to track performance metrics and gather insights into audience behavior and preferences. Monitor metrics such as watch time, audience retention, demographics, and geographic location to understand how viewers engage with your content.
- **A/B Test Variations**: Experiment with different video formats, messaging, and CTAs through A/B testing to identify what resonates most with your audience. Test variations of thumbnails, video length, content structure, and messaging to optimize performance and maximize results.
- **Measure ROI**: Calculate the return on investment (ROI) of your video marketing campaigns by comparing the costs of production and distribution to the generated revenue or other desired outcomes. Determine the ROI of individual videos or campaigns to allocate resources effectively and optimize future strategies.
- **Iterate and Improve**: Continuously iterate and improve your video marketing strategies based on performance data and audience feedback. Identify trends, patterns, and areas for improvement to refine content

creation, distribution, and optimization strategies for better results over time.

9.3 PLATFORMS FOR VIDEO MARKETING: YOUTUBE, VIMEO, SOCIAL MEDIA

Video marketing has become an integral part of digital marketing strategies for businesses worldwide, offering a dynamic and engaging way to connect with audiences and drive brand awareness, engagement, and conversions. With the proliferation of online video platforms, businesses have a plethora of options to choose from when it comes to distributing their video content.

Video marketing offers businesses a powerful platform to connect with their audience, drive brand awareness, and achieve marketing objectives effectively. By leveraging platforms such as YouTube, Vimeo, and social media, businesses can reach a diverse and engaged audience, showcase their products and services, and foster meaningful connections and relationships with their followers. Whether it's creating compelling content, optimizing for search and discoverability, or measuring performance and engagement, businesses can maximize the impact of their video marketing efforts by implementing strategic approaches tailored to each platform's unique features and audience dynamics.

9.3.1 YouTube

As the largest video-sharing platform globally, YouTube offers unparalleled reach and visibility for businesses looking to share their video content with a vast audience.

- **Massive Audience:** With over two billion logged-in monthly users, YouTube provides access to a massive and diverse audience across demographics, interests, and geographic locations.
- **SEO Opportunities:** YouTube is also the second-largest search engine globally, making it a powerful platform for improving search engine visibility and driving organic traffic to your videos and website.
- **Monetization Options:** YouTube offers monetization options such as ad revenue sharing, channel memberships, and Super Chat, allowing businesses to generate revenue from their video content.
- **Analytics and Insights:** YouTube provides robust analytics and insights into video performance, including views, watch time, engagement, audience demographics, and traffic sources, enabling businesses to track and measure the effectiveness of their video marketing efforts.
- **Community Building:** YouTube fosters a sense of community and interaction among creators and viewers through comments, likes,

shares, and subscriptions, allowing businesses to engage with their audience and build a loyal fan base.

Best Practices for YouTube Video Marketing

- Optimize video titles, descriptions, and tags with relevant keywords to improve search visibility.
- Create compelling thumbnails and titles to capture viewers' attention and entice clicks.
- Publish high-quality, engaging content consistently to keep your audience engaged and coming back for more.
- Encourage viewers to subscribe to your channel, like, comment, and share your videos to increase engagement and reach.
- Leverage YouTube's advertising options, including TrueView ads, display ads, and sponsored cards, to reach specific target audiences and promote your video content.

9.3.2 Vimeo

Vimeo is a video-sharing platform known for its high-quality, ad-free content and focus on creativity and artistic expression. While it may not have the same reach as YouTube, Vimeo offers several unique features and benefits for businesses:

- **Quality and Aesthetics**: Vimeo is renowned for its high-quality video playback and sleek, ad-free interface, making it an ideal platform for showcasing visually stunning and professionally produced content.
- **Customization Options**: Vimeo offers extensive customization options for video players, privacy settings, and branding, allowing businesses to create a seamless and branded viewing experience for their audience.
- **Audience Targeting**: Vimeo provides advanced audience targeting options, including password protection, domain-level privacy, and audience restrictions, enabling businesses to control who can access and view their video content.
- **Analytics and Insights**: Vimeo offers detailed analytics and insights into video performance, including views, engagement, playbacks, and geographic location, helping businesses track and measure the impact of their video marketing campaigns.
- **Creative Community**: Vimeo fosters a vibrant and creative community of filmmakers, artists, and content creators, providing businesses with opportunities for collaboration, inspiration, and networking.

Best Practices for Vimeo Video Marketing

- Upload high-quality, visually compelling content that aligns with Vimeo's creative and artistic ethos.
- Customize your video player, including colors, logos, and end screens, to create a branded viewing experience.
- Utilize Vimeo's privacy settings to control access to your videos and target specific audience segments effectively.
- Embed Vimeo videos on your website, blog, or landing pages to enhance user experience and drive engagement.
- Engage with the Vimeo community by liking, commenting, and sharing other users' content to build relationships and visibility.

9.3.3 Social Media Platforms

Social media platforms such as Facebook, Instagram, Twitter, LinkedIn, and TikTok have become increasingly popular channels for video marketing, offering businesses diverse opportunities to connect with their audience and drive engagement. Here's why businesses should consider leveraging social media for video marketing:

- **Wide Reach and Engagement**: Social media platforms have billions of active users worldwide, providing businesses with access to a vast and engaged audience across demographics, interests, and geographic locations.
- **Native Video Features**: Social media platforms offer native video features such as Stories, Reels, IGTV, and Live, allowing businesses to create and share a variety of video content formats tailored to each platform's audience and user behavior.
- **Visual Discovery**: Social media platforms are highly visual-centric, making them ideal for showcasing products, services, and brand stories through visually compelling and engaging video content.
- **Real-Time Interaction**: Social media enables real-time interaction and engagement with audiences through likes, comments, shares, and direct messages, fostering meaningful connections and conversations between businesses and their followers.
- **Targeted Advertising**: Social media platforms offer advanced targeting options for advertising, including demographics, interests, behaviors, and retargeting, enabling businesses to reach specific target audiences with personalized video content.

Best Practices for Social Media Video Marketing

- Tailor video content to each platform's audience, format, and best practices, including video length, aspect ratio, and content style.
- Utilize storytelling techniques, humor, and emotion to capture attention and resonate with social media users.
- Post video content consistently and at optimal times to maximize visibility and engagement.
- Encourage audience engagement through calls-to-action (CTAs), polls, questions, and interactive elements in video content.
- Leverage social media advertising options, including sponsored posts, video ads, and influencer partnerships, to amplify reach and drive desired actions.

9.4 LIVE STREAMING AND INTERACTIVE VIDEO CONTENT

In the age of digital connectivity, live streaming and interactive video content have emerged as powerful tools for communication, entertainment, and engagement. With the rise of platforms like Twitch, YouTube Live, and Facebook Live, individuals and businesses alike can reach audiences in real-time, fostering dynamic interactions and building communities like never before. Platforms for live streaming and interactive video content have revolutionized online engagement, empowering creators to connect with audiences in real-time and build thriving communities around their content. With features like real-time chat, monetization options, and immersive experiences, these platforms offer unprecedented opportunities for creativity, expression, and entrepreneurship. As technology continues to advance and consumer behaviors evolve, the future of live streaming promises even greater innovation and possibilities for creators and viewers alike.

9.4.1 The Rise of Live Streaming Platforms

Live streaming platforms have witnessed exponential growth in recent years, fueled by advancements in technology and the increasing demand for real-time engagement. Twitch, founded in 2011, initially focused on live streaming video games but has since expanded to include various categories like music, art, and lifestyle content. YouTube Live, launched in 2011 as well, offers a broader range of content and integrates seamlessly with the YouTube ecosystem, allowing creators to leverage their existing subscriber base. Facebook Live, introduced in 2016, capitalizes on Facebook's massive user base to enable live broadcasting directly within the social network.

9.4.2 Features and Functionality

These platforms offer a diverse set of features to enhance the live streaming experience for both creators and viewers. Common features include real-time chat, allowing viewers to interact with the streamer and each other, as well as monetization options such as donations, subscriptions, and advertising revenue sharing. Some platforms also provide tools for streamers to enhance their broadcasts, such as overlays, alerts, and integration with third-party applications.

9.4.3 Engagement and Community Building

One of the most significant advantages of live streaming is its ability to foster genuine engagement and community building. Unlike pre-recorded content, live streams enable direct interaction between creators and viewers in real-time, creating a sense of immediacy and intimacy. Viewers can ask questions, offer feedback, and participate in polls or Q&A sessions, fostering a sense of belonging and connection within the community.

9.4.4 Monetization Opportunities

Live streaming platforms offer various monetization opportunities for creators, allowing them to turn their passion into a source of income. Twitch, for example, enables streamers to earn money through subscriptions, donations, ad revenue, and sponsorships. YouTube Live offers similar monetization options, including ad revenue sharing, channel memberships, and Super Chat, where viewers can pay to have their messages highlighted during a live stream. Facebook Live also provides monetization opportunities through fan subscriptions, stars (virtual gifts purchased by viewers), and branded content deals.

9.4.5 Challenges and Considerations

While live streaming platforms offer tremendous opportunities for creators and businesses, they also present challenges and considerations. One challenge is the saturation of the market, with an increasing number of creators vying for viewers' attention. Standing out in a crowded landscape requires consistent quality, engaging content, and effective promotion. Additionally, creators must navigate complex monetization policies and algorithms that govern content visibility and monetization eligibility.

9.4.6 Emerging Trends and Innovations

The landscape of live streaming and interactive video content continues to evolve, driven by technological advancements and changing consumer preferences. One emerging trend is the integration of augmented reality (AR) and virtual reality (VR) technologies, enabling immersive and interactive experiences for viewers. Platforms like Twitch are exploring AR overlays that enhance gameplay streams, while VR platforms like Oculus Venues offer virtual concert experiences with interactive elements. Another trend is the convergence of live streaming with e-commerce, allowing creators to monetize their content through direct sales and affiliate marketing. Platforms like Amazon Live enable influencers to showcase products in real-time and earn commissions on sales generated through their streams. Similarly, platforms like TikTok are experimenting with live shopping features that allow viewers to purchase products directly from live streams.

9.5 VIDEO ANALYTICS AND PERFORMANCE MEASUREMENT

In the digital age, video content has become a cornerstone of online communication, marketing, and entertainment. From promotional videos to educational content and live streams, videos captivate audiences and convey messages in powerful ways. However, the success of video content isn't just about creating compelling visuals—it's also about understanding how viewers engage with it. That's where video analytics and performance measurement come into play.

Video analytics and performance measurement are integral components of any successful video content strategy. By leveraging data-driven insights, organizations can optimize their videos for engagement, drive meaningful interactions with their audience, and achieve their business objectives more effectively. As technology continues to evolve and data analysis capabilities expand, the role of video analytics in informing strategic decision-making will become increasingly critical in the digital landscape.

9.5.1 The Importance of Video Analytics

Video analytics refers to the collection, analysis, and interpretation of data related to video content. By leveraging analytics, content creators, marketers, and businesses can gain valuable insights into viewer behavior, preferences, and engagement patterns. This data-driven approach allows them to optimize their content strategy, improve audience engagement, and achieve their goals more effectively.

9.5.2 Key Metrics in Video Analytics

- **View Count:** View count indicates the total number of times a video has been viewed. While it provides a basic measure of reach, it doesn't necessarily reflect viewer engagement or satisfaction.
- **Watch Time:** Watch time measures the total amount of time viewers spend watching a video. It's a crucial metric that indicates how engaging and valuable the content is to the audience.
- **Audience Retention:** Audience retention tracks how well a video retains viewers' attention over time. It's represented as a percentage

and shows the proportion of viewers who continue watching at each point in the video.

- **Engagement Metrics:** Engagement metrics include likes, comments, shares, and click-through rates (CTRs). These metrics reflect viewer interaction with the video and indicate the level of audience engagement and interest.
- **Conversion Metrics:** Conversion metrics track actions taken by viewers after watching a video, such as signing up for a newsletter, making a purchase, or visiting a website. These metrics help measure the effectiveness of video content in driving desired outcomes.

9.5.3 Tools and Strategies for Video Analytics

- **Platform Analytics:** Many video hosting platforms, such as YouTube, Vimeo, and Facebook, offer built-in analytics tools that provide insights into various metrics like view count, watch time, audience demographics, and engagement.
- **Google Analytics:** Google Analytics can be integrated with video platforms to track user interactions, behavior flow, and conversion goals related to video content. It allows for more in-depth analysis and correlation with other website metrics.
- **Third-Party Analytics Tools:** There are numerous third-party analytics tools specifically designed for video analytics, such as Vidyard, Wistia, and Brightcove. These tools offer advanced features like heatmaps, A/B testing, and audience segmentation to optimize video performance.
- **Heatmaps and A/B Testing:** Heatmap analysis visualizes viewer engagement by highlighting areas of interest or drop-off within a video. A/B testing involves creating multiple versions of a video with slight variations and comparing their performance to identify the most effective elements.
- **Social Media Insights:** Social media platforms provide insights into video performance metrics like views, likes, shares, and comments. Analyzing these metrics helps optimize video content for specific platforms and target audiences.

9.5.4 The Role of Video Analytics in Decision Making

Video analytics play a crucial role in informing strategic decisions related to content creation, distribution, and marketing. By analyzing viewer behavior and preferences, organizations can:

- **Identify Trends and Patterns:** Analyzing video analytics helps identify trends in viewer behavior, content performance, and audience demographics. This information can inform content strategy and drive future video production efforts.
- **Optimize Content for Engagement:** Insights from video analytics enable content creators to identify areas for improvement and optimize their videos for better engagement. This may involve experimenting with different formats, lengths, and topics based on audience preferences.
- **Personalize Viewer Experiences:** By understanding individual viewer preferences and behavior, organizations can deliver personalized video recommendations and experiences tailored to each viewer's interests and needs.
- **Measure ROI and Effectiveness:** Video analytics provide quantitative data to measure the return on investment (ROI) and effectiveness of video content. By tracking metrics like conversion rates and engagement levels, organizations can assess the impact of their video marketing efforts and make data-driven decisions to optimize performance.

9.5.5 Challenges and Considerations

While video analytics offer valuable insights, there are challenges and considerations to keep in mind.

Data Accuracy and Reliability

Ensuring the accuracy and reliability of video analytics data can be challenging, especially when dealing with multiple platforms and data sources. It's essential to use consistent tracking methods and verify data integrity to make informed decisions.

Privacy and Compliance

Collecting and analyzing viewer data raise privacy concerns and may require compliance with regulations like the General Data Protection Regulation (GDPR) and the California Consumer Privacy Act (CCPA). Organizations must ensure they adhere to data protection laws and obtain consent when collecting personal information.

Interpretation and Actionability

Analyzing video analytics data is only valuable if it leads to actionable insights and informed decision-making. It's essential to interpret the data in context and translate insights into concrete strategies and actions to improve video performance.

CHAPTER 10

ANALYTICS AND DATA-DRIVEN MARKETING

10.1 THE ROLE OF DATA IN DIGITAL MARKETING

In the ever-evolving landscape of marketing, data has emerged as a game-changer, enabling businesses to make informed decisions, personalize experiences, and drive growth. Analytics and data-driven marketing have become indispensable tools for marketers, offering insights into consumer behavior, preferences, and trends.

Analytics and data-driven marketing have transformed the way businesses understand and engage with their customers. By harnessing the power of data, marketers can gain valuable insights, personalize experiences, and drive business growth. From customer profiling and personalization to predictive analytics and marketing automation, data-driven marketing offers a plethora of strategies and tactics to optimize marketing efforts and deliver measurable results. As technology continues to evolve and data analysis capabilities expand, the role of data-driven marketing in driving business success will only continue to grow in importance.

10.1.1 The Significance of Analytics and Data-Driven Marketing

Analytics and data-driven marketing involve the collection, analysis, and interpretation of data to optimize marketing strategies and campaigns. By harnessing the power of data, marketers can gain valuable insights into customer behavior, measure the effectiveness of marketing efforts, and make data-driven decisions to drive business growth. In today's digital age, where consumers are inundated with messages from various channels, data-driven marketing allows businesses to cut through the noise and deliver personalized, relevant experiences to their target audience.

10.1.2 Key Principles of Data-Driven Marketing

Data Collection

The foundation of data-driven marketing lies in collecting relevant data from various sources, including customer interactions, website analytics, social media engagement, and sales transactions. This data provides valuable insights into consumer behavior, preferences, and demographics, enabling marketers to create targeted campaigns and personalized experiences.

Data Analysis

Once data is collected, it needs to be analyzed to extract meaningful insights. This involves using analytics tools and techniques to identify trends, patterns, and correlations within the data. By understanding customer behavior and preferences, marketers can tailor their marketing strategies to resonate with their target audience effectively.

Segmentation and Targeting

Segmentation involves dividing the target audience into distinct groups based on shared characteristics or behaviors.

By segmenting their audience, marketers can create more personalized and relevant marketing messages tailored to the specific needs and interests of each segment. Targeting involves delivering these messages to the right audience through the most appropriate channels, maximizing the impact of marketing efforts.

Testing and Optimization

Data-driven marketing is an iterative process that requires continuous testing and optimization. Marketers can conduct A/B tests, multivariate tests, and other experiments to evaluate the performance of different marketing strategies and tactics. By measuring key performance indicators (KPIs) and analyzing the results, marketers can refine their approach and optimize their campaigns for better results.

Measurement and ROI

Measurement is crucial for assessing the effectiveness of marketing efforts and calculating the return on investment (ROI).

By tracking KPIs such as conversion rates, customer acquisition cost (CAC), and customer lifetime value (CLV), marketers can evaluate the impact of their campaigns and allocate resources more effectively.

10.1.3 Strategies for Leveraging Data in Marketing

Customer Profiling and Persona Development

Data-driven marketing begins with understanding your target audience. By analyzing demographic data, purchase history, online behavior, and other relevant information, marketers can create detailed customer profiles and personas. These profiles help marketers tailor their messaging and offerings to resonate with specific segments of their audience effectively.

Personalization and Customization

Personalization is a cornerstone of data-driven marketing, enabling marketers to deliver relevant and timely messages to individual customers. By leveraging data to personalize email campaigns, website content, product recommendations, and advertisements, marketers can enhance the customer experience and drive engagement and conversions.

Predictive Analytics

Predictive analytics involves using historical data and statistical algorithms to forecast future trends and outcomes. Marketers can use predictive analytics to identify potential leads, anticipate customer behavior, and optimize marketing strategies for maximum impact. Predictive modeling techniques like customer churn prediction, lifetime value prediction, and propensity modeling can help marketers make proactive decisions and stay ahead of the competition.

Marketing Automation

Marketing automation platforms streamline repetitive tasks and workflows, allowing marketers to scale their efforts and deliver personalized experiences at scale. By integrating data from various sources and automating processes like email marketing, lead nurturing, and campaign management, marketers can engage customers more effectively and drive efficiency and ROI.

Attribution Modeling

Attribution modeling is the process of assigning credit to various marketing touchpoints along the customer journey. By analyzing data from multiple channels and touchpoints, marketers can determine which marketing activities contribute most to conversions and revenue generation. This insight helps optimize marketing budgets and allocate resources to the most effective channels and campaigns.

10.1.4 Challenges and Considerations

While data-driven marketing offers significant benefits, it also presents challenges and considerations:

- **Data Quality and Privacy:** Ensuring data accuracy and compliance with data privacy regulations (e.g., GDPR, CCPA) is essential for maintaining consumer trust and legal compliance.
- **Integration and Silos:** Integrating data from disparate sources and breaking down data silos within organizations can be complex but is necessary for gaining a holistic view of the customer journey.
- **Talent and Skills Gap:** Data-driven marketing requires specialized skills in data analysis, statistics, and technology. Investing in training

and talent development is crucial for building a data-driven culture within organizations.

- **Ethical Use of Data:** Marketers must use data ethically and responsibly, avoiding practices that may infringe on consumer privacy or manipulate behavior.

10.2 INTRODUCTION TO DIGITAL ANALYTICS TOOLS

In the fast-paced world of digital marketing and online business, understanding user behavior, optimizing performance, and measuring success are paramount. Digital analytics tools serve as indispensable instruments for businesses seeking to gain insights into their online presence, customer interactions, and overall performance.

Digital analytics tools are essential instruments for businesses seeking to thrive in the digital age. By leveraging data-driven insights, businesses can understand their audience, optimize their online presence, and drive meaningful results. Whether it's tracking website performance, analyzing user behavior, or measuring the effectiveness of marketing campaigns, digital analytics tools provide the necessary tools and capabilities to navigate the complexities of the digital landscape effectively. By choosing the right analytics tool and harnessing the power of data, businesses can unlock new opportunities for growth and success in the digital realm.

10.2.1 The Significance of Digital Analytics Tools

Digital analytics tools play a pivotal role in helping businesses navigate the complexities of the digital landscape. By collecting, analyzing, and interpreting data from various online channels and touchpoints, these tools provide valuable insights into user behavior, website performance, and marketing effectiveness. Whether it's understanding customer journeys, tracking key performance indicators (KPIs), or optimizing marketing campaigns, digital analytics tools empower businesses to make informed decisions and drive growth in the digital realm.

10.2.2 Key Features of Digital Analytics Tools

Data Collection

Digital analytics tools gather data from multiple sources, including websites, mobile apps, social media platforms, email campaigns, and advertising channels. They use tracking codes, cookies, and other methods to capture user interactions and behavior across these channels.

Data Analysis

Once data is collected, digital analytics tools analyze it to uncover patterns, trends, and insights. They provide dashboards, reports, and visualization tools to help users understand and interpret the data effectively.

Audience Insights

Digital analytics tools offer audience segmentation and demographic analysis to help businesses understand their target audience better. They provide insights into demographics, interests, behaviors, and preferences, enabling businesses to tailor their marketing strategies and messages accordingly.

Website Performance

Digital analytics tools track website performance metrics such as traffic, page views, bounce rates, and conversion rates. They identify areas for improvement and optimization to enhance the user experience and drive desired outcomes.

Campaign Tracking

Digital analytics tools enable businesses to track the performance of their marketing campaigns across various channels. They provide insights into campaign reach, engagement, and conversion metrics, allowing businesses to evaluate the effectiveness of their marketing efforts and allocate resources strategically.

10.2.3 Popular Digital Analytics Tools

Google Analytics

Google Analytics is one of the most widely used digital analytics tools, offering a comprehensive suite of features for website and app analytics. It provides insights into website traffic, user behavior, conversion tracking, and audience demographics. Google Analytics is free to use and offers advanced features through Google Analytics 360 for enterprise users.

Adobe Analytics

Adobe Analytics is a robust analytics platform that offers advanced features for measuring and optimizing digital experiences. It provides real-time analytics, predictive analytics, audience segmentation, and integration with other Adobe Experience Cloud solutions. Adobe Analytics is favored by enterprise-level businesses for its scalability and customization options.

Mixpanel

Mixpanel is a user analytics platform that focuses on tracking user interactions and behaviors within web and mobile applications. It offers event-based tracking, cohort analysis, funnel analysis, and A/B testing capabilities to help businesses understand user engagement and retention. Mixpanel is popular among mobile app developers and product managers for its user-centric approach to analytics.

Heap Analytics

Heap Analytics is an easy-to-use analytics platform that automates data collection and analysis without the need for manual tracking codes. It captures every user interaction on a website or app, allowing businesses to retroactively analyze user behavior and identify insights without predefined event tracking. Heap Analytics is ideal for small to medium-sized businesses looking for a hassle-free analytics solution.

Hotjar

Hotjar is a user behavior analytics and feedback tool that combines heatmaps, session recordings, surveys, and user feedback to provide insights into website usability and user experience. It helps businesses visualize how users interact with their website, identify pain points, and optimize conversion funnels. Hotjar is popular among marketers, UX designers, and product managers for its visual approach to analytics.

10.2.4 Considerations for Choosing Digital Analytics Tools

When selecting digital analytics tools, businesses should consider the following factors:

- **Features and Functionality:** Evaluate the features and capabilities of each tool to ensure it meets your specific business needs and objectives.
- **Ease of Use:** Consider the usability and user interface of the tool to ensure it's intuitive and easy to navigate for your team members.
- **Integration:** Check if the tool integrates seamlessly with other software and platforms used in your organization, such as content management systems (CMS), customer relationship management (CRM) systems, and marketing automation platforms.
- **Scalability:** Consider the scalability of the tool to accommodate your business growth and evolving analytics needs over time.
- **Cost:** Compare the pricing plans and subscription options of different tools to find one that fits within your budget constraints.

10.3 INTERPRETING DATA AND KPIS

In the realm of business and marketing, data serves as the foundation upon which informed decisions are made and strategies are formulated. Key Performance Indicators (KPIs) play a crucial role in this process, providing measurable metrics that gauge the success and effectiveness of various activities and initiatives.

Interpreting data and KPIs is a critical component of business management and decision-making. By understanding and analyzing key metrics, organizations can gain valuable insights into performance, identify areas for improvement, and drive strategic initiatives forward. Whether it's monitoring financial health, assessing marketing effectiveness, or optimizing operational efficiency, interpreting data and KPIs provides the foundation for informed decision-making and sustainable growth. By following best practices and leveraging data-driven insights, businesses can unlock new opportunities, mitigate risks, and achieve their objectives in an ever-evolving business landscape.

10.3.1 The Significance of Interpreting Data and KPIs

Interpreting data and KPIs is essential for businesses seeking to measure progress, track performance, and drive continuous improvement. By analyzing and understanding these metrics, organizations can identify trends, make data-driven decisions, and optimize their strategies for success. Whether it's evaluating marketing campaigns, assessing operational efficiency, or monitoring financial performance, interpreting data and KPIs provides valuable insights into the health and trajectory of a business.

10.3.2 Common Types of KPIs

Financial KPIs

Financial KPIs measure the financial health and performance of a business. Examples include revenue, profit margin, return on investment (ROI), gross margin, and cash flow. Financial KPIs provide insights into revenue generation, profitability, and financial stability, helping businesses make informed decisions about resource allocation and investment strategies.

Marketing KPIs

Marketing KPIs track the effectiveness of marketing campaigns and initiatives. Examples include website traffic, conversion rate, customer acquisition cost (CAC), customer lifetime value (CLV), and return on ad spend (ROAS). Marketing KPIs help businesses evaluate the impact of their marketing efforts, optimize campaign performance, and allocate marketing budgets more effectively.

Sales KPIs

Sales KPIs measure the performance of sales teams and processes. Examples include sales revenue, sales growth, sales conversion rate, average deal size, and sales pipeline velocity. Sales KPIs provide insights into sales performance, customer acquisition, and revenue generation, enabling businesses to identify areas for improvement and optimize sales strategies.

Customer Service KPIs

Customer service KPIs assess the quality and effectiveness of customer service and support operations. Examples include customer satisfaction score (CSAT), net promoter score (NPS), average response time, first contact resolution rate, and customer retention rate. Customer service KPIs help businesses measure customer satisfaction, loyalty, and retention, guiding efforts to deliver exceptional customer experiences.

Operational KPIs

Operational KPIs track the efficiency and performance of business operations. Examples include inventory turnover ratio, order fulfillment rate, production cycle time, employee productivity, and equipment downtime.

Operational KPIs help businesses identify bottlenecks, streamline processes, and improve overall operational efficiency.

10.3.3 Best Practices for Interpreting Data and KPIs

Set Clear Objectives

Define clear objectives and goals for each KPI to ensure alignment with business priorities and strategies.

Clearly defined objectives provide a benchmark for measuring performance and guiding decision-making.

Choose Relevant KPIs

Select KPIs that are relevant to your business objectives, industry, and target audience. Avoid tracking too many KPIs or ones that don't directly contribute to your business goals, as this can lead to information overload and lack of focus.

Establish Baselines and Targets

Establish baseline values and set achievable targets for each KPI based on historical data, industry benchmarks, and business objectives. Baselines provide context for interpreting KPI performance, while targets serve as actionable goals to strive for.

Monitor Trends and Patterns

Monitor KPI trends over time to identify patterns, anomalies, and areas for improvement. Analyze historical data to understand seasonality, cyclical trends, and potential correlations between different KPIs.

Segment and Drill Down

Segment KPI data by different variables, such as demographics, geographic location, or product categories, to uncover insights and opportunities for targeted optimization. Drill down into specific data subsets to identify root causes and drivers behind KPI performance.

Benchmark Against Peers

Benchmark KPI performance against industry peers, competitors, or best-in-class organizations to gain insights into relative performance and identify areas of strength and weakness. Benchmarking helps set realistic targets and provides context for interpreting KPI data.

Iterate and Improve

Continuously iterate and refine KPIs based on changing business needs, market dynamics, and performance trends. Solicit feedback from stakeholders, adapt to evolving business conditions, and incorporate lessons learned into future planning and decision-making.

10.4 APPLYING INSIGHTS TO OPTIMIZE STRATEGIES

In the dynamic landscape of business and marketing, insights derived from data serve as invaluable assets for optimizing strategies, driving growth, and staying ahead of the competition. Applying insights effectively involves translating data-driven findings into actionable strategies that deliver tangible results.

Applying insights derived from data is essential for businesses seeking to optimize their strategies, drive growth, and stay competitive in today's digital landscape. By embracing a culture of data-driven decision-making, focusing on actionable insights, and taking an iterative approach to strategy optimization, organizations can unlock new opportunities, mitigate risks, and achieve their objectives more effectively. By following best practices and leveraging real-world examples of successful implementation, businesses can harness the power of insights to drive innovation, improve customer experiences, and achieve sustainable growth in an ever-evolving business environment.

10.4.1 The Importance of Applying Insights

Applying insights derived from data is essential for businesses seeking to maximize their potential and achieve their objectives. Insights provide a deeper understanding of customer behavior, market dynamics, and competitive trends, enabling businesses to make informed decisions and tailor their strategies for success. By applying insights effectively, organizations can identify opportunities, mitigate risks, and optimize their operations, ultimately driving sustainable growth and long-term profitability.

10.4.2 Key Principles of Applying Insights

Data-Driven Decision Making

Embrace a culture of data-driven decision-making, where insights derived from data serve as the foundation for strategic planning and execution. Base decisions on empirical evidence rather than intuition or gut feelings, ensuring that strategies are informed by objective analysis and rigorous evaluation.

Actionable Insights

Focus on generating actionable insights that can be translated into tangible strategies and initiatives. Identify key findings that have the potential to drive meaningful change and prioritize actions that are likely to have the greatest impact on business outcomes.

Iterative Approach

Take an iterative approach to applying insights, continuously refining strategies based on feedback, performance data, and evolving market conditions. Embrace experimentation and adaptability, allowing strategies to evolve in response to changing dynamics and new insights.

Cross-Functional Collaboration

Foster cross-functional collaboration and communication within the organization, ensuring that insights are shared and applied effectively across different departments and teams. Break down silos and encourage knowledge sharing to maximize the impact of insights on overall business performance.

Measure and Monitor

Establish metrics and KPIs to measure the effectiveness of strategies and monitor their impact over time. Regularly track performance against benchmarks and targets, identifying areas for improvement and optimization based on data-driven insights.

10.4.3 Best Practices for Applying Insights

- **Segmentation and Personalization:** Leverage insights to segment your audience and personalize experiences based on their preferences, behaviors, and demographics. Tailor messaging, products, and offers to resonate with different segments, maximizing relevance and engagement.
- **Optimization and Testing:** Use insights to optimize strategies through A/B testing, multivariate testing, and other experimentation techniques. Test different variables, such as messaging, imagery, and calls-to-action, to identify the most effective combinations and refine your approach accordingly.
- **Customer Journey Mapping:** Map the customer journey based on insights derived from data, identifying key touchpoints, pain points, and opportunities for engagement. Optimize the customer experience

at each stage of the journey, removing friction and providing value to drive conversion and retention.

- **Predictive Analytics:** Harness predictive analytics to anticipate future trends, behaviors, and outcomes based on historical data and statistical modeling. Use predictive insights to proactively address challenges, capitalize on opportunities, and stay ahead of the competition.
- **Continuous Learning and Improvement:** Foster a culture of continuous learning and improvement, where insights are used to inform ongoing education, skill development, and process refinement. Encourage employees to stay curious, experiment with new ideas, and embrace a growth mindset to drive innovation and excellence.

10.4.4 Real-World Examples

Netflix

Netflix leverages data-driven insights to personalize recommendations for its users, improving content discovery and retention. By analyzing viewing habits, preferences, and engagement metrics, Netflix identifies relevant content recommendations tailored to each user's interests, increasing user satisfaction and loyalty.

Amazon

Amazon uses insights derived from customer data to optimize its e-commerce platform and drive sales. By analyzing purchase history, browsing behavior, and demographic information, Amazon delivers personalized product recommendations, targeted promotions, and optimized search results, enhancing the shopping experience and driving conversion.

Uber

Uber applies insights from data to optimize its ride-sharing service and improve operational efficiency. By analyzing traffic patterns, demand trends, and driver behavior, Uber optimizes pricing algorithms, driver dispatch algorithms, and route optimization algorithms to minimize wait times, reduce congestion, and maximize driver utilization.

Nike

Nike uses insights from data to personalize marketing campaigns and product offerings for its customers. By analyzing social media engagement, purchase history, and fitness data, Nike tailors its marketing messages, product recommendations, and loyalty programs to resonate with different segments of its audience, driving brand loyalty and advocacy.

10.5 PRIVACY, CONSENT AND DATA PROTECTION

In an increasingly digital world, where personal information is constantly exchanged and utilized, ensuring privacy, obtaining consent, and safeguarding data have become critical considerations for individuals, businesses, and governments alike.

Privacy, consent, and data protection are essential considerations in today's digital landscape, where personal information is constantly exchanged and utilized. Upholding privacy rights, obtaining informed consent, and safeguarding data are fundamental for building trust, complying with regulations, and maintaining ethical standards in data practices.

By adopting best practices, implementing robust measures, and prioritizing transparency and accountability, organizations can navigate the complexities of privacy and data protection effectively, ensuring the responsible and ethical handling of personal information in the digital age.

10.5.1 Understanding Privacy, Consent, and Data Protection

Privacy

Privacy refers to an individual's right to control their personal information and decide how it is collected, used, and shared.

It encompasses aspects such as confidentiality, autonomy, and anonymity, allowing individuals to maintain boundaries and protect their personal space in the digital realm.

Consent

Consent is the voluntary agreement given by individuals to the collection, processing, and use of their personal data for specific purposes. It requires clear communication, informed decision-making, and the ability to withdraw consent at any time. Consent forms the cornerstone of ethical data practices and respects individuals' autonomy and rights.

Data Protection

Data protection encompasses the measures and regulations designed to safeguard personal data from unauthorized access, use, or disclosure. It includes principles such as data minimization, security safeguards, transparency, and accountability, ensuring that personal information is handled responsibly and in accordance with legal requirements.

10.5.2 The Significance of Privacy, Consent, and Data Protection

Privacy, consent, and data protection are essential for several reasons:

- **Trust and Transparency:** Respecting privacy, obtaining consent, and protecting data are fundamental for building trust between individuals, businesses, and institutions. Transparent data practices foster trust and confidence, enhancing relationships and enabling responsible data stewardship.
- **Legal Compliance:** Adhering to privacy regulations and data protection laws is essential for avoiding legal repercussions and regulatory penalties. Compliance with frameworks such as the General Data Protection Regulation (GDPR), California Consumer Privacy Act (CCPA), and other regional data protection laws is necessary to protect individuals' rights and avoid potential liabilities.
- **Ethical Considerations:** Upholding privacy, obtaining informed consent, and safeguarding data align with ethical principles and moral responsibilities. Respect for individuals' autonomy, dignity, and rights requires organizations to prioritize privacy and data protection in their operations and decision-making processes.
- **Business Reputation:** Demonstrating a commitment to privacy and data protection enhances an organization's reputation and credibility. Responsible data practices can differentiate businesses from competitors, attract customers who value privacy, and foster positive relationships with stakeholders.

10.5.3 Challenges in Privacy, Consent, and Data Protection

Complexity of Regulations

The evolving regulatory landscape and the proliferation of privacy laws present challenges for organizations seeking to navigate compliance requirements effectively. Keeping up with regulatory changes, understanding legal obligations, and implementing appropriate measures can be daunting tasks for businesses of all sizes.

Data Security Risks

Data breaches, cyberattacks, and security vulnerabilities pose significant risks to privacy and data protection. Protecting personal data from unauthorized access, data breaches, and cyber threats requires robust security measures, risk assessments, and ongoing monitoring and mitigation efforts.

Lack of Awareness and Education

Many individuals lack awareness of their rights regarding privacy and data protection, making it challenging for them to make informed decisions and exercise control over their personal information. Education and awareness campaigns are needed to empower individuals to understand their rights, protect their privacy, and navigate digital environments safely.

Ethical Dilemmas

Ethical considerations surrounding privacy and data protection can present dilemmas for businesses and organizations.

Balancing the need for data-driven insights with respect for individuals' privacy rights and autonomy requires careful deliberation and ethical decision-making frameworks.

10.5.4 Best Practices in Privacy, Consent, and Data Protection

Privacy by Design

Adopt a privacy-by-design approach, integrating privacy and data protection considerations into the design and development of products, services, and systems from the outset.

Consider privacy implications at every stage of the data lifecycle, from collection and processing to storage and disposal.

Transparency and Communication

Be transparent about data practices, policies, and procedures, providing clear and concise information to individuals about how their data is collected, used, and shared.

Communicate privacy notices, consent requests, and data processing activities in plain language, ensuring individuals understand their rights and options.

Informed Consent

Obtain informed consent from individuals before collecting, processing, or sharing their personal data.

Ensure consent is freely given, specific, informed, and unambiguous, providing individuals with clear information about the purposes, risks, and implications of data processing activities.

Data Minimization

Practice data minimization, collecting only the data that is necessary for the intended purposes and limiting the scope of data processing activities accordingly.

Minimize the collection of sensitive or unnecessary data to reduce privacy risks and enhance data protection.

Security Measures

Implement robust security measures to protect personal data from unauthorized access, disclosure, or misuse. Use encryption, access controls, authentication mechanisms, and other security safeguards to safeguard data integrity and confidentiality.

Data Subject Rights

Respect individuals' rights regarding their personal data, including the right to access, rectify, delete, and restrict the processing of their data. Establish processes and mechanisms for individuals to exercise their rights effectively and respond to requests in a timely and transparent manner.

CHAPTER 11

DIGITAL MARKETING TOOLS AND TECHNOLOGIES

11.1 OVERVIEW OF ESSENTIAL DIGITAL MARKETING TOOLS

In the fast-paced and ever-evolving world of digital marketing, having the right tools at your disposal is crucial for success. From managing social media campaigns to analyzing website traffic and automating email marketing, digital marketers rely on a diverse array of tools to streamline their efforts, engage with their audience, and drive results.

Digital marketing tools play a vital role in helping businesses achieve their marketing objectives, engage with their audience, and drive results in today's digital landscape. By leveraging the right tools and technologies, marketers can streamline their workflows, gain valuable insights, and deliver personalized experiences that resonate with their target audience. From analytics and SEO to content marketing and automation, the right digital marketing tools can empower businesses to succeed in a rapidly evolving digital world.

11.1.1 Categories of Digital Marketing Tools

Analytics and Data Insights

Analytics tools provide valuable insights into website traffic, user behavior, and campaign performance. They allow marketers to track key metrics, measure ROI, and make data-driven decisions to optimize their strategies. Popular options include Google Analytics, Adobe Analytics, and Mixpanel.

Search Engine Optimization (SEO) Tools

SEO tools help marketers improve their website's search engine rankings and visibility. They provide keyword research, on-page optimization, link building, and competitor analysis features to help businesses increase organic traffic and drive conversions. Examples include SEMrush, Moz, and Ahrefs.

Content Marketing Platforms

Content marketing platforms enable marketers to plan, create, distribute, and analyze content across multiple channels. They offer features such as content calendars, collaboration tools, and performance tracking to help businesses attract, engage, and retain their audience. HubSpot, CoSchedule, and ContentCal are popular options in this category.

Email Marketing Software

Email marketing software allows marketers to create, send, and track email campaigns effectively. They offer features like email templates, automation workflows, A/B testing, and analytics to help businesses nurture leads, drive conversions, and build customer relationships. Examples include Mailchimp, Constant Contact, and Campaign Monitor.

Social Media Management Tools

Social media management tools help marketers manage their social media presence, schedule posts, engage with followers, and analyze performance metrics. They support multiple platforms and offer features such as content scheduling, social listening, and audience segmentation. Hootsuite, Buffer, and Sprout Social are popular choices for social media management.

Pay-Per-Click (PPC) Advertising Platforms

PPC advertising platforms enable marketers to create and manage paid advertising campaigns across search engines, social media platforms, and display networks. They offer targeting options, bidding controls, and performance tracking features to help businesses reach their target audience and drive conversions. Google Ads, Facebook Ads, and LinkedIn Ads are leading platforms in this category.

Marketing Automation Software

Marketing automation software streamlines repetitive tasks and workflows, allowing marketers to automate email campaigns, lead nurturing, and customer segmentation. They offer features like lead scoring, CRM integration, and behavioral tracking to deliver personalized experiences and drive efficiency. Marketo, Pardot, and HubSpot are popular choices for marketing automation.

11.1.2 Significance of Digital Marketing Tools

Efficiency and Productivity

Digital marketing tools help streamline workflows, automate repetitive tasks, and improve efficiency, allowing marketers to focus on strategic initiatives and creative endeavors. By automating processes like content scheduling, email campaigns, and social media management, these tools enable marketers to accomplish more in less time.

Insights and Analytics

Digital marketing tools provide valuable insights and analytics that help marketers understand their audience, track performance, and measure ROI. By analyzing data on website traffic, user engagement, and campaign effectiveness, marketers can make informed decisions, optimize their strategies, and allocate resources more effectively.

Audience Engagement and Personalization

Digital marketing tools enable marketers to engage with their audience across multiple channels and deliver personalized experiences that resonate with individual preferences and interests. By leveraging features like segmentation, targeting, and automation, marketers can create tailored content and messages that drive engagement and build customer loyalty.

Competitive Advantage

In today's competitive digital landscape, having access to the right tools can provide a competitive advantage by enabling marketers to stay ahead of trends, capitalize on opportunities, and outperform competitors. By leveraging advanced features and capabilities offered by digital marketing tools, businesses can differentiate themselves and achieve greater success in their marketing efforts.

11.1.3 Best Practices for Using Digital Marketing Tools

Set Clear Goals and Objectives

Define clear goals and objectives for your digital marketing efforts to guide your tool selection and usage. Whether it's increasing website traffic, generating leads, or improving conversion rates, align your tool usage with your overarching business objectives.

Invest in Training and Education

Invest in training and education to ensure that your team has the necessary skills and expertise to effectively utilize digital marketing tools. Take advantage of online courses, workshops, and certifications offered by tool providers to enhance your team's proficiency and maximize the value of your investment.

Regularly Monitor and Analyze Performance

Regularly monitor and analyze performance metrics to track progress, identify areas for improvement, and optimize your strategies. Use the insights provided by digital marketing tools to make data-driven decisions and iterate on your approach based on real-time feedback.

Stay Updated on Emerging Trends and Technologies

Stay updated on emerging trends and technologies in the digital marketing space to ensure that you're leveraging the latest tools and strategies to stay competitive. Follow industry blogs, attend conferences, and participate in networking events to stay informed and ahead of the curve.

Maintain Data Security and Compliance

Ensure that you're adhering to data security best practices and regulatory compliance requirements when using digital marketing tools. Protect sensitive information, obtain necessary permissions and consents, and implement measures to safeguard data privacy and security.

11.2 AUTOMATION AND WORKFLOW TOOLS

In the fast-paced landscape of modern business, the efficient management of tasks, processes, and workflows is crucial for staying competitive and meeting the demands of customers. With the rapid advancements in technology, businesses are increasingly turning to automation and workflow tools to streamline operations, improve productivity, and enhance overall efficiency. Automation and workflow tools are indispensable assets for modern businesses seeking to enhance efficiency, agility, and innovation. By automating repetitive tasks, minimizing errors, and providing actionable insights, these tools empower organizations to optimize processes, make informed decisions, and stay ahead of the competition. While implementation challenges and workforce implications must be carefully managed, the benefits of automation far outweigh the risks, paving the way for a more productive, resilient, and digitally empowered future.

Automation and workflow tools encompass a wide range of software solutions designed to automate repetitive tasks, streamline complex processes, and facilitate seamless collaboration among team members.

These tools leverage technologies such as artificial intelligence (AI), machine learning, robotic process automation (RPA), and cloud computing to optimize workflows and drive operational excellence. From automating data entry and document processing to orchestrating complex business processes, automation and workflow tools offer diverse functionalities to meet the unique needs of different industries and organizations.

One of the primary benefits of automation and workflow tools is the significant improvement in efficiency they bring to businesses. By automating repetitive and time-consuming tasks, such as data entry, report generation, and email notifications, these tools enable employees to focus their time and energy on more strategic activities that add value to the organization. For instance, in customer service operations, chatbots powered by AI can handle routine inquiries, freeing up human agents to address complex customer issues and provide personalized support. This not only enhances productivity but also enhances the overall customer experience.

Moreover, automation and workflow tools play a crucial role in minimizing errors and ensuring consistency in processes. Unlike humans, who are prone to fatigue and distractions, automated systems can perform tasks with a high degree of accuracy and precision, thereby reducing the risk of costly errors and delays. For example, in manufacturing environments, automated assembly lines and robotic systems can consistently produce high-quality products with minimal variation, leading to improved product reliability and customer satisfaction.

In addition to efficiency gains, automation and workflow tools contribute to better decision-making by providing real-time insights and analytics. These tools often include built-in reporting and analytics capabilities that allow businesses to track key performance indicators (KPIs), monitor process metrics, and identify areas for improvement.

By harnessing data-driven insights, organizations can make informed decisions, optimize workflows, and drive continuous process improvement. For instance, in supply chain management, predictive analytics tools can analyze historical data to forecast demand, optimize inventory levels, and mitigate supply chain risks, thereby enhancing operational resilience and agility.

Despite their numerous benefits, implementing automation and workflow tools can pose challenges for businesses, particularly in terms of integration, customization, and employee resistance. Integrating automation tools with existing systems and processes can be complex and time-consuming, requiring careful planning and coordination across different departments. Moreover, customization is often necessary to tailor these tools to the specific needs and workflows of the organization, which may require expertise in software development and configuration.

Additionally, some employees may be resistant to change, fearing job displacement or loss of control over their work processes. Addressing these challenges requires effective change management strategies, including clear communication, training programs, and incentives for adoption.

Furthermore, the increasing reliance on automation and workflow tools raises concerns about job displacement and the future of work. While automation has the potential to eliminate repetitive and mundane tasks, it also creates new opportunities for innovation and skill development. Rather than replacing human workers, automation often augments their capabilities, allowing them to focus on higher-value tasks that require creativity, critical thinking, and emotional intelligence.

However, to fully harness the benefits of automation, businesses must invest in upskilling and reskilling initiatives to equip employees with the necessary digital skills and competencies. By fostering a culture of lifelong learning and adaptability, organizations can empower their workforce to thrive in the digital age.

Looking ahead, the future of automation and workflow tools is promising, driven by advancements in AI, machine learning, and robotic automation. These technologies will continue to evolve, enabling more sophisticated automation capabilities, such as natural language processing, image recognition, and autonomous decision-making.

Additionally, the integration of automation tools with emerging technologies like the Internet of Things (IoT) and blockchain will unlock new possibilities for process optimization, supply chain transparency, and decentralized collaboration. However, as automation becomes more pervasive, it is essential to address ethical considerations, such as data privacy, algorithmic bias, and the impact on society.

11.3 AI AND MACHINE LEARNING IN DIGITAL MARKETING

The digital marketing landscape is continuously evolving, driven by technological advancements and changing consumer behaviors. In this dynamic environment, businesses are increasingly turning to artificial intelligence (AI) and machine learning (ML) to enhance their marketing efforts and stay competitive.

AI and machine learning are driving a paradigm shift in digital marketing, enabling businesses to deliver personalized experiences, optimize campaign performance, and make data-driven decisions. Despite the challenges and complexities involved, the benefits of AI in digital marketing far outweigh the risks, paving the way for more effective, efficient, and innovative marketing strategies in the digital age. As AI continues to evolve, marketers must stay abreast of emerging trends and technologies to remain competitive and capitalize on the opportunities presented by AI and machine learning.

11.3.1 Understanding AI and Machine Learning

AI refers to the simulation of human intelligence processes by machines, enabling them to perform tasks that typically require human intelligence, such as problem-solving, decision-making, and natural language understanding. Machine learning, a subset of AI, focuses on the development of algorithms that allow computers to learn from data and improve their performance over time without being explicitly programmed.

11.3.2 Applications of AI and Machine Learning in Digital Marketing

Personalized Content Recommendations

AI-powered algorithms analyze user behavior, preferences, and interactions to deliver personalized content recommendations across various digital channels. By understanding individual interests and preferences, marketers can enhance engagement, drive conversions, and build long-term customer relationships.

Predictive Analytics

Machine learning algorithms analyze large datasets to identify patterns, trends, and correlations, enabling marketers to predict future outcomes and anticipate customer behavior. Predictive analytics helps optimize marketing campaigns, allocate resources effectively, and identify potential opportunities for growth.

Chatbots and Virtual Assistants

AI-driven chatbots and virtual assistants provide real-time assistance to customers, answering queries, resolving issues, and guiding them through the purchase journey.

By leveraging natural language processing (NLP) and machine learning, chatbots deliver personalized and conversational experiences, enhancing customer satisfaction and retention.

Customer Segmentation and Targeting

Machine learning algorithms segment customers based on their demographics, behaviors, and preferences, allowing marketers to tailor their messaging and offers to specific audience segments. By delivering targeted and relevant content, businesses can improve engagement rates, conversion rates, and overall campaign performance.

Dynamic Pricing Optimization

AI-powered pricing optimization algorithms analyze market dynamics, competitor pricing, and customer demand to dynamically adjust prices in real-time. By optimizing pricing strategies based on demand elasticity and market conditions, businesses can maximize revenue, profitability, and competitive advantage.

11.3.3 Benefits of AI and Machine Learning in Digital Marketing

Enhanced Personalization

AI and ML enable marketers to deliver highly personalized and relevant experiences to customers, leading to increased engagement, loyalty, and customer lifetime value. Personalized marketing campaigns drive higher conversion rates and revenue growth by resonating with individual preferences and needs.

Improved Efficiency and Scalability

Automation of repetitive tasks and processes through AI and ML increases operational efficiency, reduces manual effort, and enables marketers to focus on strategic initiatives. Automated workflows and algorithms streamline campaign management, optimization, and reporting, allowing businesses to scale their marketing efforts effectively.

Data-Driven Insights

AI and ML algorithms analyze vast amounts of data from multiple sources to extract actionable insights and trends. By harnessing data-driven insights, marketers can make informed decisions, identify opportunities for optimization, and continuously improve their marketing strategies and performance.

Better Decision-Making

Predictive analytics and machine learning algorithms empower marketers to make data-driven decisions based on accurate forecasts and models. By leveraging insights derived from AI, businesses can optimize resource allocation, marketing spend, and campaign targeting, leading to better ROI and profitability.

11.3.4 Challenges and Considerations

Data Privacy and Security

As AI and ML rely on vast amounts of data for training and analysis, ensuring data privacy and security is paramount. Marketers must comply with regulations such as GDPR and CCPA and implement robust security measures to protect sensitive customer information from unauthorized access or misuse.

Algorithmic Bias and Fairness

AI and ML algorithms may exhibit biases inherent in the data they are trained on, leading to unfair or discriminatory outcomes. Marketers need to carefully evaluate and mitigate bias in their algorithms to ensure fairness and equity in their marketing practices and decision-making processes.

Talent and Skills Gap

Implementing AI and ML technologies requires specialized skills and expertise in data science, machine learning, and programming. Marketers need to invest in training and upskilling their teams or partner with external experts to effectively leverage AI and ML in their digital marketing strategies.

11.3.5 Future Implications and Trends

Hyper-Personalization

Advancements in AI and ML will enable marketers to deliver hyper-personalized experiences tailored to individual preferences, behaviors, and contexts. AI-powered algorithms will continuously adapt and refine content recommendations, product offerings, and marketing messages to maximize relevance and engagement.

Voice Search and Conversational Marketing

The rise of voice-enabled devices and virtual assistants will reshape the way consumers search for information and interact with brands. Marketers will need to optimize their content and messaging for voice search and embrace conversational marketing strategies to engage with customers in natural language and contextually relevant conversations.

AI-Generated Content

AI-powered tools and platforms will automate the creation of content, including articles, videos, and advertisements, based on user data and preferences. Marketers will leverage AI-generated content to scale their content marketing efforts, improve efficiency, and deliver personalized experiences at scale.

11.4 EMERGING TECHNOLOGIES AND THEIR APPLICATIONS

Emerging technologies are revolutionizing industries, disrupting traditional business models, and driving unprecedented innovation across various sectors. From artificial intelligence (AI) and blockchain to quantum computing and biotechnology, these technologies hold the potential to address complex challenges, unlock new opportunities, and reshape the way we live, work, and interact.

Emerging technologies are driving a profound transformation across industries, society, and the global economy, offering unprecedented opportunities for innovation, growth, and progress. From AI and blockchain to quantum computing and biotechnology, these technologies hold the potential to address complex challenges, enhance human capabilities, and shape the future of humanity. As we navigate the opportunities and challenges of the Fourth Industrial Revolution, it is imperative to embrace a mindset of responsible innovation, collaboration, and ethical stewardship to harness the full potential of emerging technologies for the benefit of all.

11.4.1 Artificial Intelligence (AI)

AI-Powered Automation

AI enables automation of repetitive tasks and processes across industries, ranging from manufacturing and logistics to customer service and healthcare. Machine learning algorithms analyze vast amounts of data to optimize workflows, enhance efficiency, and drive operational excellence. For example, in manufacturing, AI-driven robotics automate assembly lines, increasing productivity and reducing errors.

Personalized Recommendations

AI algorithms analyze user data and behavior to deliver personalized recommendations and experiences in areas such as e-commerce, content streaming, and digital marketing. By understanding individual preferences and patterns, businesses can enhance customer engagement, loyalty, and satisfaction.

For instance, streaming platforms use AI to recommend content based on viewers' past interactions and viewing habits.

Healthcare Diagnostics and Predictive Analytics

AI-powered diagnostics and predictive analytics are transforming healthcare by enabling early detection of diseases, personalized treatment plans, and proactive interventions. Machine learning algorithms analyze medical images, genomic data, and patient records to identify patterns and trends, assisting clinicians in diagnosis and decision-making. AI also facilitates remote monitoring and telemedicine, improving access to healthcare services.

11.4.2 Blockchain Technology

Decentralized Finance (DeFi)

Blockchain technology underpins decentralized finance (DeFi) platforms, enabling peer-to-peer lending, borrowing, trading, and asset management without intermediaries. Smart contracts, powered by blockchain, automate financial transactions, enforce terms and conditions, and ensure transparency and security. DeFi applications offer financial inclusion, lower costs, and greater accessibility to global markets.

Supply Chain Management and Transparency

Blockchain enhances supply chain visibility, traceability, and transparency by recording transactions and data in an immutable, decentralized ledger. From raw material sourcing to product delivery, blockchain enables stakeholders to track and verify the provenance, authenticity, and quality of goods. This enhances trust, reduces counterfeiting, and mitigates supply chain risks.

Digital Identity and Authentication

Blockchain facilitates secure and decentralized digital identity solutions, enabling individuals to control and manage their personal data. Self-sovereign identity platforms leverage blockchain to authenticate users, verify credentials, and enable seamless access to services without relying on centralized authorities. Blockchain-based digital identities enhance privacy, security, and user autonomy.

11.4.3 Quantum Computing

Advanced Data Processing and Optimization

Quantum computing offers exponential computational power and speed, enabling complex data processing, optimization, and simulation tasks that are infeasible for classical computers. Quantum algorithms solve optimization problems, cryptography, and machine learning tasks more efficiently, unlocking new possibilities in drug discovery, materials science, and financial modeling.

Cryptography and Cybersecurity

Quantum computing poses both challenges and opportunities for cryptography and cybersecurity. While quantum-resistant encryption algorithms are being developed to protect sensitive data from quantum attacks, quantum computing also offers advancements in cryptographic techniques, such as quantum key distribution (QKD), for secure communication and encryption.

Climate Modeling and Simulation

Quantum computing accelerates climate modeling, simulation, and analysis, enabling researchers to better understand complex climate systems, predict weather patterns, and assess the impact of climate change. Quantum algorithms simulate molecular dynamics, atmospheric phenomena, and ocean currents with unprecedented accuracy and detail, aiding in climate research and policy-making.

11.4.4 Biotechnology

Gene Editing and Therapeutics

Biotechnology, including gene editing techniques such as CRISPR-Cas9, revolutionizes healthcare by enabling precise genetic modifications for treating genetic disorders, cancer, and infectious diseases.

Gene therapies and personalized medicine approaches leverage biotechnology to target specific genes, repair mutations, and enhance therapeutic outcomes, offering potential cures for previously untreatable conditions.

Agricultural Innovation and Sustainability

Biotechnology enhances crop productivity, resilience, and sustainability through genetically modified organisms (GMOs), gene editing, and precision agriculture techniques.

Biotech crops are engineered to resist pests, diseases, and environmental stressors, reducing the need for pesticides and fertilizers while increasing yields and food security. Biotechnology also enables the development of biofuels and biomaterials from renewable sources.

Synthetic Biology and Biofabrication

Synthetic biology combines engineering principles with biology to design and construct biological systems, organisms, and biomaterials with novel functionalities.

Biofabrication techniques, including 3D bioprinting and tissue engineering, create artificial tissues, organs, and implants for medical applications, regenerative medicine, and drug discovery. Synthetic biology offers solutions to environmental challenges, such as bioremediation and sustainable biofuels production.

11.4.5 Implications and Considerations

Ethical and Societal Impact

Emerging technologies raise ethical, social, and regulatory concerns related to privacy, bias, autonomy, and inequality.

Ethical frameworks and guidelines are needed to ensure responsible and equitable development, deployment, and governance of these technologies, addressing issues such as data privacy, algorithmic bias, and technological unemployment.

Collaboration and Interdisciplinary Research

Addressing complex challenges and realizing the full potential of emerging technologies require collaboration and interdisciplinary research across scientific disciplines, industries, and stakeholders.

Multidisciplinary approaches foster innovation, creativity, and holistic solutions to global challenges, encouraging partnerships between academia, industry, government, and civil society.

Education and Workforce Development

Emerging technologies demand new skills, competencies, and mindsets in the workforce, necessitating education and training programs to prepare individuals for the jobs of the future. Lifelong learning initiatives, reskilling programs, and digital literacy efforts empower individuals to adapt to technological disruptions, seize opportunities, and thrive in a rapidly changing labor market.

11.4.6 Future Prospects and Trends

Convergence of Technologies

Emerging technologies are converging and intersecting, leading to synergies and innovations at the intersection of AI, blockchain, quantum computing, and biotechnology. Convergence-driven innovations, such as quantum AI, biocomputing, and blockchain-enabled healthcare, hold the potential to address complex challenges and create new opportunities across sectors.

Responsible Innovation and Governance

The future of emerging technologies hinges on responsible innovation, governance, and stewardship to ensure ethical, safe, and inclusive development and deployment. Policymakers, regulators, and industry stakeholders need to collaborate on frameworks, standards, and policies that balance innovation with societal values, human rights, and environmental sustainability.

Democratization and Access

Advancements in emerging technologies are democratizing access to knowledge, resources, and opportunities, empowering individuals, communities, and organizations to innovate, collaborate, and solve local and global challenges.

Open-source platforms, DIY communities, and grassroots initiatives foster inclusivity, diversity, and participation in the innovation ecosystem.

CHAPTER 12

CREATING AN INTEGRATED DIGITAL MARKETING PLAN

12.1 ALIGNING DIGITAL CHANNELS AND TACTICS

In today's digital age, businesses operate in a multi-channel environment where consumers engage with brands across various digital platforms and touchpoints. To succeed in this landscape, organizations must align their digital channels and tactics cohesively to deliver a seamless and personalized customer experience.

Aligning digital channels and tactics is imperative for businesses seeking to deliver seamless, personalized, and impactful customer experiences in today's digital-first world. By adopting a customer-centric approach, embracing integrated marketing communications, and leveraging data-driven insights, organizations can optimize their digital marketing strategies for maximum effectiveness and ROI. Despite challenges such as organizational silos and technology integration, the future of digital marketing holds promise with emerging trends such as AI-powered personalization, voice search, and omnichannel automation shaping the landscape and driving innovation.

12.1.1 Understanding Digital Channels and Tactics

Digital channels refer to the platforms and mediums through which businesses interact with customers online. These include websites, social media platforms, email marketing, search engines, mobile apps, and online advertising networks. Each digital channel offers unique capabilities, audiences, and engagement opportunities, requiring tailored strategies and tactics to maximize effectiveness.

Digital tactics encompass the specific actions and techniques used to engage audiences, drive traffic, and achieve marketing objectives within digital channels. These tactics may include content marketing, search engine optimization (SEO), social media advertising, email campaigns, influencer marketing, pay-per-click (PPC) advertising, and website optimization. By combining various tactics, businesses can create integrated marketing campaigns that resonate with their target audience and drive desired outcomes.

12.1.2 The Importance of Alignment

Aligning digital channels and tactics is essential for delivering a consistent and cohesive brand experience across touchpoints, maximizing reach, engagement, and conversion rates. When digital channels and tactics are siloed or disjointed, it can lead to inconsistency, redundancy, and inefficiency in marketing efforts. By aligning strategies and coordinating activities across channels, businesses can amplify their impact, optimize resources, and achieve greater synergy in their digital marketing initiatives.

12.1.3 Key Strategies for Alignment

Customer-Centric Approach

Start by understanding your target audience, their preferences, behaviors, and journey across digital channels. Use data analytics, market research, and customer feedback to gain insights into customer needs and expectations. Develop buyer personas to segment your audience and tailor your messaging, content, and offers to address their specific pain points and interests.

Integrated Marketing Communications (IMC)

Adopt an integrated approach to marketing communications, where messages are consistent, coherent, and complementary across digital channels and offline touchpoints. Coordinate messaging, branding, and creative assets to ensure a unified brand identity and voice. Use storytelling techniques to convey your brand's values, mission, and unique selling propositions consistently across channels.

Cross-Channel Engagement

Encourage cross-channel engagement by creating seamless pathways for customers to interact with your brand across multiple touchpoints. For example, use social media to drive traffic to your website, where visitors can sign up for your email newsletter or participate in a live chat with customer support. Integrate call-to-action (CTA) buttons and links strategically to guide users through their journey and encourage conversions.

Data Integration and Analysis

Invest in robust data integration and analytics capabilities to track and measure the performance of your digital channels and tactics. Use data visualization tools, dashboards, and attribution models to gain insights into the effectiveness of your marketing efforts. Identify key performance indicators (KPIs) relevant to each channel and tactic, such as click-through rates, conversion rates, and return on investment (ROI), to assess their impact on overall business objectives.

12.1.4 Challenges and Considerations

Siloed Organizational Structure

One of the primary challenges in aligning digital channels and tactics is overcoming siloed organizational structures and departmental barriers. Different teams, such as marketing, sales, IT, and customer service, may operate independently, leading to disjointed strategies and communication. Break down silos by fostering collaboration, communication, and alignment of goals across departments, ensuring a unified approach to digital marketing initiatives.

Technology Integration

Integrating disparate digital platforms, tools, and systems can be complex and time-consuming, especially in large organizations with legacy infrastructure. Invest in marketing automation platforms, customer relationship management (CRM) systems, and data management solutions that facilitate seamless integration and data sharing across channels. Leverage application programming interfaces (APIs) and middleware solutions to connect systems and enable real-time data synchronization.

Content Consistency and Quality

Maintaining consistency and quality in content creation and distribution across digital channels can be challenging, especially when managing multiple platforms simultaneously. Develop a content strategy that aligns with your brand voice, values, and objectives, ensuring consistency in messaging and storytelling. Invest in content creation tools, editorial calendars, and content management systems (CMS) to streamline workflows and maintain editorial standards.

12.1.5 Future Trends and Innovations

AI-Powered Personalization

Artificial intelligence (AI) and machine learning (ML) technologies will play an increasingly significant role in personalizing customer experiences across digital channels. AI-driven algorithms analyze customer data in real-time to deliver personalized recommendations, content, and offers tailored to individual preferences and behaviors. Personalization enhances engagement, loyalty, and conversion rates, driving business growth and competitive advantage.

Voice Search and Conversational AI

The rise of voice-enabled devices and virtual assistants is reshaping the way consumers search for information and interact with brands online. Voice search optimization and conversational AI enable businesses to create voice-activated experiences that provide instant answers, recommendations, and assistance to users. Optimizing content and messaging for voice search and natural language processing (NLP) will be essential to capitalize on this trend and stay ahead of the competition.

Omnichannel Marketing Automation

Omnichannel marketing automation platforms will enable businesses to orchestrate personalized customer journeys across multiple digital channels seamlessly. Integrated automation workflows, triggered campaigns, and dynamic content delivery will allow marketers to engage customers at every stage of the buying cycle, from awareness and consideration to purchase and retention. Omnichannel automation drives efficiency, relevance, and consistency in marketing efforts, driving better results and ROI.

12.2 BUDGETING AND RESOURCE ALLOCATION

Budgeting and resource allocation are critical components of a digital marketing plan, guiding the allocation of financial resources and human capital to achieve marketing objectives effectively. In today's competitive landscape, where digital channels play a central role in reaching and engaging audiences, strategic budgeting is essential for optimizing return on investment (ROI) and maximizing the impact of marketing efforts.

Budgeting and resource allocation are critical components of a digital marketing plan, shaping the effectiveness, efficiency, and impact of marketing initiatives. By setting clear objectives, identifying target audiences, and allocating budgets strategically across digital channels and tactics, businesses can optimize their marketing investments and achieve measurable results. Adopting a performance-based approach, investing in data and analytics, and embracing emerging trends such as AI-powered optimization and predictive analytics will enable marketers to stay ahead of the curve and drive sustainable growth in the digital age.

12.2.1 Understanding Digital Marketing Budgeting

Setting Objectives and KPIs

Before allocating budgetary resources, it's essential to define clear marketing objectives and key performance indicators (KPIs) that align with overall business goals. Whether the objective is to drive website traffic, generate leads, increase brand awareness, or boost sales, each goal should be specific, measurable, achievable, relevant, and time-bound (SMART). KPIs such as conversion rates, customer acquisition cost (CAC), return on ad spend (ROAS), and customer lifetime value (CLV) provide quantifiable metrics for evaluating campaign performance and ROI.

Identifying Target Audience and Channels

Understanding the target audience's demographics, behaviors, preferences, and media consumption habits is crucial for selecting the most effective digital channels and tactics. Conduct market research, customer surveys, and competitor analysis to identify where your audience spends their time online and which channels resonate most with them. Whether it's search engine marketing (SEM), social media advertising, email marketing, content marketing, or influencer partnerships, prioritize channels that offer the highest potential for reaching and engaging your target audience cost-effectively.

Allocating Budgets Across Channels and Tactics

Once objectives, KPIs, and target audience segments are defined, allocate budgetary resources strategically across digital channels and tactics based on their relative importance, performance, and potential ROI. Consider factors such as channel reach, audience targeting capabilities, cost per acquisition (CPA), and conversion rates when determining budget allocations. Adopt a balanced approach that diversifies investments across multiple channels to mitigate risks and maximize opportunities for reaching and engaging diverse audience segments.

12.2.2 Strategies for Budgeting and Resource Allocation

Performance-Based Budgeting

Adopt a performance-based approach to budgeting that prioritizes investments in channels and tactics with proven ROI and scalability. Allocate a larger share of the budget to high-performing channels that drive the majority of conversions and revenue while maintaining flexibility to reallocate resources based on changing market dynamics and campaign performance. Continuously monitor and optimize campaigns to maximize efficiency and effectiveness throughout the budget cycle.

Test and Learn

Allocate a portion of the budget for experimentation and testing new channels, tactics, and creative approaches to identify opportunities for optimization and innovation. Conduct A/B testing, multivariate testing, and pilot campaigns to evaluate the effectiveness of different strategies, messaging, and audience targeting techniques. Use insights from testing to refine campaign strategies, allocate resources more efficiently, and scale successful initiatives for maximum impact.

Invest in Data and Analytics

Allocate resources for data collection, analysis, and attribution to gain actionable insights into campaign performance, audience behavior, and marketing attribution. Implement analytics tools, tracking pixels, and conversion tracking mechanisms to capture granular data on user interactions, conversions, and customer journeys across digital touchpoints. Leverage data-driven insights to optimize marketing strategies, allocate budgets effectively, and identify opportunities for improvement.

12.2.3 Considerations and Challenges

Seasonality and Market Dynamics

Consider seasonality, market trends, and industry-specific factors when budgeting and allocating resources for digital marketing campaigns. Adjust budget allocations and messaging strategies to capitalize on peak seasons, holidays, and promotional periods when consumer demand is high.

Monitor market dynamics, competitive activities, and external factors that may impact campaign performance and adjust budgets accordingly to maintain competitiveness and relevance.

Resource Constraints and Scalability

Balance budgetary constraints with scalability when planning digital marketing initiatives, especially for small and medium-sized businesses (SMBs) with limited resources. Prioritize investments in high-impact channels and tactics that offer the greatest potential for ROI and scalability while optimizing costs and resource utilization. Leverage automation tools, outsourcing partnerships, and agile methodologies to streamline workflows, maximize efficiency, and scale campaigns cost-effectively.

ROI Measurement and Accountability

Establish clear metrics and benchmarks for measuring ROI and campaign performance, ensuring accountability and transparency in budget allocation decisions. Track key performance indicators (KPIs), monitor campaign metrics in real-time, and conduct post-campaign analysis to evaluate the effectiveness of digital marketing initiatives. Communicate results, insights, and recommendations to stakeholders regularly, demonstrating the impact of marketing investments on business objectives and financial outcomes.

12.2.4 Future Trends and Innovations

AI-Powered Optimization

Embrace artificial intelligence (AI) and machine learning (ML) technologies to automate budget allocation, ad targeting, and campaign optimization processes. AI-powered algorithms analyze vast amounts of data in real-time to identify trends, patterns, and opportunities for optimization, enabling marketers to make data-driven decisions and maximize ROI.

Predictive Analytics and Forecasting

Utilize predictive analytics and forecasting models to anticipate future trends, customer behaviors, and market dynamics, enabling proactive budget planning and resource allocation. Predictive models leverage historical data, market signals, and machine learning algorithms to generate accurate forecasts and scenarios for optimizing marketing investments and mitigating risks.

Blockchain-Based Attribution and Transparency

Explore blockchain technology for transparent and secure attribution of marketing activities, ensuring accountability and trust in digital advertising ecosystems. Blockchain-enabled solutions provide immutable, tamper-proof records of ad impressions, clicks, and conversions, facilitating transparency, fraud detection, and fair compensation for publishers and advertisers.

12.3 IMPLEMENTATION AND PROJECT MANAGEMENT

Implementing a digital marketing plan requires meticulous planning, coordination, and execution to achieve desired outcomes effectively. From launching campaigns and managing digital assets to analyzing performance and optimizing strategies, project management plays a crucial role in ensuring the success of digital marketing initiatives.

Implementation and project management are essential components of a successful digital marketing plan, ensuring that strategies are executed effectively, resources are allocated efficiently, and objectives are achieved. By adopting agile methodologies, fostering collaboration, and leveraging technology solutions, businesses can navigate challenges, capitalize on opportunities, and drive sustainable growth in the digital age. With emerging trends such as AI, predictive analytics, and customer experience optimization shaping the future of digital marketing, organizations must remain agile, adaptable, and innovative to stay ahead of the curve and deliver exceptional experiences to their customers.

12.3.1 Understanding Implementation and Project Management in Digital Marketing

Defining Objectives and Deliverables

The first step in implementation and project management is defining clear objectives, goals, and deliverables that align with overall business objectives and marketing strategy. Whether the goal is to increase website traffic, generate leads, drive conversions, or enhance brand awareness, each objective should be specific, measurable, achievable, relevant, and time-bound (SMART). Clearly define project scope, timelines, and milestones to guide implementation efforts and track progress effectively.

Resource Allocation and Team Collaboration

Allocate resources, budget, and personnel effectively to support digital marketing initiatives and ensure project success. Assemble a cross-functional team with expertise in areas such as marketing, design, content creation, analytics, and technology to collaborate on project execution. Establish clear roles, responsibilities, and communication channels to facilitate collaboration, coordination, and accountability throughout the implementation process.

Technology and Tools Utilization

Leverage digital marketing tools, technology platforms, and software solutions to streamline workflows, automate processes, and optimize campaign performance. Invest in marketing automation platforms, content management systems (CMS), customer relationship management (CRM) software, analytics tools, and project management platforms to enhance efficiency, productivity, and visibility into project activities.

12.3.2 Strategies for Implementation and Project Management

Agile Methodology

Adopt an agile approach to project management that emphasizes flexibility, iterative development, and continuous improvement in digital marketing initiatives. Break down projects into smaller, manageable tasks or sprints, allowing for incremental progress, feedback, and adaptation.

Conduct regular stand-up meetings, sprint reviews, and retrospectives to assess progress, address issues, and make adjustments as needed to stay aligned with project objectives and timelines.

Clear Communication and Stakeholder Engagement

Establish open, transparent communication channels with stakeholders, team members, and external partners to ensure alignment, clarity, and accountability throughout the project lifecycle.

Hold regular meetings, update stakeholders on project status, milestones, and key decisions, and solicit feedback to foster collaboration and ownership. Use project management tools, email, instant messaging, and collaboration platforms to facilitate communication and information sharing across teams.

Risk Management and Contingency Planning

Identify potential risks, challenges, and obstacles that may impact project delivery and develop contingency plans to mitigate them effectively. Conduct risk assessments, prioritize risks based on severity and likelihood, and develop mitigation strategies to address them proactively.

Anticipate potential bottlenecks, resource constraints, and technical issues and develop alternative courses of action to minimize disruptions and keep projects on track.

12.3.3 Considerations and Challenges

Budget Constraints and Resource Limitations

Budget constraints and resource limitations can pose challenges to implementing digital marketing initiatives effectively. Prioritize investments in high-impact activities and channels that offer the greatest potential for ROI and align with strategic objectives. Leverage cost-effective solutions, outsourcing partnerships, and agile methodologies to optimize resource utilization, maximize efficiency, and achieve desired outcomes within budget constraints.

Technology Integration and Complexity

Integrating disparate digital platforms, systems, and technologies can be complex and time-consuming, especially in large organizations with legacy infrastructure. Invest in technology solutions that offer scalability, interoperability, and ease of integration to streamline workflows and enhance collaboration across teams. Leverage application programming interfaces (APIs), middleware solutions, and cloud-based platforms to connect systems seamlessly and enable data-driven decision-making.

Change Management and Adoption

Implementing digital marketing initiatives often requires cultural shifts, process changes, and organizational alignment to adapt to new technologies and ways of working. Invest in change management initiatives, training programs, and employee engagement activities to foster buy-in, enthusiasm, and adoption of digital marketing strategies and tools. Communicate the benefits, rationale, and impact of digital initiatives to stakeholders and provide support, resources, and training to empower employees to embrace change effectively.

12.3.4 Future Trends and Innovations

Artificial Intelligence and Automation

Artificial intelligence (AI) and automation technologies will play an increasingly significant role in streamlining digital marketing processes, optimizing campaign performance, and enhancing customer experiences. AI-powered algorithms automate tasks such as ad targeting, content personalization, and campaign optimization, enabling marketers to focus on strategic initiatives and creative endeavors.

Predictive Analytics and Data-driven Insights

Predictive analytics and advanced data analytics techniques will enable marketers to gain deeper insights into customer behavior, preferences, and trends, empowering data-driven decision-making and personalized marketing strategies. Predictive models analyze historical data, identify patterns, and forecast future outcomes, enabling marketers to anticipate customer needs, optimize resource allocation, and mitigate risks effectively.

Customer Experience Optimization

Customer experience optimization will remain a key focus area for digital marketers, with an emphasis on delivering personalized, seamless, and engaging experiences across digital touchpoints. Marketers will leverage customer data, AI-driven personalization, and omnichannel strategies to create cohesive customer journeys that drive loyalty, satisfaction, and advocacy.

12.4 MONITORING, EVALUATION AND CONTINUOUS IMPROVEMENT

Monitoring, evaluation, and continuous improvement are essential components of a digital marketing plan, enabling businesses to track performance, measure effectiveness, and optimize strategies for maximum impact. In today's dynamic and competitive landscape, where consumer behaviors and market trends evolve rapidly, it's crucial for marketers to adopt a data-driven approach and embrace a culture of continuous learning and improvement.

Monitoring, evaluation, and continuous improvement are essential components of a successful digital marketing strategy, enabling marketers to track performance, measure effectiveness, and optimize campaigns for maximum impact. By defining clear KPIs, implementing robust tracking and analytics, and conducting regular reviews and analysis, marketers can identify opportunities for optimization, drive better results, and achieve long-term success in the digital landscape. With emerging trends such as predictive analytics, real-time monitoring, and integrated measurement shaping the future of digital marketing, organizations must embrace innovation, agility, and data-driven decision-making to stay ahead of the curve and drive sustainable growth.

12.4.1 Understanding Monitoring, Evaluation, and Continuous Improvement

Monitoring

Monitoring involves tracking and measuring key performance indicators (KPIs), metrics, and milestones to assess the progress and performance of digital marketing initiatives. It involves collecting real-time data, monitoring campaign performance, and identifying trends, patterns, and anomalies that require attention.

Monitoring provides insights into the effectiveness of marketing strategies, channels, and tactics, enabling marketers to make informed decisions and adjustments as needed.

Evaluation

Evaluation involves analyzing and assessing the impact, outcomes, and effectiveness of digital marketing efforts against predefined objectives and benchmarks. It involves conducting post-campaign analysis, measuring ROI, and evaluating the alignment of outcomes with business goals. Evaluation helps marketers understand what worked well, what didn't, and why, enabling them to derive actionable insights and lessons learned for future campaigns.

Continuous Improvement

Continuous improvement involves using insights from monitoring and evaluation to refine strategies, optimize tactics, and enhance performance over time. It involves identifying areas for improvement, implementing changes, and iterating on processes to drive incremental gains and long-term success. Continuous improvement fosters innovation, agility, and adaptability, enabling marketers to stay ahead of the curve and drive sustainable growth in a rapidly changing digital landscape.

12.4.2 Strategies for Monitoring, Evaluation, and Continuous Improvement

Define Clear KPIs and Metrics

Start by defining clear, measurable KPIs and metrics that align with overall business objectives and digital marketing goals. KPIs may include metrics such as website traffic, conversion rates, click-through rates, engagement metrics, customer acquisition cost (CAC), and return on investment (ROI). Ensure that KPIs are specific, relevant, achievable, and time-bound (SMART) to facilitate accurate measurement and evaluation of campaign performance.

Implement Tracking and Analytics

Implement robust tracking and analytics systems to capture data on user interactions, conversions, and campaign performance across digital channels and touchpoints. Use web analytics tools, tracking pixels, and conversion tracking mechanisms to collect granular data on website traffic, user behavior, and campaign attribution. Leverage analytics dashboards, reports, and visualization tools to gain insights into trends, patterns, and opportunities for optimization.

Conduct Regular Reviews and Analysis

Schedule regular reviews and analysis sessions to review campaign performance, assess progress against objectives, and identify areas for improvement. Analyze key metrics, trends, and benchmarks to understand what's working well and what needs adjustment. Use data-driven insights to make informed decisions, prioritize optimization efforts, and allocate resources effectively to drive better results.

A/B Testing and Experimentation

Conduct A/B testing, multivariate testing, and experimentation to evaluate the impact of different strategies, tactics, and creative elements on campaign performance. Test variables such as ad copy, imagery, headlines, calls-to-action (CTAs), landing page designs, and audience targeting to identify winning variations and optimize campaign effectiveness. Use testing insights to refine messaging, targeting, and creative strategies for maximum impact.

12.4.3 Challenges and Considerations

Data Quality and Integrity

Ensure data quality and integrity by implementing robust data governance policies, processes, and controls. Validate data sources, eliminate duplicates, and address data inconsistencies to ensure accuracy and reliability of analytics insights. Invest in data quality tools, data validation procedures, and data cleansing techniques to maintain data integrity and credibility.

Attribution and Measurement Challenges

Attributing conversions and measuring the impact of digital marketing efforts accurately can be challenging due to the complexity of the customer journey and the proliferation of digital touchpoints. Implement multi-touch attribution models, cross-device tracking, and marketing mix modeling techniques to attribute conversions accurately and allocate credit to the most influential touchpoints along the customer journey.

Resource Constraints and Prioritization

Resource constraints and competing priorities may limit the ability to implement all optimization efforts and initiatives simultaneously. Prioritize optimization efforts based on their potential impact, urgency, and alignment with business objectives. Focus on high-impact activities that offer the greatest potential for ROI and allocate resources strategically to drive maximum results within budgetary constraints.

12.4.4 Future Trends and Innovations

Predictive Analytics and AI-driven Insights

Predictive analytics and artificial intelligence (AI) technologies will play a significant role in shaping the future of monitoring, evaluation, and continuous improvement in digital marketing. AI-driven algorithms analyze data patterns, predict outcomes, and recommend optimization strategies in real-time, enabling marketers to anticipate trends, identify opportunities, and automate decision-making processes for greater efficiency and effectiveness.

Real-time Monitoring and Optimization

Real-time monitoring and optimization capabilities will enable marketers to respond to changing market conditions, consumer behaviors, and campaign performance metrics instantly. Implement real-time analytics dashboards, automated alerts, and AI-powered recommendation engines to monitor campaign performance in real-time, identify anomalies, and adjust strategies dynamically for maximum impact.

Integrated Marketing Measurement

Integrated marketing measurement solutions will enable marketers to measure the holistic impact of digital marketing efforts across channels and touchpoints seamlessly. Implement cross-channel attribution models, unified analytics platforms, and integrated data ecosystems to gain a comprehensive view of the customer journey and understand the interconnectedness of marketing activities for more accurate measurement and optimization.

CONCLUSION

RECAP OF KEY LEARNINGS

- **Foundations of Digital Marketing:** This topic covers the fundamental principles and concepts of digital marketing, including understanding the digital landscape, consumer behavior online, and the importance of digital channels in reaching and engaging target audiences. It also involves exploring various digital marketing strategies, tactics, and tools available to businesses to achieve their marketing objectives in the digital age.
- **Content Making:** Content marketing involves creating and distributing valuable, relevant, and engaging content to attract, acquire, and engage a target audience. This includes various forms of content such as blog posts, articles, videos, infographics, and podcasts. The goal of content marketing is to build brand awareness, establish thought leadership, and drive customer engagement and loyalty through valuable and informative content.
- **Social Media Marketing:** Social media marketing focuses on leveraging social media platforms such as Facebook, Instagram, Twitter, LinkedIn, and TikTok to connect with target audiences, build relationships, and promote products or services. It involves creating and sharing content, engaging with followers, running targeted advertising campaigns, and analyzing performance metrics to optimize social media strategies.
- **Search Engine Optimization (SEO):** SEO is the process of optimizing a website to improve its visibility and ranking in search engine results pages (SERPs). This involves optimizing website content, meta tags, images, and URLs, as well as building backlinks and improving site speed and mobile-friendliness. The goal of SEO is to increase organic traffic to a website and attract high-quality leads through improved search engine visibility.
- **Pay-Per-Click (PPC) Advertising:** PPC advertising involves paying for ads to appear in search engine results or on websites, and advertisers only pay when users click on their ads. PPC platforms such as Google Ads and

Bing Ads allow advertisers to target specific keywords, demographics, and interests, and track the performance of their campaigns in real-time. PPC advertising is an effective way to drive targeted traffic to a website and generate leads or sales quickly.

- **Email Marketing**: Email marketing involves sending targeted, personalized emails to subscribers or customers to promote products, announce offers, and build relationships. This includes creating email campaigns, designing templates, segmenting email lists, and analyzing metrics such as open rates, click-through rates, and conversion rates. Email marketing is a cost-effective way to nurture leads, drive conversions, and maintain customer engagement over time.
- **Mobile Marketing**: Mobile marketing focuses on reaching and engaging audiences on mobile devices such as smartphones and tablets. This includes mobile-responsive website design, mobile apps, SMS marketing, and location-based marketing. Mobile marketing leverages the ubiquity of mobile devices and the growing trend of mobile usage to deliver targeted messages and offers to users wherever they are.
- **Influencer Marketing**: Influencer marketing involves partnering with influential individuals or personalities on social media to promote products or services to their followers. This includes identifying relevant influencers, establishing partnerships, and creating sponsored content that resonates with their audience. Influencer marketing can help brands reach new audiences, build credibility, and drive engagement through authentic and trusted endorsements.
- **Video Marketing**: Video marketing involves creating and sharing video content to engage and educate audiences, promote products or services, and drive brand awareness and engagement. This includes various video formats such as explainer videos, product demos, tutorials, and testimonials, as well as live streaming and user-generated content. Video marketing is an effective way to convey messages, evoke emotions, and capture audience attention in a visually compelling and memorable way.
- **Analytics and Data-Driven Marketing**: Analytics and data-driven marketing involve using data and insights to inform decision-making, optimize marketing strategies, and measure the effectiveness of campaigns. This includes collecting and analyzing data from various sources such as website traffic, social media engagement, and customer interactions to identify trends, patterns, and opportunities for improvement. Data-driven marketing enables marketers to make

informed decisions, allocate resources effectively, and achieve better results.

- **Digital Marketing Tools and Technologies:** Digital marketing tools and technologies encompass a wide range of software, platforms, and solutions designed to streamline marketing processes, automate tasks, and enhance campaign performance. This includes tools for content creation, social media management, email marketing, SEO, PPC advertising, analytics, and automation. Digital marketing tools enable marketers to manage campaigns more efficiently, optimize resources, and drive better results.
- **Creating an Integrated Digital Marketing Plan:** Creating an integrated digital marketing plan involves developing a comprehensive strategy that leverages multiple digital channels and tactics to achieve overarching business goals. This includes aligning objectives, target audiences, messaging, and KPIs across channels such as social media, search engines, email, and content marketing. An integrated approach ensures consistency, coherence, and synergy in marketing efforts, maximizing impact and ROI across the entire customer journey.

FUTURE TRENDS IN DIGITAL MARKETING AND SOCIAL MEDIA

Future trends in digital marketing and social media are shaped by evolving consumer behaviors, technological advancements, and industry innovations. Future trends in digital marketing and social media will be characterized by a focus on personalization, immersive experiences, privacy and data protection, and authentic engagement with consumers. Marketers who embrace these trends and adapt their strategies accordingly will be well-positioned to succeed in an ever-evolving digital landscape.

AI-Powered Personalization

Artificial intelligence (AI) will continue to play a significant role in enabling personalized marketing experiences.

AI algorithms analyze vast amounts of data to deliver tailored content, recommendations, and offers to individual users based on their preferences, behaviors, and demographics.

Voice Search and AI Assistants

With the rise of voice-enabled devices and virtual assistants, voice search optimization and conversational AI will become increasingly important. Marketers will need to optimize content and advertising strategies for voice search queries and leverage AI assistants to engage users in natural language interactions.

Augmented Reality (AR) and Virtual Reality (VR)

AR and VR technologies will transform the way brands interact with consumers, offering immersive and interactive experiences across digital channels. Marketers can use AR and VR to showcase products, create virtual storefronts, and gamify user engagement, enhancing brand storytelling and customer engagement.

Social Commerce and Shoppable Content

Social media platforms will continue to integrate e-commerce functionalities, allowing users to discover and purchase products directly within the social media environment. Shoppable posts, live shopping features, and in-app checkout options will blur the lines between social media and e-commerce, driving sales and revenue for brands.

User-Generated Content (UGC) and Community Building

UGC will remain a powerful tool for building brand authenticity and fostering community engagement on social media. Brands will increasingly leverage UGC campaigns, influencer partnerships, and community-driven initiatives to create authentic connections with their audience and drive brand advocacy.

Privacy and Data Protection

With growing concerns about data privacy and security, consumers will demand greater transparency and control over their personal data. Marketers will need to prioritize data protection measures, comply with privacy regulations such as GDPR and CCPA, and build trust through transparent data practices and ethical marketing strategies.

Micro-Moments and Real-Time Marketing

Marketers will focus on capturing micro-moments – brief, intent-rich moments when consumers turn to their devices for immediate information, solutions, or inspiration. Real-time marketing strategies, such as moment marketing and newsjacking, will enable brands to capitalize on these micro-moments and deliver timely, relevant content to their audience.

Video Content Dominance

Video content will continue to dominate social media platforms, with short-form video formats such as Stories, Reels, and TikTok videos gaining popularity. Brands will invest in video production, live streaming, and interactive video experiences to engage audiences and drive engagement on social media.

Social Listening and Sentiment Analysis

Social listening tools and sentiment analysis techniques will become essential for monitoring brand mentions, tracking customer sentiment, and identifying emerging trends and conversations on social media. Marketers will leverage social listening insights to inform content strategies, address customer feedback, and mitigate reputation risks in real-time.

Purpose-Driven Marketing

Consumers are increasingly drawn to brands that stand for a cause and demonstrate a commitment to social and environmental responsibility. Purpose-driven marketing initiatives, such as sustainability efforts, social impact campaigns, and diversity and inclusion initiatives, will resonate with socially conscious consumers and drive brand loyalty.

GLOSSARY

Digital Marketing: Digital marketing refers to the use of digital channels, platforms, and technologies to promote products, services, or brands to target audiences. It encompasses various tactics such as search engine optimization (SEO), social media marketing, email marketing, content marketing, and paid advertising.

Social Media Marketing (SMM): Social media marketing involves leveraging social media platforms such as Facebook, Instagram, Twitter, LinkedIn, and TikTok to connect with target audiences, build relationships, and promote products or services. It includes activities such as content creation, community management, influencer partnerships, and paid advertising on social media platforms.

Search Engine Optimization (SEO): Search engine optimization is the process of optimizing a website to improve its visibility and ranking in search engine results pages (SERPs). It involves optimizing website content, meta tags, images, and URLs, as well as building backlinks and improving site speed and mobile-friendliness to increase organic traffic from search engines.

Pay-Per-Click (PPC) Advertising: Pay-per-click advertising involves paying for ads to appear in search engine results or on websites, and advertisers only pay when users click on their ads. PPC platforms such as Google Ads and Bing Ads allow advertisers to target specific keywords, demographics, and interests and track the performance of their campaigns in real-time.

Content Marketing: Content marketing is the practice of creating and distributing valuable, relevant, and engaging content to attract, acquire, and engage a target audience. It includes various forms of content such as blog posts, articles, videos, infographics, and podcasts, with the goal of building brand awareness, establishing thought leadership, and driving customer engagement and loyalty.

Email Marketing: Email marketing involves sending targeted, personalized emails to subscribers or customers to promote products, announce offers, and build relationships. It includes creating email campaigns, designing templates, segmenting email lists, and analyzing metrics such as open rates, click-through rates, and conversion rates to optimize email marketing strategies.

Mobile Marketing: Mobile marketing focuses on reaching and engaging audiences on mobile devices such as smartphones and tablets. It includes mobile-responsive website design, mobile apps, SMS marketing, and location-based marketing, leveraging the ubiquity of mobile devices and the growing trend of mobile usage to deliver targeted messages and offers to users wherever they are.

Influencer Marketing: Influencer marketing involves partnering with influential individuals or personalities on social media to promote products or services to their followers. It includes identifying relevant influencers, establishing partnerships, and creating sponsored content that resonates with their audience, leveraging the trust and credibility of influencers to drive brand awareness and engagement.

Video Marketing: Video marketing involves creating and sharing video content to engage and educate audiences, promote products or services, and drive brand awareness and engagement. It includes various video formats such as explainer videos, product demos, tutorials, and testimonials, as well as live streaming and user-generated content, leveraging the power of video to convey messages and capture audience attention.

Analytics and Data-Driven Marketing: Analytics and data-driven marketing involve using data and insights to inform decision-making, optimize marketing strategies, and measure the effectiveness of campaigns. It includes collecting and analyzing data from various sources such as website traffic, social media engagement, and customer interactions to identify trends, patterns, and opportunities for improvement, enabling marketers to make informed decisions, allocate resources effectively, and achieve better results.

REFERENCES

Blue Ocean Strategy: How to Create Uncontested Market Space and Make the Competition Irrelevant by W. Chan Kim and Renée Mauborgne - Harvard Business Review Press, 2015.

Brand Thinking and Other Noble Pursuits by Debbie Millman - Allworth, 2013.

Building a StoryBrand: Clarify Your Message So Customers Will Listen by Donald Miller - HarperCollins Leadership, 2017.

Contagious: How to Build Word of Mouth in the Digital Age by Jonah Berger - Simon & Schuster, 2013.

Contemporary Digital Marketing: A Guide to Online Marketing Techniques by Daniel Rowles and Russell Marsh - Routledge, 2019.

Content Inc.: How Entrepreneurs Use Content to Build Massive Audiences and Create Radically Successful Businesses by Joe Pulizzi - McGraw-Hill Education, 2015.

Creativity, Inc.: Overcoming the Unseen Forces That Stand in the Way of True Inspiration by Ed Catmull and Amy Wallace - Random House, 2014.

Crossing the Chasm: Marketing and Selling High-Tech Products to Mainstream Customers by Geoffrey A. Moore - Harper Business, 1991.

Crushing It!: How Great Entrepreneurs Build Their Business and Influence-and How You Can, Too by Gary Vaynerchuk - HarperBusiness, 2018.

Digital Marketing Analytics: Making Sense of Consumer Data in a Digital World by Chuck Hemann and Ken Burbary - Wiley, 2018.

Digital Marketing For Dummies by Ryan Deiss and Russ Henneberry - For Dummies, 2020.

Digital Marketing Strategy: An Integrated Approach to Online Marketing by Simon Kingsnorth - Kogan Page, 2019.

Digital Marketing: Strategy, Implementation and Practice by Dave Chaffey, Fiona Ellis-Chadwick, Richard Mayer, and Kevin Johnston - Pearson Education, 2019.

Drive: The Surprising Truth About What Motivates Us by Daniel H. Pink - Riverhead Books, 2009.

Email Marketing Rules: Checklists, Frameworks, and 150 Best Practices for Business Success by Chad S. White - Wiley, 2017.

Epic Content Marketing: How to Tell a Different Story, Break through the Clutter, and Win More Customers by Marketing Less by Joe Pulizzi - McGraw-Hill Education, 2013.

Everybody Writes: Your Go-To Guide to Creating Ridiculously Good Content by Ann Handley - Wiley, 2014.

Good to Great: Why Some Companies Make the Leap... and Others Don't by Jim Collins - Harper Business, 2001.

Hacking Growth: How Today's Fastest-Growing Companies Drive Breakout Success by Sean Ellis and Morgan Brown - Crown Business, 2017.

Hooked: How to Build Habit-Forming Products by Nir Eyal - Portfolio, 2014.

How Brands Grow: What Marketers Don't Know by Byron Sharp - Oxford University Press, 2010.

How to Sell Anything to Anybody by Joe Girard - Simon & Schuster, 1977.

Inbound Marketing: Get Found Using Google, Social Media, and Blogs by Brian Halligan and Dharmesh Shah - Wiley, 2014.

Influence: The Psychology of Persuasion by Robert B. Cialdini - HarperBusiness, 2006.

Influencer: Building Your Personal Brand in the Age of Social Media by Brittany Hennessy - Citadel, 2018.

Jab, Jab, Jab, Right Hook: How to Tell Your Story in a Noisy Social World by Gary Vaynerchuk - HarperBusiness, 2013.

Lean Analytics: Use Data to Build a Better Startup Faster by Alistair Croll and Benjamin Yoskovitz - O'Reilly Media, 2013.

Likeable Social Media: How to Delight Your Customers, Create an Irresistible Brand, and Be Generally Amazing on Facebook (And Other Social Networks) by Dave Kerpen - McGraw-Hill Education, 2019.

Made to Market by Al Ries and Laura Ries - HarperBusiness, 1996.

Made to Stick: Why Some Ideas Survive and Others Die by Chip Heath and Dan Heath - Random House, 2007.

Marketing 4.0: Moving from Traditional to Digital by Philip Kotler, Hermawan Kartajaya, and Iwan Setiawan - Wiley, 2017.

Marketing Management by Philip Kotler - Pearson, 2019.

Marketing Warfare by Al Ries and Jack Trout - McGraw-Hill Education, 1997.

Ogilvy on Advertising by David Ogilvy - Vintage, 1985.

Permission Marketing: Turning Strangers Into Friends and Friends into Customers by Seth Godin - Simon & Schuster, 1999.

Positioning: The Battle for Your Mind by Al Ries and Jack Trout - McGraw-Hill Education, 2001.

Predictably Irrational: The Hidden Forces That Shape Our Decisions by Dan Ariely - Harper Perennial, 2008.

Purple Cow: Transform Your Business by Being Remarkable by Seth Godin - Portfolio, 2003.

Purple Squirrel: Stand Out, Land Interviews, and Master the Modern Job Market by Michael B. Junge - Amacom, 2012.

Rework by Jason Fried and David Heinemeier Hansson - Crown Business, 2010.

Selling 101: What Every Successful Sales Professional Needs to Know by Zig Ziglar - Thomas Nelson, 2003.

Selling the Invisible: A Field Guide to Modern Marketing by Harry Beckwith - Warner Books, 1997.

SEO 2021: Learn Search Engine Optimization with Smart Internet Marketing Strategies by Adam Clarke - Independently published, 2020.

Social Media Marketing All-in-One For Dummies by Jan Zimmerman and Deborah Ng - For Dummies, 2017.

Social Media Marketing Workbook: How to Use Social Media for Business (2021 Updated Edition) by Jason McDonald - CreateSpace Independent Publishing Platform, 2021.

Social Media Metrics: How to Measure and Optimize Your Marketing Investment by Jim Sterne - Wiley, 2010.

Social Media ROI: Managing and Measuring Social Media Efforts in Your Organization by Olivier Blanchard - Pearson Education, 2014.

Start with Why: How Great Leaders Inspire Everyone to Take Action by Simon Sinek - Portfolio, 2009.

The Art of Closing the Sale: The Key to Making More Money Faster by Brian Tracy - Vanguard Press, 2007.

The Art of Social Media: Power Tips for Power Users by Guy Kawasaki and Peg Fitzpatrick - Portfolio, 2014.

The Art of the Pitch: Persuasion and Presentation Skills that Win Business by Peter Coughter - Palgrave Macmillan, 2012.

The Brand Gap: How to Bridge the Distance Between Business Strategy and Design by Marty Neumeier - Peachpit Press, 2005.

The Complete Guide to Facebook Advertising by Brian Meert - AdvertiseMint, Inc., 2020.

The Digital Marketing Handbook: A Step-By-Step Guide to Creating Websites That Sell by Robert W. Bly - Career Press, 2018.

The Innovator's Dilemma: When New Technologies Cause Great Firms to Fail by Clayton M. Christensen - Harvard Business Review Press, 2016.

The Lean Startup: How Today's Entrepreneurs Use Continuous Innovation to Create Radically Successful Businesses by Eric Ries - Currency, 2011.

The Long Tail: Why the Future of Business is Selling Less of More by Chris Anderson - Hyperion, 2006.

The New Rules of Marketing & PR: How to Use Social Media, Online Video, Mobile Applications, Blogs, News Releases, and Viral Marketing to Reach Buyers Directly by David Meerman Scott - Wiley, 2020.

The Psychology of Influence: Theory, Research, and Practice by Andrew Stever - Springer, 2017.

The Start-Up of You: Adapt to the Future, Invest in Yourself, and Transform Your Career by Reid Hoffman and Ben Casnocha - Crown Business, 2012.

The Thank You Economy by Gary Vaynerchuk - Harper Business, 2011.

The Tipping Point: How Little Things Can Make a Big Difference by Malcolm Gladwell - Little, Brown and Company, 2000.

The Zen of Social Media Marketing: An Easier Way to Build Credibility, Generate Buzz, and Increase Revenue by Shama Hyder - BenBella Books, 2016.

This Is Marketing: You Can't Be Seen Until You Learn to See by Seth Godin - Portfolio, 2018.

Traction: Get a Grip on Your Business by Gino Wickman - BenBella Books, 2012.

UnMarketing: Everything Has Changed and Nothing Is Different by Scott Stratten and Alison Stratten - Wiley, 2014.

You Should Test That: Conversion Optimization for More Leads, Sales, and Profit or The Art and Science of Optimized Marketing by Chris Goward - Wiley, 2012.

Youtility: Why Smart Marketing Is about Help Not Hype by Jay Baer - Portfolio, 2013.

Zero to One: Notes on Startups, or How to Build the Future by Peter Thiel and Blake Masters - Crown Business, 2014.

INDEX

A

Accessibility 36, 95, 149, 167, 168, 179, 215, 233, 302

Affiliate Marketing 3, 10, 41, 47, 101, 273

Approach 3, 286, 308, 329

B

Blogging 3, 173, 175

Brand Awareness 4, 5, 56, 59, 67, 144, 148, 210, 263

Brand Safety 10

Browsers 10, 86

C

Channels 10, 33, 36, 58, 61, 131, 191, 254, 307, 310, 311

Collaborative Environment 6

Component 1, 37, 56, 146, 147, 263, 282

Content Marketing 3, 35, 37, 45, 55, 56, 57, 58, 59, 62, 66, 217, 293, 321, 327

Convenience 4

Cookies 10, 108, 192, 194, 280

Cross-Platform 9

Customer Behavior 4

D

Data-Driven 7, 35, 202, 237, 277, 285, 300, 322, 328

Digital Interaction 4

Display 8, 10

E

Email Marketing 3, 11, 34, 38, 42, 46, 66, 209, 210, 294, 322, 327

F

Fact-Check 109

Fake News 22, 28, 72, 76, 77, 101, 109

G

Game Advertising 7, 12

I

Influence 4, 243, 250, 329, 330, 332

Influencer Marketing 6, 38, 47, 243, 251, 252, 255, 256, 260, 322, 328

Invalid Traffic 10

J

Java 83, 119

Journalists 48, 110

K

Keywords 34, 38, 45, 61, 68, 87, 132, 161, 162, 166, 168, 169, 170, 171, 172, 173, 174, 176, 178, 180, 181, 185, 188, 189, 190, 191, 192, 193, 196,

200, 204, 205, 218, 231, 232, 267, 270, 322, 327

L

Leveraging 34, 37, 38, 44, 47, 64, 65, 75, 107, 147, 157, 174, 209, 214, 219, 227, 239, 240, 249, 252, 263, 266, 269, 271, 274, 279, 280, 283, 285, 293, 295, 299, 300, 307, 313, 321

Liability 26, 109

M

Measurement 9, 43, 70, 190, 240, 268, 274, 278, 312, 318, 319

Messaging Platforms 227, 228, 229, 233

N

Non-Linear 3

O

Online Shopping 4

P

Pay-Per-Click 3, 34, 36, 50, 183, 184, 327

Personalized 2, 8, 34, 35, 36, 37, 38, 40, 42, 44, 47, 49, 50, 51, 52, 53, 66, 113, 114, 134, 135, 202, 203, 209, 213, 216, 221, 227, 228, 229, 233, 235, 236, 238, 239, 271, 276, 277, 278, 279, 287, 293, 294, 295, 296, 298, 299, 300, 301, 302, 303, 307, 309, 310, 315, 316, 322, 323, 327

Prioritizing Clicks 8

Q

Queries 5, 37, 39, 50, 164, 165, 166, 192, 231, 232, 241, 299, 323

QZone 19, 21

R

Remarketing 7, 203, 206

S

Segmentation 6, 45, 46, 53, 66, 70, 210, 212, 219, 220, 221, 222, 224, 234, 237, 241, 278, 286, 299

SEM 1, 5, 11, 17, 18, 167, 311

SEO 1, 3, 5, 34, 35, 37, 41, 43, 44, 45, 49, 50, 52, 57, 58, 61, 62, 63, 66, 68, 132, 148, 161, 162, 163, 164, 166, 167, 168, 169, 170, 171, 172, 173, 174, 175, 176, 177, 178, 179, 180, 181, 218, 229, 230, 231, 232, 264, 269, 293, 307, 321, 323, 327, 331

SMS 1, 13, 35, 38, 49, 86, 105, 110, 112, 227, 228, 229, 233, 234, 235, 322, 328

Social Networking 11

T

Targeting 10, 36, 41, 189, 202, 206, 229, 237, 239, 245, 270, 278, 299

Tourism Marketing 8

Twitter 2, 5, 11, 33, 34, 37, 46, 49, 56, 61, 64, 69, 94, 98, 103, 104, 105, 106, 107, 108, 109, 110, 111, 112, 113, 114, 115, 116, 117, 118, 119, 120, 121, 122, 123, 128, 137, 140, 142, 146, 148, 150, 159, 183, 200, 244, 260, 271, 321, 327

U

Unparalleled 43, 233, 263, 269

Unprecedented 17, 35, 37, 272, 301, 303

V

Video Marketing 3, 266, 269, 322, 328
Viewability 10

W

Website Marketing 3

Z

Zhang 138
Zuckerberg 71, 72, 73, 74, 75, 76, 81, 82, 83, 84, 91, 94

www.ingramcontent.com/pod-product-compliance
Ingram Content Group UK Ltd.
Pitfield, Milton Keynes, MK11 3LW, UK
UKHW051028041026
15470UKWH00015B/1687

9 781787 153585